"Limiting pre-trial detention is a vital step towards reducing prison populations significantly, while recognising that unconvicted persons should never be incarcerated unnecessarily. This excellent book combines comparative studies of European pre-trial detention with in-depth analyses of their findings. It is an invaluable resource for penal reformers and students of criminal justice."

Dirk van Zyl Smit, *Emeritus Professor of Comparative and International Penal Law, University of Nottingham*

"This volume offers a comprehensive overview of the current empirical and legal issues surrounding pre-trial detention in Europe. The edition builds on more than a decade of research on remand detention across several European jurisdictions. Contributions are written by a stellar line up of experts, dealing with topics as diverse as human rights in remand proceedings and the practice of pre-trial decision-making. This book should be read by anyone who wishes to acquire valuable suggestions and develop operational strategies on how to reduce the use of pre-trial detention and expand the resort to its alternatives."

Adriano Martufi, *Assistant Professor of Criminal Law, University of Pavia/Leiden University*

"Pre-trial detention is a highly problematic penal practice. However, little is still known about its rationales and use across Europe. This book fills therefore an important gap in penological comparative scholarship. It is an excellent example of a multi-national, multi-lingual and multi-cultural qualitative comparative research on pre-trial detention, based on unique empirical data, combined with a theoretical and human rights approach."

Kristel Beyens, *Professor of Criminology and Penology, Vrije Universiteit Brussel*

"Pre-trial detention for a long time has been neglected in research. The present book is an outstanding example of comparative criminal justice research covering legal and international human rights aspects as well as an empirical stock-taking of the use of pre-trail detention in Europe. The core question how to limit and to avoid deprivation of liberty of formally innocents is developed by a comprehensive comparison of eight European countries revealing the variations and similarities of problems in different legal cultures and jurisdictions. It deserves the utmost attention of the scientific community and of practitioners interested in criminal procedure and penal policy based on empirical evidence."

Prof. Emeritus Dr. Frieder Dünkel, *University of Greifswald, Germany*

European Perspectives on Pre-Trial Detention

High levels of remand or pre-trial detention (PTD) is a matter of growing concern in many countries, and at a European level. Despite being responsible for a significant part of the prison population, PTD practice is rarely the focus of criminological and criminal justice research. This book examines pre-trial detention practices and different ways of reducing its use across Europe. Offering a range of country-specific studies, this book also offers comparative studies of major issues across the continent.

In particular, this book illustrates and examines how the actors (judges, public prosecutors, defence lawyers) work in pre-trial proceedings and make decisions; the common challenges in PTD decision-making; the factors which explain higher and lower rates of PTD across Europe; similarities and differences in practice; and the ways in which cross-border cases in Europe influence policy and practice.

Offering suggestions and recommendations for how to bring down the use of PTD in Europe, this book is essential reading for all those engaged with European penal research and practice.

Christine Morgenstern is Professor of Criminal Law and Legal Gender Studies at Freie Universität Berlin, Germany.

Walter Hammerschick is Deputy Head and Senior Researcher at the Department for Applied Sociology of Law and Criminology of the University of Innsbruck, located in Vienna, Austria.

Mary Rogan is Associate Professor at the School of Law, Trinity College Dublin, Ireland.

Routledge Frontiers of Criminal Justice

Disassembling Police Culture
Mike Rowe

Offender Rehabilitation Programmes
The Role of the Prison Officer
Laura M. Small and Paul Hackett

Sexual History Evidence in Rape Trails
Is the Jury Out
Charlotte Herriott

Penal Abolitionism and Transformative Justice in Brazil
Andre R. Giamberardino

Impending Challenges to Penal Moderation in France and Germany
A Strained Restraint
Edited by Kirstin Drenkhahn, Fabien Jobard and Tobias Singelnstein

Narratives on Prison Governmentality
No Longer the Prison of the Past
Marco Nocente

Preventing Prison Violence
An Ecological Perspective
Armon J. Tamatea, Andrew J. Day and & David J. Cooke

European Perspectives on Pre-Trial Detention
A Means of Last Resort?
Christine Morgenstern, Walter Hammerschick and Mary Rogan

For more information about this series, please visit: www.routledge.com/
Routledge-Frontiers-of-Criminal-Justice/book-series/RFCJ

European Perspectives on Pre-Trial Detention

A Means of Last Resort?

Edited by Christine Morgenstern,
Walter Hammerschick and
Mary Rogan

Routledge
Taylor & Francis Group
LONDON AND NEW YORK

First published 2024
by Routledge
4 Park Square, Milton Park, Abingdon, Oxon OX14 4RN

and by Routledge
605 Third Avenue, New York, NY 10158

Routledge is an imprint of the Taylor & Francis Group, an informa business

British Library Cataloguing-in-Publication Data
A catalogue record for this book is available from the British Library

ISBN: 978-0-367-74726-8 (hbk)
ISBN: 978-0-367-74727-5 (pbk)
ISBN: 978-1-003-15925-4 (ebk)

DOI: 10.4324/9781003159254

Typeset in Sabon
by Apex CoVantage, LLC

To all those striving to make pre-trial detention a means of last resort

Contents

Contributors

Skirmantas Bikelis is a senior researcher at the Criminal Justice Department of the Law Institute at the Lithuanian Centre of Social Sciences. Bikelis has 15 years of academic research experience (has been working at the Law Institute since 2008) and 9 years of lecturing experience at the Mykolas Romeris University (2003–2012). His main academic interests are modern legal measures for confiscation of crime proceeds (civil confiscation, extended powers of confiscation, illicit enrichment and money laundering criminalisation), coercive measures in criminal procedure, policies for the control of drug use, distribution and trafficking, prevention and control of corruption and organised crime.

Miranda Boone is Professor of Criminology and Comparative Penology at Leiden University, The Netherlands. Her expertise lies in decision-making processes in the application and enforcement of sanctions from both a social science and normative perspective.

Ioan Durnescu is Professor at the University of Bucharest, Faculty of Sociology and Social Work. He teaches and conducts research in the area of probation, prison and deradicalisation fields. His special interest is comparative probation and re-entry. He is also co-editor of the *European Journal of Probation* and co-chair of the RAN Rehabilitation Working Group. He is currently conducting a comparative research on re-entry involving Roma women and men released from prison in Romania, Bulgaria and Italy. European law and framework decisions are also of interest. Ioan Durnescu is part of several initiatives that looks into how these tools contribute to the EU Area of Freedom, Security and Justice.

Walter Hammerschick earned his Doctorate in Law at the University of Salzburg, subsequently studying Sociology at Bowling Green State University, Ohio. He has been a researcher at the Viennese Institute for the Sociology of Law and Criminology since 1991 where he stayed most of his professional life. There he was executive director from 2008 till 2021, when the institute became part of Innsbruck University. Today he is vice head and senior researcher at the new department for Applied Sociology of Law and Criminology (IRKS). He has been head and partner in many national and European studies in this field.

Anthea Hucklesby is Professor of Criminal Justice at the University of Birmingham, UK, where she holds a joint appointment in Birmingham Law School and the School of Social Policy. She has 30 years of experience of research on pre-trial detention and remand undertaking projects on pre- and post-charge police bail and court bail. Her most recent projects investigate the impact of recent legal changes on the use of pre-charge bail, release under investigation and electronic monitoring as a mechanism to measure compliance with bail conditions. A second research focus is wearable technologies arising from her work on electronic monitoring in criminal justice systems. She led the AHRC-funded Tracking People network and is co-editor of Tracking People: Wearable Technologies in Social and Public Policy (Routledge, 2023).

Pauline Jacobs is Associate Professor of Criminal Law and Criminal Procedure at Tilburg University, The Netherlands. Her research activities encompass themes in the field of criminal law and criminal procedure and human rights, with a special interest in penitentiary law, the field of law that focuses on the execution of criminal sanctions and measures.

Alexia Jonckheere works in the Department of Criminology at the National Institute of Criminalistics and Criminology (Brussels, Belgium) since 2004. She studied Law and Criminology and received her PhD in Criminology in 2011 following a study on the management of the Belgian Probation Service. She does research on pre-trial detention, the execution of community sentences and measures, the penal protection of the environment and administrative sanctions introduced at the local and regional levels. She is a member of the editorial board of the journal *Déviance et Société* and teaches at the Catholic Universities of Louvain-la-Neuve (Belgium) and Lille (France).

Joep Lindeman is Associate Professor of Criminal Law and Criminal Procedure at the Willem Pompe Institute for Criminal Law and Criminology, Utrecht University, The Netherlands. He is one of the programme leaders of the Montaigne Centre for Rule of Law and Administration of Justice. His research focus lies in Criminal Procedure and judicial organisation, in both the Netherlands and abroad.

Eric Maes holds a PhD in Criminological Sciences from the Katholieke Universiteit Leuven (2008) and works in the Department of Criminology at the National Institute of Criminalistics and Criminology (Brussels, Belgium) since 1999. His main scientific research interests and publications focus on penological topics such as (the history of) prison regimes, the implementation of prison sentences and community sanctions, electronic monitoring, conditional release, pre-trial detention and alternatives, sentence calculation and recidivism studies. He is currently involved in a EC Justice Programme–funded project "Improving judicial assessment of flight risk" (JUST-2021-JCOO, No. 101046544), together with colleague and co-author Alexia Jonckheere.

Christine Morgenstern is Professor of Criminal Law and Legal Gender Studies at the Freie Universität Berlin, moving in autumn 2023 to hold the Chair of Criminology at the Ruhr-Universität Bochum, Germany. She works at the intersection of penal law, human rights and criminology. Her research interests include penal theory, sentencing, criminal procedure and the access to justice for vulnerable groups. She is particularly keen on covering comparative and European aspects of these topics and cross-border exchange.

Gabriel Oancea is head of the Bucharest Probation Service and Associate Lecturer at the University of Bucharest, Faculty of Sociology and Social Work, Romania. He teaches effective methods for offender supervision and rehabilitation and in other areas of social work in criminal justice. He is involved in research projects on the effectiveness of preventive measures and the transfer of prisoners and probationers within the European Union.

Mary Rogan is Associate Professor at the School of Law, Trinity College, Dublin, Ireland, and Fellow of Trinity College. She is the Principal Investigator of an ERC-funded project examining prison oversight. Her work has been published in *Law and Society Review*, *Punishment and Society* and the *European Journal of Criminology*. Mary is qualified as a barrister and is a member of Lincoln's Inn, London. Mary was the first woman to be President of the International Penal and Penitentiary Foundation and is currently its Secretary General. She is a former Chairperson of the Irish Penal Reform Trust.

Acknowledgements

This book is based on the project Towards Pre-trial DETentiOn as Ultima Ratio – DETOUR, funded by the European Commission under Grant Agreement JUST/2014/JACC/AG/PROC/6606. It would not have been possible without the commitment of our authors, staying on board for a long journey, and the contributions by all the defence lawyers, public prosecutors, judges and probation practitioners, European officials and other professionals who shared their experiences with us and participated actively in our research as interviewees, organisational facilitators and workshop discussants. Through the work carried out as part of this book, it became clear to us that all those involved in decision-making face considerable challenges in carrying out their work. We wish to acknowledge the important role you all play to support the upholding of fundamental rights and European principles in the administration of justice.

We also want to express our deep gratitude to those who supported the research work throughout the project phase – Veronika Reidinger, David Perry, Aoife Hyde, Doireann O'Brien, Beth Whitney, Magali Deblock, Morgane Hovine, Eva Tanz and Hans Kromrey. Our thanks also go to the publishing team at Routledge, Tom Sutton, Paige Loughlin and Jessica Phillips, for their support and patience as well as to the copyeditors Sudha Prasad and Debashis from Apex Covantage and to Lea Pilone from the Department of Criminal Law and Legal Gender Studies, Freie Universität Berlin, who has assisted us with the editorial work. We are very grateful to everyone who has contributed to this book, and for keeping the project alive through some difficult and uncertain times.

Chapter 1

Pre-trial detention in Europe: a means of last resort? An introduction

Christine Morgenstern, Walter Hammerschick and Mary Rogan

What this book is about

"Pre-trial detention deprives innocents of their liberty" (*"Untersuchungshaft ist die Freiheitsberaubung gegenüber Unschuldigen"*, Hassemer, 1984: 40) – this apposite, perhaps provocative, definition encompasses the legal dilemmas and practical problems this book is about: how can the society's need to be protected from crime, the state's duty to prosecute and the suspects' rights to be free from undue state intervention be reconciled? Emphasising the deprivation – the German term can be translated as "robbing" – of liberty from a person, the remark serves to remind us that pre-trial detention must be thoroughly justified in the light of basic human rights.

The right to liberty and the presumption of innocence, enshrined in Articles 5 and 6(2) of the European Convention on Human Rights (ECHR), in Articles 9 and 14 of the International Covenant on Civil and Political Rights (ICCPR) and in domestic constitutional and legal provisions, guarantee that a mere suspicion may not lead to an infringement of these rights. The default option during criminal proceedings therefore is liberty for the suspect awaiting trial and conviction. Only good reasons to assume that s/he will not stand trial or that s/he will offend while at liberty may lead to the option of using coercive means to secure the criminal process and serve as the legitimate aims for any such measure. Nevertheless, neither the suspicion nor the facts that lead to the presumption that a person may not stand trial should make this person "a little bit guilty" in the eyes of judges and other decision-makers. Even if there is a need for coercive means, the state again must use the least intrusive measure to secure both the greatest possible amount of liberty and the proceedings. Accordingly, the second option is to restrict liberty for a suspect awaiting trial. One focus of this book is therefore on those means of restricting liberty, often described as "alternatives to pre-trial detention" or included in the concept of (conditional) bail. It is only if the state (through its law enforcement agencies) is able to prove that no other means will ensure that the suspect actually stands trial, or that s/he will not continue offending, that the most intrusive measure is legitimate, that is, pre-trial detention.

DOI: 10.4324/9781003159254-1

These normative arguments provide the starting point of the research for this book: the need to use pre-trial detention as ultima ratio, as a means of last resort or *ultimum remedium* (all three expressions are used synonymously in the chapters). Following them, we could commonly assume that a country's population of pre-trial detainees should be as small as possible. Instead, high levels of pre-trial detention are a matter of growing concern in many countries, and at European level. The aim of our research therefore was to understand what factors shape the use of pre-trial detention, how the use is justified in practice, whether these justifications are convincing in the light of the two basic human rights guarantees mentioned above, and what is done to reduce its use. The book consists of two major parts. In the first part of the book, we draw on experiences from eight European jurisdictions – Austria, Belgium, England and Wales, Germany, Ireland, Lithuania, the Netherlands and Romania. By using our own empirical findings and existing literature for each of these jurisdictions, we examine legal frameworks and policy contexts of pre-trial decision-making and illustrate how the actors (judges, public prosecutors, defence lawyers) work in pre-trial proceedings and make decisions on the use of pre-trial detention and its alternatives. The second part contains comparative chapters that analyse the factors which explain higher and lower rates of pre-trial detention in Europe and explore the extent to which practices are similar in the eight European jurisdictions under scrutiny, with special attention paid to alternatives to pre-trial detention, detention overuse against foreign nationals and pan-European developments.

Why pre-trial detention matters and why it must be studied

Despite being responsible for a significant part of the prison population, pre-trial practice has rarely been the focus of criminological and criminal justice research. Nevertheless, a growing body of literature worldwide mirrors the concern for unfair and harmful practices in that area. This concern instigates studies that seek to "move upstream" (Webster, 2022: 1) and explore how pre-trial detention not only sets the course for individual criminal proceedings, but, more globally, also contributes to high prison rates or even mass incarceration. Theoretical pieces highlight, for example, how the imposition of pre-trial detention as well as disproportionally severe bail conditions may in fact anticipate punishment (Freiberg and Morgan, 2004), and consider the consequences of the presumption of innocence for pre-trial measures. De Jong and van Lent (2016) describe it as a "*counterfactual principle*", which nevertheless serves as shield against intrusive state powers in the pre-trial phase, while Duff (2013) is more sceptical that it can be truly upheld in the current "*era of prevention*".

Other partly empirical studies scrutinise racial and socio-economic disparities in the pre-trial system and ask how sentencing judges may be influenced by earlier decisions that label persons as "risky" by denying bail and putting them in pre-trial detention (e.g. for the United States, Heaton et al., 2017; Maruna, Dabney and Topalli, 2012; Canada, Webster, 2022). Other studies from North America and Australia explore how risk-based approaches shape pre-trial practices in different contexts: Myers (2019), in a Canadian study, shows how private citizens can become part of a risk-focused approach when they provide a surety for the defendant and thus take over a policing function, while Travers et al. (2020) warn against merely risk-based assessments; they examine how, in Australia, therapeutic jurisprudence approaches in judicial bail decision-making may help to overcome the shortcomings of such assessments.

An important group of studies reminds us of the situation of underprivileged groups of suspects and how pre-trial practices affect different groups differently: while in Europe the focus is often the situation of the heterogeneous group of foreign national suspects (e.g. Jonckheere and Maes, 2011, for Belgium; Hammerschick and Reidinger, 2017, for Austria; Fink, 2020, for Switzerland), in other parts of the world racialised practices and the overrepresentation of indigenous persons in remand prisons are a concern to researchers (e.g. Sanderson et al., 2011, for Australia; Jones, 2013, for the United States; Webster, 2022, for Canada). For some suspects, intersectional identities as a foreign national, belonging to an ethnic minority, or being an indigenous person *plus* being a person with mental health issues, or being a young person, or being socially marginalised, may represent accumulated risks in the eyes of the criminal justice system. This is indicated by research on the situation of female defendants highlighting specific vulnerability caused by mental health or social issues (Forrester et al., 2020, for England) or their intersectional identities as female indigenous women in Australia (Radke, 2018), young indigenous suspects in Australia (Stubbs, 2010) or foreign national juveniles in the Netherlands (van den Brinck, 2019). More generally, the question of how far pre-trial practices contribute to a criminal justice system that is "punishing poverty" (Scott-Hayward and Fradella, 2019) – because it often affects homeless and indigent persons who cannot present a reliable address or cannot afford bail – remains pertinent everywhere.

Painting the bigger picture, several international policy-related studies have been published to denounce the overuse of pre-trial detention worldwide and to analyse the potential of milder measures. Often initiated by non-governmental human rights organisations campaigning for a humane and liberal criminal justice system, they vary in scientific rigour, but provide useful insights into the wider topic. For example, Berry et al. (2011) and Schönteich (2014) use case studies of various countries all over the world to demonstrate the scale of the problem of excessive use of pre-trial detention, the negative consequences for defendants, their families, and overloaded prison systems. DLA Piper (2021) take a specific perspective and explore, inter alia, examples from various jurisdictions on how the COVID-19 pandemic motivated judges to apply existing – but otherwise underused – possibilities to release remand prisoners. The international collection edited by van Kempen (2012) explores domestic legal frameworks for pre-trial decision-making with a special focus on legal safeguards for the suspect and his or her human rights during criminal proceedings. Many of the contributions emphasise that the legitimacy of pre-trial detention depends not only on the correct application of material prerequisites but also on a fair procedure. This requirement of a fair trial includes independence and impartiality of the decision-making bodies, a speedy trial, defence rights and rights to information and translation. The legal requirements are enshrined in Article 6(1) ECHR and Article 14 of the ICCPR. They correspond to what socio-legal research and socio-psychological research describe as procedural justice, namely the human need to understand what is happening to oneself, to be able to articulate one's own position ("voice") and to be treated with respect, not as an object of the state's investigation and intervention. In contrast, unfair procedures constitute a risk for the legitimacy of the criminal procedure as such (e.g. Tyler and Huo, 2002).

A further concern for academic legal and criminological writing is detention conditions for remand detainees, who often suffer harder conditions than sentenced prisoners, which, for example, the European Committee for the Prevention of Torture frequently (CPT) has identified as a pan-European problem (CPT, 2017). Prison conditions sometimes are so bad that in some countries they infringe Article 3 of the ECHR, which prohibits torture and inhuman or degrading treatment or punishment. The European Court of Human Rights (ECtHR) as well as the European Court of Justice (ECJ) have dealt with such cases (e.g. ECtHR *Savenkovas v. Litauen* (871/02, 18 November 2008); EJC, 5 April 2016, *Pál Aranyosi* [C-404/15] and *Robert Căldăraru* [C-659/15 PPU]). These conditions constitute a grave threat to human rights of those affected, but also a problem for legitimacy and trust in criminal justice systems within Europe.

In Europe, comparative research has therefore also been stimulated by the need to understand EU Member States pre-trial practices (Morgenstern, 2018). This is not only academic interest but is needed to enable cross-border solutions. Projects often have been funded by the European Union's institutions, such as the EU commission. Among the projects are the DETOUR study (see the following section), studies conducted by the non-governmental organisation Fair Trials (2017) and the Prison Litigation project, which both focus on access to justice for pre-trial detainees[1]; and the PRETRIAD project, which explores the possibilities of European judicial cooperation in pre-trial matters.[2] Other studies have analysed the potential of ECtHR jurisprudence in pre-trial detention matters, deploring, inter alia, weak standards for the use of alternatives (Martufi and Peristeridou, 2020), and emphasising the necessity of a reductionist approach to all pre-trial measures (see also the contributions in a special issue of *European Journal on Criminal Policy and Research* [2022, volume 28, issue 3], and Martufi and Peristeridou, 2022).

Studying pre-trial detention comparatively

The comparative approach

The broad overview over problems of pre-trial detention practice and research covering these problems show, on the one hand, that many problems exist independently of a specific jurisdiction, while, on the other hand, that practice – even if based on comparable human rights standards – differs significantly.

Additionally, some of the comparable problems – namely the overrepresentation of foreign nationals in pre-trial detention, but also the quest for fair and credible alternatives – may require cross-border approaches and therefore a globalised perspective. This approach is pertinent in Europe with the common human rights base, the ECHR, shared by all member states of the Council of Europe (47, including Russia, until September 2022), but also within the smaller Area of Freedom, Security and Justice that is the European Union with its 27 member states. The comparative approach in Europe therefore combines a horizontal comparison across jurisdictions with a vertical comparison with norms, jurisprudence and policy of the European institutions.

This approach, however, can only work when not only the law in the books but also the law in action is explored. A research project that provided most of the material for the country chapters in this book (except Chapter 4) and a great deal of material for the thematic chapters, the DETOUR project (see in the next section for details), therefore sought to combine desk research and empirical enquiry guided by the same research questions, the same methodology and comparable approaches to the fieldwork.

Comparative statistics

One of the initial drivers to conduct this European comparative study were the varying rates of pre-trial detainees (pre-trial prisoners per 100,000 of the resident domestic population) even among neighbouring jurisdictions bound by the same basic human rights principles, as we can see in the yearly published penal statistics by the Council of Europe ("SPACE I", Aebi et al., 2022 and earlier, Figure 1.1). These statistics show remarkable differences, ranging from 9 pre-trial detainees per 100.000 inhabitants at the end of January 2021 in Finland to 80 in Albania. The range between the jurisdictions represented in this book are 12 in Romania and almost the threefold number in Belgium (34).

Much caution is needed to interpret the figures (see, for example, Chapter 8), as not all jurisdictions consider the phase of pre-trial detention in the same way: some include time (and therefore persons) in police custody, some exclude those who are appealing their first instance conviction. Often, those convicted but not sentenced, or those convicted and sentenced but appealing, are detained (and counted) as pre-trial detainees. In other jurisdictions, however, they can start to serve their sentence and hence are not included in the statistics as pre-trial detainee. The statistics produced by the Council of Europe list several categories to identify these differences, but largely depend on the definitions used by the officials who report the domestic data. Certainly, these figures cannot be taken as single or even dominant indicator for pre-trial practice, but they can serve as a starting point to ask questions – how can a low number be interpreted, do statistical errors exist, who counts as pre-trial prisoner? If a low figure suggests legal or judicial restraint, we can further explore how this is achieved, for example, if there are many suspects under bail conditions, etc. Additionally, we can interpret longitudinal developments (see, e.g., Chapter 7, reporting on how Lithuania managed to halve the pre-trial detention rate).

Another interesting observation that triggers questions about the wider criminal justice context and that is visible *only* in the comparative approach are the markedly different levels for pre-trial and overall prisoner rates. Figure 1.1 shows that in some cases, low rates can be found for pre-trial detainees as well as for the overall prison population, for example in Finland, Norway or Slovenia. The same is true for high rates in both cases, for example in Turkey, Russia or Hungary. In other states, the rates diverge, namely in the Netherlands with a relatively high rate for remand prisoners and a very low rate for the overall prison population and comparable situations in Denmark or Switzerland. The opposite is true for some Middle and Eastern European states, such as Latvia, Lithuania, Poland and the Czech Republic,

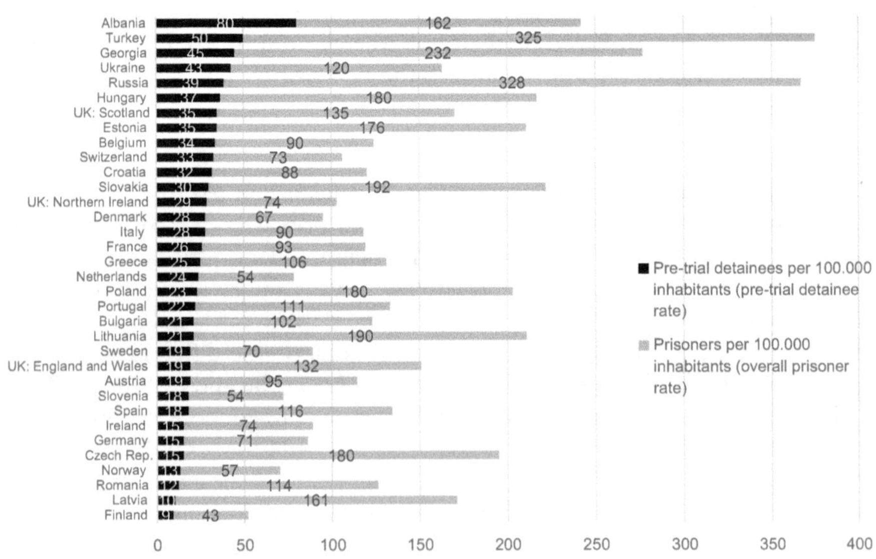

Figure 1.1 Remand prisoner rates and overall prisoner rates, 2021.

Source: SPACE I data for 31 January 2021, Aebi et al. (2022) and own calculations.

but also for Spain – here we have low pre-trial detainee rates and high rates for the overall prison population. This evokes the question whether pre-trial detention practice has to be seen as either resistant to punitive climates (as suggested, for example, for England and Wales, see Chapter 4) or, on the contrary, serves to satisfy certain societal or judicial needs even in an overall milder criminal policy climate.

Comparative methods: empirical research by the DETOUR project

Throughout this volume, the authors draw on findings from the European research project "Towards Pre-trial Detention as Ultima Ratio – DETOUR". It was funded by the European Commission in 2016–2017.[3] As a comparative criminal justice study, it combined socio-legal and criminological approaches, with theoretical starting points – as mentioned earlier – drawing on normative assumptions and statistical findings. The first steps were comprehensive reviews of national literature, statistical and jurisprudence on pre-trial detention and bail/alternatives, following guidelines the group of researchers had developed. While this meant that the research group started from the respective domestic "law in the books", regular meetings and discussions ensured that normative–descriptive considerations were widened towards a functionalist approach (Zweigert and Kötz, 1998; Michaels, 2006): Looking at pre-trial detention as a legal and cultural practice (Rogan, 2022), we concentrated on problems and the functions that pre-trial detention fulfil – the "function" serves as intersection between legal systems that become comparable entities.

Such functionalist comparative research cannot do without findings on "law in action" based on empirical findings. DETOUR opted for a qualitative approach to explore the phenomenon "pre-trial detention" and relevant contextual factors and to show possible variations within a comparative functional context. A qualitative approach is suitable particularly for comparative criminal justice research as it allows for more flexibility than a static quantitative research design with definite measuring tools. The development of the qualitative instruments used (interview guidelines, guidelines for the thematic analysis) was challenging, given the six different languages represented in the study, and the different legal and scientific backgrounds (law, criminology, sociology, social work, psychology). The necessary ongoing discussions, including the respective translation efforts by the researchers, offered the possibility to reflect constantly on the assumptions and methods of our study – an approach that is paradigmatic for qualitative research. In that way, the study also overcomes "ethnocentrism and relativism" that sometimes is attributed to comparative criminal justice research (Nelken, 2009: 291).

Practically, in an explorative first phase, we examined a number of court files, mainly to see what arrest warrants and other decisions on pre-trial detention look like, and/or we observed detention hearings (when detention is ordered or reviewed) to get an impression of how different actors influence the decision-making. The data gathered in this phase were not analysed as such but used for the development of the interview guidelines. In-depth interviews in the second phase thus were the core part of our research. In every country, around 30 interviews were conducted with judges, defence lawyers and public prosecutors, in some countries additionally with probation officers, prison staff or police officers. Altogether, a remarkable number of more than 250 qualitative interviews were carried out in the participating countries. During the DETOUR research, three workshops with practitioners served as fora for the presentation and discussion of preliminary findings, giving us important insights, in particular with regard to aspects of legal or professional traditions and cultures which are sometimes difficult to extract from research data.

Importance of socio-legal and cultural contexts

With comparative statistics – limited as they may be – and a common normative framework that is respected – or not – by the jurisdictions studied, rich material for comparative analysis seems to be at hand. Nevertheless, the legal and cultural context must be considered adequately to reach any valid conclusion on pre-trial decision-making: it is a collective social enterprise which involves different parties and individuals who mutually influence each other and who are influenced by particular historical, socio-economic, political, legal or geographical circumstances. Examples for these practice-shaping contexts are particularly high percentages of foreign nationals in pre-trial detention in Austria compared to other countries, which may have to do with the geopolitical position in the heart of Europe, or the significance of the presence of the defendant in court in countries like Germany that never accept trials in absentia. When looking at high numbers of pre-trial detainees in Lithuania, it is important to know that they have been reduced drastically, which is an achievement in a post-Soviet jurisdiction. Many more examples for these contextual factors for political, legal and judicial decision-making can be found, some of them – such as the suddenly increasing influx of war refugees and other migrants in 2015/2016 or the COVID-19 pandemic since 2020 – in several or all jurisdiction represented.

Concepts and terminology

One of the endeavours and objectives of doing comparative research is to develop a common understanding of the phenomena observed, which requires, to a certain degree, not only the use but the development of a common language. On the other hand, the audience of comparative studies – and readers of this book – must be aware that a familiar term may not be used in the same way as for domestic purposes. Some of the concepts and terms that required intensive discussions among the research team are presented in the following sections; others are discussed in the thematic chapters.

Pre-trial detention

Throughout this book, the term "pre-trial detention" (PTD) is used as uniform translation of the various different domestic terms (e.g. "investigation detention" in Germany and Austria, "preliminary detention" in the Netherlands or "preventive arrest" in Romania). Nevertheless, the period of detention comprises not only the period before trial, but also the trial period and possibly the period after conviction in case of appeal or a cassation procedure. The terms "remand detention" or "remand custody" are sometimes used synonymously. Usually, the initial arrest by the police is not counted as a period of PTD in most contexts. (This is different, for example, for the question of deduction of the final sentence for which this usually very short period of time is equally considered.)

Ultimo ratio

One of the crucial concepts for this research is the *ultimo ratio* concept itself. Since our main research question is whether PTD is the last resort in practice, we have to give a clear indication when we consider this requirement to be fulfilled and when not: PTD can only be used when it is absolutely necessary to fulfil the objectives that are intended by its use. It is therefore closely connected to legal and legitimate aims of PTD. PTD is only in accordance with the ultimo ratio principle if it is proportionate to the aims it serves. One of the inherent problems within this area is that both the aims of PTD and the concept of proportionality are fluid, with multiple possible interpretations, in particular with regard to the preventive aim. Therefore, our approach in the country chapters was to describe how these concepts were interpreted in the different countries by different practitioners and experts, and how these different interpretations can be explained. Indications for a disproportionate use – not respecting the ultima ratio principle – are an underuse of other possible strategies or measures to achieve the aims in cases where PTD is applied and the absence of considerations of such strategies, where they exist.

While they have considerable overlap, the principle of subsidiarity and the principle of proportionality have to be distinguished from the ultima ratio concept. The principle of subsidiarity refers to the use of less severe measures: such measures must always be chosen when they serve the same aim equally well as PTD (independently from the prevailing concept of alternatives explained earlier). The principle of proportionality applies to all measures: as long as the legitimate aim can be fulfilled, the least intrusive measure, for the shortest time possible, must be chosen.

Alternatives for pre-trial detention/bail

The concept of "alternatives" to PTD is difficult to grasp in the comparative context. It always refers to "more lenient", "less severe" or "milder measures" to pursue the aims of securing the proceedings or prevent recidivism that include supervision in the community in the widest sense. Referring to a categorical distinction developed by Morgenstern (2018: 756 pp.), we distinguished between two models. In the first model (substitution model), milder measures can only be ordered when the detention threshold is actually met. That means that judges have to order an arrest warrant which is then, immediately or later, suspended under conditions. We find this in Germany, the Netherlands and Belgium (on the specific Belgian model, see Chapter 3). The other model could be called the "bail model", where non-custodial measures to secure the proceedings can be ordered independently from the prerequisites for detention; PTD is just one option to choose. These measures therefore are not necessarily alternatives to PTD in the strict sense (Austria, England/Wales, Ireland, Romania, Lithuania). But even if in theory these models can be distinguished, in practice both serve the same aim and thus are not independent from the legal framework for detention. Often the non-custodial "alternative" measure is the compromise between detention and unconditional liberty regardless of the legal model. "Bail" is the concept used in England/Wales, Ireland and Romania (the Romanian terminology is "*control judiciar*" and "*control judiciar pe cautiune*"). An accused person who is granted bail (is "on bail") simply is a person who is not held in pre-trial detention while the charges against him or her are pending before the courts. Conditions, including those of a financial nature, may be attached to the accused's bail (and are, normally).

While the term "milder measures" would be more neutral, "alternatives" is the customary term, for example in the EU context. It must be emphasised, however, that framing these measures as "alternatives" reinforces the position that detention is the norm; a position that needs to be changed.

Suspect, defendant, offender

The terms "suspect" and "defendant" are legal terms that may have different meanings in different jurisdictions in different phases, depending, for example, on whether charges have been brought against a person. Often, "suspect" is used as the wider term to embrace different phases and national concepts (e.g. Cape et al., 2007). In our study, the term "defendant" is mostly used for individuals affected by pre-trial decisions, but "suspect" may be used as well. Criminological studies often also use the term "offender" regardless of the procedural stage. This, however, is to be avoided out of respect for the presumption of innocence (Article 6 ECHR): without a conviction a person must be treated as innocent and not as somebody who has committed an offence, hence as "offender".

Foreign nationals

An important aim of this study is to determine and eventually explain the proportion of non-nationals in the pre-trial population, in particular where they are grossly overrepresented (see Chapter 13). Usually, statistics (on both national and European levels) include data on nationals and "foreign nationals" in pre-trial detention. The latter is a contested term. For the purposes of this book, it is defined as individuals who are not citizens of the country where they are accused of committing an offence, that is, they have a passport or identity card from another country, are stateless or are of unknown nationality. This concept is often blurred with other concepts as, for example, irregular migrants (who are foreign nationals) or individuals from migrant and/or ethnic minority backgrounds (who are not always) and who would be interesting to be studied as groups affected by pre-trial detention, potentially affected by discriminatory practices. Foreign nationals, however, is the only group that can be identified as a delineated category and is usually captured statistically.

The country case studies and cross-cutting issues

The eight-country sample

The book includes perspectives from eight different jurisdictions. Although this is a limited number – the Council of Europe currently has 46 members – the sample is small enough to make a study manageable while it makes allowance for a range of different factors. It includes jurisdictions with a common law tradition (England and Wales, Ireland) and those with a continental civil law tradition; it includes those with higher rates of pre-trial detainees and those with lower rates (see Figure 1.1); it includes jurisdictions that can be considered as traditionally "Western" as opposed to others belonging to the former Soviet sphere of influence (Lithuania and Romania); some with high and some with middle and low percentages of foreign nationals in the domestic population and/or in pre-trial detention (see Chapter 13); and finally, it includes some that, from a criminological point of view, are traditionally deemed to have a relatively liberal approach to the criminal justice system (the Netherlands, Boone and van Swaaningen, 2013) as opposed to others that are, or were deemed to be, more punitive (e.g. England and Wales, Bell, 2013, or Lithuania, Sakalauskas, 2015). Only the Nordic countries are not represented – whether pre-trial practices are part of the "Scandinavian exceptionalism" (Pratt, 2008) or not (Ugelvik, 2012) must be left to others to examine comparatively. Nevertheless, the choice of these eight jurisdictions provides ample opportunity to examine what factors might explain different PTD practices. This is done in the part of this book that comprises eight country case studies: Austria

(Chapter 2), Belgium (Chapter 3), England and Wales (Chapter 4), Germany (Chapter 5), Ireland (Chapter 6), Lithuania (Chapter 7), the Netherlands (Chapter 8) and Romania (Chapter 9).

Common themes and cross-cutting issues

Further analysis is provided by examining specific themes and their importance for pre-trial practices across the sample. In Chapter 10, Walter Hammerschick and Skirmantas Bikelis examine the basis for decision-making. They look at the legal grounds on which pre-trial detention can be imposed under domestic and European law, but they go beyond these grounds and explore how far other factors play a role in the decision-making process and for individual decision-makers. Mary Rogan and Joep Lindeman, in Chapter 11, provide insights on the roles of different key players in the decision-making process for PTD, specifically judges, prosecutors, defence lawyers and, to a lesser degree, the probation service. They analyse the relative positions and influences of these actors, their interplay, and the legal and social cultures that surround them.

In consideration of the importance attributed to measures and strategies helping to avoid pre-trial detention, Alexia Jonckheere and Eric Maes explore in Chapter 12 the bail system, continental alternatives to pre-trial detention and their inherent dilemmas and problems: the risk of net-widening by using a variety of non-custodial measures are one concern, intrusive conditions that may violate the presumption of innocence are another and the lack of suitable measures for foreign and socially marginalised suspects are a third one. The aspect of the foreign national population in pre-trial detention is also central for Chapter 13, in which Anthea Hucklesby, Miranda Boone and Christine Morgenstern provide an overview of available data on the number of foreign nationals in pre-trial detention across Europe, analyse the situation in more depth for England and Wales, Germany and the Netherlands and examine potential measures to reduce the use of pre-trial detention for foreign nationals, including possible non-custodial measures. The discussion about how far tools of European cooperation could alleviate the situation is taken up by Christine Morgenstern and Ioan Durnescu in Chapter 14. After they have discussed the influence of European human rights law, namely decisions of the European Court of Human Rights, on PTD legislation, policy and practice, they deal with cross-border matters that affect concrete cases and would require "cross-border action" within Europe, using EU mechanisms like the European Arrest Warrant and the European Supervision Order. Finally, the editors of this book, in Chapter 15, discuss the extent to which pre-trial detention in European practice is already used with restraint – as a means of last resort – when, and why this is not the case, and what can be done to further pre-trial practice and policy that respects human rights.

Notes

1 European Prison Litigation, *Access to the law and to court in pretrial detention* at www.prisonlitigation.org/eupretrialrights/ [accessed 14 December 2022].
2 *Pretriad. Alternative pre-trial detention measures* at www.pretrial-detention.org/ [accessed 14 December 2022].
3 Grant Agreement JUST/2014/JACC/AG/PROC/6606. All reports are available online www.uibk.ac.at/irks/projekte/detour.html [accessed 3 January 2023].

References

Aebi, M.F., Cocco, E., Molnar, L. and Tiago, M.M. (2022) *SPACE I – 2021. Council of Europe Annual Penal Statistics: Prison Populations*, Strasbourg: Council of Europe.

Bell, E. (2013) 'Punishment as politics: The penal system in England and Wales', in V. Ruggiero and M. Ryan (eds) *Punishment in Europe. A Critical Anatomy of Penal Systems*, London: Palgrave.

Berry, D., English, P. and Open Society Justice Initiative (2011) *The Socioeconomic Impact of Pretrial Detention*, New York: Open Society Foundations.

Boone, M. and van Swaaningen, R. (2013) 'Regression to the mean: Punishment in the Netherlands', in V. Ruggiero and M. Ryan (eds) *Punishment in Europe. A Critical Anatomy of Penal Systems*, London: Palgrave.

Cape, E., Hodgson, J., Prakken, T. and Spronken, T. (2007) *Suspects in Europe: Procedural Rights at the Investigative Stage of the Criminal Process in the European Union*, Antwerpen a.o.: Intersentia.

CPT (European Committee for the Prevention of Torture and Inhuman or Degrading Treatment or Punishment) (2017) *Remand Detention. Extract from the 26th General Report of the CPT*, Strasbourg: Council of Europe.

De Jong, F. and van Lent, L. (2016) 'The presumption of innocence as a counterfactual principle', *Utrecht Law Review*, 12(1): 32–49.

DLA Piper (2021) *A Global Analysis of Prisoner Releases in Response to COVID-19* at https://globcci.org/wp-content/uploads/2021/06/Global-Analysis-of-Prisoner-Release-Due-to-COVID-19.pdf [accessed 14 December 2022].

Duff, R.A. (2013) 'Pre-trial detention and the presumption of innocence', in A. Asworth, L. Zedner and P. Tomlin (eds) *Prevention and the Limits of the Criminal Law*, Oxford: Oxford University Press: 115–132.

Fair Trials International (2017) *A Measure of Last Resort? The Practice of Pre-trial Detention Decision Making in the EU* at www.fairtrials.org/wp-content/uploads/A-Measure-of-Last-Resort-Full-Version.pdf [accessed 14 December 2022].

Fink, D. (2020) 'La détention avant jugement en Suisse: un état des lieux', *Nouvelle Revue de Criminologie et de Politique Pénale*, 1: 46–52.

Forrester, A., Hopkin, G., Bryant, L., Slade, K. and Samele, C. (2020) 'Alternatives to custodial remand for women in the criminal justice system: A multi-sector approach', *Criminal Behaviour and Mental Health*, 30(2–3): 68–78.

Freiberg, A. and Morgan, N. (2004) 'Between bail and sentence: The conflation of dispositional options', *Current Issues in Criminal Justice*, 15: 220–236.

Hammerschick, W. and Reidinger, V. (2017) *DETOUR – Towards Pre-trial Detention as Ultima Ratio. 2nd Austrian National Report on Expert Interviews Vienna: Institute for the Sociology of Law and Criminology* at www.uibk.ac.at/irks/

publikationen/detour-publikationen/2nd-austrian-repor_interviews.pdf [accessed 4 January 2023].

Hassemer, W. (1984) 'Die Voraussetzungen der Untersuchungshaft', *Strafverteidiger*, 4: 37–45.

Heaton, P., Mayson, S. and Stevenson, M. (2017) 'The downstream consequences of misdemeanor pretrial detention', *Stanford Law Review*, 69: 711–794.

Jonckheere, A. and Maes, E. (2011) 'Caractéristiques des personnes placées sous mandate d'arrêt et/ou en liberté sous conditions', in A. Jonckheere and E. Maes (eds) *La detention preventive et ses alternatives*, Gent, Belgium: Academia Press: 35–54.

Jones, C.E. (2013) 'Give us free: Addressing racial disparities in bail determinations', *Legislation and Public Policy*, 16: 919–961.

Martufi, A. and Peristeridou, C. (2020) 'The purposes of pre-trial detention and the quest for alternatives', *European Journal of Crime, Criminal Law and Criminal Justice*, 28: 153–174.

Martufi, A. and Peristeridou, C. (2022) 'Towards an evidence-based approach to pre-trial detention in Europe', *European Journal on Criminal Policy and Research*, 28: 357–365.

Maruna S., Dabney D. and Topalli V. (2012) 'Putting a price on prisoner release: The history of bail and a possible future of parole', *Punishment & Society*, 14: 315–337.

Michaels, R. (2006) 'The functional method of comparative law', in M. Reimann and R. Zimmermann (eds) *Oxford Handbook of Comparative Law*, Oxford: Oxford University Press.

Morgenstern, C. (2018) *Die Untersuchungshaft*, Baden-Baden: Nomos.

Myers, N.M. (2019) '"Jailers in the community": Responsibilizing private citizens as third-party police', *Canadian Journal of Criminology*, 61: 66–85.

Nelken, D. (2009) 'Comparative criminal justice. Beyond ethnocentrism and relativism', *European Journal of Criminology*, 6: 291–307.

Pratt, J. (2008) 'Scandinavian exceptionalism in an era of penal excess: Part I: The nature and roots of Scandinavian exceptionalism', *The British Journal of Criminology*, 48: 119–137.

Radke, A. (2018) 'Women's yarning circles: A gender-specific bail program in one Southeast Queensland Indigenous sentencing court, Australia', *The Australian Journal of Anthropology*, 29: 53–69.

Rogan, M. (2022) 'Examining the role of legal culture as a protective factor against high rates of pre-trial detention: The case of Ireland', *European Journal on Criminal Policy and Research*, 28: 425–433.

Sakalauskas, G (2015) 'Strafvollzug in Litauen: Blick zurück oder nach vorne?', *Neue Kriminalpolitik*, 27: 190–201.

Sanderson, J., Mazerolle, P. and Anderson-Bond, T. (2011) *Exploring Bail and Remand Experiences for Indigenous Queenslanders Research Report. Griffith University* at www.premiers.qld.gov.au/publications/categories/reports/assets/exploring-bail-and-remand-experiences.pdf [accessed 14 December 2022].

Schönteich, M. (2014) *Presumption of Guilt: The Global Overuse of Pretrial Detention*, New York: Open Society Justice Initiative.

Scott-Hayward, C.S. and Fradella, H.F. (2019) *Punishing Poverty: How Bail and Pretrial Detention Fuel Inequalities in the Criminal Justice System*, Oakland, CA: University of California Press.

Stubbs, J. (2010) 'Re-examining bail and remand for young people in NSW', *Australian & New Zealand Journal of Criminology*, 43: 485–505.

Travers, M., Colvin, E., Bartkowiak-Théron, I., Sarre, R., Day, A. and Bond, C. (2020) *Rethinking Bail*. London: Palgrave.

Tyler, T. and Huo, Y.J. (2002) *Trust in the Law: Encouraging Public Cooperation with the Police and Courts*, New York: Russell Sage Foundation.

Ugelvik, T. (2012) 'The dark side of a culture of equality: Reimagining communities in a Norwegian remand prison', in T. Ugelvik and J. Dullum (eds) *Penal Exceptionalism? Nordic Prison Policy and Practice*, London a.o.: Routledge.

Van den Brinck, Y. (2019) 'Young, accused and detained. Awful, but lawful? Pre-trial detention and children's rights protection in contemporary Western societies', *Youth Justice*, 19: 238–261.

Van Kempen, P.H. (ed) (2012) *Pre-trial Detention: Human Rights, Criminal Procedural Law and Penitentiary Law, Comparative Law*, Cambridge: Intersentia.

Webster, C. M. (2022) 'Bailing them out early: Moving upstream in the search for solutions to the over-representation of Indigenous peoples in Canadian prisons', *The Criminal Law Quarterly* (forthcoming).

Zweigert, K. and Kötz, H. (1998) *An Introduction to Comparative Law*, 3rd ed., Oxford: Oxford University Press.

Chapter 2

Pre-trial detention in Austria: a preventive approach[1]

Walter Hammerschick

Introduction

Fundamental legal principles and developments

The Austrian legal system is based on the civil law tradition. All legal provisions must comply with the provisions of the constitutional laws. It was the so-called *Große Strafrechtsreform* (major reform of criminal law) of the 1970s which coined today's criminal law and the criminal procedures in Austria. The two central codes are the Austrian Penal Code (CC), which above all regulates the elements and the definitions of a crime, and the Austrian Code on Criminal Procedure (CCP), which regulates the procedures for criminal cases. There are also provisions with respect to the preliminary criminal proceedings, the imposition of arrest and pre-trial detention are regulated. The Personal Freedom Act of 1988, a constitutional code, regulates the most important protective aspects with respect to infringements of personal freedom. Secondary legislation supplements these regulations, for instance, the Juvenile Justice Act (JGG), which provides specific regulations for juveniles and for young adults.

According to §§ 173 pp CCP, pre-trial detention is the deprivation of liberty of an untried or not yet convicted person following a decision by the court. Literally translated, the term *Untersuchungshaft* means "investigating detention" and it comprises any detention during the pre-trial phase up to the end of an appeals procedure.

The main principles found in Austrian law on pre-trial detention are as follows:

- The ultima ratio principle prohibiting any deprivation of liberty if more lenient measures are sufficient to achieve the aims.
- The principle of proportionality which according to the Personal Freedom Act prohibits pre-trial detention if it is disproportionate to the aims pursued.
- According to the prevailing Austrian doctrine, pre-trial detention may never be "anticipated punishment".

DOI: 10.4324/9781003159254-2

Additionally, the Personal Freedom Act states the imperative for a speedy procedure, prescribes the need for review and guarantees compensation in cases of unlawful arrest or detention.

The fundamental bases for today's regulations on pre-trial detention have been laid out through an amendment to the CCP in 1993, strengthening the role of the so-called Investigating Judge. This deciding authority also became entrusted with legal protection. Connected to this, the actions of the involved parties became crucial for the procedures (*Parteienprozess*). With the CCP Reform Act of 2004, which entered into force in 2008, the position of the investigating judge however was abolished. Since then, the competencies and responsibilities of the public prosecutor have been extended and all procedures during the pre-trial phase are now driven or initiated by the public prosecutor. Today, all decisions concerning encroachments of rights of suspects, including detention, are the responsibility of the newly named detention and legal protection judge (*Haft- und Rechtsschutzrichter*).

In 2010, the possibility was introduced for pre-trial detention to be executed by means of house arrest monitored by an electronic monitoring device. So far, this option however is hardly used. As it is not an alternative to pre-trial detention as such, but rather a way to execute pre-trial detention, electronic monitoring (EM) in such cases also has to be terminated if less stringent measures secure the aims. In the prevailing view of legal practitioners, EM is hardly apt to exclude the reasons for pre-trial detention. If it would do so, usually milder measures are considered sufficient to serve the purpose of pre-trial detention (e.g. Hammerschick et al., 2012: 163).

Austria ratified the European Convention on Human Rights and Fundamental Freedoms (ECHR) in 1958 on constitutional level, and it is party to the European Convention for the Prevention of Torture (CPT). The Optional Protocol to the UN Convention for the Elimination of Torture and other Cruel, Inhuman or Degrading Treatment or Punishment (OPCAT) has been implemented by an amendment to the Austrian Constitution in 2011. Since 1981 Austria has an Ombudsman Board: the *Volksanwaltschaft* (§ 148a Federal Constitution). It is entrusted with the task of examining all alleged or presumed grievances arising in connection with the public administrative system. Since 2012, the Ombudsman Board and committees of experts installed there also fulfil the task of the National Prevention Mechanism (NPM). The committees of experts regularly visit and control institutions in which people are deprived of their freedom (OPCAT– Committees).

Pre-trial detention in practice

With a rate of 22.3 pre-trial detainees per 100,000, the Austrian pre-trial detention rate right before the pandemic in January 2020 represents about the European average (Aebi and Tiago, 2021; Aebi et al., 2019).[2] Pre-trial detainees on an average make up more than a fifth of the whole prison population. Thus, this group of prisoners contributes to the prison overcrowding prevalent in Austria in recent years. The high numbers of prisoners constitute considerable problems for the prison administration not least affecting the conditions of life in prison and the treatment of prisoners. The situation of pre-trial detainees is often particularly difficult, as they are frequently spending up to 23 hours a day in their cells with little or no contact with the outside world.

A central problem of pre-trial detention in Austria is one of the highest rates of foreigners in pre-trial detention all over Europe. In recent years, foreign nationals consistently represented about 70% of all pre-trial detainees in Austria. This fact must be seen in connection with the very central geographical location of the country within Europe, with considerable migration movements since the 1990s and with tourism playing a major economical role in the state. At any point of time, the number of people staying in Austria is considerably bigger than the registered population (e.g. Fuchs, 2017). This becomes also visible when data on crime and offenders is presented.

During the COVID-19 pandemic in 2020–2021, the numbers of prisoners decreased. By the end of 2019, about 9,200 prisoners were reported, with about 1,750 pre-trial detainees. On 1 March 2021, a total of 8,449 prisoners was counted, 1,463 of them in pre-trial detention. Presumably, pre-trial detention numbers declined above all due to reduced numbers of crime. Defence counsellors reported that the practice to order pre-trial detention did not really change; courts, however, were more willing to later release detainees under conditions.

Procedures, prerequisites and the competent authorities

Authorities, procedures, deadlines and decisions

The Austrian Code on Criminal Procedure (CCP) regulates arrest (*Festnahme*) and pre-trial detention (*Untersuchungshaft*) in §§ 170–189 CCP.

The police are the authority which carries out arrests ordered by the prosecutor and approved by a judge. Only in cases of "imminent danger" are the police entitled to arrest a suspect without an order by the public prosecutor, if and when prosecutor and judge cannot be reached in time. Each arrest, each order of pre-trial detention and each prolongation of pre-trial detention must be based on a request of the prosecutor with the responsible judge. Without this request, a suspect must be released. The judge issues arrest warrants applied for, carries out the obligatory hearings and is responsible for all decision to (further) detain suspects. Prior research casts doubt on the role of the prosecutor being the leader of the investigations (Birklbauer et al., 2011). In practice, the police were reported to carry out most investigations, with little involvement or guidance of the prosecutor and arrests are mostly carried out by the police autonomously on the grounds of imminent danger.

Detention begins with the arrest and may last up to two times 48 hours. With the arrest, legally important periods begin to run.

Arrest by the police (first 48 hours)

- If apprehended without warrant immediately after arrest,
  - written instructions have to be provided on the rights of the suspect in a language the suspect is able to understand (§ 171(4) CCP);
  - a hearing is required on the reasons and requirements for pre-trial detention, on the case and the suspicion; and
  - a written and reasoned motivation of the arrest issued by the police has to be supplied (§ 171(3)).
- If the arrest was based on an arrest warrant,
  - delivery of a written arrest warrant issued by the prosecutor and ordered by a judge within 24 hours (§ 171(3) CCP).
- Within 48 hours, there must be a transfer of the detained person to the prison and an application of the prosecutor for pre-trial detention, or otherwise a release (§ 172 CCP). The prosecutor's application for detention mentioning the grounds for detention applicable is based on the police reports.

Detention at the prison (second 48 hours)

- Right after arrival at the prison, the judge hears the suspect on the suspicion, the grounds for detention and investigates into all aspects relevant for the decision.
- Before deciding on detention or release, the judge may carry out investigations or order the police to do so, if it can be expected that this will have considerable impact on the judgment. In practice however, this is hardly done (Hammerschick and Reidinger, 2017). With respect to juveniles and young adults, the court may take advantage of the Jugendgerichtshilfe (Court Aid) to learn about the person and his/her social environment. The decision must be immediately communicated orally.
- In the decision, the following criteria have to be substantiated by the judge:
  - Urgent suspicion
  - One or more grounds for detention
  - Proportionality of pre-trial detention to the seriousness, the consequences and the punishment of the offence one may face in case of conviction

- The application of alternatives to detention or justifications why milder measures do not apply
- Delivery of the written and grounded decision to all parties involved within 24 hours after the decision;
- Without a decision within 48 hours, the suspect is to be released.

Time limits

Time limits for the validity of the pre-trial detention orders are defined in § 175 CCP. If this time has elapsed, the suspect must be released, or a detention hearing (*Haftverhandlung*) has to be carried out prior to the due date (§ 176 CCP). A first detention hearing has to take place 14 days after the first pre-trial detention order has been issued. Detention can then be prolonged on the prosecutor's request by one month, followed by two more months after the second and after each further hearing (and prolongation). This means that each time the court has to check if the reasons for detention still exist and decide whether the detention has to be prolonged, or whether the suspect has to be released.

There are also fixed limits for the duration of pre-trial detention regulated in § 178 CCP. If the trial does not begin before, pre-trial detention must not exceed the following time limits:

- Two months, if detention is grounded only in the risk of collusion/obscuring of evidence
- Six months for offences with a maximum penalty of three years
- One year with respect to crimes that carry a maximum penalty of more than three years, but not more than five years
- Two years with respect to offenses with a maximum penalty of more than five years.

In general, extensions beyond six months have to be substantiated by particular difficulties and complexities of the investigations depending on the weight of the ground for detention (§ 178(2) CCP). Once the bill of indictment has been delivered to the court, no further explicit time limits apply. The suspect however can always apply for release. Once the trial has started, a person who had to be released before due to the expiry of allowed periods can only be detained again for six weeks (§ 178(3) CCP). In principle, however, this could happen several times (Nimmervoll, 2018: 273).

The prerequisites for pre-trial detention

Detention actually begins with the arrest and the grounds for arrest are largely the same than the grounds for detention. For an arrest, a mere suspicion is sufficient; while for pre-trial detention to be ordered, the suspicion must be "urgent". The principle of proportionality always has to be considered. Even if grounds for detention may be given, detention is not allowed if the objectives of pre-trial detention can be met otherwise.

The grounds for detention are as follows (§ 173 CCP):

- The risk of absconding or hiding:
  - This does not apply if a fully integrated person is suspected of a crime that carries a maximum penalty of up to five years unless concrete preparations to flee have been made;
- Tampering with evidence
- The need to prevent new crimes:
  - If the suspect is charged with a crime carrying a penalty of more than six months and if there is a substantiated risk of reoffending
  - With respect to an offence with serious consequences
  - With respect to an offence with more than slight consequences if the suspect was already convicted because of such an offence before
  - If already convicted because of such an offence twice, it is enough that the reoffending is punishable by at least six months
  - If he is charged with repetitive forms of the same offence
  - The need to prevent the continuation of the offence that the suspect is charged with

For crimes punishable with a minimum of ten years of imprisonment, until recently pre-trial detention had to be ordered unless there were substantiated reasons which exclude the grounds for pre-trial detention ("conditional mandatory" ground for detention, § 173 CCP). A decision of the constitutional court however forced the legislator to abolish this provision in 2023. In general, chances appear very small that pre-trial detention is not ordered in such cases (see, e.g., Nimmervoll, 2018: 176 f).

Procedural rights, defence counselling and detention hearings

The rules to be followed in connection with the questioning after arrest are always the following: Firstly, it must be checked whether there is a need for translation. The suspect must be informed about the offence he is charged with, that s/he has the right to remain silent and that whatever s/he says may be held against her/him in a future trial (§ 164). S/he must be informed about her/his right to contact a close person and a defence counsel. If the initial ground for arrest cannot be validated, the suspect must be released. Already at this stage, the suspect also must be released if the purpose of the arrest can be fulfilled by milder measures. This however is not common practice.

Suspects have the right to the presence of a defence lawyer/counsellor during first hearings (§ 164 CCP). Active participation of the counsellor however is restricted at this stage and, most importantly, according to § 59 CCP, the police may supervise conversations between lawyer and suspect and restrict this to general legal information if this is deemed necessary to avoid interference with the investigation or with evidence. Not much of a surprise, this is regularly criticised by counsellors (e.g. Schumann, 2016). Supervision may even be extended for up to two months during detention. In *Lanz v. Austria*, the European Court of Human Rights (ECtHR, Application No. 24430/94, 21 May 1998) stated that there have to be very weighty reasons to justify this kind of restriction of Article 6(1) ECHR. After an amendment to the Criminal Code which came into force in 2017, more suspects now take advantage of a first legal aid consultation via phone. It is still, however, a small group who ask for the presence of legal assistance at the first interrogations. Despite information leaflets being provided in many different languages, which also address the question of the costs of legal assistance, suspects still seem to be afraid of risking high costs (Hammerschick and Reidinger, 2017). Most defendants are represented by legal aid–funded lawyers. The provision of legal aid in Austria however is often criticised, mainly because defence counsellors with rather little experience in criminal matters may also be appointed (Hammerschick and Reidinger, 2017; Kolda, 2017).

With the amendment to the CCP of 2004, the suspect and his/her lawyer have been clearly entitled to see and study all documents in police and court files beginning with pre-trial detention. This right however also can be restricted until the end of the pre-trial periods in favour of securing effective investigations. This is considered to be in line with the case law of the ECHR as long as it does not interfere with the rights of defence to assess the lawfulness of pre-trial detention (Morgenstern, 2009).

During the non-public detention hearings, the presence of a defence counsel is obligatory. These hearings are generally considered important procedural events, not least highlighting the periods for the obligatory reviews of the detention decisions. Nevertheless, critique has been expressed pointing at a restriction of most hearings to formal qualities (Hammerschick and Reidinger, 2017). Exchange of information on possibilities to apply alternative measures between counsellors and the judiciary as well as preparations in this respect mostly take place outside the courtroom. If the prosecution and the court agree on a release on non-custodial measures, release regularly takes places immediately outside detention hearings (ibid).

Each decision of the court on pre-trial detention may be appealed (§§ 87 pp. CCP) to the Court of Appeals within three days of the decision. Additionally, after all regular remedies have been used, since 1992 a so-called *Grundrechtsbeschwerde* (appeal with respect to basic rights) can be addressed to the Supreme Court seeking to overturn the decision of the Court of Appeals. This appeal has to argue that the decision of the Court of Appeals infringed the right to freedom. In practice, the means to fight decisions of the courts before the trial stage are generally hardly used (e.g. Birklbauer et al., 2011: 121). Attorneys report that it is better to talk to the prosecutor than to formally take advantage of legal safeguards. Not least they are afraid that decisions of the upper court may have negative impacts on the final verdict (Hammerschick, 2019: 225).

Decision-making and relevant factors

The extensive qualitative research carried out in the course of the DETOUR project (see Chapter 1), including 35 in-depth interviews with Austrian practitioners, provides valuable insights in factors relevant to the decision-making. This chapter is largely based on these outcomes (Hammerschick and Reidinger, 2017).

Prosecutors often appear to tend to favour pre-trial detention, although in principle they also have to pursue exculpatory factors (ibid: 68). This approach is partly legitimised by the procedural division of labour, with the judge being responsible for an evaluation of the application and for the decision. This way the prosecutors see themselves on the "safe side". It however also became clear that prosecutors perform a filtering function regularly diverting out cases brought forward by the police which, under their assessment, do not justify pre-trial detention.

According to estimates of the practitioners, it is assumed that judges follow the applications of the prosecution in 85–90% of cases. When questioned about this fact, judges explain that the applications would mostly be well-grounded. Both judges and especially prosecutors refer to a high level of shared assessments, while defence counsellors view prosecutors and judges as too close, indicating that the procedural safeguard based on the system of application and decision-making may be thereby weakened. Also, judges appear to have quite some discretion in their decisions on pre-trial detention, which they consider necessary also because of the time pressure and the rather little information sometimes available to decide on. Apart from hard facts in the records, the personal impression of a person is described to be very important, although this may be more difficult to assess if communication is restricted due to language barriers. Attorneys consider the discretion of the judges to be extensive (e.g. Echseneder, 2003).

The Austrian pre-trial detention practice is very much influenced by preventive aspects. Available data and expert interviews suggest that a risk of reoffending is assumed in about 90% of all pre-trial detention cases (e.g. Birklbauer et al., 2011: 187). This is not least due to the rather detailed regulations with respect to the risk of reoffending as a ground for detention. In fact, these regulations and their practical application appear to mirror societal concerns with respect to security. The domination of the risk of reoffending among the grounds for detention apparently is also based in the frequently provided explanation that it is a strong ground which is also quite easily substantiated in many cases (Hammerschick and Reidinger, 2017: 40). This is, on the one hand, due to the unfavourable (social) background of many offenders. On the other hand, already before the current definition of the risk of reoffending came into force, Venier (2006) had pointed at risks of more pre-trail detention caused by the then prepared extension of the definition. Until then, the formulation of the CCP referred to severe offences a suspect must be charged with for the application of this ground, while the new one refers to offenses punishable with more than six months. Defence counsellors criticise the application of the risk of reoffending to be applied to extensively. While the formal prerequisites often may be fulfilled, evaluations of the real risk are said to be hardly carried out, as expressed in the following quote:

> So this prognosis of the actual risk of a further offense is hardly checked so seriously in practice. From my regrettable experience, this is really such that an automatism is carried out here in the sense of a subsumption. If the relevant conditions are met – the expected penalty or relevant previous convictions and the like – as soon as these legal requirements are met, the risk of reoffending also becomes accepted without further ado, without really seriously considering whether this danger, this assumption of danger, also seriously lurks in a specific individual case. You see, that's what I mean by this automatism.
>
> (Defence counsellor 2)

In fact, this ground is often also applied with rather minor offences with assumed "criminal tourists" who are accused of property offenses aiming at a regular income. This indicates general preventive considerations which are not supposed to influence decisions on pre-trial detention.

Risks of absconding are explained to be harder to justify, considering the rather high threshold with respect to the expected sentence and obligations to consider bail. Nevertheless, this ground for detention is also often applied, frequently in combination with a risk of reoffending. Risks of tampering with evidence or to influence witnesses, on the other hand, play a minor role practically (Birklbauer et al., 2011: 187). Closely connected to the practical dominance of the risk of reoffending ground, a central factor prosecutors and judges look at when assessing a need for pre-trial detention is the prior records of the suspect and repeated offences. Prior records actually trigger many succeeding questions aiming at the assessment of a possible need for pre-trial detention, such as the time that has passed since the last conviction, social conditions the suspect was living in at the time of prior offences, the severity of prior offences, sanctions, alternative measures applied already and, last but not least, the question whether prior offences concerned the same legal values (Hammerschick and Reidinger, 2017: 24).

Procedural efficiency appears to play an important role as well, particularly when pre-trial detention is ordered with foreigners. Although the European Arrest Warrant is valued, practitioners are afraid of delays and hassle. In view of delays of the proceedings and of administrative difficulties, it is tempting to rather try and keep the suspect in custody. The imperative of a speedy process in detention cases is stressed by prosecutors when questioned about a disputed practice seemingly broadly applied. In cases with the investigations largely completed, an application for pre-trial detention is brought in with the judge presiding the trial together with the indictment. With this approach, the trial judge has to decide on pre-trial detention while also discussing and deciding on the suspicion at this stage, a practice possibly influencing the verdict (Ortner, 2017). In this context, judges reported about cases not fully investigated at the time of the indictment, in fact causing delays and problems later on.

Central to the decisions is the principle of proportionality, which however seems to be fulfilled quite easily in practice. Not least the Austrian Supreme Court ruled that it is not necessary that the expected sentence will be an unconditional one. The principle of proportionality is fulfilled if the length of the expected sentence suffices, no matter whether it is expected to be unconditional or conditional (e.g. Nimmervoll, 2018: 149). A burglary into a home is, for instance, subject to a prison sentence of up to five years. If one would only expect a sentence of about a third of the maximum, the principle of proportionality in this respect appears to be easily fulfilled indeed.

On alternatives to pre-trial detention

The list of alternatives to pre-trial detention called "milder measures" in the Austrian legal terminology provided by § 173(5) CCP is exemplary. This means that the judge is free to order any milder measure which seems adequate and does not infringe personal rights disproportionately, including combinations. In practice, the courts hardly take advantage of this option to introduce new or individually designed alternatives. If orders require suspects to get in contact with certain institutions, to participate in counselling, in therapy or similar measures, it is most often up to the client to organise those himself/herself. It is also up to them to provide proof to the court that they did follow the order, like confirmations issued by the respective institutions.

Regularly, orders concern the place of residency, pledges not to leave it and not to impede the proceedings, regular reports to the police as well as obligations to keep away from certain areas (e.g. in cases of domestic violence) or not to get in contact with certain persons (e.g. victims). In cases of domestic violence, there is an accompanying counselling available at so-called Men's Counselling Centers (*Männerberatungsstellen*) which as well may be ordered by the judge, including psychotherapy and specific trainings for the prevention of violence. To restrict mobility, documents can be confiscated and to avoid problematic situations, alcohol and substance abstinence can be ordered, controlled by institutions which also offer support in this respect. If drug problems are considered central reasons for offending behaviour, pledges to undergo dependency treatment are in fact often accepted as an alternative to pre-trial detention. Parts of such treatment may also cover the development of a work structure and leisure activities. Other orders may be directed at stable employment and structuring daily life. (Financial) Bail plays a very minor role in Austria, not least due to the fact that it can only be ordered for a risk of absconding being the only ground for detention (Hammerschick and Reidinger, 2017: 45).

Preliminary probation may be applied if the court assumes that the support and supervision by a probation officer will suffice to secure proceedings and to stabilise the situation of life of a suspect. It is regularly applied with juveniles and young adults, hardly however with adults. This may be due to a prevailing view which considers probation above all as a pedagogic tool and, therefore, less likely to succeed with adults (Hammerschick, 2021: 19). In this view, however, the potential of support to positively influence suspects in difficult situations of life and thereby reducing risks relevant in prosecuted cases is ignored (Hammerschick and Reidinger, 2017: 43).

Pre-trial detention is only to be applied as a last resort. Therefore, alternative measures to pre-trial detention must be given priority (§ 173/1 CCP). Consequently, the prosecutor and court have to establish reasons why alternatives are not implemented. In practice, alternatives to pre-trial detention are reported to be regularly used with juveniles and young adult, but rarely with adults. Unfortunately, no empirical data is available on the use of alternatives to pre-trial detention. According to estimates of practitioners, alternatives are applied in 5–15% of all cases for which pre-trial detention has been applied for (ibid). The high rate of foreigners in pre-trial detention, of course, also has to be considered an obstacle to order alternatives more often, but there seems to be a generally prevailing reluctance to order alternatives more often. Many judges and prosecutors quite obviously do not have sufficient trust in the potential of alternative measures to substitute pre-trial detention and to sufficiently exclude the risks (ibid: 50). Despite there being an obligation on judges to assess the possible application of alternatives, it is the counsellors whose initiative on this subject is above all expected with respect to alternative measures. Their performance in this respect however has been described to be sometimes improvable as well. Apart from the need to actively pursue alternatives, they were said to need more creativity with respect to the design of possible alternatives (ibid: 69). It is the responsibility of the public prosecution in charge of the case to supervise the compliance of suspects with the orders given.

It is a broadly acknowledged fact that the information available to the court to base the detention decision on is often rather poor. This is particularly true for information on the suspect and on social aspects (ibid: 39). It can be assumed that this is part of the reasons why alternatives are not applied more often. An option not or hardly used in practice is that of preparatory enquiries by probation services, which can be ordered by the court to obtain more information on the suspect and his/her social situation before preliminary probation may be ordered to avoid pre-trial detention. A supportive measure enquiring into the social surrounding of young people at risk and into their socio-economic situation to be considered in detention decisions is the so-called court assistance for juveniles and young adults (*Jugendgerichtshilfe*). It regularly also points out specific measures which seem to be necessary either to solve specific problems or to reduce risks. The court assistance is regularly employed and valued by the courts in juvenile cases. Again, with young people, the so-called social net conferences (SONEKO) can be carried out to possibly convince the judge to terminate pre-trial detention. At the conferences, plans are elaborated for the future that may help the youths to stay out of trouble, with the other participants (the social net) taking over tasks and responsibilities in this respect. Both court assistance and social net conferences are not available in adult criminal cases; however, they might have a potential to avoid pre-trial detention more often (Hammerschick, 2021: 21).

Data on pre-trial detention

Austria observed a considerable increase of the prison population in the early years of the century when the average numbers of prisoner rose from <7,000 in 2000 to almost 9,000 in 2007 (Bundesministerium für Justiz, 2020b). Since then, the numbers have been rather stable or slightly increasing. This was primarily due to increased numbers of foreigners in Austrian prisons. The number of detainees with Austrian citizenship, on the other hand, has been constantly decreasing. Figure 2.1 shows that this is also true for pre-trial detainees. In 2019, the number of Austrians in pre-trial detention represented 73% of the number in 2001. The number of persons without Austrian citizenship in pre-trial detention on the contrary increased dramatically by 81% till 2018, even though a decrease to 166% was observed in 2019.

It does not seem likely that Austrian nationals "improved" that much with respect to offending behaviours. In the context of the DETOUR project, practitioners confirmed that the practice has become more lenient with Austrians but rather harsh with foreign nationals (e.g. Hammerschick and Reidinger, 2017: 9). However, it also has to be pointed out that the number of foreign national suspects has also increased considerably.

In Figure 2.2, the dark grey column shows that only about a quarter of all entries into pre-trial detention in 2016–2018 were Austrian citizens. Another quarter of all entries were European citizens (light grey and grey), however only 3% of the EU 15, most of them Germans. Within the group of the "new" EU member states (EU 16–28), Romanians are the nationality most

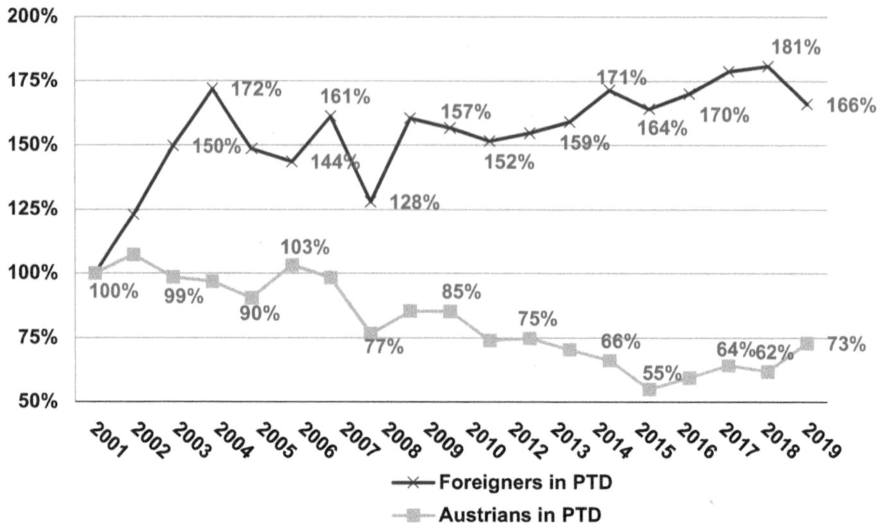

Figure 2.1 Development of the number of prisoners in pre-trial detention: Austrians and foreigners.

Note: Security report of the Ministry of Justice 2019 with own adjustments: annual date of data collection 1.9, start out point 2001 = 100%.

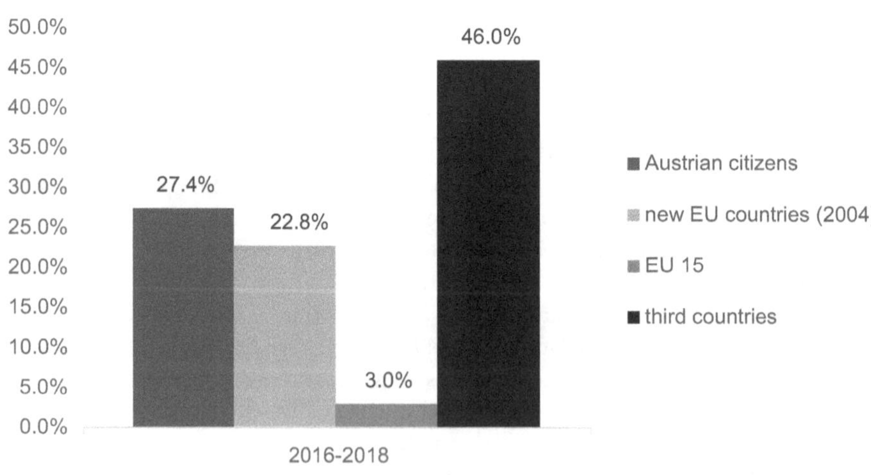

Figure 2.2 Nationality of pre-trial detainees 2016 and 2018: percentages of entries.

Source: Author's own calculations based on data provided by the General-Directorate of the penal system in Austria (2020).

often taken into custody in Austria, followed by Slovakian citizens and Hungarians. Citizens of Third Countries (black column) represented 46% of all entries into pre-trial detention in Austria. Most entries of this group were Serbians, followed by Afghan nationals and Nigerian (Bundesministerium für Justiz, 2020b). It has to be assumed that the refugee movements of the recent years have added to the high rate of suspects from Third Countries.

Since 2004, the average length of pre-trial detention has constantly increased. With an average of 86 days, the average length of pre-trial detention in 2019 was more than 20 days longer than in 2004 (Bundesministerium für Justiz, 2020b). Most often suspects are held in pre-trial detention because of property offences (e.g. theft), followed by drug offences. Both these kinds of offences are most often observed with foreigners. For Austrian citizens, sexual offences and offences against health and life are predominant (Hammerschick, 2021: 30).

Pre-trial detention rates vary considerably in different Austrian regions. In particular, an east (Vienna)–west (Innsbruck) divide has to be pointed out, which has already been observed in the 1990s (Hanak et al., 1998). In 2016–2018, an offender in Vienna (dark grey column) had a likelihood to be ordered pre-trial detention almost three times as high compared to an offender in Innsbruck (black column – see Figure 2.3). Of course, population trends and crime structure also show regional differences. In the Vienna region, slightly more serious crimes[3] are reported. The proportion of foreign

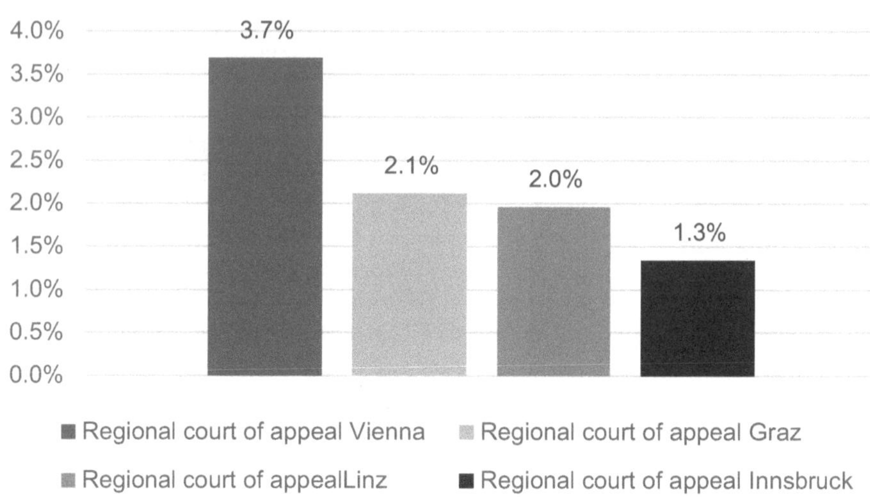

Figure 2.3 Regional distribution of pre-trial detention rates entries 2016–2018 in relation to suspects.

Source: Own calculations based on data provided by the General-Directorate of the penal system in Austria and on the Crime Statistics 2016–2018 (Ministry of Interior, 2019).

suspects altogether does not, however, show major differences. In the district of the Court of Appeal of Innsbruck, a slightly higher portion of suspects from Third Countries is observed, while in the Eastern-Austrian region slightly more suspects from "new" EU member states are detained. These differences however cannot explain the considerable differences with respect to the detention rate. The differences indicate a rather wide margin of discretion and a differing use of it, not least also coined by differing approaches of the Regional Courts of Appeal (Hammerschick, 2020: 41).

The burden pre-trial detention may mean for detainees becomes terribly visible when we look at suicide rates. In comparison to sentenced prisoners, the suicide rate among pre-trial detainees per 100,000 in 2019 was almost five times higher: 154.8 for pre-trial detainees versus 32.1 for sentenced detainees (Bundesministerium für Justiz, 2020b). Even more striking is a comparison with the general Austrian population, which reveals a rate more than ten times higher.

European aspects and their meaning for national pre-trial detention practice

For Austria, European cooperation is an urgent matter, also because of the high number of foreigners in Austrian prisons. Cooperation among European member states in criminal matters requires clear regulations, clear and functional organisational paths and not least mutual trust. The partly considerable differences with respect to the standards of detention in the member states are for instance a problem of practical relevance when it comes to extraditions and the execution of sentences in home countries of offenders. The CJEU decision in the cases *Aranyosi and Căldăraru*[4] has been reported to also have effects on decisions of Austrian courts with respect to the execution of European Arrest Warrants (EAW), an EU-wide arrangement which replaces traditional extradition procedures. For the year 2019, the Austrian Ministry of Justice reported 202 suspects to have been transferred to other EU countries based on a European Arrest Warrant (EAW, Bundesministerium für Justiz, 2020b: 306). The number of persons who have been transferred to Austria based on an EAW in 2019 was 192 (ibid). Until 2014, both transfers to and from Austria had been rising constantly. Since then, the numbers vary, but they are consistently higher than before 2014. According to the Austrian Ministry of Justice, the EAW is considered a success story which considerably simplified and accelerated the transfer of suspects (Bundesministerium für Justiz, 2020a: 262).

The European Supervision Order (ESO), a tool to supervise defendants in their home countries instead of detaining them in the country in which they face trial (see Chapter 14 for details), has been implemented in Austria in 2013. Until now however, hardly any cases have been reported with Austria asking another member state to take over the supervision of an alternative to pre-trial detention and the same is true the other way round. Considering the numbers of European citizens in pre-trial detention in Austrian prisons, this provokes the question what is wrong with the ESO not to be applied? The research carried out for the DETOUR project revealed that in 2017 most practitioners did not yet know about the ESO and seemingly this has not changed much recently.[5] The prevalent reactions of the practitioners were sceptical, quickly referring to administrative and bureaucratic burdens as well as to additional hassle if suspects would not appear for trial (Hammerschick and Reidinger, 2017: 83). Another argument regularly brought forward was the time needed for the transnational organisation. The organisational and administrative requirements would restrict the ESO to only a few cases with expectantly rather long times of pre-trial detention. Furthermore, different standards within the European Union with respect to the judicial systems as well as with respect to supervision measures and their availability were among the expressed concerns.

An option frequently used by Austrian authorities is the transfer of criminal cases to other European member states for prosecution according to Article 21 of the European Treaty on Legal Assistance in Criminal Cases and § 74 of the Austrian Code on Extraditions and Legal Assistance. Here it seems Austrian authorities trust in the work and the decisions of authorities in other member states. Such transfers may be applied for with other member states if this is viewed to be in the interest of finding the truth, or useful with respect to sentencing or sentence execution. The number of such cases involving Austrian authorities has been constantly rising during recent years reaching a new high of 2,799 in 2019. Of these cases, 80–90% regularly concern Austrian applications with other member states (Bundesministerium für Justiz, 2020a: 265; Bundesministerium für Justiz, 2020b: 306). These applications are mostly granted (84% in 2019).

Conclusions

The rather high pre-trial detention rates in Austria appear to be not least due to a broad definition of grounds for detention aiming at preventive goals combined with a practice additionally valuing preventive grounds. A backdrop most relevant in this respect is the high number of foreign suspects regularly apprehended in Austria. By widely applying preventive grounds, judges and prosecutors may see themselves in line with many people who are worried about rather high numbers of foreign suspects, sometimes additionally exaggerated by political actors. In such a political climate, general preventive motives can easily find their way into pre-trial detention decisions, which definitely are no ground for detention. In practice, the ambitions of judges and prosecutors to avoid pre-trial detention with foreigners may additionally be restricted due to procedural economics which may be at a higher risk in such cases. Most foreign suspects have a poor social background in common, which in turn makes it easier to substantiate the grounds for detention. Although pre-trial detention can be legitimised in most of these cases, there is a discriminatory quality to many cases with foreign suspects. Of course, criminal law cannot solve social problems, but criminal law practice should be careful not to unnecessarily aggravate them.

Looking at the main actors, pre-trial detention practice in Austria appears rather harmonic. In most cases, judges apply detention as requested by the prosecution and attorneys rarely challenge the decisions. Legal counsellors comment critically on the practices of the judges seldom denying applications of the prosecutor and most often insufficiently assessing the risks assumed in pre-trial detention cases. They themselves are however often reluctant to fight pre-trial detention decisions referring to strategic reasons. Appeals on detention decisions may provoke decisions or substantiations of the Courts of Appeal which in the end can have negative effects on the final verdict. When assessing chances of successful appeal, legal counsellors look at the regular jurisprudence of the courts of appeal which also is the main guideline for prosecutors and judges. As a consequence of this practice of the prosecutors, the judges and also the counsellors, the principally well-constructed legal safeguards lose parts of their teeth. Not least in light of a rather wide margin of discretion of the judges, this is a deficit. Some more "conflict orientation" of all actors involved would serve the legal culture, the continuing development of the legal system and the protection of the rights of individual suspects.

If Austrian judges and prosecutors do not apply alternative measures nationally, it is not much of a surprise, they are not applying them with the ESO in other member states. There remains a need for awareness raising about the gravity of the intrusiveness of pre-trial detention in the lives of persons affected and about the need to strengthen the ultima ratio principle. The DETOUR project indicated that there is some room for development in the realisation of the latter. A redesigning and strengthening of the detention hearings as well as a requirement of more substantial groundings for denials to apply alternatives could present valuable approaches. With respect to the ESO, it becomes visible that there continues to be an urgent need for opportunities for practitioners to meet colleagues from other countries, to exchange, to learn about and with each other and, not least, to aim for the realisation of common standards. The lack of knowledge about the ESO also calls for dissemination strategies and considering the defensive stance of many practitioners in cross-border matters, low-threshold support and counselling structures appear valuable. There will always be cases in which pre-trial detention will hardly be avoidable. Before this conclusion is reached however, procedures must be adhered to which ensure the protection of the rights of suspects, the adherence to the ultima ratio principle, to the principle of proportionality and the appropriate and well-assessed evaluation of suitable alternatives.

Notes

1 This chapter is largely based on reports elaborated in the run of the DETOUR project (see Chapter 1), on articles derived from these as well as on a report published in the context of the project PRETRIAD – alternative pre-trial detention measures (Hammerschick and Reidinger, 2016; Hammerschick and Reidinger, 2017; Hammerschick, 2019; Hammerschick, 2020; Hammerschick, 2021).
2 The latest available figure for a European median rate presented here is for September 2016.
3 Severe crimes (*Verbrechen*) are considered offences with a possible penalty of more than three years.
4 CJEU C-404/15 and C – 659/15, 5 April 2016: The CJEU decided that conditions of detention violating human rights can be a reason to deny the execution of European Arrest Warrants.
5 This is indicated in expert interviews carried out in the run of the project PRETRIAD – alternative pre-trial detention measures.

References

Aebi, M.F. and Tiago, M.M. (2021) *SPACE I – Council of Europe Annual Penal Statistics: Prison Populations, Survey 2020*, Council of Europe at http://210330_FinalReport_SPACE_I_2020 (unil.ch) [accessed 21 December 2022].

Aebi, M.F., Tiago, M.M., Berger-Kolopp, L. and Burkhardt, C. (2017) *SPACE I – Council of Europe Annual Penal Statistics: Prison Populations. Survey 2016*, Strasbourg: Council of Europe at https://wp.unil.ch/space/files/2019/02/SPACE-I-2016-Final-Report_Updated_190207.1.pdf [accessed 21 December 2022].

Birklbauer, A., Soeryer, R. and Stangl, W. (2011) *Die Rechtspraxis des Ermittlungsverfahrens nach der Strafprozessreform*, Wien-Graz: Neuer wissenschaftlicher Verlag.

Bundeministerium für Justiz (2020a) *Sicherheitsbericht 2018*, Bundesministerium für Justiz at www.justiz.gv.at/home/justiz/daten-und-fakten/berichte/sicherheitsberichte~2c94848525f84a630132fdbd2cc85c91.de.html [accessed 21 December 2022].

Bundeministerium für Justiz (2020b). *Sicherheitsbericht 2019*, Bundesministerium für Justiz at www.justiz.gv.at/home/justiz/daten-und-fakten/berichte/sicherheitsberichte~2c94848525f84a630132fdbd2cc85c91.de.html [accessed 21 December 2022].

Echseneder, H. (2003) 'Verteidigungspraxis im Vorverfahren und Reformvorhaben', in R. Soyer (ed) *Strafverteidigung – Realität und Vision – 1. Österreichischer StrafverteidigerInnentag*, Wien-Graz: Neuer wissenschaftlicher Verlag.

Fuchs, W. (2017) *Öffentliche Sicherheit in Wien*, Vienna: Institute for the Sociology of Law and Criminology (Research Report) at http://wp_öffsi.pdf (uibk.ac.at) [accessed 21 December 2022].

Hammerschick, W. (2019) 'Empirische Forschung zur Praxis der Anordnung von Untersuchungshaft als Reflexionsangebot', *Journal Für Strafrecht*, 6(3): 221–227.

Hammerschick, W. (2020) 'Zur Praxis der Untersuchungshaft in Österreich – Ermessenspielräume und Kontrolle', *Neue Zeitschrift für Kriminologie und Kriminalpolitik*, 1(1): 39–45.

Hammerschick, W. (2021) *Annex 3 – Austria in Hammerschick, W. D2.1. Literature Review: Legislative Analyses and Pre-trial Detention Impacts*, Department for the Sociology of Law and Criminology of the University of Innsbruck (Research

Report) at www.uibk.ac.at/irks/publikationen/2021/pdf/d2.1.-a-literature-review-on-pre-trial-detention.pdf [accessed 21 December 2022].

Hammerschick, W. and Reidinger, V. (2016) *DETOUR – Towards Pre-trial Detention as Ultima Ratio – Working Paper 1st National Report*, Vienna: Institute for the Sociology of Law and Criminology (Research Report) at http://1st-austrian-report.pdf (uibk.ac.at) [accessed 21 December 2022].

Hammerschick, W. and Reidinger, V. (2017) *DETOUR – Towards Pre-trial Detention as Ultima Ratio – Working Paper 2nd National Report*, Vienna: Institute for the Sociology of Law and Criminology (Research Report) at Microsoft Word – 2nd Nat Report-Part AT corr fin221217.docx (uibk.ac.at) [accessed 21 December 2022].

Hammerschick, W., et al. (2012) *Evaluation des Elektronisch Überwachten Hausarrests*, Vienna: Institute for the Sociology of Law and Criminology (Research Report).

Hanak, G., Karazman-Morawetz, I. and Stangl, W. (1998) *Die Praxis der Untersuchungshaft im Jahr 1996: Eine empirische Studie zur regionalen Anwendung des Haftrechts in Österreich und zur Auswirkung der Haftrechtsreform durch das Strafprozeßänderungsgesetz 1993*, Vienna: Institute for the Sociology of Law and Criminology (Research Report).

Kolda, J. (2017) Verfahrenshilfe: Mehr Roulette als Garantie. *Die Presse*, 2 February 2017.

Morgenstern, C. (2009) 'Austria', in A.M. Kalmthout, M.M. Knapen and C. Morgenstern (eds) *Pre-trial Detention in the European Union: An Analysis of Minimum Standards in Pre-trial Detention and the Ground for Regular Review in the Member States of the EU*, Nijmegen: Wolf Legal Publishers.

Nimmervoll, R. (2018) *Haftrecht – Freiheitsentzug im Strafverfahren*, Wien: Lexis Nexis Orac Verlag.

Ortner, M. (2017) 'Über den unmittelbaren Strafantrag mit Antrag auf Verhängung der Untersuchungshaft', *Journal Für Strafrecht*, 4(2): 117–120.

Schumann, S. (2016) 'Rechtstatsachenforschung', in A. Stuefer and W. Pleischl (ed) *Strafrecht und Strafverteidigung – Beiträge zum Symposium für Richard Soyer zum 60. Geburtstag*, Wien: Verlag Österreich.

Venier, A. (2006) 'Strafprozessreform und Haftrecht', in R. Moos, U. Jesionek and O.F. Müller (eds) *Strafprozessrecht im Wandel: Festschrift für Roland Miklau zum 65. Geburtstag*, Innsbruck and Wien: Studienverlag.

Chapter 3

Well meant is not always well done: pre-trial detention in Belgium[1]

Eric Maes and Alexia Jonckheere

Introduction

"*148 gedetineerden moeten in Belgische cel op de grond slapen*" [148 detainees have to sleep on the floor in Belgian cells], the Flemish newspaper *De Standaard* stated on 22 March 2021; *Le nombre de détenus dormant sur le sol dans les prisons belges augmente* [The number of inmates sleeping on the ground in Belgian prisons is increasing], the French-language public broadcaster RTBF reported that same day. The aforementioned figure was recently released by the Belgian Minister of Justice Vincent Van Quickenborne in response to a parliamentary question from Flemish senator Annick Lambrecht.[2] This distressing situation in Belgian prisons has everything to do with the problem of prison overcrowding, which has been gripping the country for decades.

Belgium has somewhat less than 100 inmates per 100,000 inhabitants (94.9),[3] which is lower than the European average (119.8 on 1 January 2019; Aebi and Tiago, 2020: 30), but (much) higher than neighbouring countries such as the Netherlands (43.7) and Germany (69.7), and in particular the Scandinavian countries (Finland: 49.8; Sweden: 59.7; Norway: 60.4). Nevertheless, Belgium has a high prison overcrowding rate, even one of the highest within the whole of Europe (14%; 10,514 inmates for a prison capacity of 9,219 places, on 20 September 2019; Beyens and Maes, 2020). Especially the use of pre-trial detention seems to contribute strongly to this; according to the recent communication of the Minister of Justice to the aforementioned parliamentary question, 38% of the prison population are persons in pre-trial detention.

This situation raises many questions. More than 30 years ago, in 1990, the pre-trial detention system was thoroughly reformed. Stricter criteria for the use of pre-trial detention and the introduction of (new) alternatives were introduced and were intended to solve the experienced "abuse" of pre-trial detention. Situations of crisis, such as long-lasting and large-scale strikes in Belgian prisons and specific policies and measures adopted to combat the COVID-19-pandemic, at a given moment appeared to be able to turn the

DOI: 10.4324/9781003159254-3

situation around, but the question remains what the long-term impact of the so-called alternatives to pre-trial detention is:

> If it is seemingly "easy" to reduce pre-trial detention during a time of crisis, it begs the question: Why wouldn't it be feasible to do so in ordinary times?
>
> (Maes and Jonckheere, 2020)

Or, otherwise stated, did the "alternatives" to pre-trial detention in the long run (in "normal" times) fail to produce the desired effects?

Legal framework and alternative options to pre-trial detention

In Belgium, the imposition and execution of pre-trial detention and alternatives is situated within a complex institutional structure that, since the first State reform in 1980, has been constantly evolving. Important areas of competence relating to the judicial area or closely related to it are spread across various state entities.

Belgium is a federal state with three Communities divided mainly according to language (the Dutch-speaking Flemish Community, the French-speaking French Community and the German-speaking Community) and three regions aspiring to greater economic autonomy (the Flemish Region, the Brussels Capital Region, and the Walloon Region). Issues such as Justice and Home Affairs are mainly the competence of the federal state, with some exceptions like the probation service in charge of executing sentences and measures in the community.[4] In this way, the implementation of custodial measures that can be applied in the pre-trial stage fall within the federal state (organisation of the judiciary and prison service), whereas the execution of alternative measures belongs to the competence of the Communities (probation service).

Criminal proceedings and pre-trial detention

Criminal proceedings are laid out in the Code of Criminal Procedure, but specifically with respect to pre-trial detention and alternatives, a separated legislation is provided by the Pre-Trial Detention Act (hereafter PTD-Act).[5] This legislation envisaged two major reforms. On the one hand, in addition to the existing possibility to release on (money) bail, a new alternative option to pre-trial detention was introduced – the possibility to release a suspect under conditions. On the other hand, new procedural guarantees strengthened the rights of the defence.

In principle, and in most cases, a criminal case is opened for any offence known to the public prosecutor. After receiving the initial police report of the offence, this prosecutor may decide to conduct the investigations with the assistance of police, a process called *information*. S/he may also decide to refer the case to an investigating judge. In this case, an *instruction* is opened and the investigations take place under the responsibility of the investigating judge and the judicial council, a special chamber of the district court in first instance. If the prosecutor requests special measures such as an arrest warrant, s/he must ask to open an *instruction*.[6] The police can arrest a person judicially for a maximum of 48 hours.[7] After this period, the deprivation of liberty can only be prolonged by the decision of an investigating judge, ordering a pre-trial detention under an arrest warrant (to be executed in prison or under electronic monitoring).

Grounds for pre-trial detention and defence counselling

Under Belgian law, such a coercive measure is only possible when it is absolutely necessary for public security, when the criminal offence is punishable with a prison sentence of one year or more and when serious indications of guilt exist.

Furthermore, if the maximum sentence for the criminal offence does not exceed 15 years of imprisonment, remand in custody or alternatives have to be based on additional grounds: risk of recidivism, absconding, collusion or destroying evidence. Since the Law of 3 August 2016 which was adopted to guarantee the protection of society,[8] this additional ground is no longer required in case of "terrorist" offences that are punishable with more than five years of imprisonment.

Especially since the 2011 legislation related to a decision by the European Court of Human Rights (ECtHR), *Salduz v. Turkey* (36391/02, 27.11.2008), particular attention has been paid to the rights of the defence: anyone deprived of freedom of movement has access to a lawyer of choice from the moment of arrest and prior to the first questioning by the police or, failing that, by the public prosecutor or the investigating judge (Article 2bis PTD-Act). If the suspect has not chosen a lawyer or this lawyer is not available, the Bar Council's *pro bono* unit is contacted. A suspect who does not have adequate resources can benefit from full or partial free legal aid.[9]

Duration of pre-trial detention and procedural guarantees

Pre-trial detention is always a temporary measure. Although Belgian law does not stipulate a maximum duration, an accused person has to be taken to court within a reasonable time. This reasonable time is stipulated in Article 5, paragraph 3 of the European Convention on Human Rights (ECHR) and is considered in the light of the jurisprudence of the European Court of Human Rights (ECtHR). This means that the judge has to verify, on the basis of the concrete circumstances of the case, '*la durée tant effective que relative de la détention, le degré de complexité de l'instruction, la manière dont celle-ci fut conduite, le comportement de l'inculpé et celui des autorités compétentes'* [the actual and relative duration of the detention, the degree of complexity of the investigation, the manner in which it was conducted, the behaviour of the accused and that of the competent authorities] (Roggen, 2012: 6–7). In that respect, the Court of Cassation, the highest court in the country, recently recalled that '*l'existence d'un intérêt public à la poursuite de la détention ne peut s'apprécier qu'à l'issue d'un examen actualisé, précis et personnalisé des éléments de la cause, puisque la privation de liberté est l'exception et que les raisons l'ayant justifiée peuvent perdre leur pertinence au fil du temps*' [The existence of a public interest in continued detention can therefore only be assessed after an updated, precise and personalised examination of the elements of the case, since deprivation of liberty is the exception and the reasons that justified it may lose their relevance over time].[10] For example, in the context of the COVID-19 health crisis, it was decided that the increased risk of contagion in prison and the related limitations of prisoners' rights are elements to be taken into account when assessing the need to maintain, or not, pre-trial detention (Kennes, 2020). To ensure that the principle of "reasonable time" would be respected, a new provision was introduced in 2005 that provided for an automatic control, by the chamber of indictment, of cases in which the accused was in pre-trial detention and the investigation process was still ongoing, six months after the issuing of the arrest warrant.[11] This protective measure, however, has been abolished.[12]

The investigating judge's first decision on pre-trial detention is valid for five days, from the moment of execution. Within that period, a special chamber of the district court, the judicial council, has to decide if the pre-trial detention is to be maintained. If the judicial council does not take a decision within five days, the suspect must be released. Before taking its decision, the judicial council must take note of the investigating judge's report as well as the prosecutor's requests. It should also hear arguments of defence from the accused party and, if relevant, the lawyer. The judicial council checks the legal conditions for detention and assesses whether the pre-trial detention should be continued. If there is an irreparable nullity, such as a detention based on an irregular warrant of arrest, the judicial council cannot repair the act and has to order the release of the accused. As long as pre-trial detention is still ongoing and the investigation is not completed, the judicial council will review the detention, twice on a monthly basis and then bi-monthly.[13]

Both the suspect and the prosecutors have the right to appeal against the decisions of the judicial council before the chamber of indictment and a further appeal against the decision of the chamber of indictment can be made to the Court of Cassation. In order to reduce the workload of the Court of Cassation, the legislator decided by Law of 5 February 2016 to limit this possibility of appeal in cassation (Michiels and Kerzmann, 2016); however, the Constitutional Court annulled this restriction in its judgment of 21 December 2017.[14]

At the end of the *instruction*, the investigating judge hands the case file over to the public prosecutor. If there is no demand for any further investigation, the judicial council examines the file and then decides whether or not to refer the case to court. Additionally, the court decides whether pre-trial detention should continue or if the individual is eligible for release under conditions. After this decision, the judicial council no longer conducts an automatic review for the pre-trial detainee, who can still, from month to month, introduce a request for release. For a suspect released under conditions, the sentencing court may decide to deliver an arrest warrant if the suspect does not respond to summons or in the case of new and serious circumstances.

Alternative options to pre-trial detention (in prison)

Belgian legislation provides for different "alternative" solutions to (pre-trial) detention in prison. In cases where pre-trial detention may be ordered or maintained, the competent judicial authorities (investigating judge, judicial council or chamber of indictment) may decide on an alternative measure or another way of executing the arrest warrant or pre-trial detention: electronic monitoring, release on (money) bail and/or release under conditions.

Electronic monitoring

Since 1 January 2014, it is possible to use electronic monitoring in the context of pre-trial detention.[15] More specifically, according to Belgian legislation, electronic monitoring is considered as a "modality of execution"[16] of an arrest warrant (and thus not, a real "alternative" in a stricter sense). This means that the investigating judge (or investigating courts) will first decide whether an arrest warrant has to be issued (or prolonged) and then, in a second step, will decide where the arrest warrant will be executed: in prison or at the suspect's home (or at another assigned residence).

At this stage of the criminal justice process, suspects are monitored using GPS technology, without limitation in time. In case of non-compliance or other specific circumstances (e.g. technical problems), electronic monitoring can be converted into pre-trial detention in prison. The continuation of electronic monitoring will be reviewed on a regular basis, just as would have been the case were the suspect detained in prison.

A suspect under electronic monitoring is not allowed to leave the assigned place of residence except for a limited number of movements allowed for medical reasons, in case of *force majeure*, or in relation to the criminal investigation process (e.g. hearings by judicial authorities and police interrogations). As such, electronic monitoring in the pre-trial stage appears to be a form of "24-hour home detention". Similar to "classic" pre-trial detention, the electronic monitoring system *can* also be "individually modulated", that is, a prolonged term of "prohibition of free communication" is possible, in terms of contacts with the outside world (i.e. individuals or institutions listed individually in the arrest warrant) by way of correspondence, visits and telephone contacts. Since the possibilities to leave the assigned residence are very limited, it seems, as a consequence, very difficult, if not impossible, to engage in a professional activity.

(Financial) bail

In cases in which pre-trial detention can be ordered or maintained, the investigating judge can, *ex officio* or at the request of the public prosecutor or the suspect, determine an amount for bail on the basis of the suspect's actual or presumed income, without any legal restriction. The suspect can then be released following prior and complete payment. The idea behind bail is to encourage a person to remain at the disposal of the justice system until the trial. If the suspect was present at all the proceedings and has presented himself/herself in order to serve his/her sentence, the bail is returned to him/her.

There has been almost no scientific research about this topic and there is no updated data that can inform us about the application of this measure. Nevertheless, it seems that, in practice, financial bail is not used very often. According to some, this mainly has to be related to the culture of the country (Burssens, 2011; Tange, 2011). However, critical voices also report that, from the point of view of principle, freedom and the "absolute necessity for public security" (one of the preconditions for pre-trial detention) cannot be bought off (Vandermeersch, 2015), and that it threatens the equality of citizens. Although members of parliament thought that financial bail does not imply discrimination between those with no or little income and others who can afford to pay bail, to the extent that investigating judges can always impose other conditions on release,[17] some authors maintain that the measure is unequal. Those who have no financial resources will find it more difficult to offer to pay an amount that will reassure the judge (Kennes, 2011). Furthermore, doubts can subsist as to the legality of the money (risk of money laundering by the State). Though it was announced by the former Minister of Justice in January 2016 that the legislation on pre-trial detention would be reformed on this point,[18] no initiative has been taken since then.

Release under conditions

The most common alternative is to release the suspect on one or several conditions. Such release under conditions can occur either without a prior arrest warrant or after time is spent in detention (or under electronic monitoring). Primarily because of structural obstacles (Jonckheere and Maes, 2020: 10), most releases under conditions follow pre-trial detention (Jonckheere and

Maes, 2017; Maes and Jonckheere, 2017), thereby rather reducing length of pre-trial detention than preventing detention (in prison or at home).

When deciding on release under conditions, the judge must determine how long these measures will last. However, release under condition cannot be imposed for an initial period longer than three months (Article 35, paragraph 1 PTD-Act). Before deciding on the measure, a social enquiry report – either an extensive enquiry report or a concise social information report[19] – can be requested from the Probation Service to obtain information on the suitability of release under conditions (Article 35, paragraph 1 PTD-Act). The latter aims at answering only precisely formulated questions and was introduced in 1999 to simplify and speed up the procedure (Beyens and Scheirs, 2010). Before the termination of the first period of release under conditions, the judge may decide to extend the conditions for a new period and determine the duration, which once again cannot exceed three months. This possibility continues to be available to the judge throughout the *instruction*.

Acting *ex officio* or at the request of the public prosecutor, the investigating judge may also impose one or several new conditions, as well as withdraw, modify or extend the conditions already laid down in whole or in part. At the end of the *instruction*, the judicial council may decide to maintain or withdraw the conditions. Finally, after the *instruction* is completed, it is up to the trial court handling the case to decide whether to extend the existing conditions, always for a maximum period of three months and until the ruling at the latest. It may also withdraw or dispense with compliance with some of them, but it may never impose new ones (Article 36).

The type as well as the number of conditions is left to the judges' discretion. The PTD-Act does not provide for an exhaustive list of conditions that can be imposed. In practice, certain standard conditions are systematically applied: not committing new offences, responding to convocations, having a fixed residence, following the guidance of the probation officer and providing evidence of compliance with the conditions. These standard conditions are most often supplemented by other conditions that relate or refer to daily occupation (e.g. looking for work or following a training), to psycho-medical-social counselling, to the protection of victims (e.g. not approaching the victim),[20] to prohibitions (not leaving the country, not entering and drinking in a bar or coffee shop, not being in contact with other suspects, etc.), to budgetary and/or administrative assistance and to medical control (e.g. urine or blood tests for drug users).

Although the judge may choose which conditions are imposed, it seems that some conditions are systematically imposed in specific cases. For example, in cases of domestic violence, often the following conditions are imposed: not contacting the victim, recovering one's personal belongings through a third-party intermediary or the police, and solving problems related to the custody and visitation of children through an attorney or legal service. In the case of drug use, the following conditions are commonly imposed: staying away from drug-using environments, following therapeutic treatment (more details are sometimes included regarding the nature of the therapy, the frequency of contact, means to provide proof, etc.) and holding a regular job.

The number of conditions to be met can be high. In some cases, 15 conditions may be imposed. The Probation Service (of the French-speaking Community) has noticed a trend towards increasing the weight of conditional measures, particularly for offences related to membership in terrorist networks (Administration générale des maisons de justice, 2016).

In most cases, the Probation Service is called on to verify that conditions are being met. Adherence to conditions of prohibition (the prohibition to visit cafés, former inmates, certain neighbourhoods, etc.) must also be verified by the police (Article 38), but in practice, this verification is organised quite differently from one place to another: in some cases, police verification that the conditions are met, is solely reactive, while in other cases verification is pro-active.

If the conditions are verified by the Probation Service, it is also responsible for providing social assistance to the individual. The probation officer – a social worker, and not a judicial officer – regularly writes and sends a report to the judicial authority that ordered the release under conditions; by doing so, probation officers can draw the attention of the judges to the difficulties encountered by the person and request, for example, a modification of the conditions or the removal of some of them. Such reports must be issued in the case of non-compliance with the conditions or if a problem of compliance arises. In any case, a report must be written no more than 15 days before the period of release under conditions ends (Article 38, paragraph 1).

Non-compliance with the conditions does not constitute an offence in Belgium, in contrast to, for example, the situation in Canada (Vanhamme, 2020: 16). In the event of a breach of conditions, depending on the stage of the proceedings, the investigating judge, the judicial council or the chamber of indictment may deliver an arrest warrant. In fact, it is observed that this option is rarely used: releases under conditions are revoked in only 3% of the cases (Administration générale des maisons de justice, 2016). However, this percentage may be underestimated, as probation officers are not always informed of the delivery of an arrest warrant. In some instances, judges prefer to impose new conditions or adapt the conditions to the situation of the individual concerned.

The length of releases under conditions is extremely variable. In some cases, it only lasts three months; in other cases, the measure may last for a few years. In some judicial districts, releases under conditions are automatically prolonged, while this never happens in other districts. Different reasons may explain a prolonged period of supervision, such as a heavy workload of probation officers (not being able to provide support to suspects in their first period of release) or expectations of (investigating) judges with regard to the necessity of a continuation of the guidance; because the suspect encounters difficulties in respecting the imposed conditions, or on the contrary, because the suspect respects the conditions such as therapeutic treatment so well that it seems preferable to reconfirm these conditions.

In practice, releases under conditions are, on average, longer than pre-trial detention. A possible explanation is that a lower priority is reserved for cases in which the person is not detained, and because the law provides for a maximum length which is then easily fully used by judges.

Research and statistics on pre-trial detention in Belgium

Growing prison population numbers, sustained criticism of the use of imprisonment and increasing attention paid to the efficiency of criminal justice proceedings have led to several proposals for reform and new Belgian legislation in the domain of (criminal) justice in recent decades, especially in the area of criminal justice proceedings and pre-trial detention. As already indicated, major legislative reforms concerning pre-trial detention were enacted in 1990 (the new PTD-Act), 2005, 2011 (the so-called Salduz legislation), 2012 (electronic monitoring at the pre-sentencing stage) and 2016 (strengthening the protection of society in the context of terrorism, and "Salduz-bis" or "Salduz+").[21]

Consequently, quite a lot of literature has been produced on pre-trial detention (and alternatives) in recent times, both by criminal justice practitioners (judges, prosecutors, lawyers) and by scholars at universities and public research institutions.

Apart from juridical contributions (*doctrine*) published in specialised journals and important "reference works" in which proposals for legislative reform, newly introduced legislation and/or highly relevant jurisprudence are commented on and discussed, as well as national overviews in legal-comparative studies,[22] a significant amount of empirical scientific research has been conducted on pre-trial detention and alternatives in Belgium since the late 1980s.[23] Within this research literature, three major types of research can be distinguished:

- Contributions that describe and comment on (quantitative) developments in the use of imprisonment and alternative measures or sanctions, and/or that describe profiles (specific characteristics) of the populations concerned. Information on these topics with respect to pre-trial detention/alternatives is provided as part of more general descriptions of the prison population or alternatively sanctioned offenders, or is specifically devoted to the pre-trial detainees or suspects subjected to an alternative pre-trial measure.
- Research into factors that influence the decision to remand suspects in custody and the length of pre-trial detention, using quantitative multivariate

analyses of data gathered through analyses of judicial files and research on underlying decision-making processes, using qualitative research methods like interviews and observations.

- Research that evaluates the effects of already introduced legislative or practical reforms or that assesses the desirability and/or possible impact of proposed legislative or practical reforms (e.g. increasing the eligibility threshold for the application of pre-trial detention, developing "positive" or "negative" lists of offences, limiting the length of pre-trial detention and introducing electronic monitoring as an additional alternative/ execution modality).

This scientific criminological research on pre-trial detention and alternatives produced some interesting findings. First, it has become clear that the PTD-Act of 1990 has had no substantial reducing effect on the remand prison population in Belgium. From a European perspective, Belgium has a prison population rate below the European rates (adjusted figure in 2016[24]: 93.6 prisoners per 100,000 inhabitants versus a European average of 122.1 and a median of 110.6; SPACE I, Aebi et al., 2018: 53). However, the rate of "prisoners not serving a final sentence" (30.0 in 2016) is higher than the respective European average (27.0) and median (27.1) (SPACE I, Aebi et al., 2018: 77). Although stabilised during almost 15 years, between 2003 and 2016 (on a daily average of around 3,500–3,600 pre-trial detainees and non-definitively convicted prisoners), this population has more than doubled between 1990 and 2019 (on average 3,969 pre-trial detainees and non-definitively convicted prisoners) (Figure 3.1).

The significant drop in the (total) prison population after the introduction of depopulation measures in response to COVID-19[25] to below the limit of 10,000 (see, e.g., Maes and Nève, 2020: 14) was, somewhat predictably, only short-lived. While on 14 May 2020 there were still 9,614 detainees in prison – a decrease of the population, which seems partly also due to shifting policies in the use of pre-trial detention (Maes and Nève, 2020: 17) – the number increased again after the measures were stopped. In June 2020, the prison population rose rapidly to its former level, up to about 10,600 inmates. When the second wave of infection had started, the prison population remained initially very high, reaching 10,838 inmates on 23 November 2020 (Maes and Beyens, 2021). Nevertheless, it seems that the pandemic influenced pre-trial detention practices: as such, the number of electronically monitored suspects in Flanders, for example, has increased significantly, by 60%, in 2020 (945 new EM supervision orders in the pre-trial stage versus 590 in 2019).[26]

Previous studies on possible legislative reforms to reduce the remand prison population have shown that only (very) "radical" legislative reforms would have any significant impact, for example, the introduction of a list of "eligible" offences (e.g. only violent offences). Current legislation actually

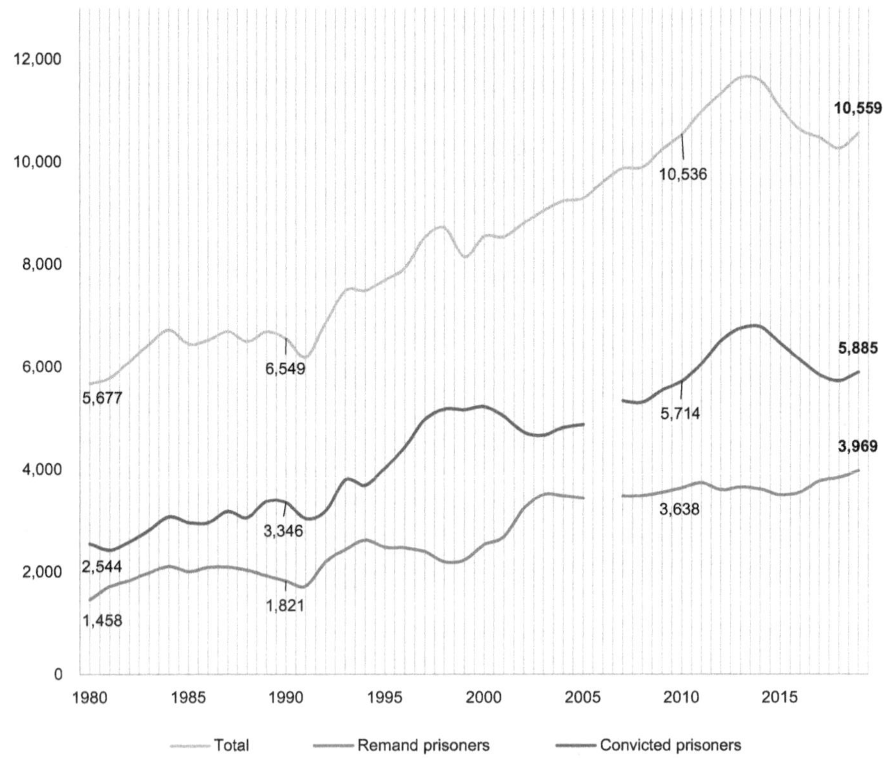

Figure 3.1 Evolution of the prison population (daily average): total number (1951–2019) and according to legal status (remand and convicted prisoners, 1980–2019).

Source: Beyens et al. (1993) and Beyens and Tubex (2002) (data for 1951–1994); unofficial data from the prison administration (data for 1995–2005); Annual Reports Prison Service (for 2007–2016); brochure "Justitie in cijfers 2015–2019" (FOD Justitie, 2020; for 2017–2019).

provides sufficient guarantees for a careful use of pre-trial detention. An extensive application of pre-trial detention therefore rather depends on the practical implementation of the legislation. In practice, current legal grounds (risk of recidivism, absconding) can be justified quite easily (e.g. Maes and Deblock, 2017: 16–18; Jonckheere, 2017: 7), particularly with regard to the risk of recidivism, which is considered to be a "catch-all concept" giving considerable discretionary power to the investigating judge (Jonckheere, 2017: 8). The motivation of the decision is often stereotypical, standardised (especially in larger districts) and, in later stages of the procedure, it is not unusual that decisions to keep the suspect in custody just refer to the fact that the motivation of the initial decision is still valid (e.g. Maes and Deblock, 2017: 65–67).

Many factors influence the decision to issue an arrest warrant as well as the length of pre-trial detention, case-specific characteristics (e.g. presence of co-suspects and their eventual arrest), geographical differences, as well as individual features (e.g. nationality or origin, residence status, criminal history, and social, financial, psychological or drug problems) (Burssens et al., 2015). Besides that, it seems that pre-trial detention is sometimes also used as a kind of "short sharp shock-detention" (De Man et al., 2009: 146; Maes and Deblock, 2017: 9 and 21; Jonckheere, 2017: 9) or as a reaction to/consequence of (prison) sentence implementation policies (non-execution of prison sentences/conversion into EM/early automatic release schemes) (De Man et al., 2009: 138 and 164; Beyens et al., 2010; Burssens, 2011: 60; Tange, 2011: 82; Maes and Deblock, 2017: 8–9 and 40; Jonckheere, 2017: 9).

Another explanatory factor could be the fact that shifts in social sensitivity, expectations of the public (together with the rise of social media) and sometimes highly critical reporting by traditional media puts pressure on and/or effectively affect public prosecutor's policies.[27] Regular settlement of cases on the level of the public prosecution may become less used, at least where it concerns specific criminal phenomena (e.g. intra-familial violence, hit-and-run), thereby favouring referral for judicial *instruction* with requests for pre-trial detention (Maes and Deblock, 2017: 8). That public prosecutors themselves propose alternatives, remains an exception, in the further course of the criminal proceedings (at judicial review hearings), that is, after the decision initially has been taken by an investigating judge to issue an arrest warrant (Maes and Deblock, 2017: 25–26; Jonckheere, 2017: 18).

As a possible explanation for the large number of arrest warrants, magistrates (also) indicated a potentially greater sensitisation and willingness to report by victims of specific offences (sex offences, intra-familial violence, etc.), an increasing degree of elucidation through progress in forensic and criminal investigation techniques, and changes in the nature of crime (e.g. more international and organised character, namely in case of human trafficking, drug production and traffic, property crimes) (Maes and Deblock, 2017: 8; Jonckheere, 2017: 2), and organisational problems that prevent, for example, an immediate care of a person at risk (for example, a person in crisis with psychiatric disorders) in a specialised shelter (Jonckheere, 2017: 9).

In any case, the increase in pre-trial detention does not seem to result from a global increase in crime. Indeed, crime figures suggest that the overall crime rate did not increase over the last two decades; on the contrary, rather a "crime drop" can be observed, at least since 2012. While the federal police service reported more than one million offences in the year 2000, this overall number dropped to 898,057 in 2019 (Federale Politie, 2020 – closing date 24 October 2020). Nevertheless, with regard to cases admitted to the prosecutorial services (College van Procureurs-generaal, Statistisch analisten, 2018; Maes, 2018, slide 86), some types of criminal phenomena seem to increase over time (between 2003 and 2015), such as manslaughter and murder

(+20.3%), sexual assault and rape (+16.6%) and assault and battery (+2.6%) On the other hand, a significant decrease of "violent theft" has been reported at the level of the prosecution office (–20.7%).

With respect to the use of alternatives, some (structural) obstacles still exist (Maes and Deblock, 2017: 36–39; Jonckheere, 2017: 26–27): quasi automatic exclusion of foreign nationals without residence in Belgium (Jonckheere and Maes, 2010); lack of adequate extra-mural mental health and social care services in some regions; not enough capacity; long waiting lists; difficulties to organise intake interviews with pre-trial detainees; some suspects not asking for treatment or being difficult to "motivate"; problems with (native) language; strict exclusion criteria towards clients with multiple problems, towards justice clients in general, or more specific for pre-trial detainees, rejection because not yet being convicted and still being presumed innocent (Maes and Jonckheere, 2017).

Despite these obstacles, "alternatives" for pre-trial detention are very "popular". The annual number of committals to prison and placements under community supervision before final judgment ("release under conditions") within the framework of pre-trial detention (supervised by the Probation Service),[28] amounts, in 2019, to almost 14,500 confinements and almost 6,000 new "release under conditions" orders (compared to only 600 mandates in the year 1995) (Figure 3.2). The question arises whether release under conditions replaces freedom/release without conditions rather than imprisonment (pre-trial detention), that is, the question of net-widening (Maes et al., 2016: 29; Burssens et al., 2015: 55–56 and 66).

It seems that defence lawyers contribute to a certain extent to such net-widening. In their defence strategy, they do not longer ask for release without conditions as they would have done earlier, but plea more generally for the imposition of alternatives, as they also seem to experience that what can be called "old habits" are not appropriate any longer. Often, they use the stricter electronic monitoring option to convince indecisive, hesitating magistrates and avoid prison for their client ("*out is out, whatsoever how*"); in some cases, this also works (Maes and Deblock, 2017: 9 and 26; Jonckheere, 2017: 18).

Electronic monitoring (EM), as mentioned earlier, formally no alternative but an execution modality of an arrest warrant, has, certainly in the first years of implementation, been much less popular than the measure of "freedom or release under conditions". Also, the variation in practices between judicial districts is remarkable. There are several reasons why electronic monitoring in the pre-trial stage was – at least in the early years – not so often used in Belgium (e.g. EM stock on 17 September 2018: $N = 320$[29]; *DGEPI Daily Prison Population*): lack of knowledge/information about (technology of) EM; fear for additional administrative workload; questions about the ability to prevent risks of collusion and the ability to effectively prevent absconding or recidivism; the very "strict" EM regime (more flexibility required?);

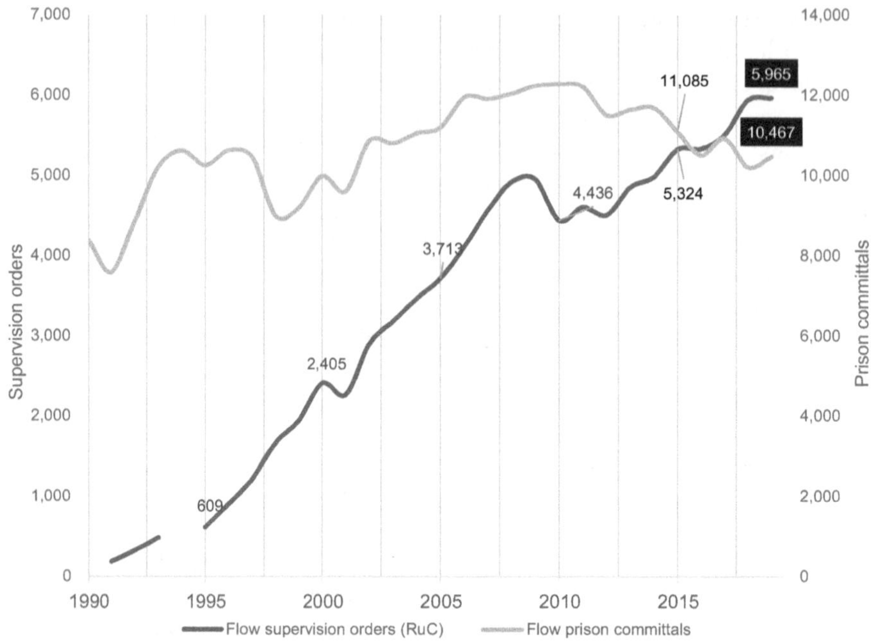

Figure 3.2 Evolution of the annual number of new supervision orders within the framework of pre-trial detention (release under conditions) and the number of prison committals (flow) (1990–2019).

Source: Prison committals PTD: Beyens et al. (1993: data for 1980–1991); personal analysis of raw prison data (data for 1992–1995: see Deltenre and Maes, Panopticon 2002: 210–211); brochure "Justitie in cijfers" (data for 1996–2010); Annual Reports Prison Service (data for 2011–2015; exclusively minors for 2015–2016); brochure "Justitie in cijfers 2015–2019" (FOD Justitie, 2020; data for 2016–2019).

Supervision Orders RuC: Evaluation Reports Service Social d'Exécution de Décisions Judiciaires (data for 1991–1993, 1995, 1997–1998); statistics Dienst Maatschappelijk Werk Strafrechtstoepassing (data for 1996); brochure "Justitie in cijfers" (data for 1999–2010); Annual Reports Probation Service data for 2011–2014); datawarehouse Probation Service (data for 2015); brochure "Justitie in cijfers 2015–2019" (FOD Justitie, 2020; data for 2016–2019).

discriminatory aspects (unequal quality of EM "detention" places); "negative" impact of EM on suspects and their families (e.g. psychological pressure, social life, family relations – "pains of EM"); "bad" experiences (e.g. consent of cohabitants) (Maes and Deblock, 2017: 50–51; Jonckheere, 2017: 13).

In 2019, more than 7,500 persons experienced one or another kind of "judicial supervision", awaiting a final sentence,[30] compared to "only" 1,800 suspects in Belgian prisons in 1990, when release under conditions and electronic monitoring did not yet exist (Figure 3.3). So, over 30 years, the total

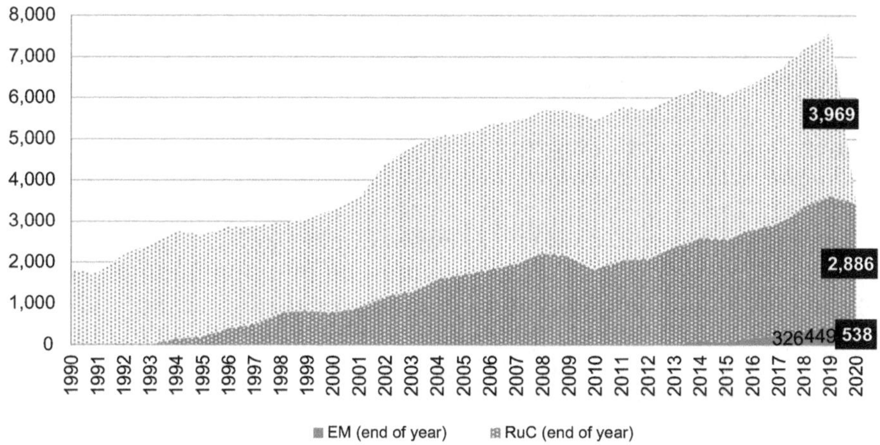

Figure 3.3 Evolution of the daily population "under judicial control" within the framework of pre-trial detention (remand custody in prison, release under conditions, electronic monitoring, 1990–2019/2020).

Source: EM population: Annual Report Probation Service (data for 2014); data obtained from *Centre de Surveillance Électronique* (data for 2015–2016: daily population on 1 January 2016, resp. 2017); data obtained from the cabinet minister of Justice (data for 2017: population on 28 December 2017); information obtained from the different Probation Services in February–March 2021 (data for 2019–2020)

RuC population: Annual reports Probation Service (data for 1994–2003); brochure "Justitie in cijfers" (data for 1999–2004); data obtained from Paul Verhaeghe (data for 2006); data obtained from the Flemish Probation Service in February 2021 (for 2005 and 2007–2009); Annual Reports Probation Service (data for 2010–2014); information obtained from the different Probation Services in February–March 2021 (data for 2015–2020).

PTD population: Beyens and Tubex (2002) (data for 1980–1994); data obtained from Samuel Deltenre (Prison Service; data for 1995–2005); Annual Reports Prison Service (data for 2007–2016; exclusively minors in 2015–2016); Brochure "Justitie in cijfers 2015–2019" (data for 2015–2019).

number of persons under judicial supervision before the final trial has more than quadrupled. The question arises if the "alternatives" to pre-trial detention meet their objectives. Do we still need "alternatives" (see Maes and Jonckheere, 2017) or would it be better to return to the pre-1990 situation, when alternatives did not exist and significantly fewer people were placed under judicial supervision?

European watchdogs and instruments

As foreigners, even from EU member States,[31] often seem to be excluded from alternative measures,[32] with pre-trial detention being the "default position" for them, one may wonder whether European instruments designed to improve EU-wide cooperation, based on mutual trust – in particular the

European Arrest Warrant (EAW) and the European Supervision Order (ESO) – could bring any solution.

With respect to European developments and its impact on domestic legislation and jurisprudence, first of all, and more generally, it must be stated that Belgium has always been supportive of the idea of European social and economic integration. Belgium was one of the founding members of the Council of Europe (CoE) in 1949 and of the European Economic Community (EEC) in 1957, which integrated into the European Union (EU).

Belgium ratified the European Convention on Human Rights (ECHR) on 14 June 1955 and the European Convention for the Prevention of Torture and Inhuman or Degrading Treatment or Punishment (ECPT) on 23 July 1991. The new PTD-Act and other legislation on the deprivation of liberty before trial were significantly influenced by the case law established by the ECtHR, especially the decisions in the cases of *Lamy v. Belgium* (10444/83, 30.03.1989; access to file information and "equality of arms"), *Bouamar v. Belgium* (9106/80, 29.02.1989; detention of minors in remand centres) and *Pauwels v. Belgium* (10208/82, 26.05.1988; deprivation of liberty of military soldiers) (Van den Wyngaert et al., 2009). As mentioned already, more recently, the cases of *Salduz v. Turkey* (36391/02, 27.11.2008) and *Bouglame v. Belgium* (16147/08, 02.03.2010) impacted on Belgian legislation and led to important modifications of the PTD-Act, where it concerns access of lawyers to police interrogations and the hearing by the investigating judge (Law of 13 August 2011).

In one of her contributions, Beernaert (2016) assessed whether the Belgian legislation on pre-trial detention conforms to the standards set by the ECHR and the European Court's case-law. Although she concluded that Belgian law (on pre-trial detention) is/was in conformity with the main principles of the Convention, the question arises as to whether the practice of pre-trial detention infringes important requisites of the convention; e.g. when the placement in pre-trial detention or its continuation is motivated in a summary, abstract and stereotyped way, or when this is done without taking into account the evolution of the situation and the progress of the proceedings; when alternatives to deprivation of liberty have not been seriously considered or have been refused without a convincing and detailed motivation; or when the proceedings are not conducted with all diligence that is desired.

In any case, the Belgian State was convicted (again) by the ECtHR, because of unreasonable length of pre-trial detention (*Lelièvre v. Belgium*, 11287/03, 8 November 2007; remand in custody of seven years and ten months – violation of Article 5, § 3 ECHR), and because of inhuman or degrading detention conditions due to prison overcrowding in Belgian prisons (*Vasilescu v. Belgium*, 64682/12, 25.11.2014, *Sylla and Nollomont v. Belgium*, 36467/13–36467/14, 16.05.2017, *Pîrjoleanu v. Belgium*, 26404/18, 16.03.2021 – violation of Article 3 ECHR).

In addition, the European Committee for the Prevention of Torture and Inhuman or Degrading Treatment or Punishment (CPT) repeatedly criticised the situation in detention facilities, and especially the detention conditions in remand prisons. After having visited the remand centre of Vorst/Forest in Brussels in 2012, the CPT concluded that the detention conditions as mentioned in its report, and more specifically those in certain wings of the Forest prison, could be considered as resembling an inhuman and degrading treatment to inmates who experience this situation, a conclusion that was not even contested by the Belgian authorities that were interviewed during the visit.[33] Strikes of prison guards in 2016 attracted the attention of the CPT and, following a visit in order to "*examine on the spot the impact of this industrial action . . . on the situation of inmates*", the CPT held "high-level talks" with the then Minister of Justice and a member of the Private Office of the Belgian Prime Minister.[34] Such situation also poses problems in terms of international cooperation. For example, some European member states sometimes refused to extradite their own nationals to Belgium because of the poor detention conditions (Jonckheere and Maes, 2020).[35]

With regard to EU legal instruments, Belgium adopted legislation in order to implement the European Arrest Warrant (EAW)[36] and more recently, the so-called European Supervision Order of 2009 (ESO) that was transposed into domestic legislation by a Law of 23 March 2017.[37] Belgium was one of the last countries to adopt appropriate legislation in this respect, at the time being (interviewed) practitioners did not seem familiar with this instrument; they had never heard about it, or only had some vague notions (Maes and Deblock, 2017: 70). While the ESO could bring some kind of solution to the question of the pre-trial detention of (EU) suspects not permanently (and officially) residing in Belgium – who are often taken into custody quasi-automatically, as conditions could not be controlled by the foreign authorities in the home country – there were some critical comments, whether or not based on experiences with other EU instruments. It was, for example, referred to as too much "bureaucracy", a lot of additional paper work, complicated and maybe long-lasting procedures, language problems, problems of co-ordination and of "trust" or "recognition" (Maes and Deblock, 2017: 70).

In a recent evaluation report on Belgium (Council of the European Union, 2021), it was noted that the problems identified by the Belgian authorities in the application of the ESO concerned the complexity of the legislation; the lack of awareness of those instruments on the part of practitioners; the multiple national authorities involved in the application of the instrument; the perception that the instrument seems unsuitable for the types of cases in which a measure is ordered as an alternative to (pre-trial detention), that is, serious cases; and, uncertainties as to whether or not the decision on supervision measures is recognised, the time limits within which the issuing state will be notified of any failure to comply with the conditions (the concept of "without delay"), and the arrangements for exercising the supervision carried out in the executing state. Given the multiplicity of actors competent at the national level for the application of the ESO, there exists no statistical data on its application on the national level. Nevertheless, it appears that, until now, there are only very few cases in Belgium in which it is applied.

Conclusion

For many years now, voices have been raised in Belgium to strictly limit the use of pre-trial detention. Criticism is not only expressed by the scientific community; also, socio-legal professionals (including judges, sometimes members of the highest courts in the country), the political world and even the media advocate cautious use of pre-trial detention. Nevertheless, there is at the same time another underlying – and just as powerful – discourse, which rejects any possible risk of (re)offending. This seemingly paradoxical situation shows the discrepancy between theory and practice; otherwise stated, "thinking" well is not the same as "doing" well. The recent DETOUR research (see Chapter 1 for details), financed by the European Union, indicated that countries that focus more frequently on (preventive) grounds relating to public security (e.g. Belgium) to justify pre-trial detention – and where motivations are thus more often based on perceived risks of recidivism – have higher pre-trial detention rates than those countries that focus primarily on securing the criminal investigation, the trial and the execution of punishment (risks of absconding, destroying evidence).

In addition, the (very) complicated Belgian institutional landscape and excessive fragmentation of governmental powers do not really favour mutual understanding, and as a consequence, fluent cooperation between the various actors within the criminal justice chain, each of them working in different organisational frameworks and under the responsibility of other (subsidising) authorities. Only concerted and politically supported actions can allow to hope for a more reasoned use of pre-trial detention and alternative measures.

Notes

1 This chapter is to a large extent based on previous publications, especially on some (national) reports produced within the framework of the DETOUR project (Maes et al., 2016; Maes and Deblock, 2017; Jonckheere, 2017) and on a book chapter published as Jonckheere and Maes, 2019. Where relevant and available, most of the (previously reported) quantitative data and statistics were updated for the occasion of this contribution.

2 Q&A, Senate, session 2020–2021, Written question No. 7–1137, 5 March 2021 (answer received on 18 March 2021).

3 For Belgium, these data concerning the total number of inmates, as reproduced in SPACE I, relate to December 2019 (instead of 31 January 2019) and were retrieved from www.prisonstudies.org/country/belgium (see Aebi and Tiago, 2020: 33).

4 Under the authority of the Communities since 1 January 2015 (Jonckheere, 2016).

5 The Pre-trial Detention Act of 20 July 1990 does not include the proceedings for juvenile detention which are not discussed in this contribution.
6 The legislator has recently expanded the prosecutor's prerogatives in the preliminary stage of a criminal procedure. Since the Law of 5 February 2016, the public prosecutor can also validly request a search warrant in the context of a "*mini-instruction*", that is, with no involvement of the investigating judge (De Valkeneer, 2017; Masset and Monville, 2016).
7 For many years, Belgium had a maximum length of judicial arrest (by the police) of 24 hours, extendable in some cases up to 48 hours, but this time limit has been modified by an amendment of the Belgian Constitution in 2017. Since then, judicial arrest by the police is allowed for a period of 48 hours, which is not extendable.
8 Law of 3 August 2016 providing miscellaneous provisions for combating terrorism, *Belgian Official Journal*, 11 August 2016, 50.973. For more information on this legislative reform and other measures introduced to prevent and combat terrorist crimes within the framework of the criminal investigation process, see Schotsaert and Van Linthout (2018). Further proposals for legislative changes with respect to pre-trial detention and alternatives in terrorist cases were recently, for example, formulated by Walter Damen (Damen, 2018).
9 See the two laws strengthening recently the rights of the defence: Law of 13 August 2011 (*Belgian Official Journal* 5 September 2011, 56.347) and Law of 21 November 2016 (*Belgian Official Journal* 24 November 2016, 77.974).
10 Cassation, 2nd Chamber, 18 March 2020, *Journal des tribunaux*, 2020, 384.
11 Law of 31 May 2005 modifying the law of 13 March 1973 on the compensation in case of unjustified pre-trial detention, the law of 20 July 1990 on pre-trial detention and some dispositions of the Code of Criminal Procedure, *Belgian Official Journal*, 16 June 2005, 27.390.
12 Law of 5 February 2016 modifying penal law and criminal procedural law and containing several dispositions relating to justice, *Belgian Official Journal*, 19 February 2016, 13.130.
13 New legislation entered into force on 1 July 2016 (Law of 5 February 2016 amending criminal law and criminal procedure and introducing various provisions in the field of justice, *Belgian Official Journal*, 19 February 2016, 13.130).
14 Constitutional Court, Judgment No. 148/2017 of 21 December 2017, *Belgian Official Journal*, 12 January 2018, 1.393.
15 Law of 27 December 2012 introducing various provisions relating to justice, *Belgian Official Journal*, 31 January 2013, 5.286.
16 As a consequence, time spent in pre-trial detention under electronic monitoring is deducted from the prison sentence that would be imposed. This does not apply for the time spent on the "alternative" of release under conditions.
17 *Parl. Doc.*, Senate, *Projet de loi relatif à la détention préventive, Rapport fait au nom de la commission Justice*, Doc. No. 658–2 (1988–1989), 5 June 1990, p. 111.
18 Commission Justice de la Chambre des Représentants, *Compte-rendu intégral*, 27 January 2016, CRIV 54 COM 324, p. 6.
19 This latter type of report aims at answering to some precisely formulated questions and was introduced in 1999 to simplify and speed up the procedure (Beyens and Scheirs, 2010).
20 The issue of compensation to the victim at this stage of the proceedings is controversial due to the presumption of innocence.
21 The so-called Salduz-bis Law of 21 November 2016 relating to certain rights of persons subject to interrogation has significantly extended the right to counsel during a hearing (Giacometti, 2018).

22 See some publications with chapters on Belgium: Van Kalmthout et al. (2009), Van Kempen (2012).
23 For an overview, see also Burssens (2012), the first Belgian rapport within the framework of the DETOUR research project (Maes et al., 2016), and more recently, Jonckheere and Maes (2019).
24 Belgium did not provide (comparable) data for subsequent SPACE I reports (i.e. published reports for the years 2018 and 2019).
25 Interruption of sentence execution "Coronavirus COVID-19" for detained convicted offenders, early release from prison as of six months before the end of the sentence, deferral of sentence implementation for some convicted offenders, etc.
26 https://dwvg.be/jaarverslag20/cijfers-elektronisch-toezicht (accessed 12 July 2021).
27 Certain files transmitted to the investigating judge are therefore very "light", the request for an arrest warrant being formulated as a precautionary measure (Jonckheere, 2017: 34–35).
28 In Belgium, the intervention of the Probation Service for a suspect released under conditions is not obligatory. The judge may release under conditions someone, while having him/her supervised by the police. There is no statistical data on this police supervision. Due to the lack of these data, the number of releases under conditions in Belgium is therefore slightly underestimated.
29 Compared to 538 on 31 December 2020 (information obtained from the different Probation Services in February–March 2021).
30 On average 3,969 persons were detained in prison (on a daily basis); in addition, on 31 December 2019, 3,178 were on release under conditions and 449 underwent pre-trial detention under electronic monitoring.
31 According to the prison administration, in 2017, 44.2% of the total prison population (DGEPI 2019: 46) are non-Belgian citizens.
32 In previous research, we showed that foreign nationals were much more represented in the pre-trial population than in the population released under conditions (Jonckheere and Maes, 2010: 121–122).
33 See for CPT reports on Belgium: www.cpt.coe.int/documents/bel
34 www.cpt.coe.int/documents/bel/2016-06-22-eng.htm (accessed 12 July 2021).
35 See, for example, the refusal (suspension) of extradition by the *Internationale Rechtshulpkamer* of the Amsterdam court on 31 May 2016, at www.demorgen.be/nieuws/nederland-schort-uitlevering-van-verdachten-aan-belgie-op~b2092bab/
36 Law of 19 December 2003 concerning the European arrest warrant, *Belgian Official Journal*, 22 December 2003.
37 Law of 23 March 2017 on the application of the principle of mutual recognition of decisions relating to control measures pronounced as an alternative to pre-trial detention, *Belgian Official Journal*, 19 May 2017, 57.946.

References

Administration générale des maisons de justice (2016) *Rapport Annuel 2015*, Bruxelles: Fédération Wallonie-Bruxelles.

Aebi, M.F. and Tiago, M.M. (2020) *SPACE I – 2019 – Council of Europe Annual Penal Statistics: Prison Populations*, Strasbourg: Council of Europe.

Aebi, M.F., Tiago, M.M., Berger-Kolopp, L. and Burkhardt, C. (2018) *Annual Penal Statistics. SPACE I. Prison Populations*, Strasbourg: Council of Europe.

Beernaert, M.-A. (2016) 'La détention préventive sous le regard de la Cour européenne des droits de l'homme', in L. Aubert (ed) *Détention préventive: Comment sans sortir?*, Bruxelles: Bruylant: 37–57.
Beyens, K., Clémence, F. and Scheirs, V. (2010) 'Les juges belges face à l'(in)exécution des peines', *Déviance et Société*, 34(3): 401–424.
Beyens, K. and Maes, E. (2020) 'Het lappendeken van tien jaar strafuitvoering in België', *Panopticon*, 41(1): 10–41.
Beyens, K. and Scheirs, V. (2010) 'Encounters of a different kind. Social enquiry and sentencing in Belgium', *Punishment & Society*, 12(3): 309–328.
Beyens, K., Snacken, S. and Eliaerts, C. (1993) *Barstende muren. Overbevolkte gevangenissen: omvang, oorzaken en mogelijke oplossingen*, Antwerpen: Kluwer.
Beyens, K. and Tubex, H. (2002) 'Gedetineerden geteld', in S. Snacken (ed) *Strafrechtelijk Beleid in Beweging*, Brussel: VUBPress: 139–177.
Burssens, D. (2011) 'Voorlopige hechtenis (z)onder voorwaarden', in A. Jonckheere and E. Maes (eds) *De voorlopige hechtenis en haar alternatieven. Onderzoekers en actoren in debat*, Gent: Academia Press: 57–72.
Burssens, D. (2012) 'De voorlopige hechtenis in België. Synthese van bestaand empirisch onderzoek', *Fatik*, 133: 17–23.
Burssens, D., Tange, C. and Maes, E. (2015) *Op zoek naar determinanten van de toepassing en de duur van de voorlopige hechtenis. A la recherche de déterminants du recours à la détention préventive et de sa durée (Onderzoeksrapport No 39).* Brussel: NICC.
College van Procureurs-Generaal. Statistisch analisten (2018) *Jaarstatistiek van de correctionele parketten en het federaal parket – Opsporing en vervolging van strafzaken door de parketten van de rechtbanken van eerste aanleg (Jaarstatistiek 2015)* at www.om-mp.be/stat/corr/jstat2015/n/home.html [accessed 12 July 2021].
Council of the European Union (2021) *Evaluation Report for the Ninth Round of Mutual Evaluations – Ninth Round of Mutual Evaluations on Mutual Recognition Legal Instruments in the Field of Deprivation or Restriction of Liberty – Report on Belgium*, Brussels, 29 April 2021 at https://data.consilium.europa.eu/doc/document/ST-12996-2020-REV-2-COR-1/en/pdf [accessed 12 July 2021].
Damen, W. (2018) 'De advocaat aan het woord', in J. Kerkhofs, Ph. Van Linthout and A. Schotsaert (eds) *Contra-Terrorisme. De gerechtelijke aanpak van terrorisme in België*, Brussel: Larcier: 357–403.
Deltenre, S. and Maes, E. (2002) 'Effectmeting van enkele mogelijke wetswijzigingen op het vlak van de voorlopige hechtenis', *Panopticon*, 23(3): 196–211.
De Man, C., Van Brakel, R., Maes, E. and Mine, B. (2009) *Toepassingsmogelijkheden van het elektronisch toezicht in het kader van de voorlopige hechtenis. Possibilités d'application de la surveillance électronique dans le cadre de la détention préventive* (Rapports INCC/NICC), Institut national de criminalistique et de criminologie; INCC/NICC at https://nicc.fgov.be/upload/publicaties/rapport_23.pdf [accessed 12 July 2021].
De Valkeneer, C. (2017) 'L'information et l'instruction', in M. Cadelli and Th. Mozeto (eds.) *La loi pot-pourri II*, Bruxelles: Larcier: 91–131.
DGEPI (Directoraat-Generaal Penitentiaire Inrichtingen) (2019) *Jaarverslag 2017*, Brussel: Federale Overheidsdienst Justitie.

Federale Politie (2020) *Politiële criminaliteitsstatistieken – België – 2000–1e semester 2020* at www.stat.policefederale.be/assets/pdf/crimestat/nationaal/rapport_2020_trim2_nat_belgie_nl.pdf [accessed 12 July 2021].

FOD Justitie (2020) *Justitie in Cijfers 2015–2019* at https://justitie.belgium.be/sites/default/files/jic-nl-2015-2019.pdf [accessed 12 July 2021].

Giacometti, M. (2018) *Mandat d'arrêt : Retour des formalités prescrites à peine de remise en liberté*, Cahiers du CRID&P, UCLouvain.

Jonckheere, A. (2016) 'L'informatique dans la tourmente de la 6ème réforme de l'Etat', *Pyramides*, 2013/2 & 2014/1(26 & 27): 87–106.

Jonckheere, A. (2017) 'DETOUR-towards pre-trial detention as ultima ratio. Report on (French-speaking) expert interviews', in *DETOUR-Towards Pre-trial Detention as Ultima Ratio. 2nd Belgian National Report on Expert Interviews*, Brussels: INCC-NICC.

Jonckheere, A. and Maes, E. (2010) 'Opgesloten of vrij onder voorwaarden in het kader van het vooronderzoek in strafzaken? Analyse van het profiel van verdachten onder aanhoudingsmandaat en vrij onder voorwaarden (VOV) op basis van justitiële databanken (jaar 2008)', in L. Pauwels, S. De Keulenaer, S. Deltenre, L. Deschamps, H. Elffers, J. Forceville, J. Goethals, R. Kerkab, E. Maes, S. Pleysier, P. Ponsaers and E. Van Dael (eds) *Criminografische ontwikkelingen: Van (victim)-survey tot penitentiaire statistiek*, Antwerpen: Maklu: 107–140.

Jonckheere, A. and Maes, E. (2017) 'Actualités autour des alternatives à la détention préventive', in Y. Cartuyvels, C. Guillain and Th. Slingeneyer (eds) *Les alternatives à la détention en Belgique: Un état des lieux, à l'aune du Conseil de l'Europe*, Bruxelles: La Charte: 145–162.

Jonckheere, A. and Maes, E. (2019) 'Pre-trial detention and alternatives in Belgium: Standards, practices and research', in C. Mincke, D. Brutyn, D. Burssens, A. Lemonne, E. Maes, B. Renard and L. Robert (eds) *20 Years of Criminology at the NICC. A Scientific Journey and its Perspectives*, Oud-Turnhout: Gompel&Svacina: 53–83.

Jonckheere, A. and Maes, E. (2020) 'Les mesures avant jugement en Belgique: Une éternelle insatisfaction', *Neue Zeitschrift für Kriminologie und Kriminalpolitik/Nouvelle Revue de Criminologie et de Politique Pénale/New Journal of Criminology and Crime Policy (NKrim/NCrim)*, 1(1): 5–11.

Kennes, L. (2011) *La libération sous caution: Le prix d'une liberté très provisoire* [Justice en ligne] at www.justice-en-ligne.be/La-liberation-sous-caution-le-prix [accessed 12 July 2021].

Kennes, L. (2020) 'L'influence de la pandémie sur la détention préventive', *Journal Des Tribunaux*, 16(6812): 292–295.

Maes, E. (2018, Septembre 25) *De gevangenisbevolking en de situatie in gevangenschap: Een penale en maatschappelijke contextualisering – Cijfermatige benadering*, Leuven: Gespecialiseerde opleiding voor toekomstige magistraten van de strafuitvoeringsrechtbanken (Instituut voor Gerechtelijke Opleiding, FOD Justitie).

Maes, E. and Beyens, K. (2021) 'Waarheen met de strafuitvoering?', *Panopticon*, 42(1): 1–6.

Maes, E. and Deblock, M. (2017) 'DETOUR-Towards pre-trial detention as ultima ratio. Report on (Dutch-speaking) expert interviews (Flanders)', in *DETOUR-Towards Pre-trial Detention as Ultima Ratio. 2nd Belgian National Report on Expert Interviews*, Brussels: INCC-NICC.

Maes, E. and Jonckheere, A. (2017) 'Quo vadis ? Dilemma's rond alternatieven voor voorlopige hechtenis', *Panopticon*, 38(6): 401–411.

Maes, E. and Jonckheere, A. (2020) 'Dealing with crime in ordinary times as in times of crisis: A solution to reduce pre-trial detention?', *Newsletter CEP (Confederation of European Probation)* at www.cep-probation.org/dealing-with-crime-in-ordinary-times-as-in-times-of-crisis-a-solution-to-reduce-pre-trial-detention/ [accessed 12 July 2021].

Maes, E., Jonckheere, A., Deblock, M. and Hovine, M. (2016) *DETOUR-Towards Pre-trial Detention as Ultima Ratio. 1st Belgian National Report*, Brussels: INCC.

Maes, E. and Nève, J. (2020) 'Detentie in tijden van Corona. Impact van COVID-19-maatregelen inzake strafuitvoering op de omvang van de gevangenisbevolking', *Fatik*, 37(166): 12–18.

Masset, A. and Monville, P. (2016) 'La réforme de l'enquête préliminaire: Peau de chagrin ou requiem pour l'instruction?', in M. Cadelli and Th. Moreau (eds) *La loi "pot-pourri II": Un recul de civilisation?*, Limal: Anthemis: 39–59.

Michiels, O. and Kerzmann, L. (2016) 'Nouveautés en matière de détention préventive ou les droits de la défense à prix bradés: Une fausse bonne affaire?', in M. Cadelli and Th. Moreau (eds) *La loi "pot-pourri II": Un recul de civilisation?*, Limal: Anthemis: 61–82.

Roggen, F. (2012) 'Le délai raisonnable : Principes, contrôles et sanctions de son dépassement. Développements jurisprudentiels récents', in *Actualités en droit pénal*, Bruxelles: Bruylant: 1–33.

Schotsaert, A. and Van Linthout, P. (2018) 'Het procedureel terrorismestrafrecht', in J. Kerkhofs, Ph. Van Linthout and A. Schotsaert (eds) *Contra-Terrorisme. De gerechtelijke aanpak van terrorisme in België*, Brussel: Larcier: 99–147.

Tange, C. (2011) 'La détention préventive: Pis-aller du système pénal?', in A. Jonckheere and E. Maes (eds) *La détention préventive et ses alternatives. Chercheurs et acteurs en débat*, Gent: Academia Press: 73–101.

Van den Wyngaert, C., De Smet, B. and Van Dromme, S. (2009) *Strafrecht en strafprocesrecht in hoofdlijnen*, 7th ed., Antwerpen: Maklu.

Vandermeersch, D. (2015) 'La détention préventive de la personne présumée innocente et la privation de liberté de l'étranger', *Revue de droit pénal et de criminologie*, 6: 602–619.

Vanhamme, F. (2020) 'La détention provisoire au Canada: Inflation, processus et contexte', *Neue Zeitschrift für Kriminologie und Kriminalpolitik/Nouvelle Revue de Criminologie et de Politique Pénale/New Journal of Criminology and Crime Policy (NKrim/NCrim)*, 1(1): 12–18.

Van Kalmthout, A.M., Knapen, M.M., Morgenstern, C., Bahtiyar, Z., Lambertinal, P.S., Van der Linden, W.A.M. and Rozel, M. (2009) *Pre-trial Detention in the European Union. An Analysis of Minimum Standards in Pre-trial Detention and the Grouds for Regular Review in the Member States of EU*, Nijmegen: Wolf Legal Publishers.

Van Kempen, P.H. (ed) (2012) *Pre-trial Detention. Human Rights, Criminal Procedural Law and Penitentiary Law, Comparative Law. Détention Avant Jugement. Droits de l'homme, droit de la procédure pénale et droit pénitentiaire, droit comparé*, Cambridge: Intersentia.

Chapter 4

A systemic approach to reducing custodial remands

The experience of England and Wales

Anthea Hucklesby

Introduction

Under English law, defendants awaiting trial or sentence may be remanded on bail, with or without conditions, or in custody. When incarcerated, the term used is remand prisoners. The Bail Act 1976 provides the legal framework for remand decisions. It provides for a presumption in favour of bail in most cases. The fundamentals of the remand system have not changed significantly since it was overhauled in the 1970s. Pressure built during the 1960s to introduce a legal framework which promoted the use of bail and limited the use of "money" bail, thereby reducing the number of defendants remanded in custody. Although the prison remand population has fluctuated since, it continued to fall over the decade prior to the COVID pandemic. It is now one of the lowest per capita pre-trial detention populations in the world.

This chapter will examine the legal framework governing the use of bail and pre-trial detention in England and Wales and explore the reasons for its resilience and apparent success. It will also suggest that much more pervasive problems are the growth in the use of bail conditions, which can severely restrict defendants' liberty whilst presenting a veneer of freedom, lack of opportunities to review the remand status as cases progress through the criminal process and the increasing use of technology to facilitate remote remand hearings.

The legal framework for remand decision

Remand decisions are governed by the Bail Act 1976. The Bail Act 1976 remains largely intact and has widespread support from those who work with it. Research shows that practitioners from all parts of the system (judges, magistrates, prosecutors and defence lawyers) view the Bail Act 1976 as good law, which is fit for purpose (Grech, 2017; Hucklesby, 2011). One contributory factor to its success and longevity is the evidence-based and deliberative process used to create it. This involved the setting up of a Working Party (Home Office, 1974) comprising representatives of relevant organisations,

DOI: 10.4324/9781003159254-4

which heard evidence from many sources and drew on robust research studies before making its recommendations which were largely followed (Bottomley, 1970; King, 1971; Simon and Weatheritt, 1974).

The fundamental tenet of the Bail Act 1976 (s. 4) is a presumption of unconditional bail which can only be overturned in specific circumstances. The three original exceptions to the right to bail are that there is a substantial risk of failing to surrender to court; offending; or, interfering with witnesses or the administration of justice (Schedule 1, Bail Act 1976). Additional exceptions to the presumption of bail have been added to the original Act, including when the court *believes* that defendants are on bail at the time of the offence and/or breached conditions or failed to appear at a time when they were on bail previously. The use of "believes" as the criterion is important as it provides ample room for the use of discretion and does not conform to the standards of evidence and legal proof usually required in criminal cases.

None of these exceptions apply if defendants are unconvicted, as opposed to convicted but unsentenced, *and* there is no real prospect that they will receive a custodial sentence. This requirement was legislated for in the Legal Aid, Sentencing and Punishment of Offenders Act 2012, with the intention of limiting the use of custodial remands. Early research suggested that it was at the forefront of practitioners' minds and may have changed practices, but it does not appear to have led to less use of custody (Grech, 2017). Instead, it appears that it was presentational, that is, had no real effect on decision-making and was enacted for political purposes. This is a common theme with bail law. Legal changes often reinforce current practice, post-date changes in decision-making and/or duplicate existing law which already addresses the issue under scrutiny (Hucklesby and Marshall, 2000; Simon and Weatheritt, 1974). Generally, decision-makers are resistant to Government attempts to increase the use of custodial remands.

The Bail Act 1976 includes other, much less used, exceptions. The presumption of bail can be rebutted for defendants' own protection, for instance, if there is a serious risk of them being harmed because of the nature of alleged offences,[1] if there is insufficient information on which to make decisions, or if defendants are serving prisoners. There are also minor differences to the legal framework for imprisonable and non-imprisonable offences, but these are rarely material given that most offences dealt with by the courts are imprisonable.[2] Exceptions vary for summary (less serious offences) as opposed to either way or indictable (more serious) offences.[3] These have the effect of making it more difficult to rebut the presumption in favour of bail in summary cases. As a result, in these cases, bail may only be refused on the grounds of risk of failing to surrender if defendants have a history of failing to surrender, and/or if they have failed to surrender or breached conditions previously *and* there are substantial grounds to believe that they would fail to surrender, commit an offence and/or interfere with witnesses. Only the exception relating to risk of offending on bail does not need to be supported with evidence of previous breaches of bail. Importantly, bail may be refused if courts believe that defendants would commit an offence, which is likely to cause physical or mental injury to an associated person (relatives, spouse/civil partner, cohabitants or those in an intimate relationship of a significant duration) or lead to them fearing such injury. This provision is intended to directly address concerns about protecting victims of domestic abuse.

The legal framework provides a number of grounds, which are reasons for applying exceptions to bail. These include the nature and seriousness of the offence, strength of the prosecution case and defendants' offending and bail histories. Importantly, the nature and seriousness of the alleged offence is not an exception to the presumption of bail, but research has suggested that many decision-makers treat it as such (Hucklesby, 1997). Research has demonstrated that decision-makers often rely on all three, or at least two, exceptions when refusing bail, recognising that defendants who they deem to pose a bail risk overall often do so on multiple grounds, that the exceptions to bail are interlinked and single grounds can be used to support more than one exception (Hucklesby, 1996). Historically, the bail system focused on preventing absconding, but overtime, preventing offending has become the dominant rationale for pre-trial detention and the imposition of conditions (Grech, 2017; Hucklesby and Marshall, 2000). This trend fits squarely into the broader narrative about reducing offending and protection of the public as the primary purpose of the criminal justice system. Getting justice done and ensuring the efficient operation of the courts, both rationales linked to ensuring that defendants appear for trial, remain important but their prominence in official narratives has decreased.

An important exception to this trend are cases involving foreign national defendants. In these cases, risk of flight appears to be paramount in the minds of decision-makers partly because these defendants often lack, or are assumed to lack, community ties, the ease of travel between jurisdictions and difficulties of extraditing individuals from overseas jurisdictions. To partially address concerns about defendants leaving the country, defendants may be required to surrender their passports and/or deposit a security with the court – a sum of money which can be forfeited if they abscond. Yet, this results in different standards of justice for foreign nationals as opposed to "British Nationals" (Robson, 2022).

There are a number of circumstances in which the presumption of bail does not apply. These include cases of murder, manslaughter, rape and other serious sexual offences where bail may only be granted if exceptional reasons exist and if defendants have not been convicted previously of a similar offence in the UK or EU (s. 25(2) Criminal Justice and Public Order Act 1994). In cases of alleged murder, bail cannot be granted by magistrates (s. 115(i) Coroners and Justice Act 2009). It may only be granted if it is believed that there is no significant risk that an offence will be committed which would cause physical or mental injury (s. 114 Coroners and Justice Act 2009). As part of efforts to channel drug using defendants into treatment (see the following section), defendants who refuse to submit to a drug test whilst in police custody also have their right to bail removed (Hucklesby et al., 2007; Hucklesby, 2010).

Types of bail

There are several distinct phases in the pre-trial process where bail decisions are required. The first of these is before defendants are charged with any offences and is known as pre-charge bail or bail before charge.[4] When individuals are suspected of committing an offence but there is insufficient evidence to charge them, and this will not be forthcoming within the legal time limits for detaining individuals in custody (usually 24 hours which can be extended in certain circumstances), the police are able to bail suspects to return to the police station to allow further enquiries to be conducted. Recently, pre-charge bail has been very controversial because of the high numbers of suspects on bail and the length of time some suspects spend on pre-charge bail (Cape, 2016; Cape and Edwards, 2010; Hucklesby, 2021). This resulted in several changes in the law. First, the Policing and Crime Act 2017 limited the use of pre-charge bail and introduced a process of review by courts (Hucklesby, 2021). This led to pre-charge bail being used much less and being replaced with "Release Under Investigation" (RUI) which had no basis in law (Hucklesby, 2021). RUI is the extremely problematic. Suspects remain under investigation but are released without any obligations and no conditions can be imposed. No date is set for the investigation to be reviewed or concluded. Suspects can be rearrested at any time without warning. This new law was heavily criticised and was amended by the Police, Crime, Sentencing and Courts Bill 2021. This reversed the presumption against the use of bail and amended the review process to encourage greater use of bail and less use of RUI. Whether the changes will succeed is an open question because RUI remains available albeit now on a statutory footing and is an extremely valuable and efficient way for the police to investigate alleged offending, without the same level of hassle and bureaucracy involved in imposing bail (Hucklesby, 2021).

Remand decisions are made when suspects are charged with an offence following arrest and detention by the police. At this stage, the police decide to either bail defendants, with or without conditions, until their first court appearance or detain them to appear in court at the next available opportunity (usually within 24 hours). Around 10% of defendants were detained by the police which has remained constant between 2016 and 2020 despite a decline in the number of arrests (MoJ, 2021d). The purpose of police bail is to minimise the detention of suspects awaiting court appearances as well as reducing pressure on courts to deal with "overnight" cases at short notice. There are no time limits on police bail, but most defendants spend a relatively short time awaiting their first court appearance, around 30 days (Home Office, 2020; House of Commons Library, 2020; Ministry of Justice, 2022).

Research shows consistently that there is a correlation between police and later court bail decisions (Bottomley, 1970; Hucklesby, 1996). If defendants are bailed by the police, courts almost never remand them in custody. Courts, however, do bail defendants detained by the police, but a significant proportion are remanded in custody. In many ways, it is not surprising that courts seem to follow the police's lead given that they rely largely on the same information, including taking as fact the police version of events. However, the significant influence the police have on court decision-making and their decisions means that they must be carefully monitored and scrutinised. Currently, this is hampered by a lack of data availability, and little interest in this part of the process by academics and others.

Court remand decisions take place any time from the first court appearance to the conclusion of the case. For all but the most serious of cases, initial bail decisions are taken by magistrates' courts. The remand decision-makers in these courts are a mix of District Judges, who are paid legally qualified professionals, and magistrates, who are lay members of the community who are advised by legally trained professionals. If magistrates' courts refuse bail on two occasions, defendants are able to make an application to a "Judge in Chambers" for the decision to be reconsidered. This is a purely paper-based application, which is made to a Crown Court Judge who makes the decision "in camera", that is, not in open court. The Crown Prosecution Service also has the right to appeal against a decision to grant bail in cases where it opposed it and the alleged offence is imprisonable (s. 1 Bail Amendment Act 1993).

The final stage when bail decisions may be made is when convicted individuals lodge an appeal against their conviction or sentence. In these cases, individuals apply for bail which may be granted with conditions. Bail may be granted by the Crown Court or Court of Appeal depending upon the nature of the appeal. It is rare for those appealing their sentence to be bailed (Criminallawyer.co.uk., 2018).

Bail conditions

Although no statistics are published on the number of defendants released on conditional bail as opposed to unconditional bail, observational research suggests that conditional bail has become the norm (Grech, 2017; Hucklesby et al., 2007; Hucklesby, 2011). Conditions were introduced as a mechanism to reduce custodial remands, but they also have other functions including risk management, providing reassurance to decision-makers and victims that identified risks are being mitigated and, importantly, allowing decision-makers to defend their decisions if unwanted events subsequently happen (Hucklesby, 2009). Section 3(6) of the Bail Act 1976 enables conditions to be imposed if they are *necessary* to ensure defendants turn up to court and/or do not commit offences on bail or interfere with witnesses or obstruct the course of justice in another way. Breaching conditions is not an offence, but defendants may be arrested and brought before the court for bail to be reconsidered (s. 7 Bail Act 1976). In these circumstances, bail may be refused, conditions added, strengthened, for example, by increasing curfew hours or removed in full or in part. No guidance exists on criteria which should be considered when making such decisions, but the nature and seriousness of the breach is an obvious factor. Failure to surrender to bail is a criminal offence (s. 7 Bail Act 1976) and theoretically means that defendants who do not appear at the date and time required by the court have committed such an offence. In practice, the courts use their discretion particularly when defendants surrender themselves to court quickly after their original appearance date/time.

The law does not stipulate the conditions which may be imposed (except in the case of electronic monitoring) or which conditions should be used to meet the risks associated with specific exceptions. Consequently, decision-makers have wide discretionary power to impose whatever conditions they deem appropriate. In practice, courts stick to a relative small menu of conditions which has remained constant over time (Grech, 2017; Hucklesby, 1996; Raine and Willson, 1996). It includes residence, curfews, reporting to police stations and banning defendants from contacting specific people (victims, witnesses or associates) or going to particular places – shops, pubs, houses or much wider areas, including whole towns or cities. A constant concern has been the enforceability of conditions. Historically, enforcement has relied on *ad hoc* rather than systematic methods to uncover breaches, for example, the police spotting defendants in exclusion zones, victims or witnesses reporting sightings and so on. Although the police are responsible for enforcement, the resources required are significant and checking compliance with bail conditions for all but the highest profile defendants and/or the highest risk cases, is not usually a priority. There are also consistent complaints by the police and others that the courts simply bail defendants again with the same conditions after being arrested for breaching conditions. Consequently, the police have little incentive to arrest suspects for breaching conditions unless they believe that a new offence has been committed (Hucklesby, 2011; Hucklesby et al., 2007). From the perspective of the courts, the threshold for overturning decisions to grant bail on the basis of breaching bail conditions is likely to be substantial. There is no evidence or available data about the effectiveness of bail conditions as a mechanism to divert defendants from custody or as a measure to prevent unwanted behaviour and/or promote positive behaviours.

Curfews have always been widely used bail conditions, but the problem of how to enforce them was ever present. Historically, significant police resources were used for this purpose, whereby police would visit defendants' homes randomly. The introduction of electronic monitoring (EM) in the 2000s provided a mechanism to systematically and remotely monitor compliance, thereby saving police resources (Hucklesby and Holdsworth, 2016). Curfews are the most common use of EM, whereby radio frequency technology is used to monitor whether defendants remain at their curfew address during specified hours (Hucklesby and Holdsworth, 2016). Curfew hours are not stipulated in law. Theoretically, they can be imposed for 24 hours a day, but they are usually imposed overnight for around 12 hours, seven days a week (Hucklesby, 2009; Hucklesby and Holdsworth, 2016). EM using Global Positioning Scheme (GPS) technologies was introduced in 2019, which is currently available to enforce exclusion zones, curfews and ensure that defendants attend appointments. Trial monitoring can also be used to track defendants' movements and can be interrogated to match individuals' movements to known crimes (Hucklesby and Holdsworth, 2020). Whatever GPS technology is used, the police are able to request information about the whereabouts of specified individuals at particular times to exonerate them from involvement in known offences. As a result, there is a very real danger that these data will be used more widely in law enforcement in the future, raising considerable human rights and privacy issues, which are heightened by the unconvicted status of some wearers.

The use of EM to monitor bail conditions is increasing. In March 2020, 3,621 defendants were subject to EM bail conditions compared with 2,795 in 2018 (MoJ, 2021e). Better enforcement was a key driver for the introduction and use of EM bail, but another reason was to reduce custodial remands. Evidence is scant and dated about the effectiveness of this strategy, although two studies suggest that around half of those on EM bail would have been remanded in custody (Lobley and Smith, 2000; Mair and Mortimer, 1996). The other half may have been subject to non-EM curfews or no curfew requirements at all. Even at this level of exchange, EM appears to make a significant contribution to reducing the prison remand population.

Two other types of bail conditions raise concerns because they require positive engagement from defendants. Defendants in the pre-trial process are legally innocent, but a worrying trend is for this stage of the criminal justice process to be viewed as an opportunity to intervene into defendants' lives and start treatment or another intervention which would historically have been mandated only as sentence requirements. Bail conditions are therefore increasingly being used as vehicles to begin the process of change required to bring about desistance *before* defendants are convicted (Freiberg and Morgan, 2004). The first condition which illustrates this trend requires defendants who have tested positive for drugs at the police station, thereby suggesting that their alleged offence was drug-related, to attend an assessment and engage with treatment (Hucklesby et al., 2007). The fact that defendants rarely refuse means that bail is almost never withheld, but bail is being used as an incentive to direct defendants into treatment before they are even found to be legally guilty (Hucklesby et al., 2007). The amount of coercion involved is open to debate but there is no mistaking the intention.

The second illustrative condition is the requirement to cooperate with the Bail Accommodation and Support Service (BASS), which also arguably wraps up coercion into a veneer of help and support (Hucklesby, 2011; MoJ/HMPPS, 2018). The purpose of BASS, an outsourced service, is to provide accommodation for defendants who have no suitable housing and support is also provided (Nacro, 2021). The aim is to reduce custodial remands, increase compliance with bail conditions and assist defendants to lead crime-free lives. An evaluation of a similar pilot scheme suggested that defendants found it helpful, but there was evidence of a gap between what the scheme promised and what it delivered and whether services were provided consistently (Hucklesby, 2011) and lack of spaces remains a problem.

Suitable accommodation is a requirement of courts to grant bail. There is a significant minority of defendants who do not have anywhere to reside or who cannot reside at their normal residence because of the nature of their alleged offence(s), for example, if they are accused of domestic violence. Between April 2020 and March 2021, 728 defendants on bail were accommodated by BASS (MoJ, 2021b). This scheme does not capture all of those individuals who have an accommodation need. For example, many more defendants are housed temporarily with family and friends. What is less clear in relation to BASS is whether all of the defendants who require accommodation also need the "support" which comes with it. There is a very real danger that a form of net-widening is happening, which is of particular concern if defendants are acquitted. Historically, accommodation has been provided in Approved Premises (hostels run by the probation service or voluntary organisations), but very few defendants on bail are now accommodated in them (HMIP, 2017).

Remand detention in England and Wales

In 2008, the prison remand population stood at around 12,000 and comprised 16% of the prison population, having risen by a tenth since 1996 (Hucklesby, 2009). Figure 4.1 provides data for the period 2009–2019 and demonstrates a significant decline in the pre-trial detention population from 13,276 in 2009 to 9,145 in 2019 (MoJ, 2020c). This is a drop of nearly a third at a time when the prison population as a whole remained stable. As a result, the proportion of the prison population on remand declined to 11%. By March 2020, there has been a slight increase in the pre-trial population, which stood at 10,043 (Table A1.1, MoJ, 2020d). The COVID-19 pandemic makes it impossible to map trends thereafter (see Figure 4.1).

A line graph has years from 2009 to 2019 in increments of 2 along the x-axis and numbers from 0 to 90000 in increments of 10000 along the y-axis. The two lines on the graph represent remand population, which is around 10000 all along, and prison population, which is at around 80000 all along.

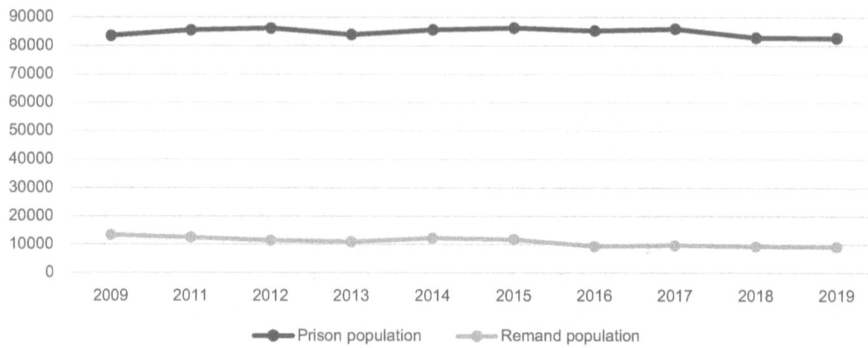

Figure 4.1 Prison population of England and Wales on 30 June 2009–2019.
Source: Ministry of Justice (2020d: Table A1.1).

These data demonstrate that England and Wales has one of the lowest per capita rates of pre-trial detention in Western Europe – 16 per 100,000 in 2020 – demonstrating a significant drop from 24 per 100,000 in 2010 (Walmsley, 2021; see also chapter 1). It is now one of the lowest in the World (Walmsley, 2021). There has been a fall in both the unconvicted population, that is, those awaiting trial, decreasing from 8,730 in 2009 to 5,996 in 2019, and the convicted unsentenced population, that is, those who have been found guilty and remanded in custody pending sentencing, usually to allow specialist reports to be prepared, which dropped from 4,546 to 3,149 over the same period. These figures represent falls of around a third in both groups (MoJ, 2020c: Table A1.1).

The remand population on any given day provides only a partial picture because of the churn in the remand population can be significant. As a result, it is important to consider the number of individuals received into prison on remand. Figure 4.2 clearly shows that the drop in the number of individuals on remand at any given time reflects a decrease in the number of individuals received in prison. Between 2015 and 2019, first receptions of remand prisoners decreased by 24% from 13,136 to 9,970 in a three-month period from April to June. This decrease is present in both the untried and unsentenced populations with a slightly greater drop for the untried (27%) compared with the unsentenced population (21%) (MoJ, 2016: Table 2.2a; MoJ, 2019a: Table 2.4b).

Court remand decisions

The number of remand receptions reflects bail decisions by the police and courts. This section explores these critical decisions.

The number of defendants remanded in custody by the courts in 2019 was 51,084. This represents a drop of 26% on the 2014 figure of just

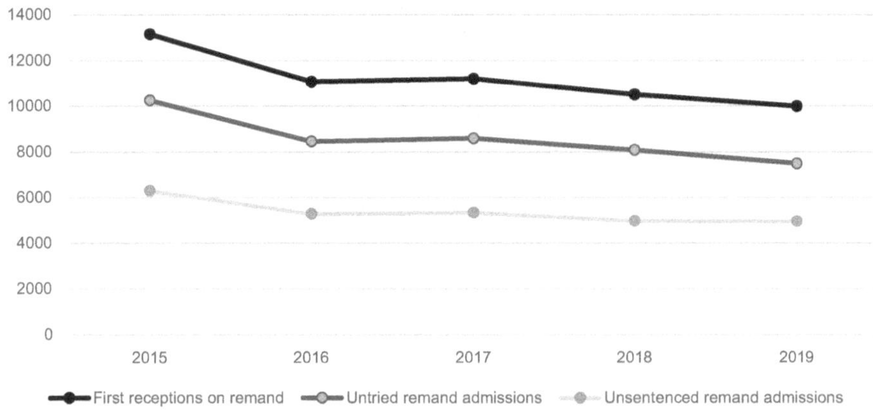

Figure 4.2 Remand receptions April–June 2015–2019.

Source: MoJ (2015, 2016, 2017, 2018, 2019a: Tables 2.1 and 2.2a).

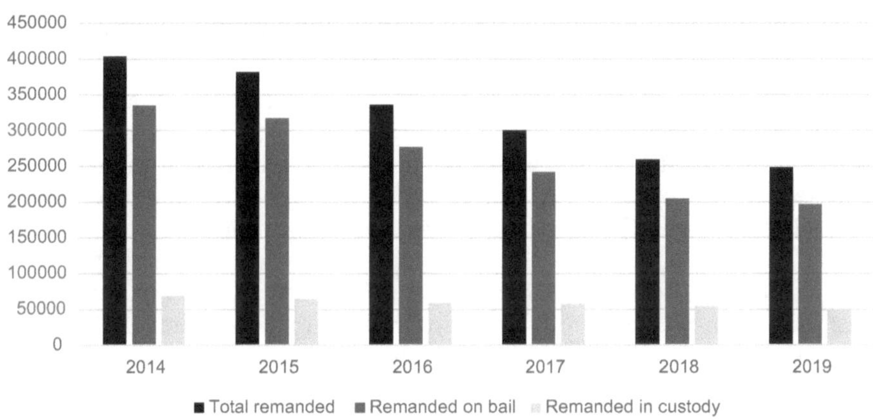

Figure 4.3 Number of defendants remanded by magistrates' courts in England and Wales 12 months to September 2014–2019.

Source: MoJ (2014, 2019a: Table Q4.2).

below 69,000 and will have fed through into a reduced number of prison receptions. However, there does not appear to have been a shift from the use of custodial remands to bail. Figure 4.3 shows a drop in the number of defendants remanded on bail of over 148,000 between 2014 and 2019 representing a 44% fall. As a result, there has been an increase in the proportion of remanded defendants who were remanded in custody from 17% to 21% over this period. Instead, the decline in custodial remands reflects the steep decline in the number of defendants remanded by the courts. As

Figure 4.3 shows, the number of defendants remanded decreased by two fifths (39%) from over 400,000 in 2014 to just under 250,000 in 2019 (MoJ, 2014, 2019a).

The decrease in the use of custodial remands and bail is visible for all offence categories except summary motoring offences. As would be expected, the steepest decline in custody rates between 2016 and 2019 was a drop of over a third for the least serious summary non-motoring offences (MoJ, 2014, 2019a: Table Q2.4b). However, custody rates also declined by 12% for the most serious offence category (indictable only). All offence categories also showed a fall in the use of bail, from 40% for summary non-motoring offences to 23% for the most serious indictable only offences (MoJ, 2014, 2019a: Table Q2.4b).

The fall in the number of defendants remanded by the courts reflects both changes in the pre-trial process, for example, a higher proportion of cases completed at first appearance and a significant drop in defendants appearing in magistrates' courts. In terms of the latter, the number of defendants appearing in magistrates' courts dropped from 1,559 million in 2016 to 1,442 million in 2019, which has continued the trend of previous years (MoJ, 2020b: Table Q4.1) reflecting a drop in recorded crime and changing crime patterns (ONS, 2022).

Police decisions have also changed resulting in fewer defendants appearing in court from police custody. The number and proportion of defendants who appear in magistrates' courts who have not been remanded by the police increased by 10% from 1.034 million to 1.109 million between 2016 and 2019 (MoJ, 2020b: Table Q4.1). The number and proportion of defendants appearing in court having been arrested and bailed has decreased by two fifths (41%) from 351,000 in 2016 to 207,000 in 2019. The number of defendants appearing from police custody has also dropped by over a fifth (22%) from 157,700 in 2016 to 123,700 in 2019, thereby reducing the pool of likely candidates for custodial remands.

Taken together these data illustrate the ongoing direction of policy to divert as many cases as possible away from the formal criminal justice process focusing specifically, but not exclusively, on defendants accused of less serious offences (Hucklesby, 2009). At the same time, a package of measures has been introduced to speed up court processes and incentivise both defendants and criminal justice practitioners to complete cases at the first court appearance. These policies have had a significant impact on the remand process demonstrating that measures to tackle high prison remand populations do not simply need to focus on providing alternatives measures such as EM. They also need to look at the process as a whole and identify ways in which defendants can be diverted, dealt with differently before remand decisions need to be taken, and/or implement measures to speed up the processing and disposal of cases.

The COVID pandemic and remand

At the time of writing the pandemic, which began in March 2020, is not over, but it is clear from official statistics that it has already had significant impact on both bail decision-making and the prison remand population, which is explored in this section.

As a result of the pandemic, the number of cases reaching the courts dropped significantly from 1,432 million in 2019 to 1,135 million in 2021 (MoJ, 2021a: Table Q4.2). Over the same period, courts made greater use of remand with the proportion of defendants remanded increasing from 17% to 25% (MoJ, 2021d: Table Q4.2). In turn, this led to the courts making greater use of bail with the number of defendants bailed rising from 196,600 in 2019 to 232,000 in 2021, representing an increase from 79% to 83% of those remanded (MoJ, 2021d: Table Q4.2). In the same period, the number of defendants remanded in custody decreased from 51,600 to 46,700 reflecting a drop from 21% to 17% of all those remanded (MoJ, 2021d: Table Q4.2). These patterns were consistent for nearly all offences categories – indictable only, either-way and most summary offences. These trends are likely to be linked to a number of factors, including a greater number of cases being adjourned rather than dealt with at first appearance; pressure to keep defendants out of prison to reduce the health risks and keep people safe; and recognition of increased court waiting times because of temporary court closures and the challenges of running a criminal justice system during a pandemic. EM bail has been put to greater use during the pandemic. On 31 March 2021, 6,001 defendants were subject to EM bail, representing a rise of two-thirds since March 2020 (MoJ, 2021e). This suggests that it may have been used as a mechanism to keep defendants out of custody.

Despite a drop in the number of defendants remanded in custody, the prison remand population rose during the pandemic to reach 12,990 on 30 September 2021 (MoJ, 2021c: Table 1.1). Both the unconvicted and unsentenced population increased by 30% between 2019 and 2021 (MoJ, 2021c). Two thirds (65%) of the population were unconvicted on 30 September 2021. The number of remand prisoners entering prison increased only slightly (3%) from April–June 2020 to 2021 from 9,065 to 9,359, suggesting that the rise in the prison remand population was driven by increased time spent awaiting trial and/or sentence because of the backlog of cases in the courts (MoJ, 2021c: Table 2.1). Worryingly, the number of women received into custody during this period increased disproportionately compared to men, rising by 9% compared with under 3% for men (MoJ, 2021c: Table 2.1).

Composition of the prison remand population

This section discusses the composition of the prison remand population and identifies trends in remand decision-making, which indicate that defendants are not treated equitably in the current system. The majority of individuals held on remand are adult males. Just over a tenth of the prison remand population were under the age of 21 on 30 June 2019 (MoJ, 2020c: Table 1.1). Of these, 173 were aged between 15 and 17. Similarly, the vast majority (94%) of the population were men, with just over 500 women in prison on remand (MoJ, 2020c: Table 1.1). The majority of both men and women were unconvicted, with women slightly less likely to be held after conviction awaiting sentence (29% compared to 35% of men). Men and women had similar offence profiles, with the majority of both groups being remanded for violence against the person (25%), drugs (19%) or theft (13%) offences. Data from criminal courts shows that women are less likely than men to be remanded in custody with 23% of women and 39% of men remanded in custody in 2019 (MoJ, 2020d: Table 4.2). However, an increasing proportion of women are remanded in custody rising to its 2019 level from 19% in 2015 whilst the proportion of men remained stable (MoJ, 2020c). The proportion of women not remanded increased from 13% to 23% between 2015 and 2019 having the effect of shrinking the number of women on bail (MoJ, 2020a).

Despite publishing data on the composition of the whole prison population by ethnic origin, these data are unavailable for the remand population. Data on court remand decisions shows that White defendants (38%) are less likely to be remanded in custody than any other ethnic group who have rates of 40% for Asians, 45% mixed race and 46% for Black, Chinese and others for those charged with indictable offences in the Crown Court (MoJ, 2019b). Data published on foreign national remand prisoners shows that they comprise a higher proportion of the prison remand population than the prison population as a whole, suggesting that they are more likely to be remanded in custody than British nationals (see Chapter 13).

Effectiveness of remand decisions

Remand decisions are not just about minimising the use of prison. An important element is measuring their effectiveness in terms of whether remand decisions militate the risks posed by defendants and/or result in the expected outcome. This section explores these questions.

Data are published on how many defendants fail to surrender to court which shows that nearly 15,000 defendants, 7% of those bailed in the 12 months to March 2020, did not appear. This compares to 4% of those not remanded in the same period, which might suggest that bail is less effective than no obligations to ensure attendance at court, although the populations may be significantly different (MoJ, 2020d: Table Q4.4). The rates are the same as those published in 2014, suggesting that rates remain stable, despite the decreasing number of defendants on bail and in custody (MoJ, 2020d: Table Q3a). The published data needs to be viewed cautiously given the complexity and ambiguity with which these offences may be dealt with and recorded. These data only include defendants convicted of the offence of failing to surrender to bail rather than everyone who did not turn up at court at the appointed time. The way the law is framed in terms of failure to surrender is different in England and Wales from other jurisdictions. For example, in Scotland the law makes an explicit distinction between a risk of absconding and failing to appear at court as grounds to refuse bail (s. 23c(1) Criminal Procedure (Scotland) Act 1995). Absconding suggests a wilful and planned decision to evade justice whereas not appearing at court may happen because of poor planning, lack of organisation and so on. English law leaves the court with a great deal of discretion about how to deal with defendants who do not comply with the letter of the law by arriving late.

The second set of available outcome data provide details of how cases ended. These data are often used as a measure of the effectiveness of remand decisions. It may be argued that high rates of community sentences amongst those remanded in custody mean that initial remand decisions were wrong. However, the process from first remand decision to sentence is often a long one and a lot may change during this time making it difficult to judge a decision retrospectively. The criteria on which remand decisions are made are also different from those which are relevant to sentencing and time spent in custody awaiting trial may result in sentencers deciding that sufficient time has already been spent in prison and a community sentence is appropriate. Nonetheless, the data suggest that the potential exists to reduce the number of defendants received into prison on remand.

Of most concern is that in the 12 months to March 2020, 7,625 defendants spent time in remand detention only to be acquitted[5] or the case dismissed[6] (MoJ, 2020d: Table Q4.4). This equates to 10% of defendants whose cases were heard in the Crown Court and 9% of those who cases were held in the magistrates' courts. Just over a fifth of defendants (n = 46,200) were acquitted or their case was discharged having spent time on bail (MoJ, 2020d: Table Q4.4). This time will have disrupted the lives of these individuals and particularly of those remanded in custody, yet no compensation or other support is available.

Table 4.1 shows the outcomes of proceedings for those sentenced in the 12 months to March 2020 (MoJ, 2020d: Table Q4.4). It demonstrates the correlation between remand status and sentence outcomes. As expected, the most likely sentence if individuals were not remanded is a fine, a community sentence if individuals were on bail and a sentence of imprisonment for those remanded in custody. However, a quarter of those remanded in custody did not receive a custodial sentence. This represents a slight decrease from 2016, but it still means that a considerable number of defendants who serve time in custody pre-sentence have non-custodial sentences imposed (MoJ, 2014: Q3a).

Different groups have different outcomes. Women who are remanded in custody are less likely than men to receive a custodial sentence. In 2019, only

Table 4.1 Sentence outcomes for 12 months ending March 2020

	Not remanded		*Bailed*		*Remanded in custody*	
Sentence	*n*	%	*n*	%	*n*	%
Imprisonment	31,017	3	13,419	13	31,076	75
Suspended sentence	17,568	2	18,377	18	3,800	9
Community sentence	42,304	4	37,849	38	3,079	7
Fine	880,958	87	20,408	20	1,390	3
Other	41,258	4	11,428	11	2,378	6
Total	1,014,698	100	101,481	100	41,723	100

Source: MoJ (2020d: Table Q4.4).

60% of women remanded in custody were sentenced to imprisonment (MoJ, 2020a). Similarly, defendants from all minority ethnic groups are slightly less likely than their White counterparts to receive a custodial sentence having been remanded in custody (73% compared with 69–72%) (MoJ, 2019a).

Despite periodic references in the media to cases in which defendants have allegedly committed serious or large numbers of offences on bail or absconded, no data are available on some key measures of the effectiveness of bail, including the extent of offending on bail, compliance with bail conditions and the extent to which victims and witnesses are kept safe. These gaps, alongside other significant missing data such as the number and type of conditions imposed, mean that it is impossible to assess the appropriateness and effectiveness of bail decisions. The lack of data also does not allow decisions to be monitored to ensure that they adhere to fundamental principles of a fair and just criminal justice process.

Bail procedures

Research in England and Wales has consistently highlighted areas in court bail procedures which are concerning. The link between all of these is the focus on getting justice done quickly and efficiently at minimal cost, which has been a priority of successive governments. This coupled with a misguided trust in criminal justice agencies, and their ability to prosecute and convict only those that are factually guilty, results in procedures and safeguards, whose purpose is to minimise mistakes, being overridden, sidelined or ignored. This section will briefly examine some of these issues.

Legally remand hearings are adversarial. The prosecution is required to prove that defendants pose a substantial bail risk and that the right to unconditional bail should be rebutted. In turn, the role of the defence is to challenge the prosecution's objections to unconditional bail, putting forward relevant information to support the granting of bail. In practice, most bail hearings are uncontested (Grech, 2017; Hucklesby, 1997; Smith, 2021). This includes a significant minority of cases in which the prosecution is requesting custodial remands and nearly all cases in which defendants are granted bail. One consequence is that many hearings are completed very quickly (Doherty and East, 1985; Cape and Smith, 2016). Another consequence is that limited information is presented in court by either the prosecution or defence because they do not need to justify the proposed outcome to the same extent if they had disagreed. However, the problem of a lack of information extends beyond these uncontested hearings. Remand decisions need to be taken very early in the criminal justice process, and at a stage in the case where only limited information is likely to be available to support the prosecution case or an application for bail. Whilst there are often calls to increase the quantity and quality of information available (see Smith, 2021), the practical difficulties are significant given that time is very short and a balance needs to be struck between minimising the time suspects are detained in police custody and maximising relevant information.

A proven and effective method for providing additional information to courts are Bail Information Schemes (Hucklesby, 2011). These schemes which work in courts and/or prisons are operated by probation or prison staff or NGOs, and collate and verify relevant information about defendants for the courts, for example, address and employment status. They are also key to accessing accommodation and other services. Unfortunately, these schemes have all but disappeared in England and Wales. The once vibrant and successful schemes operated under ring-fenced funding have been victims of funding cuts, a lack of focus on remand policy and the reluctance of probation services to provide pre-trial services.

The law requires reasons for custodial remands and the imposition and varying of bail conditions to be given in open court, but the way this is done in practice is not always helpful or informative, making decisions difficult to challenge (Hucklesby, 1997; Hucklesby et al., 2007; Smith, 2021). Whilst reasons are nearly always provided when defendants are remanded in custody, they are much less likely to be forthcoming when conditions are imposed (Hucklesby, 1997; Hucklesby et al., 2007; Smith, 2021). When reasons are provided, they tend to be formulaic. They are structured around the main exceptions to bail and do not routinely identify the reasoning or even the legal grounds in any detail. Even when detailed reasoning is provided orally in court, it is questionable whether defendants are able to fully understand and memorise what is said, although this is arguably an important role for defence lawyers. In theory bail notices, which are written records of decisions, deal with this problem. However, decisions are recorded via tick boxes, structured according to the exceptions and grounds in the Bail Act 1976. This has the advantage of making the process of recording reasons quick and consistent, but it provides very little detail and encourages a formulaic approach instead of clear and accessible reasons for overturning the presumption in favour of unconditional bail as the law requires.

Prior to the Criminal Justice Act 1988, remand hearings took place every seven days. At each of these hearings, defendants appeared in court in person and could apply for bail, even if their circumstances had not changed. This process was viewed as unnecessary and costly in terms of both time and resources for the court and prison service. The number of bail applications defendants can make was limited to two throughout the process in the Criminal Justice Act 1988. After two applications defendants need to prove that there has been a change in circumstances before a further application is allowed. This means that after the first two hearings, hearings only take place when the case is ready to progress, which may be many weeks. Even when hearings are scheduled, defendants are required to make written bail applications at least two days prior to the hearing (Rule 14.7 Criminal Procedure Rules). The application must contain specific details, including the reasons for the original court decision, why the court should not withhold bail, further information or legal argument about what has changed and proposed bail conditions. As suggested by several defence lawyers' websites, it is not a simple process, taking time to prepare, which is made more difficult when defendants are in prison with limited access to lawyers and the outside world. It also relies on defendants being aware that something relevant has changed. These issues bring to the fore the role of defence lawyers who should play a key role in protecting the rights of defendants during the remand process, but successive research questions whether they do so in practice (Hucklesby, 1997; McConville et al., 1994; Newman, 2013).

A similar process is in place for prosecutors to request that remand decisions are reviewed, but the Criminal Procedures Rules envisage applications only to withhold bail or to impose or vary conditions and not to request the release of defendants or the grant of unconditional bail. The effect is to make it extremely difficult for initial bail decisions to be reviewed. Rather than reviews of bail status being a routine part of case management, they are only reviewed when proactively initiated by either party, which may have greater impacts on those defendants with less agency and resources.

Many of the hearings now take place remotely using "live-link" technologies whereby defendants appear on screens in court rooms from prison. It is possible that all hearings related to a case take place remotely. Although mechanisms are in place for private conversations between defendants and their lawyers, it is qualitatively different from being in the same room. This process was already underway prior to the pandemic but has since become significantly more widespread. As a result, concerns have been raised by lawyers and others about the impact on defendants' access to justice and their ability to actively participate in their cases (O'Brian, 2020). Historically, attending court has been an opportunity to meet with defence lawyers and family to discuss progress with the case and ask for additional work to be done in relation to any bail applications, and this is no longer routinely available to defendants.

Since the mid-1980s, custody time limits (CTLs) have been in place to limit the time spent in custody awaiting trial. They were introduced by s. 22 Prosecution of Offences Act 1985 and set down different time limits for cases to be completed depending on the category of offence.[7] If time limits are reached, there is a requirement for defendants to be released on bail, with or without conditions. The Crown Prosecution Service may also apply for CTLs to be extended in specific circumstances. Whilst CTLs were set pragmatically in the first place, so that the impact on case processing times was negligible, there is no doubt that they focus the minds of prosecutors to ensure that cases do not run out of time. As a result, they have helped to keep the prison remand population in check. Applications to extend CTLs are rare, but anecdotal evidence suggests that they are nearly always granted.

The COVID pandemic has led to an unprecedented situation in courts (National Audit Office, 2021). Government health advice meant that courts were unable to function normally for an extended time period. As a result, some CTLs were extended. Whilst the time limit for cases dealt with in magistrates' courts remained in place, the limits for Crown Court cases was increased from 182 to 238 days. It was also made easier to extend time limits if it was clear that the cause was pandemic related rather than prosecution delays (CPS, 2020). These changes fuelled the increase in the prison remand population described earlier. The original time limits have now been reinstated but the backlog in the courts means that lengthy periods spent on remand will continue to be a problem for some time. There are no limits on the time taken to complete cases when defendants are on bail. As a result, defendants may be subject to restrictive conditions for lengthy periods of time. An inevitable downside of CTLs is that bail cases go to the back of the queue.

Concluding comments

On the surface it might appear England and Wales has achieved the aim of reducing its prison remand population because it now has one of the lowest per capita rates in the world. The success has been a result of a need to contain the prison population within the available estate rather than because of a commitment to the presumption of innocence and/or bail. Less use is being made of remand (on bail and in custody) because more cases are completed at first appearance. This all appears positive but threatens many of the fundamental principles of a justice system that prides itself on only convicting the legally guilty. It has also left a situation in which it is too easy to say that all the issues relating to pre-trial detention and bail have been addressed. There are still around 40,000 people remanded in custody every year (MoJ, 2020e), some of which do not need to be imprisoned which causes unnecessary harm to those individuals and their significant others. The barriers to applying for bail initially, and particularly later in the process, also remain. Consequently, once in prison, it is difficult to get out, even if there are significant changes to cases and/or defendants' personal circumstances. The conditions in which remand prisoners are confined remain very problematic (HMIP, 2012). The pandemic has resulted in defendants spending lengthy periods of time in pre-trial detention, which is likely to continue for some time. Much of the last two years has seen remand prisoners "locked-down" in their cells with little or no association within prisons and few visits from outside (Fair Trials, 2021).

Whilst attention has been focused on pre-trial detention, conditional bail has become the norm, restricting defendants' freedom whilst they await trial in the community. Lack of data relating to conditions makes monitoring and scrutinising their use impossible. The focus of defendants and representatives on getting out of custody also means that less attention is devoted to whether conditions are necessary and proportionate. Practices seem to have changed little since the early 1990s when defence lawyers suggested a package of conditions as a way of leveraging bail (Hucklesby, 1996). The rudimentary attention given to meaningful reasoning for the imposition of conditions and custodial remands means that defendants and anyone working with them struggles to identify ways for them to be rebutted. There are limited opportunities for an ongoing and meaningful review of whether all conditions remain necessary and proportionate during the trial process, and there is a very real risk that defendants remain subject to some conditions which become unnecessary. The increasing use of technologies to monitor bail conditions makes them even more onerous and intrusive, and compliance becomes harder as a result. The maxim of innocent until proven guilty is also threatened because of the use of conditions designed to address "offending behaviour". As a result, there is a very real risk that defendants are set up to fail, leading to greater use of custody in the longer term.

Notes

1 If they are accused of sexual offences and there is a possibility of revenge attacks.
2 All offences in England and Wales are categorised as imprisonable or non-imprisonable offences by way of the maximum sentences which are available upon conviction. In theory, all but the most minor offences can attract a prison sentence, although in practice they often do not.
3 Offences are classified as summary, either way or indictable only in law. These categories relate to the courts which will adjudicate on the case. Summary offences are the less serious and are dealt with by magistrates' courts. Indictable only cases are the most serious and are dealt with by the Crown Court. All either way cases begin in magistrates' courts but those which are deemed too serious are committed to the Crown Court to be dealt with.
4 There is also a little used police power of "Street Bail" which allows the police to bail suspects "on the street" without arresting them and detaining them in custody (Hucklesby, 2004).

5 Defendants who are found not guilty after a trial.
6 Cases in which the Prosecution decides there is no case to answer.
7 The time limit for summary cases is 56 days, for summary cases dealt with in magistrates' courts 70 days and 182 days for indictable only and either way cases dealt with at Crown Court (CPS, 2021).

References

Bottomley, A.K. (1970) *Prison Before Trial*, Occasional Paper in Social Administration, 39, London: Bell and Son.

Cape, E. (2016) *What If Police Bail Was Abolished*, London: Howard League for Penal Reform at https://howardleague.org/publications/what-if-police-bail-was-abolished/ [accessed 29 September 2022].

Cape, E. and Edwards, R.A. (2010) 'Police bail without charge: The human rights implications', *Cambridge Law Journal*, 69(3): 529–560.

Cape, E. and Smith, T. (2016) *The Practice of Pre-trial Detention in England and Wales: Research Report*. Project Report, Bristol: University of the West of England at www.fairtrials.org/wp-content/uploads/Country-Report-England-and-Wales-MASTER-Final-PRINT.pdf [accessed 4 January 2021].

Criminallawyer.co.uk (2018) *Appeals Against Sentence* at www.crimelawyer.co.uk/news/tag/Bail+pending+appeal [accessed 18 July 2022].

Crown Prosecution Service (CPS) (2020) *Coronavirus Crisis Protocol for the Effective Handling of Custody Time Limit Cases in the Magistrates' and the Crown Court* at www.cps.gov.uk/sites/default/files/documents/legal_guidance/Revised-Coronavirus-Protocol-for-CTL-cases-signed-07042020.pdf [accessed 12 December 2021].

Crown Prosecution Service (CPS) (2021) *Custody Time Limits* at www.cps.gov.uk/legal-guidance/custody-time-limits-including-coronavirus-protocol [accessed 12 December 2021].

Doherty, M. and East, R. (1985) 'Bail decisions in magistrates' courts', *British Journal of Criminology*, 25: 251–266.

Fair Trials (2021) *Locked up in Lockdown: Life on Remand During the Pandemic* at www.fairtrials.org/sites/default/files/Locked%20up%20in%20lockdown%20-%20Life%20on%20remand%20during%20the%20pandemic.pdf [accessed 10 January 2022].

Freiberg, A. and Morgan, N. (2004) 'Between bail and sentence', *Current Issues in Criminology*, 15(3): 221–236.

Grech, D. (2017) *Culture Before Law? Comparing Bail Decision-Making in England and Canada*, University of Leeds PhD thesis at https://etheses.whiterose.ac.uk/19704/ [accessed 24 May 2023].

Her Majesty's Inspectorate of Prisons (HMIP) (2012) *Remand Prisoners: A Thematic Inspection* at www.justiceinspectorates.gov.uk/hmiprisons/wp-content/uploads/sites/4/2012/08/remand-thematic.pdf [accessed 7 July 2022].

Her Majesty's Inspectorate of Probation (HMIP) (2017) *Probation Hostels' (Approved Premises) Contribution to Public Protection, Rehabilitation and Resettlement* at www.justiceinspectorates.gov.uk/hmiprobation/wp-content/uploads/sites/5/2017/07/Probation-Hostels-2017-report.pdf [accessed 7 July 2022].

Home Office (1974) *Bail Procedures in Magistrates' Courts*, Report of the Working Party, London: HMSO.

Home Office (2020) *Police Powers: Pre-Charge Bail: Government Consultation* at www.gov.uk/government/consultations/police-powers-pre-charge-bail [accessed 7 July 2022].

House of Commons Library (2020) *Court Statistics for England and Wales*, Briefing Paper CBP 8371, 22 December 2020 at https://researchbriefings.files.parliament.uk/documents/CBP-8372/CBP-8372.pdf [accessed 7 July 2022].

Hucklesby, A. (1996) 'Bail or Jail? The practical operation of the Bail Act 1976', *Journal of Law and Society*, 23(2): 213–233.

Hucklesby, A. (1997) 'Remand decision makers', *Criminal Law Review*, April: 269–281.

Hucklesby, A. (2004) 'Not necessarily a trip to the police station: The introduction of street bail', *Criminal Law Review*, October: 803–813.

Hucklesby, A. (2009) 'Keeping the lid on the prison remand population: The experience in England and Wales', *Current Issues in Criminal Justice*, 21(1): 3–23.

Hucklesby, A. (2010) 'Pre-trial initiatives', in A. Hucklesby and E. Wincup (eds) *Drug Interventions in Criminal Justice*, Buckingham: Open University Press.

Hucklesby, A. (2011) *Bail Support Schemes for Adults*, Bristol: Policy Press.

Hucklesby, A. (2021) 'Pre-charge bail and release under investigation (RUI). An urgent case for reform', *Criminal Law Review*, 2: 79–94.

Hucklesby, A., Eastwood, C., Seddon, T. and Spriggs, A. (2007) *The Evaluation of Restriction on Bail Pilots: Final Report*, RDS Online Report 06/07, London: Home Office.

Hucklesby, A. and Holdsworth, E. (2016) *Electronic Monitoring in England and Wales* at www.emeu.leeds.ac.uk [accessed 7 July 2022].

Hucklesby, A. and Holdsworth, E. (2020) *Electronic Monitoring and Probation Practice*, HM Inspectorate of Probation Academic Insights 2020/08 at www.justiceinspectorates.gov.uk/hmiprobation/wp-content/uploads/sites/5/2020/12/Academic-Insights-Hucklesby-and-Holdsworth-FINAL.pdf [accessed 12 December 2021].

Hucklesby, A. and Marshall, E. (2000) 'Tackling offending on bail' with E. Marshall', *Howard Journal*, May, 39(2): 150–170.

King, M. (1971) *Bail or Custody*, London: Cobden Trust.

Lobley, D. and Smith, D. (2000) *Evaluation of Electronically Monitored Restriction of Liberty Order*, Edinburgh: Scottish Executive Central Research Unit.

Mair, G. and Mortimer, E. (1996) *Curfew Orders with Electronic Monitoring*, Home Office Research Study 163, London: Home Office.

McConville, M., Hodgson, J., Bridges, L. and Pavlovic, A. (1994) *Standing Accused: The Organisation and Practice of Criminal Defence Lawyers in Britain*, Oxford: Clarendon Press.

Ministry of Justice (2014) *Criminal Justice Statistics Quarterly, March 2014* at www.gov.uk/government/statistics/criminal-justice-statistics-quarterly-april-2013-to-march-2014 [accessed 20 December 2021].

Ministry of Justice (2015) *Prison Receptions April to June* 2015 at www.gov.uk/government/statistics/offender-management-statistics-quarterly-april-to-june-2015 [accessed 12 December 2021].

Ministry of Justice (2016) *Prison Receptions April to June 2016* at www.gov.uk/government/statistics/offender-management-statistics-quarterly-april-to-june-2016 [accessed 12 December 2021].

Ministry of Justice (2017) *Prison Receptions April to June 2017* at www.gov.uk/government/statistics/offender-management-statistics-quarterly-april-to-june-2017 [accessed 12 December 2021].
Ministry of Justice (2018) *Prison Receptions April to June 2018* at www.gov.uk/government/statistics/offender-management-statistics-quarterly-april-to-june-2018 [accessed 12 December 2021].
Ministry of Justice (2019a) *Prison Receptions April to June 2019* at www.gov.uk/government/statistics/offender-management-statistics-quarterly-april-to-june-2019 [accessed 12 December 2021].
Ministry of Justice (2019b) *Statistics on Race and the Criminal Justice System 2018* at https://assets.publishing.service.gov.uk/government/uploads/system/uploads/attachment_data/file/849200/statistics-on-race-and-the-cjs-2018.pdf [accessed 12 December 2021].
Ministry of Justice (2020a) *Statistics on Women and the Criminal Justice System 2019* at https://assets.publishing.service.gov.uk/government/uploads/system/uploads/attachment_data/file/938360/statistics-on-women-and-the-criminal-justice-system-2019.pdf [accessed 12 December 2021].
Ministry of Justice (2020b) *Criminal Court Statistics Quarterly*, October to December 2019 at www.gov.uk/government/statistics/criminal-court-statistics-quarterly-october-to-december-2019 [accessed 12 December 2021].
Ministry of Justice (2020c) *Offender Management Statistics Quarterly October to December 2019 and Annual 2019* at www.gov.uk/government/statistics/offender-management-statistics-quarterly-october-to-december-2019 [accessed 12 December 2021].
Ministry of Justice (2020d) *Criminal Justice Statistics Quarterly, March 2020* at www.gov.uk/government/statistics/criminal-justice-system-statistics-quarterly-march-2020 [accessed 12 December 2021].
Ministry of Justice (2020e) *Prison Receptions January to March 2020* at www.gov.uk/government/statistics/offender-management-statistics-quarterly-january-to-march-2020-2 [accessed 12 December 2021].
Ministry of Justice (2021a) *Criminal Justice Statistics Quarterly, June 2020* at www.gov.uk/government/statistics/criminal-justice-system-statistics-quarterly-june-2020/criminal-justice-statistics-quarterly-june-2020#remands [accessed 10 December 2022].
Ministry of Justice (2021b) *Bail Accommodation and Support Service* at https://data.justice.gov.uk/contracts/bass#:~:text=Bail%20Accommodation%20and%20Support%20Services,a%20permanent%20place%20to%20live [accessed 10 December 2021].
Ministry of Justice (2021c) *Prison Population 30th September 2021* at www.gov.uk/government/statistics/offender-management-statistics-quarterly-april-to-june-2021 [accessed 12 December 2021].
Ministry of Justice (2021d) *Criminal Justice Statistics Quarterly*, June 2021 at www.gov.uk/government/statistics/criminal-justice-system-statistics-quarterly-june-2021 [accessed 12 December 2021].
Ministry of Justice (2021e) *Justice Data: Electronic Monitoring* at https://data.justice.gov.uk/contracts/electronic-monitoring [accessed 12 December 2021].
Ministry of Justice (2022) *Criminal Court Statistics Quarterly October-December 2022* at www.gov.uk/government/statistics/criminal-court-statistics-quarterly-october-to-december-2021 [accessed 18 July 2022].

Ministry of Justice/HMPPS (2018) *Bail Accommodation and Support Service Policy Framework* at https://assets.publishing.service.gov.uk/government/uploads/system/uploads/attachment_data/file/767313/bass-policy-framework.pdf [accessed 18 July 2022].

Nacro (2021) *Nacro Bail Accommodation and Support Service* at www.nacro.org.uk/services/bass/nacro-bass/ [accessed 10 December 2021].

National Audit Office (NAO) (2021) *Reducing the Backlog in the Courts*, HC 732, MoJ and HMCTS at www.cps.gov.uk/legal-guidance/custody-time-limits-including-coronavirus-protocol [accessed 12 December 2021].

Newman, D. (2013) *Legal Aid Lawyers and the Quest for Justice*, London: Bloomsbury.

O'Brian, M. (2020) 'Live video link tech is hindering access to justice', *Law Society Gazette*, 2 January 2020 at www.lawgazette.co.uk/commentary-and-opinion/live-video-link-tech-is-hindering-access-to-justice/5102599.article [accessed 04 January 2022].

Office for National Statistics (ONS) (2022) *Crime in England and Wales Year Ending March 2021* at www.ons.gov.uk/peoplepopulationandcommunity/crimeandjustice/bulletins/crimeinenglandandwales/yearendingmarch2021 [accessed 18 July 2022].

Raine, J. and Willson, M. (1996) 'The imposition of conditions in bail decisions', *Howard Journal*, 35(3): 256–270.

Robson, M. (2022) *A Suspect Population? An Examination of Bail Decision-Making for Foreign National Women in Criminal Courts in England and Wales*, London: Griffins Society.

Simon, F. and Weatheritt, S. (1974) *The Use of Bail and Custody by London Magistrates' Court Before and After the Criminal Justice Act 1967*, Home Office Research Study no. 20, London: HMSO.

Smith, T. (2021) 'Rushing remand: Pre-trial detention and bail decision-making in England and Wales', *Howard Journal*, 60(1): 46–74.

Walmsley, R. (2021) *World Pre-trial/Remand Imprisonment List*, 4th ed., Institute for Criminal Justice Policy Research (ICPR) at www.prisonstudies.org/sites/default/files/resources/downloads/world_pre-trial_list_4th_edn_final.pdf [accessed 18 July 2022].

Chapter 5

Pre-trial detention in Germany: a liberal approach, but not for all

Christine Morgenstern

Introduction

Pre-trial detention (*Untersuchungshaft*) in German law is the deprivation of liberty of an untried or not finally convicted person.[1] It can be preceded by a temporary detention by the police of a maximum of 48 hours. Any further detention must be ordered by a judge. According to German law and doctrine, the main objectives of pre-trial detention are to ensure the public right to a thorough investigation of an offence and a criminal procedure according to the rule of law. Nevertheless, the prevention of a new crime is also accepted as one objective of pre-trial detention. The only way to supervise a suspect or accused in the community and as such the only "alternative" to pre-trial detention is the suspension of an arrest warrant. Usually, conditions and obligations apply, such as to provide a financial surety, to report to the police regularly, etc.

After shedding some light on its historical development and use in practice, this chapter introduces the legal and constitutional characteristics of pre-trial detention in Germany. It then takes a closer look on decision-making processes as decisive factor for current practices and explains the relatively small role of non-custodial alternatives to pre-trial detention. Additionally, it studies the discreet, but noticeable influences by European institutions and norms. The chapter draws on official statistics, legal materials, case law and existing studies as well as own research from two studies conducted between 2014 and 2017: *Untersuchungshaft in Europa*, funded by the German Research Agency (Morgenstern, 2018)[2] and the DETOUR project as described in Chapter 1.[3]

Characteristics of pre-trial detention in Germany: development and statistics

Historical development

The legal embodiment of pre-trial detention stems from the 1870s and did not change much until the end of the Weimar Republic in 1933. After the

DOI: 10.4324/9781003159254-5

erasement of the rule of law under the Nazi regime, the post-war legislator restored the legal situation of the pre-1930s in 1950. This included the restriction to only two grounds to remand an individual in custody: the risk of absconding and the risk of obscuring evidence. It took until 1964 for the risk of re-offending to be introduced as an additional preventive ground. At the same time, the gravity of the offence alleged became the fourth ground to order pre-trial detention. As part of the criminal justice reform discussion of the 1960s and 1970s, scholars became increasingly critical of these expansions. Nevertheless, the legislator extended the scope of the preventive ground. Rising numbers of inmates in remand custody were a result of increasing numbers of arrest warrants and longer durations of detention (Dünkel and Vagg, 1994).

Critical voices became louder and pre-trial detention practice was accused of being "contrary to the rule of law, in opposition to social concerns and hopelessly outdated" (Wolter, 1981: 452). Even the Minister of Justice shared this assessment and spoke of "excessive" pre-trial detention (Engelhard, 1986: 359). Although this did not translate into legislative action, it seems to have had influence on practitioners. Slowly, the detention practice and culture changed: 4,8% of all persons included in the Conviction and Sentencing Statistic (*Strafverfolgungsstatistik*) had been in pre-trial detention in 1975. This ratio dropped to 3.2% in 1985, which led to a significant decrease in absolute terms (Morgenstern, 2018).

Development since 1992

The German reunification in 1990 as a period of societal changes brought with it a time of uncertainties for many and a rise in both crime data and prisoner numbers. Figure 5.1 shows the development of prison stock data for Germany in its reunified shape. While the number of sentenced prisoners continued to rise until 2004, peaking at more than 65,000, the number of remand prisoners started to descend earlier. After the all-time high in 1994 with about 21,700 remand prisoners, the number was halved twenty years later (31 March 2013: 10,560). The share of pre-trial detainees then fell below 17%. The rate per 100,000 inhabitants as comparative measure sank to 13. It should be noted, however, that there is considerable variation between the Federal States that only partly can be explained by different demographics: When the overall German rate stood at 13 in 2013, the regional rates varied between 7.0 and 20.9 (Morgenstern and Kromrey, 2017).

After 2013, the trend has reversed: the number of sentenced prisoners continued to decrease moderately, while the number of pre-trial detainees increased significantly to more than 14,000, a growth by 30% within five years. Their share rose to 23% of the overall prison population and even overcrowding became an issue again in a few prisons (Morgenstern, 2018). Data for 2019 and 2020 show a decrease, but it remains to be seen whether this is a new trend or influenced by the COVID-19 pandemic and its implications for the Criminal Justice System (Dünkel and Morgenstern, 2022).

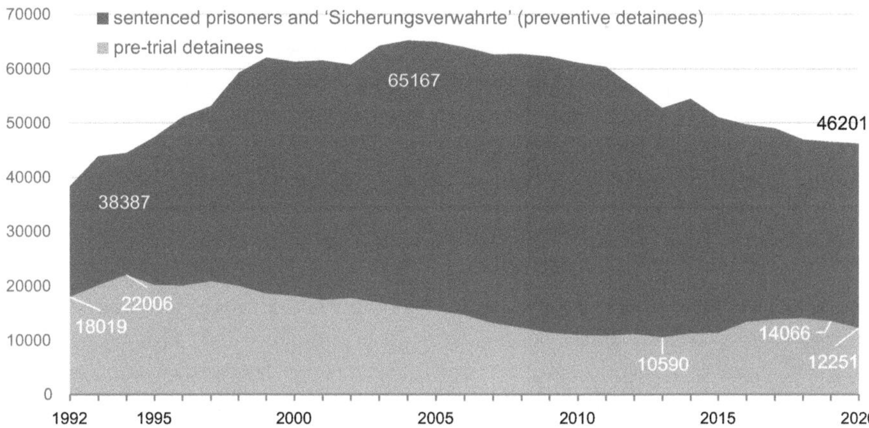

Figure 5.1 Prison population (stock data) in Germany, 1992–2020.
Source: Statistisches Bundesamt (2021a), data for 31 March of each year.

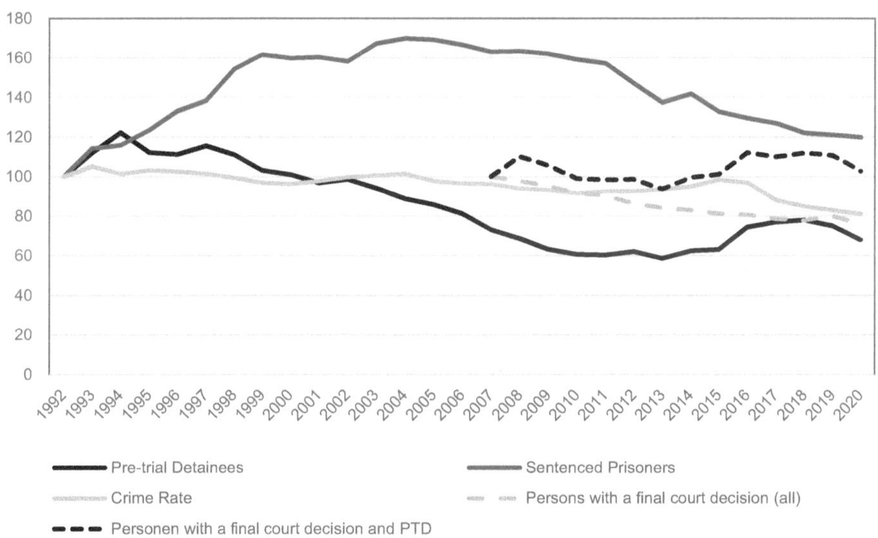

Figure 5.2 Context data over time (indexed for 1992 and 2007: 100%).
Source: Statistisches Bundesamt (2021a, 2021b), Bundeskriminalamt (2021).

Prisoner stock data are only a rough indicator for developments in criminal justice. Unfortunately, official statistics on pre-trial detention practice in Germany are scarce. Figure 5.2 is an attempt to put some indicators into context by showing different trends, taking 1992 as a starting point and adding the development of yearly crime data per 100,000 of the population (all criminal offences) as well as data from the Conviction and Sentencing Statistics. The latter include all persons that received a final court decision in a given year[4] and provide data for the whole of Germany since 2007. This date was therefore chosen as starting point for data on sentenced persons as a rough indicator of influx into the system.

This context data reveals that a decrease in the overall crime level may have had some effect on the reduced use of pre-trial detention. More refined analyses that consider the development of more severe offences (violent crime, robbery, etc.) with an increased likelihood of pre-trial detention confirm this trend, because they also have been declining for many years (Morgenstern, 2020). The context data also underline that trends between the number of sentenced prisoners and pre-trial prisoners may differ significantly. Only in recent years we observe converging developments, although – as Figure 5.2 shows – the overall number of persons that have been tried and received a final court decision has clearly decreased while this is not the case for the subgroup of those who underwent pre-trial detention. Here, we find a first indication that judicial restraint to order pre-trial detention may have come to a halt.

The population of pre-trial detainees is predominantly male and adult: On 31 March 2019, merely 5.5% were female. This corresponds roughly to their share of 6% among sentenced prisoners; neither has changed much over the last couple of years. 11% of pre-trial detainees are 21 years or younger, 2.6% are aged 18 or below.[5] Most importantly, German defendants have become a minority in pre-trial detention over the last years. While no regular official statistics exist, a clear picture of overrepresentation emerges from the scattered data available[6]: non-nationals form more than 60% of the pre-trial population according to the latest data available (2017) as opposed to 12% of the resident population, 31% of suspects registered by the police and 30% of all persons with a final court decision. Only 32% of all sentenced prisoners were foreigners in the same year. When looking at flow data, it becomes evident that non-nationals have a significantly higher risk to be detained provisionally: while the overall rate stood at 3.3% in 2017, it was 1.9% for Germans and 6.5% for foreigners, meaning a threefold increased risk for this group (Morgenstern, 2020). Since 2008, in particular since 2014, both number and percentage of foreigners in the statistics in all these categories have shown increases, albeit to very different degrees.

In this timespan falls the so-called refugee crisis in 2015–2016. During this time, many refugees from war-torn regions and other migrants reached the European Union, Germany registered almost 900,000 refugees in 2015 alone. In a societal and political climate of initial solidarity and understanding, soon critical and hostile voices became louder, accusing young male migrants of frequent criminal behaviour. Some incidents were extensively covered by the German and international media. During 2015–2016 New Year's Eve celebrations, mass sexual assaults and numerous thefts were reported in several

German cities. Suspects were mainly North African men, often asylum seekers. Police coined the term *Nafris* (which stands for "North African" but also for "North African Intensive Offender"), which sometimes is still used as a pejorative chiffre for a certain type of offender.

Overall, the gross overrepresentation of foreigners affected by pre-trial detention cannot be explained by developments in the other groups described. Its scope has a strong impact on German pre-trial detention practice as such. The difference between sentenced persons and those undergoing pre-trial detention is particularly alarming. It indicates that many of those foreigners that have been in pre-trial detention do not serve a prison sentence – at least not in Germany. How many of them are expelled from the country is unknown, but we can assume that many are convicted of crimes that are not severe and do not merit a prison sentence.

This, however, is a phenomenon observed not only for foreign suspects but also for others affected. It is highly problematic regarding the principle of proportionality. In Germany, most of those who were in pre-trial detention are later convicted.[7] However, many of them do not receive an unconditional prison sentence as one would expect under the principle of proportionality. More than 45% of all cases ended with a non-custodial sanction – about 9% with a fine and about 34% with a suspended prison sentence. These figures are stable for many years. The data is published without further information on citizenship, but we can assume from what was said earlier that foreigners who committed smaller crimes are particularly affected.

Reform discussion

Some explanations for the development of German pre-trial practice over the last two decades have been discussed already, highlighting a change of culture in the 1980s and the practice regarding foreigners more recently. It must be added that legislative changes played a minor role, if any. The only reform project for pre-trial detention legislation for many years aimed at strengthening the procedural rights of suspects. Most importantly, since 2010 a defence lawyer (paid by the state, if necessary) was obligatory in all cases where remand detention is enforced; in 2019 this provision has been extended to all cases in which pre-trial detention is requested (see the following section).

Scholarly rhetoric has always found stark words for problems of pre-trial detention – seeing it as "as the trouble spot of criminal procedure" because of its nature as a "both dangerous and tempting instrument of state power", which makes it a "touchstone for the thresholds of the rule of law and of public welfare provided by the [German] constitution" (Arbeitskreis Strafprozessreform, 1983: 1). Nevertheless, only a small body of scholarly works exists. A productive phase in the 1980s saw two comprehensive legal-theoretical studies published (Arbeitskreis Strafprozessreform, 1983; Paeffgen, 1986) that aimed at legislative reform to restrict the use of pre-trial detention. The most comprehensive empirical study also dates back to that period (Gebauer, 1987), which provided insights for example in pre-trial detention decision-making relying on extra-legal motives.

Later studies focused on analyses of jurisprudence, including that of the Federal Constitutional Court (FCC) and the European Court of Human Rights (ECtHR), or looked at different legal grounds of pre-trial detention (Dessecker, 2007; for a detailed research review see Morgenstern, 2018). An important and more recent strand of research studied the impact of defence counselling on pre-trial detention, according to which the early consultation of a defence lawyer reduces the time spent in pre-trial detention (see, e.g., Busse, 2008). A renewed scholarly interest in pre-trial detention was visible in recent years, partly triggered of European and cross-border developments (Morgenstern, 2018; Wolf, 2017).

None of this has had much influence on the legislator. While there is generally great appetite for criminal law reform, often introducing new offences or making existing ones severer, and despite reform calls by some scholars and defence lawyers associations (König, 2015; Wolf, 2017) to introduce legal restrictions for pre-trial detention, no such plans exist.

Legal and constitutional framework

Basic principles

The German criminal justice system belongs to the continental civil law tradition. The criminal procedure is designed to establish the truth about an alleged offence, and the prevailing theory of punishment is based on the "principle of individual guilt" while the enforcement of all sentences must strive for social reintegration (Morgenstern, 2015). If there are indications that a crime was committed, the public prosecution must initiate an official investigation (*Legalitätsprinzip*) and, if evidence permits, it must bring charges. As "master of the investigation" (*Herrin des Ermittlungsverfahrens*), the Public Prosecution dominates the investigative stage within the non-adversarial German system. Once the bill of indictment is with the court, it is the court's duty to pursue further official investigations. Only courts may impose criminal sanctions, but since the 1970s, more and widely used possibilities exist for the public prosecution to discontinue proceedings conditionally or unconditionally. It is unknown in how many of these cases pre-trial detention is ordered but presumably their number is low (Morgenstern, 2018). Depending on the case, criminal courts consist of professional judges who are trained lawyers, and lay judges. The latter are never involved in decisions on pre-trial detention. Trial and conviction "in absentia" are not possible (only few exceptions apply).

Pre-trial detention is regulated in the Code of Criminal Procedure (CCP), but the German constitution, the *Grundgesetz* ("Basic Law" [BL]) plays an important role for the criminal procedure. Its first part consists of a charter for individual human rights (fundamental rights (*Grundrechte*), Article 1–19 BL). Article 20 enshrines the rule of law (*Rechtsstaatsprinzip*, Article 20 BL) which includes the fair trial principle and the presumption of innocence. The European Convention on Human Rights (ECHR) serves as an additional source for procedural principles. The Basic Law provides for so-called fundamental procedural rights (*Prozessgrundrechte*), among them the court's duty to maintain neutrality and the Habeas Corpus guarantees that require, among others, a judge's decision on any form of detention no later than 48 hours after apprehension (Article 104 BL).

Germany is characterised by a federal organisation of its political and legal system. The legislative competences are split up between the Federal system and the Länder, with the Federation being responsible for the parameters of the criminal justice system (i.e. the "if" of an order to pre-trial detention) while the *Länder* are in charge of the prison system (the "how" of enforcing pre-trial detention). Regional varieties can be observed and must be seen as part of German legal culture, as the aforementioned variation of pre-trial detention rates show.

Another part of German legal culture is the significance of fundamental rights in everyday judicial practice, not least elicited by the jurisprudence of the FCC as guardian of the constitution. Since the 1960s, the court has influenced and restricted the practice of pre-trial detention by many important decisions, emphasising the right to liberty, the principle of proportionality and the presumption of innocence. Fundamental rights and the jurisprudence by the FCC play a major role in the professional socialisation of young lawyers.

Pre-trial detention legislation

The requisites for ordering and reviewing pre-trial detention are codified in §§ 112–130 CCP. It is imposed by a written judicial order (arrest warrant, *Haftbefehl*) following an oral hearing. The judge must observe the constitutional time limit mentioned earlier and must issue the warrant not later than the end of the day following arrest, meaning a maximum of 48 hours. As police and public prosecution may have used much of the time, judges may end under significant time pressure.

The CCP holds two cumulative prerequisites for pre-trial detention: a strong suspicion (*dringender Tatverdacht*) at the time of arrest, implying the high likelihood that the suspect will be found guilty, and a ground to remand him or her in custody. Additionally, pre-trial detention "may not be ordered if it is disproportionate to the significance of the case or to the penalty or measure of reform and prevention likely to be imposed".

The four grounds foreseen in the CCP are as follows:

- Flight or the risk of flight (absconding)
- The risk of tampering with or obscuring evidence

- The risk of repeating or continuing a listed offence of a (relatively) serious nature (re-offending)
- The gravity of the offence in cases of very serious allegations, mainly capital offences

It is important to note that the risk of absconding is more than the risk that a person will not stand trial, as the wording of § 112(2) CCP shows:

> A ground for detention exists, when, on the basis of facts, 1. it is established that the accused is absconding or in hiding, 2. considering the circumstances of the individual case, there is a risk that the accused will evade criminal proceedings (risk of flight).
>
> (translation my own)

"Evading" and "hiding" indicate intentionality.

The risk of re-offending (§ 112a CCP) faces scholarly criticism, as it aims at the prevention of future deviance in a "police-like manner" (Arbeitskreis Strafprozessreform, 1983: 45). It often is considered to serve general preventive aims and therefore problematic regarding the presumption of innocence and the procedural objectives (Paeffgen, 1986; Roxin and Schünemann, 2022). Nevertheless, the FCC confirmed this ground to be constitutional (FCC, 30 May 1973 [BVerfGE 35, 185]).

The FCC has, however, not accepted the seriousness of the offence as a stand-alone fourth ground. It had already been criticised by scholars for systematic reasons: If there is no risk for the proper conduct of the criminal procedure, there is no legitimate need to detain. The mere quality of the offence itself does not impede the process nor does it justify detention for preventive reasons – public dismay does not suffice. Therefore, according to the FCC in its first key decision on pre-trial detention, the provision only meets constitutional requirements when one of the other grounds to remand is at least plausible (FCC, 15 December 1965 [BVerfGE 19, 342]).

Several forms of judicial control of pre-trial detention exist. The most important is the "detention review" (*Haftprüfung*). For the most part, it is up to the accused and their lawyers to have remedies filed, although the court and the prosecution service formally are obliged to reassess ongoing detention *ex officio* at any stage of the proceedings. Additionally, and with the strongest impact on the system, an *ex officio* judicial review of the imposition and prolongation of remand detention exists after six months: The Higher Regional Court (*Oberlandesgericht*) then must review the case because the regular duration of remand detention expires. Empirical data suggest that these decisions have helped to reduce the overall use or at least the length of remand imprisonment and slowly but steadily have influenced lower courts (Dessecker, 2007). An extension of detention according to the law may only be allowed in cases of "particular difficulty" or because of "the unusual extent of the investigation" or "another important reason". Statistics show that despite this restriction, a quarter of all remand detainees had been serving more than six months of pre-trial detention at the time of their conviction (Morgenstern, 2020). The six-month deadline is met once the application for a continuation order is filed with the Higher Regional Court or the main proceedings commenced, so that detention in complicated cases or those that are appealed may last much longer. In 2014, the FCC stated that remand detention of more than one year can only be justified in "very exceptional cases" (FCC, 30 July 2014, 2 BvR 1457/14). Statistically, the effect of this decision has not been visible; on the contrary: in 2015, about 1,500 persons spent one year or more in pre-trial detention, in 2020, this number has risen to more than 2,200 (Statistisches Bundesamt, 2021b). The backlog of cases that piled up in 2020 and 2021 during the COVID-19 pandemic will increase this problem (Dünkel and Morgenstern, 2022).

Decision-making

General practice and legal culture

It was suggested earlier that the development of German pre-trial practices followed rather a changing legal culture or decision-making style than legislative reform or different crime rates. This was confirmed partly in the DETOUR study,[8] as some respondents assumed that the sensitivity for the suspects' rights has increased:

> I do have the impression that the readiness to issue arrest warrants among courts is reduced significantly, . . . I think judges are somewhat more sensitive today.
>
> (Interview 32, lawyer)

> I am rather reluctant. I think detention is a very serious decision. And a serious interference with a person's life. We have the presumption of innocence, the arrest warrant interferes with it, and this is why the detention decision is the last one you must take.
>
> (17, Judge)

Fundamental rights awareness was mentioned as important for legal training:

> Only this question of reasons to detain makes it clear for many [legal trainees] what responsibility they will have to take when they start their working life. And if they are good, they will understand why we have this system, why we have the division of power, why a state claims it can lock up fellow citizens, and what particular task it is to care for them in pre-trial detention.
>
> (19, Public Prosecutor)

Some interviewees, however, observed a harsher practice more recently:

> I think there is a shift in paradigms for the last 3 to 4 years. I think the law is applied more harshly.
>
> (25, Prison Social Worker)

Despite these seemingly contradictory findings, the assumption can be confirmed that it is not law that shapes everyday practice but changing cultures that can be volatile.

Actors and their roles

One particular interest of the DETOUR research was to see how the different actors assessed their own influence and responsibility in decision-making. In several interviews the respondents used the image of a filtering system:

> The first preliminary test runs already with the police, which looks at what is going on, which direction it might take, which offence, is here a prison sentence in question or not. Then here with us at the prosecutor's office, where really the course is almost set. And once again more careful, with more peace and quiet . . . the judge. These are different filters; I always imagine it that way.
>
> (19, Public Prosecutor)

The constitution and the CCP attribute the responsibility for the detention decision to the judge, but it is the Public Prosecution who has, according to the German CCP, the overall leading role during the investigative stage of the criminal proceedings. Earlier research (Gebauer, 1987; Busse, 2008) suggests that only about 10% of all requests for arrest warrants by the public prosecution are rejected, this was confirmed in our study. Answers to our question who in practice dominates the decision-making process in detention matters varied to an astonishing degree. Most lawyers attributed the most influential role to the public prosecution. Several public prosecutors and even some judges agreed. Most judges, however, insisted that it was them who have and take on the responsibility for the decision and see themselves as the dominating actors.

The role of the defence in pre-trial detention matters was strengthened with the reform 2010, making the assignment of a (state-paid, if necessary) defence lawyer obligatory in all cases where pre-trial detention is enforced. In the eyes of many practitioners, this was a half-baked reform because the appointment came too late – at an "*absurd point of time*" (12, lawyer). Meanwhile, European legislation has forced the German legislator to go further: With the transposal of EU Directive 2016/1919 on Legal Aid, the CCP since December 2019 foresees mandatory defence "as soon as [the suspect] is supposed to be brought before the judge for a decision upon detention or preliminary placement", § 141 (2 Nr. 1) CCP. In our study not only lawyers, but also judges had a positive view on this reform: they argued that an early appointment professionalises the proceedings, speeds them up and increases fairness for suspects. One judge explained that it "*make[s] my life easier*" (10, judge). This is interesting in so far as it highlights what is expected from the lawyers: to provide necessary information to facilitate the decision-making:

> [T]hose lawyers that are involved in an early stage . . . they could bring something new. Admittedly it is not really their task, but it would be a possibility that they would do it. For example, positive developments, living situation, job perspectives.
>
> (13, Judge)

It remains to be seen how the new regulation of 2019 influences detention decisions. Under the legal situation relevant during our fieldwork and irrespective of the question of mandatory counsel, suspects were (and are) entitled to seek advice and support by a defence lawyer at any stage of the proceedings. Indeed, in many cases suspects have lawyers quickly after the arrest but their possibilities to influence the decision are limited because they are usually involved only very shortly before the first detention hearing. As indicated earlier, they become more important for review hearings. The suspect usually does not play an active role in the proceedings and hardly articulates him- or herself in the detention hearings. Interviewees agreed across the board that there are no quality differences between state-paid and privately paid lawyers in detention matters, but that there is a certain problem of uninspired lawyers mainly interested in getting fees for sometimes useless review requests.

Grounds and motives to detain

From the four grounds available, the risk of absconding is by far the most often applied, accounting for 92% of all impositions of pre-trial detention in 2020 (Statistisches Bundesamt, 2021b). The risk of tampering with or obscuring evidence accounts for 5% of all arrest warrants while the risk of reoffending with currently only 3% has even lost significance over the last years. Interviewees thought that tradition, difficulties to substantiate the second and the legal construction of the latter ground as subsidiary were decisive for this situation. To ensure that the trial can take place seems to be crucial:

> So, it in first instance secures the trial and in second instance the execution of the sentence. This means, when I have to fear that somebody will not show up at the trial that can have whatever result, I principally have to keep him here.
>
> (15, Judge)

> If need be, the risk of flight is always a ground one could construct.
>
> (23, Public Prosecutor)

This and similar remarks show that practitioners factually interpret the legal provisions in a way that overstrains the narrow legal meaning of absconding or hiding.

Higher courts and legal scholars have developed an elaborated catalogue of requirements for a lawful judicial prognosis for the individual's risk of absconding (Morgenstern, 2018). For the detention judge on the ground, this requires a comprehensive check of the factual circumstances not only of the case, but also of the personal background of the suspect. Judges, however, do not cope well with these expectations. Our file study confirms earlier research (Gebauer, 1987; Kowalzyck, 2008) that the written decision to detain usually comprises of a few lines and includes very few considerations, mainly about the expected sentence as "flight stimulus".

While it was explicitly acknowledged by some of our interviewees that the expected sentence may not be the sole argument to base a decision on, it nonetheless plays a central role when the risk of flight is considered. Once a "perceptible" sentence is expected, the general assumption is that the suspect would try to avoid it. When asked for thresholds, very diverse answers were given. They ranged from a six-month ("*you can try it*", interview 8, Public Prosecutor) to five years prison sentence ("*almost impossible to avoid PTD*", several respondents). Often the threshold of a directly enforceable prison sentence was mentioned – in Germany only prison sentences of up to two years can be suspended. Such a huge range of different assessments of a sentence severe enough to stimulate flight is an indicator for an incoherent and somewhat irrational judicial practice.

The expected sentence also was considered to assess proportionality – this was to be expected as it is a legal requirement. Proportionality restrictions, however, did not seem to play a role for socially marginalised suspects without fixed abode that are repeat offenders; here even petty cases such as minor shoplifting often lead to detention:

> For trivial offence it [the arrest warrant] is out of the question. Except you have definite indications for flight or rather such a situation of neglect, that means no social bonds, that you have to say you can't seriously conduct the proceedings at all [without arrest warrant].
>
> (31, judge)

> [T]hey get at most a suspended sentence, if at all. But I cannot conduct the proceedings when I do not lock them up, because then they are gone.
>
> (15, Judge)

This means that proportionality considerations are at least for some overridden by the commitment to secure the proceedings and enforce the law, ultimately therefore also for reasons of general prevention.

Previous convictions play a role in so far as they may increase the expected sentence. Regarding other personal circumstances that may trigger or hinder PTD, housing in the form of a permanent postal address was the most relevant factor. Stable family bonds and employment or education were additionally mentioned as stabilising factors (and if missing, as indicators for the risk of absconding). This had major significance also for foreign nationals. According to our research, they do not *per se* run a greater risk of being detained, but the risk of absconding is linked to stable living conditions in Germany. Therefore, certain subgroups often cannot avoid detention: so-called travelling offenders, those with insecure residence status or who are already illegal, and, due to particular political or media pressure after the incidents mentioned earlier, certain groups of young men coming from Northern Africa and Arab countries as one interviewee stated: "*Reason to detain? Nafri!*" (26, lawyer).

German nationals with contacts abroad (bank accounts or second homes) would be detained because the risk of flight as well. It was mainly for them that lawyers pointed out that the risk of flight is grossly overstated:

> [M]aybe 10% of all people that actually are taken into custody because of a risk of flight would actually abscond . . . most of the people do not go into hiding, because flight means unbelievable stress. Financially, the fewest have the possibility . . . not being at home is permanent anxiety, most people don't stand this.
>
> (5, Lawyer)

Drug addiction is a feature often mentioned regarding pre-trial detention practice, while the problem of a rising number of mentally ill suspects that is discussed in the literature was only recognised by some interview partners. They, however, pointed out that it is an "*exploding problem*" (26, Lawyer; similar 19, Public Prosecutor) and very difficult to handle for an unaware and understaffed judicial system.

Necessities, strategies, constraints: procedural aspects

The strict time limit after a suspect's arrest means that all actors usually must act under time restraints and with usually only a thin case file containing scarce information. By far the most prosecutors said they take their time but indicated that one needs to "*act instinctively*" and that it was not possible to "*waste much time*" with detailed requests for arrest warrants (3, PP). Judges equally found that they had "*all the time I need*" (10, judge), only some referred to organisational problems such as quickly finding translators. This cognitive dissonance could perhaps be explained with habituation and adaptation to the situation.

In several interviews new tendencies to use speedy procedures (Morgenstern, 2021) or at least a particularly speedy approach in the normal procedure were mentioned. Sometimes this was supported in particular for petty cases:

> [S]he has that first conviction, four months suspended, and two weeks later she comes back. Now she is in detention. Even if they don't go into the speedy procedure, they have their verdict after six weeks. That is all okay.
>
> (13, Judge, about a repeat shoplifter from another country)

All interviewees reported a lot of informal communication – in the early phase of the proceedings between Police and Prosecution and later with judges, possibly with the result that requests for arrest warrants are declined because they are not substantiated in the eyes of the next decision-maker in the decision-chain. Once a lawyer is involved, they also communicate informally, sometimes on practical issues, sometimes cases are "*negotiated*" in a "*consensual form of defending the client*" (9, lawyer).

Marked deficits were visible in information-gathering because responsibilities were unclear or shifted from one actor to the other:

> One of the facts that make me unhappy personally is that people operate with insufficient information. Positive circumstances are not considered because they have not been ascertained . . . this is the task for the court and the public prosecution. They have this duty ex officio to investigate positive aspects. . . . I want to emphasise that it is not their [the lawyers'] job, but in the forensic reality it is the standard that if something is presented concerning the personal circumstances, it comes from the defence.
>
> (13, Judge)

Often only review hearings can remedy this deficit. Reviews aim at either a revocation of the arrest warrant or the suspension of its execution. The latter happens far more often – even if it sometimes is a foul compromise in cases where detention could legally be challenged because either the suspicion is not strong enough or the facts do not properly justify a ground for detention.

Avoiding pre-trial detention: the use of alternatives

Alternatives to pre-trial detention play a comparably small role in Germany. This partly is due to the overall procedural concept: In a first step, detention judges – upon request by the public prosecution – must consider if an arrest warrant is necessary in the case and if all legal requirements are fulfilled. Only in a second step, judges can (and must) consider if less restrictive means are sufficient to secure the proceedings. If so, the suspect must be released, possibly under conditions (suspension of the arrest warrant,

Außervollzugssetzung, § 116 CCP). In practice and in our fieldwork, this is called "to spare the suspect from detention" (*Haftverschonung*); indicating that if coercive measures are deemed necessary, pre-trial detention is the norm and other measures the exception.

No statistics exist on suspensions of arrest warrants. Estimates during our fieldwork confirmed existing research (Gebauer, 1987; Busse, 2008): A suspension rarely happens in the first hearing after the initial arrest. In later hearings, usually in the first review, according to personal experience of our interviewees between 20% to 40% of all arrest warrants are suspended. Some reported that these suspensions happen more often and earlier than some years ago, namely in the first detention review that after the reform of 2010 takes place much earlier than before, usually after two to three weeks.

There was consensus that defence lawyers in most cases take the initiative in this regard and suggest possible conditions, mainly obligations to report to the police. Money bail is hardly used and only some practitioners in higher courts thought that it should be used more often. According to the great majority of practitioners of all professional groups, alternatives generally worked well and those under suspended warrants did indeed appear before court, fulfilled their obligations, and stood trial. This is why defence lawyers understandably requested judges to show more courage – if they were not able to dismiss the request for an arrest warrant, they should at least suspend it. Even if that form of compromise is not how the German system is constructed, it seemed to be acceptable, pragmatism reigns:

> The silver bullet is just to issue an arrest warrant and then to suspend with suitable conditions, then both sides are usually happy.
>
> (17, Judge)

Equally, a defence lawyers argued that neither for her nor for the client there was a big difference between the rejection of an arrest warrant or the suspension, as long as detention is avoided; at least not when only the usual obligation to report to the police is the only condition attached since this is not a very restrictive measure.

Defence lawyer's associations have argued in recent years that it is necessary to broaden the use of alternatives and some propagated electronic monitoring as a condition to a suspended arrest warrant (König, 2016). So far, this possibility is used only in the Federal State of Hesse (Bräuchle and Kinzig, 2017). Most interviewees did not support it because they saw no additional value in it:

> I think it [EM] is unsuitable for the suspension of execution of the warrant, because if I trust someone so little that I have to control him with an ankle bracelet then I have to think about whether I want to release that person in the first place. And if he wears it, . . . I can perhaps solve a

criminal offense in retrospect, but I can under no circumstances prevent something. That is why I find this from a practical point of view a wrong idea and under legal aspects I have not thought further about it.

(26, Lawyer)

European aspects

Both the Council of Europe and the European Union play a role for the development of German pre-trial practice. Germany has been convicted a few times by the ECtHR for the unjustified length of detention because the court denied that the cases were overly complex,[9] or criticised a lack of adequate promotion of the proceedings by the judiciary,[10] thus declaring it an infringement of Article 5 (3) ECtHR. However, in more recent cases the ECtHR upheld the now more thoughtful approaches of the German law enforcement agencies and the reasoning of the courts given in their decision on the prolongation of the pre-trial detention.[11] This indicates that the ECtHR rulings may have had some influence on German practice.

A second area with directly visible impact of decisions by the ECtHR is the right to inspect case files in pre-trial detention cases. Traditionally, the Prosecution could deny access to files for defence lawyers and their clients when access would have "endangered the purposes of the criminal investigations". Under the principle of equality of arms (Article 6 ECHR), however, the accused must have sufficient information for his procedural defence against the arrest warrant. According to the ECtHR especially the practice to preselect parts of the files accessible or to inform merely orally violated Article 6 ECHR.[12] In a direct reaction to this jurisprudence, the German legislator amended the law in 2010. In our DETOUR study, access to files was described as straightforward, even if sometimes time-consuming, by all professional groups. The ECHR or decisions by the ECtHR were hardly mentioned.

This was different for questions around the cross-border cooperation within the European Union. As mentioned earlier, the EU Directive 2016/919 on Legal Aid had direct impact on German legislation on mandatory assignments of defence counsels. Equally, some cooperation tools are accepted in practice – the European Arrest Warrant, for example, is widely used (Morgenstern, 2018). It is questionable, however, in how far German courts in practice accept and use detention-avoiding cooperation tools within the EU, namely to contact and summon foreign defendants in their home country, or whether they still prefer to detain them safely in Germany. We found contradictory signs in the DETOUR study:

With EU citizens you completely have to leave aside that they are "foreigners" at all. When I was on duty in X-court the last time, the judge completely left aside that they were from other EU countries, Romania and Lithuania on that day. [She said] you could summon the suspects in

> their home countries without problem. In both cases no arrest warrant was issued.
>
> (8, Public Prosecutor)

Equally indicating overall acceptance, another judge referred to the possibility of formally submitting so-called penalty orders (convictions in a written procedure) within the EU for *„small and middle-ranged criminality"* (4, judge). It is possible, however, that the acceptance of EU mechanisms is at best superficial and has not sunken in fully:

> [laughing] . . . in the past you could lock up everybody coming from a foreign country, you always had a risk of flight. But meanwhile you say, that within Europe you find people relatively quickly and extradite them. You have to consider that now.
>
> (29, Judge, similar 15, Judge)

Another judge acknowledged the need for equal treatment of EU foreigners "*in theory*" but said that in practice it is irrelevant to him and gave the example of professional thieves, who would "*straightaway disappear to Eastern Europe*" if released (16, judge; similarly with regard to "*travelling offenders*" 15, judge). Other practitioners were therefore rather frustrated:

> [O]n every occasion you talk about a unified Europe, but when you look at detention judges' decisions, you would find often enough arrest warrants saying "He does not have a fixed abode in Germany" and then the court is not fussed about this person having in the neighbouring country Poland the same address for 20 years, because they are too lazy . . . to get that information.
>
> (26, Lawyer)

Scepticism, sometimes ignorance, was clearly visible regarding the specific instrument of the European Supervision Order (ESO), that aims at facilitating pre-trial supervision in the community "at home" within the EU (see Chapter 14). This reluctance was shown already by the German legislator who transposed the Framework Decision only with considerable delay in 2015 into unwieldy provisions in the Legal Cooperation Act, IRG (§§ 90 o-90 y). Most of our respondents did not know it, only two had practical experience and found the procedure cumbersome – the judge interviewed said that the defence lawyer involved "*begged him not to repeat this exercise*" (3, judge). Others did not want to try it because they were "*deterred by all the bureaucracy*" (10, judge). A lawyer assumed that a detention judge would probably declare him "*completely off my mind*" when he would request such as thing, "*even it was in the domestic law like all the other provision on pre-trial detention*" (26, lawyer). There is no evidence that the ESO has become more popular recently.

Conclusion

Our research shows that the accusation of pre-trial detention being ordered "too often, too quickly, too long" in Germany (Arbeitskreis Strafprozessreform, 1983: 25) is not true across the board: The presumption for liberty in the pre-trial phase and the principle of proportionality do play a role in practice, as the long trend of declining use of pre-trial detention since the 1990s shows. It can be assumed that it is the practice of public prosecutors who drives the development – the judicial rejection quote of about 10% of all requests of arrest warrants was stable over the years, so that falling numbers of pre-trial detainees must be attributed to fewer requests. Additionally, shorter detention periods may play a role.

There are groups, however, where these rather liberal principles are thrown overboard to maintain functionality and to have the suspect "at hand" for trial. Citizenship at least for foreigners who reside in Germany permanently plays not the decisive role *per se*, but the risk to be detained prior or during trial increases significantly for those who are socially marginalised. This is true for homeless persons and many foreign suspects and is visible both in statistics and in our fieldwork. Other shortcomings in decision-making relate to insufficient investigations in personal circumstances that could prevent detention and an unjustified reservedness towards alternatives. Suggested legal reforms, for example, once again to refine the reasons to detain or to strengthen alternative solutions, may not be sufficient to tackle this problem unless practical solutions are found, for example shelters for persons without abode in Germany that provide them with the necessary "fixed address" to summon them are established.

The need for better data and more empirical research, in particular on unequal treatment of certain groups, is apparent. Additionally, there seems to be a lack of adequate training, among others on European developments. Training events could be important for interprofessional exchange and to reflect own practice. While it is true that the workload of practitioners is large and they need to be updated on many different things, detention as fundamental interference with personal liberty merits a deeper understanding.

Notes

1 In this chapter, the terms "pre-trial detention", "remand detention" and "remand custody" are used synonymously.
2 Untersuchungshaft in Europa. Eine vergleichende Untersuchung unter rechtsdogmatischen, kriminologischen und europarechtlichen Aspekten" – Deutsche Forschungsgemeinschaft (DFG) – Projektnummer 219315043.
3 www.uibk.ac.at/irks/projekte/detour.html.de.
4 The Conviction and Sentencing Statistics (*Strafverfolgungsstatistik*) combines data for those prosecuted and either convicted (typically 80% and more), acquitted (3%)

or discharged conditionally or unconditionally by a judge (about 17%, mostly juveniles) in a given year and counts them as category "persons with a final court decision". The statistics also identify a subgroup of persons who were in pre-trial detention.

5 They are thus (usually) treated under the Juvenile Justice Act with special rules for procedure and sentencing and will therefore not be covered in this chapter.

6 It must be acknowledged that comparisons are difficult because offenders are counted irrespective of their state of residence and may be travelling. A more detailed account can be found in Chapter 13.

7 According to the Conviction and Sentencing Statistics, in 2019 only 5% of all defendants with pre-trial detention were not convicted: 1.5% of defendants were acquitted (compared to 3% of all defendants), 2% were discharged by the court, 1% received an isolated preventive measure (usually for mentally ill defendants).

8 In the German part of the DETOUR study, 31 semi-structured interviews were conducted with 11 judges, 8 public prosecutors, 9 defence lawyers and 3 prison officials in 3 different German regions (Mecklenburg Western Pomerania, North Rhine-Westphalia and Berlin), represented here in quotes with the interview number and the professional role of the interviewee.

9 ECtHR, *Erdem v. Germany*, 5 July 2001, 38321/97.

10 ECtHR, *Dzelili v. Germany*, 10 November 2005, 65745/01; ECtHR, *Patalakh v. Germany*, 8 March 2018, 22692/15.

11 ECtHR, *Ereren v. Germany*, 6 November 2014, 67522/09.

12 ECtHR, *Mooren v. Germany*, 13 December 2007, 11364/03.

References

Arbeitskreis Strafprozessreform (1983) *Die Untersuchungshaft. Gesetzentwurf mit Begründung*, Heidelberg: Müller.

Bräuchle, A. and Kinzig, J. (2017) *Rechtspolitische Perspektiven der elektronischen Aufenthaltsüberwachung*, Tübingen: TOBIAS-lib.

Bundeskriminalamt (2021) *Polizeiliche Kriminalstatistik 2020* (and earlier), Wiesbaden: Bundeskriminalamt at www.bka.de/DE/AktuelleInformationen/Statistiken-Lagebilder/PolizeilicheKriminalstatistik/PKS2020/pks2020_node.html [accessed 10 October 2022].

Busse, U. (2008) *Frühe Strafverteidigung und Untersuchungshaft*, Göttingen: Universitätsverlag.

Dessecker, A. (2007) 'Die Begrenzung langer Untersuchungshaft: eine Rechtsprechungsanalyse', *Höchstrichterliche Rechtsprechung*, 8: 112–118.

Dünkel, F. and Morgenstern, C. (2022) 'Germany', in F. Dünkel, S. Harrendorf and D. van Zyl Smit (eds) *The Impact of Covid-19 on Prison Conditions and Penal Policy*, London: Routledge.

Dünkel, F. and Vagg, J. (eds) (1994) *Untersuchungshaft und Untersuchungshaftvollzug – Waiting for Trial*, Freiburg: Max-Planck-Institut für ausländisches und Internationales Strafrecht.

Engelhard, H.-A. (1986) '"Die Freiheit eines Beschuldigten darf nur eingeschränkt werden, wenn es nachweislich notwendig ist"', *Zentralblatt für Jugendrecht*, 73: 359–362.

Gebauer, M. (1987) *Die Rechtswirklichkeit der Untersuchungshaft in der Bundesrepublik Deutschland*, Göttingen: Fink.

König, S. (2016) 'Reform des Untersuchungshaftrechts?', in Strafverteidigervereinigungen (eds) *Welche Reform braucht das Strafverfahren? Texte und Ergebnisse des 39. Strafverteidigertages in Lübeck, 6. – 8.3.2015*, Berlin: Organisationsbüro.

Kowalzyck, M. (2008) *Untersuchungshaft, Untersuchungshaftvermeidung und geschlossene Unterbringung bei Jugendlichen und Heranwachsenden in Mecklenburg-Vorpommern*, Monchengladbach: Forum.

Morgenstern, C. (2015) '"Der Resozialisierungsgrundsatz" – Social Reintegration as the dominant narrative for community punishment in Germany?', in G. Robinson and F. McNeill (eds) *Community Punishment. A European Perspective*, London: Routledge.

Morgenstern, C. (2018) *Die Untersuchungshaft. Eine Untersuchung unter rechtsdogmatischen, kriminologischen, rechtsvergleichenden und europarechtlichen Aspekten*, Baden-Baden: Nomos.

Morgenstern, C. (2020) 'Aktuelle Entwicklungen in Recht und Praxis der Untersuchungshaft in Deutschland', *Neue Zeitschrift für Kriminologie und Kriminalpolitik/ Nouvelle Revue de Criminologie et de Politique Pénale*, 1: 19–28.

Morgenstern, C. (2021) 'Need for speed: Die neue Beschleunigungsfreude im Strafverfahren am Beispiel der Untersuchungshaft', *Zeitschrift für Rechtssoziologie*, 40: 90–116.

Morgenstern, C. and Kromrey, H. (2017) *1st German National Report. Working Paper, DETOUR Project (Pre-trial Detention as Ultima Ratio)* at www.uibk.ac.at/irks/projekte/detour.html.de [accessed 10 October 2022].

Paeffgen, U. (1986) *Vorüberlegungen zu einer Dogmatik des Untersuchungshaft-Rechts*, Köln a.o.: Heymanns.

Roxin, C. and Schünemann, B. (2022) *Strafverfahrensrecht*, 30th ed., München: C.H. Beck.

Statistisches Bundesamt (2021a) *Bestand der Gefangenen und Verwahrten in den deutschen Justizvollzugsanstalten Januar bis Dezember 2021* (and earlier), Wiesbaden: Destatis at www.statistischebibliothek.de/mir/receive/DEHeft_mods_00143126 [accessed 10 October 2022].

Statistisches Bundesamt (2021b) *Strafverfolgung – Fachserie 10, Reihe 3–2020* (and earlier), Wiesbaden: Destatis at www.destatis.de/DE/Themen/Staat/Justiz-Rechtspflege/_inhalt.html#_ls3012ksz [accessed 10 October 2022].

Wolf, L. (2017) *Die Fluchtprognose im Untersuchungshaftrecht. Eine empirische Untersuchung der Fluchtgefahr nach § 112 Abs. 2 Nr. 2 StPO*, Baden-Baden: Nomos.

Wolter, J. (1981) 'Untersuchungshaft, Vorbeugungshaft und vorläufige Sanktionen', *Zeitschrift für die gesamte Strafrechtswissenschaft*, 93: 452–506.

Chapter 6

Pre-trial detention in Ireland

Emphasising alternatives?

Mary Rogan

Introduction[1]

Ireland's pre-trial detention rate is relatively low by European and international standards, standing at around 14 pre-trial detainees per 100,000 population (based on figures drawn from Irish Prison Service, 2021). Until the 1990s, the use of pre-trial detention in Ireland was very limited, partly due to a Supreme Court decision from 1966 which held that pre-trial detention on the grounds of the risk of offending was constitutionally impermissible. This decision influenced practice for many years and continues to do so in important ways. However, a critical moment in the history of pre-trial detention in Ireland occurred in 1997, when a referendum was passed to amend the constitution in order to permit the use of pre-trial detention in circumstances where a court felt the accused person was likely to commit serious offences if not detained. Since then, Ireland has built a prison originally designed to house those detained pending their trial (Rogan, 2011) and has seen its pre-trial detention population rise, though it has been relatively stable over the last decade.

The long-established alternative to pre-trial detention in Ireland is bail. As will be described later, this usually comes with conditions attached, but support services and intensive supervision of those on bail are not widespread practices in the case of adults. It is therefore important to clarify terminology at the outset. While the term *bail* in other contexts often refers to the actual financial guarantee provided to secure attendance at trial, the term *bail* in the Irish context is used to describe the alternative to custody in its entirety. An accused person who is granted bail or is described as "on bail" is simply a person who is not held in pre-trial detention while the charges against him or her are pending before the courts. Conditions, including those of a financial nature, may be attached to the accused's bail.

There has been limited examination of pre-trial detention in Ireland from an empirical point of view, though several analyses of the legal provisions exist (see, for example, O'Malley, 2009). The empirical work available shows that, among children, there was often confusion about the terms of bail and

DOI: 10.4324/9781003159254-6

there was a significant lack of support to comply with bail conditions (Freeman, 2008; Seymour and Butler, 2008; Carroll and Meehan, 2007). Research has also found that legal actors did not consider the European Court of Human Rights (ECtHR) to have had a major impact on pre-trial detention practice in Ireland (Irish Penal Reform Trust, 2016). This research also concluded that the conditions attached to bail were too often disproportionate and too numerous.

This chapter explores the contours of how pre-trial detention is used in Ireland. With a comparatively low rate of pre-trial detention in European terms, Ireland offers an interesting case study by which to explore the factors which influence such decision-making. The chapter draws on official figures concerning the use of pre-trial detention, as well as qualitative interviews with members of the judiciary, prosecution and defence lawyers, and members of the probation service conducted as part of the DETOUR project (see Chapter 1). The experience of Ireland suggests that the risk of offending pending a trial ground for using pre-trial detention is likely a key influence on higher rates of detention. The comparatively late introduction of this ground has meant that a strong judicial and legal culture which favours the use of bail has proven quite enduring. This is so even in the absence of well-developed social supports or probation supervision. The influence of European developments will also be examined, something of particular concern in light of the outsize effect of Brexit on Ireland, as well as concerns that the legal culture giving rise to lower pre-trial detention rates in Ireland is being eroded.

Pre-trial detention in practice

Ireland has seen significant increases in its prison population generally during the late 1990s and 2000s, with a fall in the 2010s and something of a plateauing since then, as seen in Figure 6.1. For several years, the numbers of people in pre-trial detention remained quite static, though the proportion of pre-trial detainees within the prison population overall has grown, as seen in Figure 6.2. This situation is explained in part by decline in overall committals to prison in Ireland, particularly for those serving sentences. However, there is also evidence that the average number of detainees in any given month has increased since 2016 (Figure 6.2). Though the data are limited as the lengths of time people are spending in pre-trial detention have only been published in recent years, the numbers of people spending longer periods in detention (over one year) are increasing (Figure 6.3) and there is also an indication that both lawyers and judges are concerned about increasingly lengthy delays in holding trials (Carolan, 2021). A former Director General of the Irish Prison Service has also stated the view that pre-trial detainees are being held for longer than before (Irish Prison Service, 2021: 2). A particularly striking increase has occurred in the use of pre-trial detention for women, with a 37% increase in the number of women detained in pre-trial detention over the period 2013–2019 (Finn, 2020). It is notable that 19 prisoners had spent over two years in pre-trial detention by October 2021 with a further 58 spending one to two years by this point.[2]

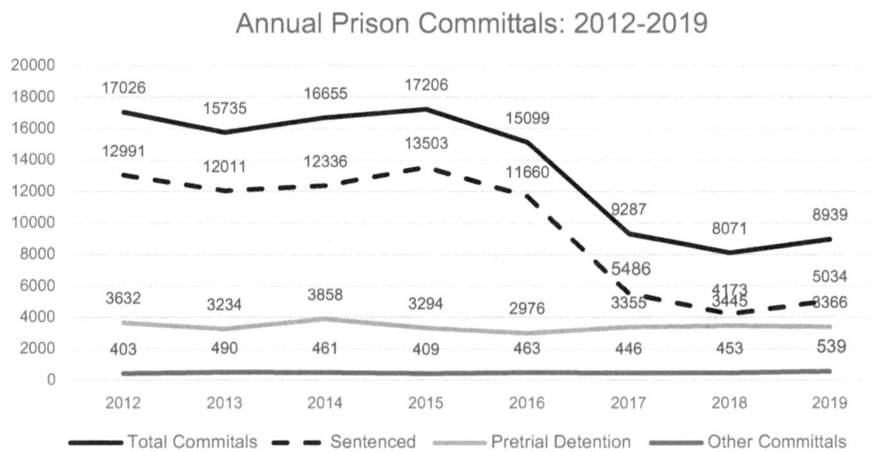

Figure 6.1 Committals to prison by type 2012–2019.

Source: Irish Prison Service Annual Reports.

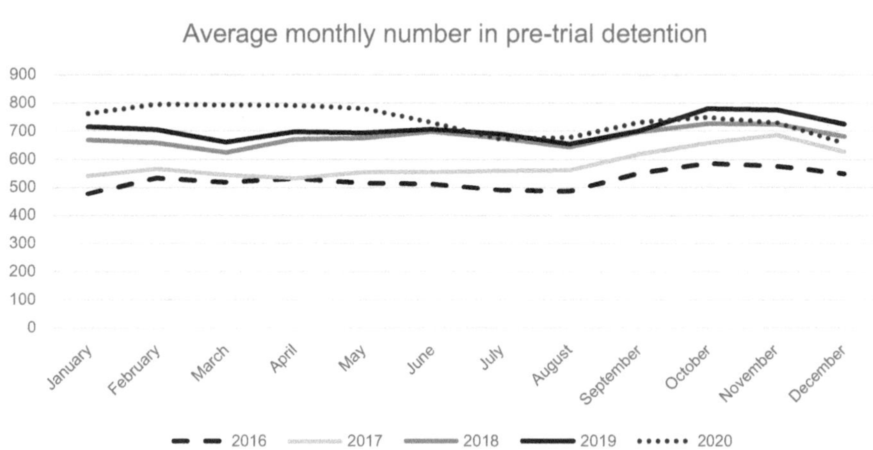

Figure 6.2 Average monthly numbers in pre-trial detention 2016–2020.

Source: Irish Prison Service monthly notes.

A line graph depicts average monthly number in pre-trial detention with the months of the year along the x-axis and numbers from 0 to 900 in increments of 100 along the y-axis. The five lines on the graph represents the years from 2016 to 2020.

Legal framework

Ireland is a common law jurisdiction, a legacy carried over from its colonial days under the rule of the United Kingdom. Ireland introduced a written constitution, Bunreacht na hÉireann in 1937. The Constitution contains

Table 6.1 Numbers of people in pre-trial detention classified by length of time in pre-trial detention at the time of data collection

	<1 Month	*1–3 Months*	*3–6 Months*	*6–9 Months*	*9–12 Months*	*1–2 Years*	*2 Years plus*
October 2019	241	146	139	49	30	29	3
October 2020	183	135	134	60	37	53	7
October 2021	188	152	84	64	40	58	19

Note: This table and Figure 6.3 are from Irish Prison Service monthly reports. These figures relate to people who are in pre-trial detention awaiting trial or sentence only and not those who are already serving a sentence and who are also awaiting trial.

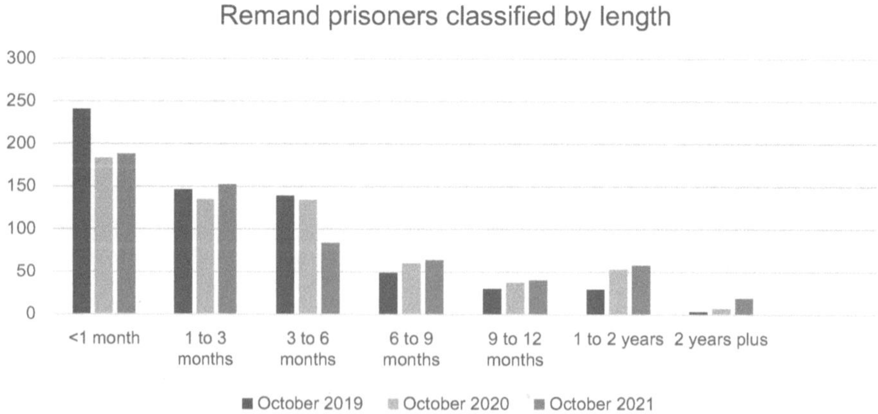

Figure 6.3 Numbers of people in pre-trial detention categorised by length of time in pre-trial detention at the time of data collection, 2019–2021.

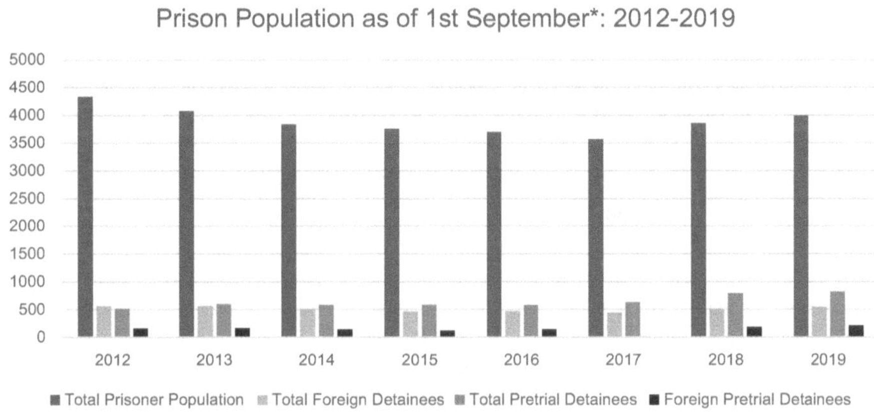

Figure 6.4 Prison population composition, 2012–2019.

Source: Council of Europe, SPACE-I. Data for 2018 and 2019 are from 31 January not 1 September. No SPACE I report was available for 2017, so data for that year are from the Irish Prison Service Monthly Information Note for the population on 31 August. There was no information on foreign pre-trial detainees for 2017.

explicit protections for the presumption of innocence, the right to liberty and the right to a fair trial. The law governing pre-trial detention derives from a mixture of case law, statute and the Constitution. There are several statutory provisions which allow the police (Garda Síochána) to detain people for investigative reasons before a charge is made. Such detention is for a finite period of time, usually a maximum of seven days, with various increments within that overall period subject to extension through the approval of either senior police officers or judges. For example, Section 4 of the Criminal Justice Act (1984) permits the detention of a person for a total period of 24 hours, while Section 50 of the Criminal Justice Act (2007) permits the detention of a person arrested for certain serious offences, including murder or an organised crime offence, for a total of 144 hours.

When a person is actually charged with an offence, an important feature of Irish law is the *prima facie* (on its face) entitlement to be released on bail pending the resolution of the charges (*Vickers v. DPP*, 2009). The foundational decision of *People (Attorney General) v. O'Callaghan* (1966) held that detaining a person in custody simply on the basis that s/he has been charged with an offence is inconsistent with the presumption of innocence. Some additional factor is necessary to justify the use of pre-trial detention. The *O'Callaghan* decision held that there were two such permissible grounds for pre-trial detention: the risk of not turning up for trial, and the risk of interfering with witnesses. These were the only two permissible grounds for pre-trial detention until 1997, when a new ground – the risk of offending while on bail – was introduced. Irish law currently recognises three objections to bail or bases for pre-trial detention:

- Where it is probable that the accused will abscond or otherwise evade justice by failing to appear at court to answer the charges (*People [Attorney General] v. O'Callaghan, 1966*); the court must be satisfied that there is a likelihood of such matters happening, but need not be satisfied beyond a reasonable doubt.[3]
- Where it appears "reasonably probable" that the accused will pervert the course of justice by interfering with prospective witnesses and jurors, tampering with evidence, or disposing of illegally acquired property (*People [Attorney General] v. O'Callaghan, 1966; People [DPP] v. McGinley, 1998*).
- Where there is a real risk that the accused will commit serious offences if granted bail.

In all cases, it is for the prosecution to prove the existence of these grounds to the satisfaction of the court.

The third ground noted earlier, where a risk of offending is considered to exist, was introduced into Irish law by means of a referendum in 1996, following a period of disquiet about crime in rural parts of Ireland and a perceived upsurge in organised crime, along with the murder of a journalist investigating such crimes, Veronica Guerin. This period has been described as a "textbook case" of a moral panic (O'Donnell and O'Sullivan, 2003: 48). Until then, the Supreme Court's interpretation of the Constitution as preventing the use of preventive detention held sway. Article 40.4.6 was inserted into the Constitution to overturn this position. The insertion of this new article was then followed by the enactment of Section 2 of the Bail Act (1997), which provides that, where a person is charged with a serious offence, a court may refuse an application for bail. The court may do so if "satisfied that such refusal is reasonably considered necessary to prevent the commission of a serious offence by that person". This has become known as a *section 2 objection*.

A section 2 objection can only be made where the accused has been charged with certain offences, and it must also be a "serious offence" which is feared to be committed. Under the Schedule to the Bail Act (1997), these offences include murder, manslaughter, serious assaults, kidnapping, rape and robbery, theft or damage to property. The scope of the Bail Act 1997 is therefore wide. The prosecution need not prove that there is a risk that a serious offence will be committed pending the trial beyond a reasonable doubt, but the court must be satisfied that the risk is a real one (*Vickers v. DPP*, 2009). The Bail Act (1997) sets out considerations which the court must weigh up when making such a decision. These include the seriousness of the offence charged, the accused's previous convictions, especially while on bail, and whether the accused is addicted to drugs. A court can consider other factors, including the likely date of trial (*Maguire v. DPP, 2004*).

Following another period of concern about offending, in this case burglaries, the Criminal Justice (Burglary of Dwellings) Act (2015) was passed to deal specifically with factors which a court must consider when a person aged over 18 makes an application for bail in respect of a charge of burglary of a dwelling and a section 2 objection is made by the prosecution. This complex legislation essentially creates a situation whereby pending charges or recent convictions for burglary of a dwelling can be taken as evidence of likelihood to commit such offences while on bail, with the stated purpose of making it more difficult for accused persons in such circumstances to obtain bail.

Once a person has been charged with an offence and placed in pre-trial detention, there is no maximum duration of that period of detention set out in Irish law. There are, however, time limits for the periods between which a person must appear again before the District Court, for example, generally for a maximum of eight days from the person's first appearance in the District Court (Section 24, Criminal Procedure Act, 1967; Order 19, Rules of the District Court); these time limits can be extended by the court. Similar time limits do not, however, apply to pre-trial detention in respect of proceeding before higher courts. In the situation where a person is detained in pre-trial custody on the basis of a section 2 objection, if the trial has not started within four months of the date of refusal of bail, the accused person may apply to the court for bail on the basis of a delay by the prosecution and the court may release that person if the interests of justice so require (Section 3, Bail Act, 1997). There have been sweeping changes proposed to decision-making on pre-trial detention in Ireland through the Bail Bill (2015), the Bail (Amendment) Bill (2016) and the Bail (Amendment) Bill (2017). All of these efforts are framed as ways to make it more difficult to avoid pre-trial detention but have not progressed into law.

Decision-making and the use of pre-trial detention in Ireland

At the pre-trial stage, both the police and courts may grant bail, though this power is given to the police in limited circumstances (Section 31, Criminal Procedure Act, 1967). Where a person is charged with a criminal offence, s/he must be brought before the District Court, the lowest court in terms of the hierarchy of courts in Ireland, as soon as practicable. In most cases, the District Court will decide on bail, but this power is reserved to the High Court for some offences, including murder (Section 29(1), Criminal Procedure Act, 1967). There is a right of appeal against the decision to impose pre-trial detention (Section 28(3), Criminal Procedure Act, 1967).

Before all courts where bail may be granted, it is up to the prosecution to make an objection to the grant of bail and seek pre-trial detention. It is usual practice that the accused person will be represented by a lawyer at all hearings regarding pre-trial detention, and the vast majority will receive funded legal assistance (Criminal Justice [Legal Aid] Act, 1962; Legal Aid [Custody Issues] Scheme). At the District Court level, it is usually the case that a member of the police service (Garda Síochána) will represent the prosecution, while the accused person will usually be represented by a solicitor or a barrister, or both. At the High Court level, the prosecution will usually be represented by a barrister and a solicitor acting for the Director of Public Prosecutions. The accused person will normally be present for the hearing. Hearings are almost always in public, and those concerning bail do not have a specific list or time, instead taking their place amongst a variety of other criminal matters.

At the District Court level, the typical practice is for the prosecution to present its bail objections, calling any witness evidence necessary. The accused, or the accused's legal representatives may cross-examine any such witnesses. The accused may then present her/his own evidence, which can also be questioned by the prosecution. Both the prosecution and defence then have the opportunity to make arguments to the judge about whether or not to grant bail and it is for the judge to decide. The District Court judge makes the decision alone. At the District Court level, there can be great variation in the length of bail hearings and the degree of formality which they follow.

At the High Court level, decisions concerning pre-trial detention arise out of appeals from refusals to grant bail by the lower courts, or the High Court may hear applications *de novo* for certain serious offences. These hearings have a dedicated list, and the accused person must swear a written affidavit describing the basis for the application for bail and relevant circumstances. These hearings are also generally in public. As with the District Court, a judge of the High Court hears the evidence and/or arguments from both sides and makes the decision alone. In the case of Section 2 objections, Section 2A of the Bail Act (1997) allows a senior police officer (Chief Superintendent) to give evidence of her/his belief that pre-trial detention is reasonably necessary to prevent the commission of a serious offence and this evidence is to be considered as evidence that pre-trial detention is reasonably necessary.

At both High and District Court levels, while prosecution and defence representatives sit on either side of the courtroom, there is no distinction between them in terms of their distance from the judge or their respective physical elevations.

Agreement to the release of the person on bail on conditions is not uncommon and the court can make a "consent order" to reflect this agreement. While this is the formal legal position, the factors which influence this picture in practice have only recently come under scrutiny. As noted in the introduction, the study presented here is part of the DETOUR project. The present study was carried out of Irish pre-trial detention decision-making, using observations of bail hearings, and interviews with judges, prosecution and defence lawyers, and members of the probation service (Rogan and Perry,

2017). That study indicates a number of key elements in Irish practice which suggest that there is an emphasis on bail over the use of pre-trial detention. This emphasis is partly derived from the historical approach which did not favour the use of the risk of offending ground as a basis for pre-trial detention, as well as certain equality between prosecution and defence.

The constitutional position of bail

The experience of Ireland suggests that the formal legal position concerning the use of pre-trial influences practice. The presumption of innocence, as well as the presumption in favour of bail set down in the *O'Callaghan* case, were strongly expressed as reasons for the low use of pre-trial detention in Ireland in this study.

> Essentially, it starts with the presumption that somebody will get bail.
> (3, Judge)

> Certainly the first thing that always comes to my mind that there is a presumption in favour of the applicant for bail on the basis of O'Callaghan. So, every applicant does have a constitutional advantage of getting bail.
> (1, Prosecution Practitioner)

As one judge put it:

> [A]dmission to bail is what's to be expected, that's the norm.
> (2, Judge)

A prosecutor said:

> [S]o the default position is that a person will be entitled to bail . . . it's the default position is the difference, isn't it.
> (3, Prosecution Practitioner)

These findings suggest that the long-standing and constitutionally protected position of bail in Ireland has been influential, across all actors in the process. This position was felt to have largely inhibited the influence of the Bail Act (1997) and its introduction of the risk of offending ground as a basis for pre-trial detention.

> Has it changed? I don't really think so, it's just as lenient now as it was, certainly whenever I first started.
> (5, Defence Practitioner)

> It seems to be the same old same old really.
> (2, Defence Practitioner)

It was clear from participants that they did not consider Section 2 of the Bail Act (1997) to have made a major impact on bail practice, and that, amongst the available grounds for pre-trial detention, the most important one was the likelihood of turning up for trial. It was evident that the *O'Callaghan* decision and grounds continues to dominate practice in the area of bail in Ireland. One judge put it very simply:

> The be all and end all of bail in Ireland is the O'Callaghan case. And it's, you know, quoted in criminal courts across the country every day of the week again and again and again and it's taken seriously.
>
> (3, Judge)

The *O'Callaghan* principles for the denial of bail were very much to the forefront in participants' responses to being asked what the grounds for pre-trial detention in Ireland were. Section 2 was also a prominent response, but it was clear that the *O'Callaghan* principles remain dominant.

As one prosecution participant stated:

> It's really you know. . . . Someone who won't show up.
>
> (7, Prosecution Participant)

Another participant said:

> I think that O'Callaghan is still the main game in town.
>
> (4, Prosecution Practitioner)

Section 2 was considered to require a very high bar in terms of evidence and was most often used as a kind of "belt and braces" approach, or an added objection to bail in circumstances where pre-trial detention was very much wanted by the prosecution. However, many participants felt that the offence of burglary was one which made it more likely for a court to impose pre-trial detention. Participants also felt that the political and media climate were broadly hostile to the use of bail, but that judges in Ireland are upholding a regime which favours liberty in spite of popular and political pressure, though, as will be explored further later, there was concern that this resistance was eroding.

An extremely strong theme to emerge from the interviews was the influence of not turning up for court in the past, or getting *bench warrants*, that is, warrants for arrest made by a judge when a person fails to turn up in court. As one defence lawyer put it:

> Warrant history. Always warrant history. It's the first question asked: how many warrants? . . . But the first thing is always warrant history.
>
> (10, Defence Practitioner)

Judges shared this view. The number of warrants, that is, the number of occasions where the person had failed to attend court was, for many participants, a much more important factor even than the number of prior convictions a person had. Bench warrants were of such importance that some participants felt that this factor alone could sway a court, particularly at District Court level. This focus on bench warrant history suggests an interesting feature of the Irish system. The bail regime in Ireland is, primarily, focused on past behaviour, and, specifically, past failures to comply with bail conditions. A risk of offending is not so important under the Irish system in most cases, and, as such, the bail system is not especially future oriented. Practitioners in the Irish system examine past failures to turn up for court as evidence to predict the likelihood of turning up for court in the future. However, this is the primary calculation entered into by participants in Ireland, rather than an examination of a risk of future criminal behaviour in the form of committing criminal offences. One judge put this in very clear terms:

> Well generally speaking you're looking to the past, I mean there are exceptions, . . ., but generally speaking you're looking to the past.
>
> (3, Judge)

The next most important factor for participants was the seriousness of the charge. Practitioners felt that judges were more likely to impose pre-trial detention when a person has allegedly been injured or affected badly by the criminal actions in question; the seriousness of the offence was also considered to influence the likelihood of objections to bail. While this is so, there was complexity in the responses, with many participants noting that bail is possible even for the most serious offences, especially if a person had a good record of turning up for trials. However, it was felt that, in the recent past, offences related to organised crime were becoming extremely unlikely to result in bail being granted.

Influential actors and decision-making

The vast majority of defendants in Ireland are eligible for and receive funded legal aid, which entitles them to receive state-funded legal services from a solicitor, and, in serious cases, a barrister. The overwhelming majority of defendants in pre-trial decisions are therefore legally represented. Ireland does not have a "public defender" system, and, as noted earlier, many barristers (lawyers who act more frequently in court) work for both the prosecution and defence. There cannot be said to be a significant imbalance in the quality of legal representation afforded to both sides, with the major caveat that the prosecution has the resources of the State at its disposal. Participants described the role of the prosecutor as being to object to bail and give evidence for those objections, while the defence's task is to seek to add context to information put forward by the prosecution, question evidence, and provide assurance to the court that the person may be released on bail. The judge was viewed as a type of referee, with considerable discretion. No party was considered to be especially dominant by most participants:

> I think there's generally a good balance between the parties. Both sides are heard . . . and there seems to be enough safeguards in relation to it to make it reasonably fair.
>
> (1, Defence Practitioner)

> Generally speaking, it's a pretty level playing field, the Guard (police) says his bit and the [defence] solicitor will say their bit. Generally everyone has their say, I think.
>
> (3, Defence Practitioner)

> Evenly matched with, obviously the prosecution having the advantage of access to Garda (police) records.
>
> (4, Judge)

Some, however, felt that the prosecution did often have a strong influence on the judge, with others considering the defence had a strong role. Practitioners noted a strong theme of judicial variation to the point where some defence practitioners would avoid making an application for bail before certain judges as they felt it was unlikely they would succeed.

Another interesting feature of practice surrounding the use of pre-trial detention in Ireland is the relatively common phenomenon of the prosecution and defence agreeing terms of bail and permitting a person's release, known as *consent to bail*, which a judge would be extremely unlikely to refuse to implement. This practice was reported at all levels of court practice. Prosecutors did not have a major difficulty with this system, considering it to be an efficient use of time and resources, and a way of ensuring that pre-trial detention was not unnecessarily used. There was a clear sense that prosecution participants were open to discussions about negotiating bail conditions:

> If there's a chance of getting bail and it's not a very, very serious offence and you don't have the Guards (police) absolutely gung-ho to say there's no way this can happen you'll work around it.
>
> (4, Prosecution Practitioner)

The work of defence lawyers was crucial in this process, with evidence from the interviews that defence lawyers were very active in their pursuit of a possible bail agreement. This was often done under great time pressure, perhaps in the minutes before a hearing. Defence lawyers reported placing a lot of emphasis and putting a lot of time into having discussions with Gardaí or with the representatives of the prosecution before a case is called on. Most participants stated that it would be unlikely for a judge to probe a consent application for bail. Most judges, the participants felt, would simply accept the consent order and move on. Some judges confirmed this practice:

Interviewer: [W]ould you be likely to probe consent?
Judge 1: No, no. No.
I think, by and large, the view is that criminal trials are adversarial as the decision to seek bail or to resist bail is part of the adversarial process. And if the parties have a common position it would be rare for a judge to go behind it.

(3, Judge)

This practice of consent to bail is a manifestation of an important aspect of the legal culture surrounding the use of pre-trial detention in Ireland which involves a certain degree of collaboration between prosecution and defence. While the decision-making hearing may be extremely robust and adversarial, it emerged in interviews that there was a sense of respect between both sides and an effort to make hearings run smoothly where possible. This speaks to the way in which values and understandings around the use of pre-trial detention are not radically different between prosecution and defence lawyers for the most part. Prosecution self-restraint and a willingness to accept bail (with conditions generally) seems to be another reason influencing low pre-trial detention rates in Ireland. It was also notable from this research that the defence is considered to be very active, and that this played a weighty role. Besides seeking to undermine the prosecution's objections to bail, defence lawyers also play a key role in suggesting conditions which would alleviate the court's concerns about granting a person bail. Notably, Ireland does not have formal involvement of the probation service in decisions on the use of pre-trial detention, nor is there any form of supervision of bail conditions by the probation service for adults.

Bail and alternative solutions

Bail

As noted earlier, the term bail is *the* alternative to pre-trial detention in Ireland, though the specific conditions which apply to liberty will vary from case to case. Financial bail or a financial guarantee may be part of those conditions, but the term bail is broader in the Irish context. A court granting bail must apply the condition that the person must appear before the court when required, refrain from committing any offence while on bail, and otherwise be of good behaviour. After that, a court has wide discretion as to what conditions to impose and may impose any it "considers appropriate having regard to the circumstances of the case" (Section 6(1)(b), Bail Act, 1997). Common conditions include requiring a person to reside in a particular place or district, a condition to "sign on" or report to a specified police (Garda) station at particular times; a condition to stay away from particular places or people, a curfew, a requirement to surrender one's passport, a requirement to give a mobile phone number to the police and keep that mobile phone charged and in credit, or a condition that the accused person engage with certain rehabilitative services. Any condition must be justified on the basis of evidence and should not be an unreasonable restriction on liberty (*Ronan v. Coughlan*, 2005). A financial bond is also required. In some cases, the accused person might be required to lodge a specified sum of cash with the courts in advance of taking up bail, which will be lost in the event of non-compliance with bail conditions. However, it is not always necessary for the accused person to actually lodge money up front before being released on bail, and s/he can enter a bond to do so. A court may also require an independent surety or guarantor.

It is notable that there is limited discussion in Irish academic or legal work about the nature of conditions and their necessity, with the exception of work carried out by the NGO the Irish Penal Reform Trust (2016). While several participants pointed to examples of particular conditions being disproportionate, participants generally did not consider the operation of the system of conditions itself to be a core reason why pre-trial detention is not used as frequently in Ireland as elsewhere. Participants generally take these conditions for granted, rather than thinking of them as a system of graduated restrictions on liberty. A strong theme to emerge was the sheer variety of conditions which could be imposed, which is a manifestation of the high levels of discretion afforded to judges and the flexibility of the Irish approach. The players in the process did not describe the presence of the wide variety of conditions which can be attached to bail as a core reason for the lower rates of pre-trial detention found in Ireland than in other countries, however, I argue that this is because those conditions and their use is so deeply entrenched in legal practice and culture that their effects on liberty have become barely noticed. While we can read the Irish case as one which favours liberty over detention, it is not an unrestricted liberty which is on offer. The choice when making decisions about pre-trial detention in Ireland is by no means between liberty and detention *simpliciter*, but rather between gradations or degrees of liberty, shaped by the conditions placed on bail. Having such a variety of flexible conditions may lend comfort to judges deciding to avoid pre-trial detention and may provide an explanation for a lower use of pre-trial detention in Ireland than elsewhere.

Financial guarantees are a very common condition of bail in Ireland. An offer of money, either by the accused or a surety/guarantor, is viewed as being highly influential in a case, with an independent surety being viewed more favourably. Under Irish law, the amount should be set by reference to the means, condition and ability of the accused as well as the nature of the offence and should not be "so large as would in effect amount to a denial of bail and in consequence lead to inevitable imprisonment" (*People (Attorney General) v. O'Callaghan*, 1966, para. 518). In *DPP v. Broderick* (2006), the Supreme Court held that the court must conduct an inquiry into the accused's means and take account of same before fixing bail. Likewise, in *Li Jiuan Choong v. DPP* (2014), the Supreme Court held that a judge must consider all the circumstances of the case in setting the amount required of an independent surety, including the surety's ability to pay, the nature and gravity of the offence and the probability that the accused will fail to appear for trial.

If a person fails to appear in court or does not abide by the condition of bail, the court can order that any money entered by the accused or the surety may be *estreated*, that is, forfeited. It is also a criminal offence to breach bail conditions by not appearing in court (Section 13, Criminal Justice Act, 1984). The extent to which people are actually prosecuted for failure to abide by conditions in practice is hard to identify, but participants reported very limited formal enforcement of conditions. By contrast, however, failure to turn up for court proceedings or trial would invariably result in the issue of an arrest warrant by the judge, which can be executed by any member of the police. Participants felt that the Irish system was very different from that found in the United States of America in that vast sums of money are usually not required, however, defence practitioners did report that the emphasis on financial bail could disadvantage those of limited means.

Many cases will involve a fairly standard list of conditions, specifically a requirement to attend at a police (Garda) station on particular days, curfews, residence restrictions and a requirement to have a mobile phone switched on and able to receive calls from the police. These are considered fundamental bail conditions. It was considered that these were applied in a *pro forma* way, regardless of whether or not there was a real need for them in the particular case. This is considered to be especially the case concerning the use of a curfew:

> I have no difficulty saying that some of the conditions are just put there, sometimes there's no real reason for them, you know.
>
> (1, Prosecution Practitioner)

> There is a kitchen sink approach sometimes, which there shouldn't be.
>
> (3, Prosecution Practitioner)

> [Conditions are imposed] by and large probably in a blanket way . . . it's almost like a ticking the box exercise.
>
> (2, Defence Practitioner)

Some defence practitioners also felt that extensive conditions were imposed as a kind of compensation to the prosecution if bail was granted. Defence lawyers also noted that their clients were very unlikely to object to conditions, even if they were extremely restrictive, as they did not want to jeopardise the decision not to put them in detention. Some judges, however, stated that they did tailor conditions carefully:

> You do apply the conditions to the person as you think fit which is why although there are standard conditions you vary them, you'd rarely have the same set of conditions in every case.
>
> (5, Judge)

> [I]f the State look for conditions . . . I want to know why are they setting that condition.
>
> (6, Judge)

A lack of stable housing is a common problem for many accused persons in Ireland (O'Neill et al., 2016; Gulati et al., 2018). This can be a significant problem for people seeking to avoid pre-trial detention as there may be a residence condition which is very challenging to fulfil. There was no clear consensus as to whether a person without stable housing was more likely to be denied bail, though it was very clear that the lack of accommodation was a growing problem.

Judges did not consider a lack of a stable address made it more likely that they would refuse bail.

> I can't recall any occasion when somebody would be refused bail because they couldn't provide an address.
>
> (3, Judge)

> I never refused bail because somebody is homeless.
>
> (6, Judge)

Defence participants, however, did relate instances where they felt their clients had been denied bail because of a lack of housing. Some felt that a lack of housing when combined with a poor record of turning up for trial made it likely that bail would be refused. Some participants described practical efforts to achieve a solution where a person did not have a stable housing situation, with defence practitioners reporting considerable work trying to find accommodation with homelessness services or putting forward alternative conditions such as signing on at a police station.

Electronic monitoring

Ireland remains an outlier in European terms for its lack of use of electronic monitoring at the pre-trial stage, though it was introduced in law by Section

6B of the Bail Act (1997), which provides the courts with the jurisdiction to impose a condition regarding the electronic monitoring of an accused person released on bail where the person has been charged with a serious offence and where there is a condition on release such as residing at a particular place or reporting to a police (Garda) station. This statute has not, however, been commenced and was amended by the Criminal Justice Act (2017), which requires the prosecution to make an application for electronic monitoring (EM). The Department of Justice chaired a Working Group on EM and the Minister for Justice has stated that discussions are underway to seek an expert to advise on tendering for such services (Dáil Debates, 2019) though, at the time of writing, no further developments had been made public. EM is used for some sentenced prisoners on temporary release.

European aspects

The European Convention on Human Rights was incorporated into Irish law in 2003 (European Convention on Human Rights Act, 2003). All public bodies are to have regard to the Convention's principles and the courts are bound to interpret laws, as far as possible, in line with Convention obligations. A domestic court may make a declaration of incompatibility with the Convention, but this does not mean the law immediately becomes invalid; an Act of the Oireachtas (parliament) is required (Section 5 of the European Convention on Human Rights Act, 2003; De Londras, 2013). Decisions of the European Court of Human Rights have had extremely little impact on day-to-day decision-making, and are cited only very rarely before courts making such decisions (*Brennan v. Brennan* (2009)). While it is not clear that Convention law has shaped Irish practice directly, many of the foundational principles of Irish law on bail are in line with those of the Convention. In fact, the European Commission of Human Rights' requirement that a plausible danger of offences pending trial may be a justification for pre-trial detention (ECtHR, *Matznetter v. Austria*, 2178/64, 10 November 1969) offers less protection to the presumption of innocence than Irish law's requirement for a "real risk" of serious offences (Section 2, Bail Act, 1997). The Convention has also been cited as a reason for refusing amendments to bail law proposed by the then opposition, with the then Minister for Justice arguing that restrictions on the use of bail were inconsistent with European human rights law (Dáil Debates, 2018).

Ireland has only recently transposed the EU Framework Decision 200/909/JHA on the European Supervision Order (ESO; see Chapter 14) and was referred to the Court of Justice of the European Union by the European Commission in December 2020.[4] The ESO was transposed by the Criminal Justice (Mutual Recognition of Decisions on Supervision Measures) Act (2020), which commenced on 5 February 2021. Ireland will not consent to the forwarding of a decision on supervision measures, nor will it apply Article 14(1) of the ESO which allows issuing authorities to revoke an ESO for the benefit of the subject.[5]

In interviews, there was generally low awareness of the ESO, though most felt it would be of benefit and mean the use of pre-trial detention would be reduced for people with limited links to the state. By contrast, the European Arrest Warrant (EAW) is very well known amongst practitioners in Ireland and regularly used. Participants considered that the EAW makes a difference in how pre-trial detention is used for EU nationals compared to non-EU nationals. The EAW was considered to make it less likely that an EU national would be detained when compared with a non-EU national:

> If the perceived flight risk, if the country is a non-European Arrest Warrant country, that will be a big factor as well.
>
> (8, Prosecution Practitioner)

> A good point that you can raise if someone is considered a flight risk and it's because they're from France or from a Member State then, judges often [are] reassure[d]. . . . So there's often someone from another Member State, the flight risk issue is less troublesome [than] for someone who's from further afield, Brazil or you know wherever.
>
> (1, Defence Practitioner)

While this may be the experience, it must not be overlooked that the proportion of people without an Irish passport is higher in pre-trial detention than in the general prison population, as seen in Figure 6.3.

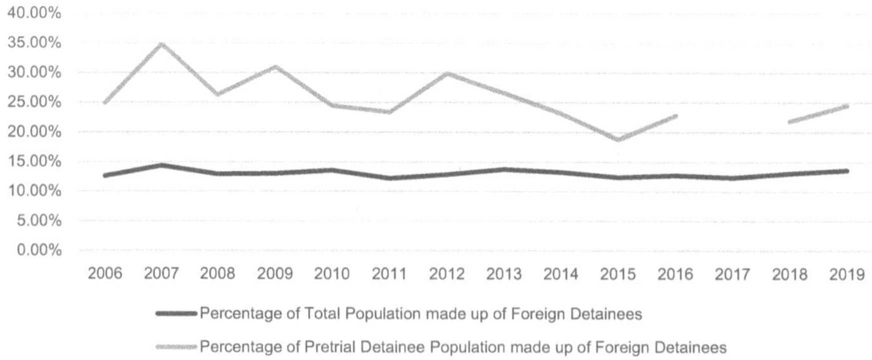

Figure 6.5 Percentage of foreign national detainees in prison and in pre-trial detention.

Source: From Council of Europe SPACE-I. Data for 2018 and 2019 are from 31 January not 1 September. No SPACE-I report was available for 2017; those data are from the Irish Prison Service Monthly Information Note for the population on 31 August. There was no information on foreign national pre-trial detainees for that year.

Conclusion

Ireland's comparatively low rate of pre-trial detention suggests that the legal frameworks for decisions on pre-trial detention plays a central role in shaping how that decision-making operates in practice. The emphasis placed on the constitutional position of bail and the presumption in favour of bail, by and large, tend to be taken seriously by the players in the process. A key aspect of this position is the relatively short history of using risk of offending as a ground for pre-trial detention and that its use has been more limited and muted than might have been expected when the law was changed in 1997, though rates of pre-trial detention have increased since that time. This experience suggests that the risk of offending ground may be a key driver in higher rates of detention in other countries, and merits careful review and narrow and judicious application.

While important contributions to understanding have been made through qualitative assessments, we still do not have a quantitative examination of decision-making on pre-trial detention in Ireland, which can be attributed, in part, to inaccessible and poor criminal justice data (Rogan, 2012). Such a study is essential to test the findings noted earlier. It will also be important to monitor the implementation of the European Supervision Order following its recent transposition.

Ireland must avoid becoming complacent about its comparatively low levels of pre-trial detention. The data on which this chapter is based were collected in 2016–2017 and, at that time, practitioners were sounding concern that there was an increasing use of pre-trial detention emerging in the Irish courts, attributable in part to what was seen as an increase in organised crime, especially involving firearms, as well as a tougher approach by the judiciary. Indeed, the average number of people in pre-trial detention has increased considerably since 2016, indicating that changes in practice are occurring. Recent years have seen a series of legislative attempts to make laws on pre-trial detention more restrictive and increase the use of pre-trial detention. The position described in this chapter could be eroded, and perhaps is being eroded, very quickly, with negative consequences for Ireland's prison system but also its protection of fundamental rights.

Notes

1 I wish to acknowledge with very warm thanks, the support of David Perry BL and Doireann O'Brien in the development of the work on which this chapter draws.
2 These figures refer only to those solely held on awaiting trial or sentence and not those serving a sentence and also waiting for a trial.
3 The *O'Callaghan* decision held that the factors which should be considered by a court when deciding on this should include the seriousness of the charge; the strength of the evidence; the likely sentence on conviction; a failure to answer bail in the past; and the length of time the accused would spend in pre-trial detention.

4 https://ec.europa.eu/commission/presscorner/detail/en/ip_20_2190 (accessed 3 January 2023).
5 www.ejn-crimjust.europa.eu/ejn/libdocumentproperties/EN/3393 (accessed 3 January 2023).

References

Bail Act 1997, Irish Statute Book (1997).

Bail (Amendment) Bill 2016, 32nd Dáil Éireann (2016).

Bail (Amendment) Bill 2017, 32nd Dáil Éireann (2017).

Bail Bill 2015, 31st Dáil Éireann (2015) Bunreacht na hÉireann, art. 40.4.6.

Brennan v. Brennan [2009] IEHC 303 (Unreported, High Court, Peart J., 18th June, 2009).

Carolan, M. (2021) 'Frustration mounts over court delays as more judges sought', *The Irish Times*, 11 November 2021, at www.irishtimes.com/news/crime-and-law/courts/criminal-court/frustration-mounts-over-court-delays-as-more-judges-sought-1.4726210 [accessed 30 December 2022].

Carroll, J. and Meehan, E. (2007) *The Children Court: A National Study*. Association for Criminal Justice Research and Development Ltd at www.acjrd.ie/images/PDFs/research/The_Children_Court_A_National_Study.pdf [accessed 30 December 2022].

Council of Europe (2019) *Council of Europe Annual Penal Statistics, SPACE-I* at https://wp.unil.ch/space/space-i/annual-reports/ [accessed 29 May 2023].

Criminal Justice Act 1984, Irish Statute Book (1984).

Criminal Justice Act 2007, Irish Statute Book (2007).

Criminal Justice Act 2017, Irish Statute Book (2017).

Criminal Justice (Burglary of Dwellings Act) 2015, Irish Statute Book (2015).

Criminal Justice (Legal Aid) Act 1962, Irish Statute Book (1962).

Criminal Justice (Mutual Recognition of Decisions on Supervision Measures) Act (2020), Irish Statute Book (2020).

Criminal Procedure Act 1967, Irish Statute Book (1967).

Dáil Debates, 970 (8). Minister Flanagan's Statement on Bail (Amendment) Bill 2017 (27 June 2018) at www.justice.ie/en/JELR/Pages/SP18000214#:~:text=A%20Cheann%20Comhairle%2C&text=The%20number%20of%20offences%20committed,even%20should%20have%2C%20been%20prevented [accessed 30 December 2022].

Dáil Debates, Question no. 234 (5 March 2019) at www.oireachtas.ie/en/debates/question/2019-03-05/234/ [accessed 30 December 2022].

De Londras, F. (2013) 'Declarations of incompatibility under the ECHR act 2003: A workable transplant?', *Statute Law Review*, 35(1): 50–65.

DPP v. Broderick [2006] IESC 34 [2006] 1 I.R. 629.

European Convention on Human Rights Act (2003).

Finn, G.C. (2020) *Women on Remand – Interim Report for IPRT Analysis of PIMS*, 13 August 2020, at https://pips.iprt.ie/progress-in-the-penal-system-pips-2020/part-2-measuring-progress-against-the-standards/reducing-the-use-of-imprisonment/10-pre-trial-detention-as-an-exceptional-measure/#cite_ref_220 [accessed 30 December 2022].

Freeman, S. (2008) 'The experience of young people remanded in custody: A case for bail support and supervision schemes', *Irish Probation Journal*, 5: 91–102 at https://arrow.tudublin.ie/cgi/viewcontent.cgi?article=1033&context=aaschsslarts [accessed 30 December 2022].

Gulati, G., Keating, N., O'Neill, A., Delaunois, I., Meagher, D. and Dunne, C.P. (2018) 'The prevalence of major mental illness, substance misuse and homelessness in Irish prisoners: Systematic review and meta-analyses', *Irish Journal of Psychological Medicine*, 36(1): 35–45.

Irish Penal Reform Trust (2016) *The Practice of Pre-trial Detention in Ireland*. Dublin: Irish Penal Reform Trust 2016 at https://www.iprt.ie/site/assets/files/6382/ptd_country_report_ireland_final.pdf [accessed 24 May 2023].

Irish Prison Service (2021) *Annual Report* available at https://www.irishprisons.ie/wp-content/uploads/documents_pdf/IPS-Annual-Report-21_Final.pdf [accessed May 24 2023].

Li Jiuan Choong v. DPP [2014] IESC 35 [2014] 2 I.R. 721.

Maguire v. DPP [2004] 3 IR 241.

O'Donnell, I. and O'Sullivan, E. (2003) 'The politics of intolerance: Irish style', *British Journal of Criminology*, 43(1): 41–62.

O'Malley, T. (2009) *The Criminal Process*. Dublin: Round Hall.

O'Neill, C., Smith, D., Caddow, M., Duffy, F., Hickey, P., Fitzpatrick, M., Caddow, F., Cronin, T., Joynt, M., Azvee, Z., Gallagher, B., Kehoe, C., Maddock, C., O'Keeffe, B., Brennan, L., Davoren, M., Owens, E., Mullaney, R., Keevans, L. and Kennedy, H.G. (2016) 'STRESS-testing clinical activity and outcomes for a combined prison in-reach and court liaison service: A 3-year observational study of 6177 consecutive male remands', *International Journal of Mental Health Systems*, 10(1).

People (Attorney General) v. O'Callaghan [1966] IR 501.

People (DPP) v. McGinley [1998] 2 IR 408.

Rogan, M. (2011) *Prison Policy in Ireland: Politics, Penal-Welfarism and Political Imprisonment*, London: Routledge.

Rogan, M. (2012) 'Improving criminal justice data and policy', *Economic and Social Review*, 43(2): 303–323.

Rogan, M. and Perry, D. (2017) 'Country briefs, Ireland', in *DETOUR – Towards Pre-trial Detention as Ultima Ratio, Country Briefs* at www.uibk.ac.at/irks/publikationen/detour-publikationen/country-briefs_detour.pdf [accessed 30 December 2022].

Ronan v. Coughlan [2005] IEHC 370 [2005] 4 I.R. 274.

Seymour, M. and Butler, M. (2008) *Young People on Remand*, Office of the Minister for Children and Youth Affairs, Department of Health and Children at https://arrow.tudublin.ie/cserrep/14/ [accessed 30 December 2022].

Vickers v. DPP [2009] IESC 58 [2010] 1 IR 548.

Chapter 7

Pre-trial detention in Lithuania: transition in legal culture and pre-trial detention trends

Skirmantas Bikelis[1]

Introduction

As a former Soviet country, Lithuania had experienced dramatic social and cultural transformations in the last 30 years, something it has in common with other Eastern European countries. As such, its experience with pre-trial detention offers important and interesting lessons. Escaping from the Soviet Union in 1990, and entering the European Union in 2004 led, among other things, to a gradual but fundamental shift in understanding the importance of the right to freedom and other human rights. In the criminal justice system, this shift may be seen in the gradual transition from the highly punitive and extremely pro-incarcerating Soviet legal penal culture to the legal culture based on liberal and humanistic Western values. The transition also includes the change in practices of implementation of pre-trial detention and other coercive measures. It progresses gradually but steady under the impact of both objective and professional–cultural factors. The objective factors that shape the trend are changes in legislation (i.e. introduction of new coercive measures), decisions of the European Court of Human Rights (ECtHR), developments in international cooperation, etc. The professional–cultural factors are the abandonment of wrongful practices, increase in quality standards for the requests and decisions, advancing competence of the criminal justice authorities and other changes. Both sets of factors that make an impact on the trends in practices of coercive measures application shall be considered in this chapter.

The professional–cultural factors of pre-trial detention practices have been little researched in academic studies so far. These factors are difficult to identify from legal sources, file analysis or statistical data. However, the intense dynamics of the pre-trial detention trend under a relatively stable national legal framework, along with remarkably different rates of pre-trial detention in different countries with relatively similar legal frameworks, suggest the key role of the professional–cultural factors for the trends in practices of the pre-trial detention use.

Therefore, this research had a particular focus, with the objective of exploring factors arising out of judicial, legal and prosecutorial cultures which

DOI: 10.4324/9781003159254-7

influence the use of pre-trial detention. The main research tools for examining these cultures were interviews with criminal justice officials and defence attorneys. In Lithuania we performed 42 interviews: 23 with prosecutors (18 with county prosecutors and 5 with district (higher level) prosecutors who head the prosecution for serious and very serious crime), 15 with judges (13 county judges and 2 district judges) and 4 with defence attorneys (three of them working mostly with serious organised, financial, economic cases and one state-paid attorney working with low profile cases like thefts, illegal crossings of state border, etc.). Geographically, we covered both bigger cities and small towns in six (out of ten) regions of Lithuania. Defence attorneys had experience in different geographical areas of Lithuania. Thirty-seven interviews were conducted in the first quarter of 2017 in the framework of the DETOUR project (see Chapter 1 and Bikelis and Pajaujis, 2017, for more details) and additional five interviews with prosecutors (which had a particular focus on the latest developments in electronic monitoring practices) took place in January 2021. Additional research methods used were court files analysis, analysis of the legal framework, the jurisprudence of the ECtHR, and academic studies. Court files analysis covered 58 criminal proceedings where decisions concerning pre-trial detention had been made. The analysis focused on the grounds for detention and the motives used to justify or deny the grounds. It covered 18 proceedings concerning non-serious violence, 16 proceedings concerning illegal trafficking of drugs (except large and very large quantity), 13 proceedings concerning thefts, and 4 proceedings concerning other crimes. The court files analysis covered decisions of years 2014–2015 and the first half of 2016.

Statistics

Statistics on incarceration in Lithuania in the European context

The heritage of Soviet penal culture, where the restrictions on the liberty of a person had never been a big concern for the authorities and where imprisonment had been considered a rather *prima facia* than *ultima ratio* measure against the suspects and convicts, has left long-lasting (although steadily fading) footprint in the Lithuanian penal policy. The penal statistics reflect this. Since the restoration of independence in 1990 until now Lithuania is among the European countries with the highest imprisonment rates, trailing behind the Western European countries by double, triple or even quadruple numbers. The total prison population rate per 100,000 inhabitants in Lithuania varied between 232 in 2018 and 410 in 1999 (Sakalauskas et al., 2019: 17). With the historically lowest number 232 at the end of 2018 and the beginning of 2019, Lithuania still had the highest prison population rate in the European Union (Aebi and Tiago, 2020: Table 3). By comparison, in 2019, other EU states had lower prison population rates, with, for example, 56.4 in the Netherlands and the highest 137.9 in England and Wales (ibid).

The imprint of the Soviet penal tradition may be seen also in the Lithuanian statistics on pre-trial detention. In this chapter, we argue that Lithuania has undergone an incredible "healing" process as part of its transition towards Western European penal culture in recent nearly 20 years. However, there is still room for improvement to catch up with the standards of most other EU member states.

Before examining SPACE I data on detainees' statistics (Aebi and Tiago, 2020), an important adjustment of the Lithuanian data must be done. Until 2019, Lithuanian statistics on pre-trial detainees did not include the category "sentenced inmates who have appealed or who are within the statutory limit to do so", but attributed this category to prisoners serving the sentence (Aebi and Tiago, 2020, notes to tables 8, 9, 10 and 11). The methodology had been changed and that category of inmates has been included in the number of pre-trial detainees since 2019 (adjusted number shall be provided for SPACE I surveys 2020 and later; personal communication with the specialist of statistics at the Prison Department at the Ministry of Justice). The formerly excluded group made up significant numbers. For example, 173 inmates, who have appealed or who were within a statutory limit to do so, should be added to the 606 detainees reported for SPACE I 2019 statistics (ibid).

Comparing adjusted numbers for the end 2018/beginning of 2019 (Aebi and Tiago, 2020), Lithuania appears to have the seventh highest pre-trial detainee rate among EU countries (27.9) and appears to be ahead of Slovak Republic (29), France (30.4), Greece (30.8), Italy (32.6), Latvia (51.1) and Luxemburg (52.6).[2] Pre-trial detainee rates in other countries represented in the DETOUR project were 99 for Romania, 16.6 for Ireland, 16.8 for Germany, 17.1 for the UK, 23.7 for Austria and 24 for the Netherlands (Aebi and Tiago, 2020).

However, an important contextual factor should be considered when making comparisons of detention rates in different countries – the number of foreign pre-trial detainees. Migrant inflows into the Eastern states of the EU are significantly lower than into the Western states of the EU. The numbers of foreign suspects and foreign pre-trial detainees also significantly differ. The non-resident suspect's lack of social bonds in the state where a criminal investigation is taking place is not definitive but is still a very significant factor for evaluation of the risk of flight from justice and, subsequently, for a decision on detention. Lithuania and Romania, and the aforementioned Slovakia and Latvia, belong to the group of seven EU countries, where the share of non-resident pre-trial detainees is <7%. In contrast, in other countries with statistically high detention rates the share of foreign detainees is remarkable: in Luxemburg, this number is 79.6%, in Greece 62.8%, in Italy 38.9%, in France 29.5%. Other DETOUR project partners also had significantly higher foreign detainees' shares than Lithuania (except Romania): in Austria

70%, in the Netherlands 26% and in Ireland 25% (Aebi and Tiago, 2020: Table 12).[3] This context indicates that the differences in practices of treating national suspects between most of the South and Western EU countries and Lithuania are more remarkable than the differences in statistics of total detention rates might imply.

Dynamics of domestic statistics on pre-trial detention

Lithuanian statistics for more than 15 years show an immense decline in pre-trial detention use. Presumably, this is the result of multiple changes in Lithuanian society – "healing" of social problems and, consequently, improvement of the criminological situation as well as, in parallel, the perception of European standards in respect of suspects' liberty in the criminal justice system.

Speaking of the social context in recent years in Lithuania, we can see a sharp decline of the symptoms that indicate a precarious situation in society: aggressive behaviour and overuse of alcohol: from 2009 to 2019 the number of deaths from assaults declined by nearly three times from 6.3 to 2.2 per 100,000 of the population, fatal traffic accidents dropped from 14.4 to 7.7, the number of suicidal deaths declined from 36 to 23.5, deaths related to overdose of alcohol fell from 10.7 to 5.9 (Department of Statistics of Lithuania, 2020). Since 2004, economic prospects for unemployed and underpaid workers improved together with the opening of the EU labour market. Over the period 2004–2019, more than 680,000 Lithuanians emigrated (European Migration Network, 2020). This equates to roughly 24% of the current Lithuanian population. The economic situation of underpaid workers (and their families) who did not emigrate also improved a little, since the minimum wage increased from inhumanely precarious €144.81 per month in 2004 to €555 per month in 2019 (Eurostat, 2020).

Declining levels of aggression, overuse of alcohol and decline of the number of people trapped in the precarious economic situation have been accompanied by the sharp decline of serious violent criminal offences, robberies and thefts. These are the categories of offences that bring a large share of the total number of detained suspects.[4] From 2004 to 2020, the number of people suspected with manslaughter or assault causing serious bodily injuries decreased more than twice from 585 to 257, the number of suspects for robberies decreased more than four times from 1,863 to 391, and the number of suspects for thefts also decreased more than four times from 11,366 to 2,772 (Department of Technologies and Communication at the Ministry of Interior, 2021).[5]

It is difficult to say how much bearing these social and criminological changes have had on statistics concerning detention. Findings based on qualitative research of the detention practices that will be presented in the next chapters show that the detention practices have changed significantly too, and certain questionable patterns for decision-making are fading away. Thus, we assume that the trends in the statistics have been affected by multiple factors.

We have looked at two different sets of detention statistics data. Figure 7.1 shows data provided by the Prison Department at the Ministry of Justice. The Prison Department also provides data for Council of Europe SPACE I reports. These data show the number of detainees and the rate of detainees per 100,000 population on the last day of the year. Data include both detainees in pre-trial investigation and on trial, except convicted detainees who have appealed or who are within the statutory limit to do so. The latter category is included only in data for the years later than 2018. This change in methodology makes the comparison of the data prior and later than 2019 incomparable.

Figure 7.1 shows a nearly twofold decline in detention rate from 2004 to 2011 when this rate peaked.[6]

Another set of data is methodologically different in many ways. It is provided by the Information Technology and Communications Department at the Ministry of Interior that operates the statistics of pre-trial investigations. The data shows the total number of suspects in the completed pre-trial investigations and the total number of suspects who were detained during the pre-trial investigation. Data has been collected from the pre-trial investigations which have been completed in the respective year.

Statistics on detention use in pre-trial investigations (Figure 7.2) show a colossal, more than tenfold drop in 17 years. The increasing gap between the total number of suspects and suspects that have been detained is a positive indicator that practices of pre-trial detention use might have been improving. Of course, this gap should not be taken too literally. The relatively stable

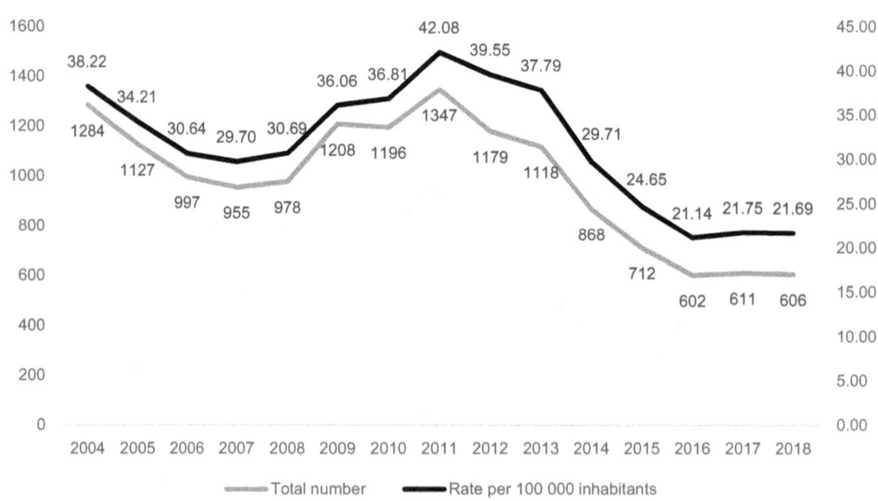

Figure 7.1 Numbers and rates of pre-trial detainees on the last day of the year.

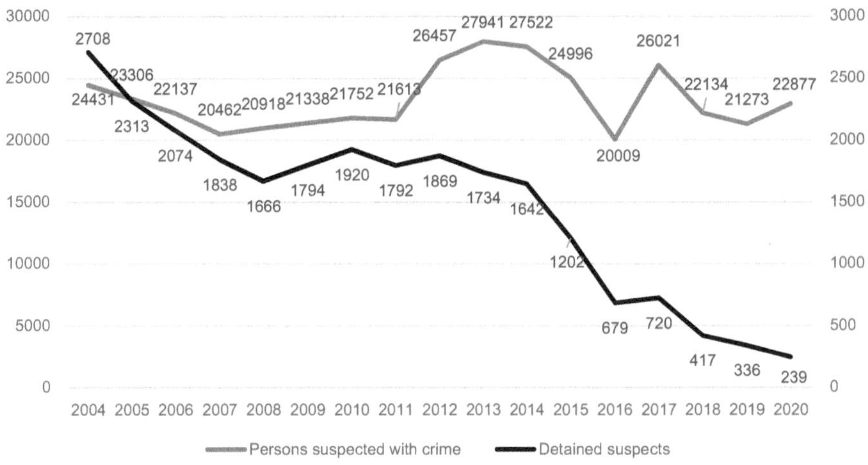

Figure 7.2 Suspects (natural persons) for crimes and detained suspects.

total number of suspects was affected by the specific penal policy steps that resulted in a sharp increase of suspects in the cases where detention was not likely.[7] But still, even considering all the different factors that made some impact on the statistics trends, we can assume that a change in detention practices definitely played an important role. This was confirmed by the findings in qualitative research we conducted.

Regulations on coercive measures, issues and trends in their application in practice

The system of coercive measures

The Lithuanian Penal Procedure Code (PPC)[8] provides for a rather extensive list of coercive measures. However, quantity does not necessarily mean quality. The questions of whether the measures are effective, practical, necessary and have the potential to reduce the use of pre-trial detention are open for discussion.

Coercive measures in the Lithuanian PPC might be classified into three groups by the severity and by the authority competent to apply them in the phase of pre-trial investigation[9]:

1 Measures that might be imposed by the police and other officers of pre-trial investigation with later notice to the prosecutor. No authorisation of the court or the prosecutor is required. Also, a prosecutor or a pre-trial

investigation judge have the authority to impose these measures. These are as follows:

- Seizure of personal documents
- Commitment not to leave the country
- Obligation to report to the police
- Suspension of specific right (e.g. driving license)
- For a soldier – observation/supervision by the command of the unit where he or she is s doing his or her service
- For a minor – committal to the supervision of parents, guardians or foster parents or the administration of a children's institution.

2 A measure that might be imposed by a prosecutor or a pre-trial investigation judge:

- Financial bail

3 Measures that might be imposed only by a pre-trial investigation judge:

- Obligation to live separately from or stay away from the victim
- House arrest
- Intense supervision (electronic monitoring)
- Detention

All the measures may be combined, except for detention.

Article 119 Section 7 of the PPC explicitly declares the principle that detention should be considered only as the measure of last resort. It provides that detention may be imposed only in the case where other measures do not allow to secure their aims: (1) ensuring the presence of the suspect at the proceedings, (2) prevention of an obstruction of the proceedings and (3) prevention of further crimes. However, this declaration may have little effect if restrictive attitudes in the authorities' mindset prevail and the founding of the decisions with the motives based on the facts of the case and also realistic estimation of the possible risks for the proceedings is not the part of professional culture of the authorities. In June 2015, legislators made an attempt to push the professional practices towards proper reasoning of the decisions and reinforced this declaration with the legal duty to indicate, when ordering pre-trial detention, the factual circumstances and arguments that allowed to believe that less strict measures were not sufficient in that case.[10] The pressure on practices in this direction grew with the recent ECtHR judgment in the case *Leonienė v. Lithuania* (61264/17, 10 November 2020) where the Court found the violation of Article 5 § 1 of the European Convention on Human Right (ECHR), and among other things, the Court noted, that the decisions of the courts that decided on detention of the applicant did not contain any reference to any of the other measures or an explanation why they would not be sufficient to ensure the applicant's appearance at trial.[11]

In general, poor reasoning for the decisions on coercive measures has been a long-term issue in the Lithuanian criminal justice system. The first major official address to this problem appeared in the survey of jurisprudence on implementation of detention and house arrest and extension of the detention (Supreme Court, 2004). In 2010, the ECtHR found the violation of Article 5 § 3 ECHR in the case *Balčiūnas v. Lithuania* (17095/02, 20 July 2010), because the reasons given in the detention orders remained general, theoretical and nearly identical throughout time, without examining the personal circumstances of the applicant, and therefore were clearly insufficient to satisfy the requirements of Article 5 § 3 ECHR.[12] In the interviews we conducted, judges and prosecutors repeatedly confirmed a shift in quality of decision motivation:

> Nowadays there are fewer decisions to detain suspects, the prosecutor's request for pre-trial detention is rarer, the grounds for pre-trial detention they provide are more substantial. Prosecutors filter the flow of pre-trial detention requests strongly, more carefully in recent years. I receive much fewer groundless requests for pre-trial detention.
>
> (1, Judge)

> A formal approach where a judge might be satisfied with the plain statement of the grounds for the pre-trial detention and where he or she would not require for sufficient facts proving substantial risks for the proceedings is no longer frequent in practice.
>
> (12, Prosecutor)

> Difference in quality of the requests for pre-trial detention years ago (especially before 2015–2016) and now is evident. Since we have the electronic system (IBPS), I can see that there are still some weaker requests, but in general, quality is much better, requests are founded with more evidence and the judges request for more. During the initial interrogation, the police now ask questions not only about circumstances related to the alleged offence but also about the facts that might be relevant for the decision on coercive measures.
>
> (20, Prosecutor)

Gradual reception of the principle of equality of arms in practice may be considered as another significant factor that contributed to the implementation of higher standards in decision-making. Inspired by the ECtHR decision in *Garcia Alva v. Germany* (23541/94, 13 February 2001), the Supreme Court of Lithuania (2004) in the jurisprudence survey declared that in the decision-making on pre-trial detention the principle of equality of arms should prevail over the principle of secrecy of investigation files. Therefore, the defence side should have access to all case files presented to the judge by the prosecution during the hearing on detention. The relevant rule was explicitly established in the law by the amendments to the Article 121 PPC on 25 June 2015. Our interview partners confirmed that this rule was already followed in practice a decade before the enactment of the amendments of the law (prosecutor 5). The principle of equality of arms has multiple effects. It strengthens the capacity of defence at the hearings and at appeals and forces up the standards of the decision-making and motivation. It also forces the prosecution to make the tactical choice – do they request pre-trial detention and reveal the evidence in the file and also tactics of investigation to the defence, or do they keep files in secret at the cost of giving up seeking incarceration of the suspect. A prosecutor noted during an interview that this dilemma indeed prevents prosecutors from requesting pre-trial detention in cases where the evidence for the grounds of pre-trial detention are not strong (prosecutor 5).

Less severe measures than pre-trial detention

This section will examine some foundational questions, including: how much potential for securing their aims do coercive measures other than pre-trial detention really have? Are they reliable when a suspect has the intention to flee justice, continue his or her criminal activities or obstruct proceedings? If a suspect has no such intentions, are these measures really necessary?

It seems that some lenient measures – obligation to report to the police, commitment not to leave, seizure of personal documents – often have a merely symbolic role and a rather vague function. They are "paper" measures (prosecutor 22). They are applied to the low-risk suspects who are eager to cooperate with the prosecutor anyway:

> Speaking of all those lenient measures, that we are used to applying them very often, that is to say, automatically, to avoid reprimands that we did not take precaution measures. On the other hand, suspects infringe them just like that and hardly anyone notices it. They travel without giving a notice, but you can reach them by means of communication and they come upon request. As long as they cooperate, we do not mind their infringements. Also, it is not uncommon that a suspect reports to the police by phone (in case of prolonged application of the measure), although a measure like this actually does not make much sense. The problem with the seizure of personal documents is that suspects need them on daily basis for job interviews, in the bank etc., so they write requests to return their documents and I spend much of my time dealing with their requests.
>
> (19, Prosecutor)

Besides, some prosecutors noted that the seizure of documents is not even a reliable measure to prevent the flight of a suspect, unless a suspect is an unexperienced one (5, 19, 20, 24, prosecutor).

Article 133 of the PPC provides that financial bail is a monetary instalment deposited to a court or the office of prosecution. Though many interviewed practitioners expressed positive attitudes towards financial bail as "very promising", in Lithuania financial bail is the second rarest measure in practice (after the house arrest, which is nearly never used in practice anymore). In 2004–2020, the number of suspects who were bailed with a monetary deposit in the pre-trial investigation stage varied in total merely 49–162 (0.2–0.6% of all suspects). The lowest number was observed in 2020.[13] During interviews, a common explanation for the rare application or even no application of financial bail was the poor financial situation of suspects:

> Suspects of the crimes we deal with, like thefts, domestic violence etc. do not have money. If you would impose it, they would refuse to pay. Where PTD is not necessary in the case, there is no way to convince a suspect to pay bail.
>
> (6, Prosecutor)

> People here in the province do not have money, probably it is different in the capital, maybe there it might be applied.
>
> (17, Prosecutor)

The law does not provide for a minimum amount of financial bail, but recommendations of the Prosecutor General provide that bail instalments should be no less than 30 standard social units (SCU) (currently, one SCU equals €50), which makes a minimum sum of €1,500 (Prosecutor General, 2015, 2019). Could lowering this threshold expand the application of financial bail? On the other hand, would low-value bail have a preventive effect and still make sense? Wouldn't it contribute to the net-widening of restrictions imposed on a suspect without significant preventive effect in situations where actually fewer or no measures are necessary? In some cases, low financial bail could work as an alternative to other measures with low preventive efficiency (like reporting to the police, seizure of documents, commitment not to leave). But again, would suspects agree to pay it, freeze their money and risk losing them while other coercive measures do not carry such risk? The added value of low financial bail carries some doubts.

During the interviews, just a few categories of cases were indicated where financial bail under the present conditions was realistic in practice: "white collar" crime (economic and financial offences, corruption cases) and organised crime, including suspected foreign truck drivers in cigarettes smuggling cases. A prosecutor 20 explained that in recent years in his practice bail is usually applied in combination with electronic monitoring (EM) for national organised crime suspects after the court refuses to extend pre-trial detention. Foreign suspects with organised crime involvement (who are mostly citizens of non-EU countries) may expect nothing else but pre-trial detention no matter how large the amount of bail (€30,000, €50,000, €100,000) is offered by their side because their risk of flight from justice is very high and the chances of their extradition are considered to be low or even non-existing where countries do not extradite their citizens (Russia, Belarus).

Having been introduced into the law in January 2015 and being technically available since April 2016, intense supervision that is electronically monitored is the second most severe coercive measure following pre-trial detention.[14] Being intensely supervised, the suspected person is obliged to (a) to have an EM device (an ankle bracelet) on, and (b) to follow his/her regulated daily agenda (e.g. regularly attend a therapeutic course). The court orders the restrictions to be attached to EM. The prosecutor has the right to remove restrictions that are unnecessary upon the request of a suspect or at his or her discretion. Being under EM does not mean complete lockdown at home. It is not uncommon that a suspect may leave his or her residence for work or other purposes within designated hours with the permission of a prosecutor.

Why has this highly restrictive, very uncomfortable for a suspect and relatively expensive measure been introduced? The preamble of the Council of Europe's Recommendation CM/Rec (2014) 4 on electronic monitoring as the relevant pan-European soft law states that electronic monitoring used in the framework of the criminal justice process can help reduce resorting to deprivation of liberty while ensuring effective supervision of suspects and offenders in the community, and thus helping prevent crime. The Recommendation also warns that where EM is used at the pre-trial phase special care needs to be taken not to net-widen its use.

However, the explanatory memorandum to the draft of the relevant amendment of the Lithuanian PPC states the contrary – the aim of the introduction of EM is to provide the alternative to the other measures when no grounds for pre-trial detention exist. Does this constitute poor wording of the same idea or the completely opposite intentions than those expressed in the Recommendation?

First, the question should be raised if it is realistic to expect that EM could replace pre-trial detention when the risks for the proceedings or the risk of reoffending are at hand? We conducted some interviews in 2021 when EM was already in practice for five years, and prosecutors shared rather pessimistic opinions. They assumed EM is not suitable for suspects who are determined to flee. Prosecutors shared stories from their own or their colleagues' practices of cases where suspects cut the bracelets off and absconded (prosecutors 21 and 22). They shared the opinion that EM might play a preventive role for suspects who are casual offenders (not members of organised crime) (prosecutor 22). However, considering that the flight risk of such suspects often is not high, it is not clear if EM would play a role in securing the proceedings. Also, the general concern should be raised if using very restrictive measures against low profile suspects would be proportionate measures.

Prosecutors also shared their experience that EM had little preventive effect on repeated offending, for example, drug trafficking. A suspect with a bracelet may communicate from his or her residence. A suspect may travel for work and thus contact people and continue his or her trafficking activities:

> I had a case in my practice, where a suspected member of organized drug trafficking was ordered to EM, but soon a few more charges for trafficking drugs followed. EM does not prevent from continuing criminal activities.
>
> (22, Prosecutor)

However, some prosecutors are still rather enthusiastic about EM as

> one of the best contemporary measures, suitable for any situation, having it we need no other measures (other than pre-trial detention).
>
> (20, Prosecutor)

EM is a specific measure that requires a special technical availability check. During our early interviews in 2017 right after the introduction of EM, judges expressed their cautious attitude. Some of them explained that they would never apply EM on their own initiative, but if the prosecutor requested for EM, that should mean the prosecutor was sure it would be possible technically to execute EM in the case (judge 9). In 2020–2021, tables turned and judges are more enthusiastic about EM. Now, prosecutors avoid imposing EM for technical reasons (shortage of devices), but the courts that do not bother about the availability of devices apply EM rather often:

> In Spring 2020 the police circulated information asking to refrain from the application of EM because of shortage of devices, so we prosecutors request or apply it very rarely. But the courts do impose EM when we request PTD and especially when we request PTD extension, sometimes in combination with financial bail.
>
> (19, prosecutor)

It seems that EM was well accepted by the courts and the prosecutors. We may assume that by having an option of a restrictive measure that is nicely branded as "modern", the courts have more determination to release suspects from pre-trial detention. But some doubts remain if a good image of EM is well deserved. After the interviews with the prosecutors, there remain doubts that the EM restrictions work efficiently. Doubts also remain if the use of EM is proportionate in most cases it is actually applied. We cannot rule out, that net-widening effects take place and EM is applied too easily in some cases (quasi-automatically) without proper consideration if a suspect is indeed prone to absconding or re-offending and if some more lenient measures (for example, financial bail and seizure of documents) would be sufficient or maybe no measures would be necessary at all.

Pre-trial detention in law and practice

Article 122 of PPC provides that pre-trial detention may be imposed on a suspect, accused or convicted during the proceedings on offences that are punishable with imprisonment and the maximum sanction is at least one year. Actually, it is a negligible limitation as far as all criminal offences fall into this category except misdemeanours. Article 122 PPC also provide four grounds for pre-trial detention:

1 A request for extradition, made by a foreign country or international court, or a pending European Arrest Warrant.
2 The risk that the suspect would impede the proceedings.
3 The risk that the suspect, who is suspected with serious or very serious offences or offences of mid-seriousness against property, would commit said offences before the judgement is passed in the proceedings.
4 The risk that the suspect would abscond.

Among all the risks that may serve as a ground for pre-trial detention, the risk that the suspect would impede the proceedings is the rarest in practice. The results of the file analysis showed that reference to the risk of impeding proceedings appeared only in 13% of the decisions to detain suspects. A significant turning point in the practice of the application of this ground for pre-trial detention was the Supreme Court Survey (2004) where the Court declared that only retrospective grounds establishing the risk of impeding proceedings may be a valid motive for pre-trial detention. To establish the risk of impeding the proceedings the suspect should have had either a history of impeding proceedings or should have been caught in *flagrante delicto*, "*for instance, when the suspect is caught burning the documents during the search in the investigation of financial crimes*" (judge 2). In practice, rare exceptions are allowed, mostly in cases of human trafficking, sexual crimes and sometimes with organised crime cases (with reference to the ECtHR case *Podeschi v. San Marino*, 13 April 2017, 66357/14) where this ground for pre-trial detention has been approved solely on the basis of the nature of the sophisticated financial crime).

Another turn in the practice of the application of this pre-trial detention ground was related to the interpretation of the right to silence or non-confession of the suspect, his or her reluctance to give testimony about the location of the relevant items (e.g. stolen goods), accomplices, etc. Before the Supreme Court Survey (2004), non-cooperation of the suspect used to be commonly interpreted as impeding the proceedings and thus providing a legitimate ground for detention:

> Nowadays prosecution and courts became modern – non-cooperation of the suspect and non-confession may not have any significance for the

> decision on detention of a suspect because a suspect has a right but not a duty to testify.
>
> (2, Prosecutor)

The risk that a suspect would further commit certain crimes was considered as the second common ground by the majority of the interviewed practitioners. Only a few interviewees held the ground of re-offending for the leading one, which is, however, being mostly established in combination with a flight risk. Typically, this ground for pre-trial detention is used where the suspect is suspected with a series of thefts, also in cases of drug trafficking and serious cases of domestic violence. According to the file analysis, detention was motivated with the risk of re-offending in approximately 56% of the examined case files and was the second most applied pre-trial detention ground next to the risk of absconding.

The risk of absconding is the most commonly used ground for detention in practice in Lithuania. It was most often referred to as the most frequent among the interviewees. The file analysis of 63 court decisions on the imposition of detention indicated that this ground was employed in 89% of the decisions to detain suspects (often in combination with another ground for detention, namely the risk of re-offending).

As far as the risk of absconding is the most frequently used ground for pre-trial detention, the changes in the interpretation of this ground may be assumed a significant factor for the dynamics of pre-trial detention use. As has been mentioned already, over the last 15 years the standards for quality and motives of the requests for pre-trial detention have increased gradually. Based on the insights from the interviews, we assume that the prosecutors do tend to reflect seriously on actual risks of absconding. Also, we noted some progressive practices in dealing with absconding if it actually happened, where communication with the suspects is preferred over immediate efforts to detain them (see the following text).

How common is absconding? The chief prosecutor of Vilnius county prosecution office (the office that deals with all offences except the very serious and some serious ones) provided statistics that at the beginning of 2021 the office had 3,200 open investigations and 160 suspects were on the run. But it would not be correct to extrapolate from these numbers that around 5% of suspects absconded. The share of absconded suspects is much lower. The number of investigations was provided for a certain moment but the number of absconded suspects accumulated over time. Some of them are unaccounted for since 2010–2012. Most long-term fugitives were suspected of non-serious and non-extraditable offences (a big share of them were suspected with failure to support their child, Article 164 PC which is not a criminal offence in some other countries, some were suspected with non-serious thefts). Since these suspects reside in foreign countries the perspectives of their prosecution are very vague.

Most of our interview partners estimated the risk of flight in general as low, except for the risk for organised crime members from non-EU countries.[15] They could recall only few examples of absconding in their careers. Some shared their reflections showing that they were aware of the complicated reality of the flight and did not take circumstances, that might indicate some risk of flight, lightly and out of context:

> It is difficult to flee to the third countries where the suspect is basically alone and needs money and visas. Meanwhile here, in the EU (in the area of operation of EAW), law enforcement works well enough to find him/her. It could take a year but, in the end, we would find him.
>
> (5, Prosecutor)

> A suspect needs advanced life experience or support from relatives or friends abroad to be capable in successful hiding. The decision to face the high pressure (stress) of the absconding is difficult to make.
>
> (6, Judge)

A higher court judge emphasised that every case is decided individually and provided examples where the suspects in the cases of homicide, criminal association or drug trafficking-related offences were not detained and attended the court hearings nevertheless:

> We have got proceedings against a criminal association which is charged with drug trafficking, overall 30 suspects, but only four of them are in custody.
>
> (5, Judge)

This example is in line with an interview with a defence attorney, who recalled their talks with clients who were charged with very serious drug offences and faced the perspective of long-term imprisonment and still had no motivation to abscond. The clients told them that they did not see any sense to abscond because it was too costly to live in hiding. The terms of statutes of limitation are very long, they simply could not afford to spend so many years in hiding (attorney 1).

Some suspects leave the country (technically, they abscond) but they still keep contact with the prosecutors and are willing to cooperate. Typically, they are emigrant workers, who return to Lithuania for holidays and get into trouble which result in a criminal investigation (drunk fighting, violation of public order, domestic violence, theft, etc.). Despite the order not to leave or even before receiving such order they return to their residence country avoiding losing their job. After the prosecution contacts them, they promise to come back on their nearest return on the next holidays and they indeed return. Sometimes they even recover the damages for the victim while absconding and working in their country of residence. A prosecutor (21) told us in an interview that in most cases in which an emigrant leaves for his or her job, the prosecution does not request a European Arrest Warrant (EAW), but keeps communicating with him or her and patiently wait for them to return. The prosecution would apply for an EAW only in case of a serious offence. The chief prosecutor of Vilnius county prosecutor's office provided that in the beginning of 2021 they had up to 20 of such suspects.

Prosecutor 21 also reported the case where online interrogation of the suspect was organised (the suspect came to the embassy to participate in the interrogation) thus eliminating the need for him or her to return temporarily to Lithuania. However, such cases are very rare. The prosecutor (21) explained that the online method of interrogation during pre-trial investigation is still not regulated in the Code of Penal Proceedings (though it is already regulated for at the trial stage) and therefore prosecutors avoid using it. He also suggested that this method might be limited to investigations for the cases that are usually conducted in speedy proceedings: cases of not serious offences, where the circumstances of the case are clear and the suspect confesses.

The practices that allow avoiding the unnecessary application of pre-trial detention are encouraged by the rules for issuing the EAW adopted by the minister of Justice and the Prosecutor General that provide that EAW may be issued only when other methods to ensure the participation of the suspect in the proceedings are already exhausted (Ministry of Justice and Office of the Prosecutor General, 2004).

The length of pre-trial detention is another important factor defining the level of incarceration during pre-trial investigation. The developments in practices concerning the length of pre-trial detention may serve as an example showing the key role of the mentality of the authorities in reducing the levels of incarceration.

Lithuanian legislation (Article 127 of PPC) provides that pre-trial detention may be ordered for no longer than a period of three months at once. Pre-trial detention can be extended for up to a maximum of three months but no more than six months in general. However, a higher (regional) court may extend the length of detention for up to three more months under two circumstances: (a) due to an extraordinary complexity (e.g. organised or white-collar crimes), or (b) the scale of the case (e.g. a significant number of suspected and accused individuals, victims or witnesses). The total length of detention during pre-trial investigations may be no longer than nine months. This limit was reduced from 18 months in 2015 (the law on amendment of Articles 121, 123, 125, 126, 127, 130, 131 and 181 of the Penal Procedure Code, 2015). In cases where a grave or a serious crime may have been committed, or the suspects/accused may have committed a crime in a group of accomplices, an organised group or a criminal association, or the individuals are detained in a foreign country, pre-trial detention may not last longer than eighteen months. The same amendment in 2015 provided also the overall limit for pre-trial detention during the whole criminal proceedings (including trial in first and appellate stages of the trial) – two-thirds of the maximum length of imprisonment possible for the offence the suspect is charged with.

It is very unlikely that setting maximum limit for the overall pre-trial detention term or reducing maximum pre-trial detention terms possible during the proceedings for non-serious offences could have a direct and significant impact on the level of incarceration. That long pre-trial detention terms are extremely rare if ever applied. On the other hand, changes in the legislation of this kind may serve as the policy message to the practice to consider the length of pre-trial detention with more scrutiny in the light of the *ultima ratio* principle.

Most of our interview partners noted a significant shift in judicial practices concerning short term pre-trial detention:

> Now it is not like years ago when we used to request for 3 months (maximum length of PTD) and used to get 3 months. Now you get 10–14 days.
>
> (19, Prosecutor)

> Nowadays practices have changed fundamentally. Now we see, that even for a suspect with murder less than 3 months (of PTD) are imposed. Prosecutors do narrow down their requests – request for 1–2 months. The courts order 1 month or 20 days.
>
> (20, Prosecutor)

> The courts became more lenient. Even for high profile leaders of organized groups, PTD for more than 6 months is unrealistic.
>
> (22, Prosecutor)

During the interviews, some changes in practices in specific cases were reported. They reflect in fact a combination of changes in the interpretation of the grounds for pre-trial detention. Also, we assume they contributed significantly to the decrease of levels in the use of pre-trial detention. A prosecutor (prosecutor 22) noted that years ago they used to request for pre-trial detention in every case of illicit drug trafficking, without regard to the quantity of drugs, no matter if a suspect was only 20 years old, had a job or was unemployed. Gradually the practice made a turn so that nowadays requests for pre-trial detention in such cases for Lithuanian suspects caught with a drug quantity not large are rather rare. Another prosecutor (20) noted:

> Years ago, in the cases of group violence, where a severe injury was caused by one strike, two months of PTD for all the participants of the group was a routine measure. Nowadays they would be arrested for 48 hours and then released.

Concluding remarks

In Lithuania, during the last 15 years, practices with respect to the application of coercive measures changed significantly. Though it is impossible to measure the exact impact of the changes in practices on the impressive drop of pre-trial detainees' rates in last decades statistically (other factors, like drop in crime rates, also had their impact), we can affirm the positive and significant trend in continuing shift from Soviet incarceration-orientated professional culture to the culture that respects suspects' right to liberty.

We could detect very few legislative developments that contributed to this shift (joining the EAW area, the introduction of EM, not to mention some legislative initiatives that established rules that had already been accepted in practice years before). The key development that contributed to the decrease of pre-trial detention use was a shift in the professional standards and culture of the criminal justice authorities. Indeed, often it is not so much the legislation that makes the impact on practice, but the professional mentality and standards of the prosecution and the judges.

Our interview respondents also shared similar ideas concerning the main reasons for changes in pre-trial detention practices in Lithuania in recent decades. First, the change of generations of practitioners has been mentioned. Judicial and prosecution systems received a substantial influx of new young judges and prosecutors who have good knowledge of recent European standards for the protection of human rights and of the principles of rule of law and have no experience and ties with former (more restrictive) practices (judge 2, prosecutor 5). As a rule, the position of a pre-trial judge is a starting point for newly appointed judges, where they usually serve for the first couple of years. Secondly, respondents mentioned gradual overall developments of the Lithuanian legal professional mentality, its transition from (post-Soviet) deterrent and security-focused attitude to a more liberal, more human rights-focused approach, which is stimulated by the precedents of the ECtHR and the highest courts of Lithuania, as well as by the recommendations of the Prosecutor General and public academic discussions (attorney 1; judges 1 and 2; prosecutors 5, 12 and 13). One judge pointed out straightforwardly in the interview:

> It feels like judges are less afraid to release the suspect without pre-trial detention nowadays.
>
> (6, Judge)

Though we recorded many examples in recent pre-trial detention use practices that reflect high standards in respect of suspects' right to liberty, comparative pre-trial detention statistics suggest that Lithuania still needs to promote, enhance and develop liberal practices in pre-trial detention use to catch up with the standards of the leading EU countries.

Notes

1 I want to thank my colleague Virgilijus Pajaujis for his valuable contribution to the research.
2 This comparison does not include Belgium and Malta that did not provide data on the number of detainees for SPACE I 2019 (Aebi and Tiago, 2020).
3 Belgium, Germany and the UK did not provide data on foreign inmates, but see the country chapters in this volume.
4 Though thefts of relatively low-value property are not serious crimes, they are often committed in series and high frequency for living by socially vulnerable offenders (often with drug addictions). In these circumstances, many prosecutors see detention as the only effective measure to prevent further offending (interview 6, Prosecutor).
5 Among the reasons for the decrease in thefts was the penal law amendment (active since 2015) that decriminalised theft of low-value property (under €150) if no aggravated circumstances present. The same amendment reclassified thefts of property under €250 without aggravated circumstances into misdemeanours, thus excluding this category from the scope cases where detention is allowed.
6 The starting point of the year 2004 has been chosen for two reasons: 2004 is the first full year with the new Penal and Criminal procedure Codes in force (both entered into force on 1 May 2003). Also, Lithuania entered the EU on 1 January 2004.
7 After the priority for the prosecution of domestic violence has been set, the number of suspects for minor violence rose from 780 in 2011 to 7,541 in 2013 and was stable at this level until recent years. In statistics of 2015 and 2016, we see the result of decriminalisation of minor theft. Since 2017, the number of suspects increased again since the criminalisation of drunk driving without causing an accident was introduced on 1 January 2017. That year the number of suspects in criminal traffic cases jumped from 628 to 4,373 and has been more or less stable until recent years.
8 Code of Criminal Procedure of the Republic of Lithuana//OG, 2002, No 37–1341.
9 During the trial phase, only a judge is responsible for the imposition of any measure on a defendant.
10 This amendment came into force on 11 July 2015.
11 The disputed court decisions have been passed between the end of 2016 and mid-2017.
12 The Court assessed the orders that were passed in 1998–2002.
13 Calculations based on open data from the Department of Technologies and Communication at the Ministry of Interior, Open data set in form 1G-A " Data on Suspects (accused) and victims in the Republic of Lithuania", www.ird.lt.
14 Unfortunately, statistics of EM use are being collected since September 2020 only, so no statistics for the popularity of this measure are available.
15 The fact that Russia, Belarus and many other countries do not extradite their citizens weighs for pre-trial detention of foreign suspects in serious crimes. On the other hand, if the predictable sanction is a fine, financial bail equal to the value of the predictable fine is usually imposed (i.e. for truck drivers in cigarettes trafficking cases). However, in the interviews, prosecutors assured us that there is no automatic rule that every foreigner from a non-EU country who risks imprisonment sentence, gets pre-trial detention. The example was given that a citizen of India, who was suspected of trafficking a very large quantity of drugs, was ordered for EM during the proceedings and did not abscond (23, Prosecutor).

References

Aebi, M.F. and Tiago, M.M. (2020) *SPACE I – 2019 – Council of Europe Annual Penal Statistics: Prison Populations*, Strasbourg: Council of Europe.

Bikelis, S. and Pajaujis, V. (2017) *DETOUR – Towards Pre-trail Detention as Ultima Ratio, 2nd Lithuanian Report on Experts Interviews* at www.uibk.ac.at/irks/projekte/detour.html.de [accessed 4 January 2023].

Council of Europe Recommendation CM/Rec (2014) *4 of the Committee of Ministers to Member States on Electronic Monitoring*, Strasbourg: Council of Europe Publishing.

Department of Statistics of Lithuania (2020) *Deaths by Cause of Death, Deaths per 100 000 Population* at https://osp.stat.gov.lt/statistiniu-rodikliu-analize?hash=6e74d488-d1d3-448b-b934-6e6f134fea73#/ [accessed 1 February 2020].

Department of Technologies and Communication at the Ministry of Interior (2021) *Open Data Set in form 1G-A 'Data on Suspects (Accused) and Victims in the Republic of Lithuania'* at www.ird.lt [accessed 1 February 2021].

European Migration Network at https://123.emn.lt/ [accessed 4 January 2023].

Eurostat (2020) *Minimum Wages in Europe*. Lithuania at https://ec.europa.eu/eurostat/statistics-explained/index.php?title=Minimum_wage_statistics [accessed 4 January 2023].

The Law on Amendment of Articles 121, 123, 125, 126, 127, 130, 131 ir 181 of the Penal Procedure Code of the Republic of Lithuania//OG, 2015–07–10, Nr. 11239.

Ministry of Justice and Office of the Prosecutor General, *Order No 1R-195/I-114 on the Rules for Issuing the European Arrest Order and Surrendered persons*//OG, 2004, Nr. 134–4886; sec. 4.4. Vilnius: Ministry of Justice.

Prosecutor General (2015, 2019) *Recommendations on Application and Supervision of the Measures, Except Detention, in the Pre-trial Proceedings*, No. I-306 at https://e-seimas.lrs.lt/portal/legalAct/lt/TAD/ceff71e0986e11e5a69681f9674b7edd [accessed 1 February 2021].

Sakalauskas, G., Jarutienė, L., Kalpokas, V. and Vaičiūnienė, R. (eds) (2019) *Kalinimo sąlygos ir kalinių socialinės integracijos prielaidos (Conditions of Imprisonment and Prerequisites for Social Integration of Prisoners)*, Vilnius, Lithuania: Žara: 512.

The Supreme Court of Lithuania (2004) *Order of the Lithuanian Supreme Court Senate No 50 on Promulgation of the Survey of Jurisprudence on Implementation of Detention and House Arrest and Extension of the Detention*, 30 December 2004, Vilnius: The Supreme Court.

Chapter 8

Pre-trial detention in the Netherlands

Absolutely low, relatively high

Joep Lindeman, Pauline Jacobs and Miranda Boone

Introduction

In this chapter, we give an outline of Dutch legislation and practice of pre-trial detention. We also consider some important facts and figures relating to pre-trial detention and we will address the extensive academic debate on pre-trial detention that has been continuing over the last years in the Netherlands. As partners in the DETOUR research project (see Chapter 1 for details), we have carried out comprehensive empirical research in 2016 and 2017, which has been documented in a National report on the Netherlands (Boone et al., 2017). In this chapter we elaborate on these findings that are still very much relevant today, complemented by more recent research findings in the area of pre-trial detention in the Netherlands and case law from the European Court of Human Rights (ECtHR). We will also share some findings on the effect of COVID-19 on pre-trial detention in the Netherlands.

The Dutch criminal justice system

The pre-trial phase plays a pivotal role in the Dutch criminal justice system (a civil law system with a moderate inquisitorial character). During this phase, virtually all evidence is gathered, assessed and documented by the police and the prosecution (Van Toor, 2020). Defence lawyers have a marginal role in this phase. The Public Prosecution Service (PPS) is responsible for all criminal investigations and has authority over the police in that matter. Also, based on the opportunity principle (*opportuniteitsbeginsel*), public prosecutors have the monopoly (and broad discretionary powers) on the decision to prosecute a case or not and/or to enter in out-of-court proceedings (e.g. by way of a penal order, *strafbeschikking*) (Holvast and Lindeman, 2020; Brinkhoff et al., 2019: 115–119; Fedorova, 2019: 17). In the cases that do appear before a judge, the application of unconditional prison sentences is relatively scarce (Meijer et al., 2022).

DOI: 10.4324/9781003159254-8

Prison population and numbers of pre-trial detainees

According to the SPACE statistics of the Council of Europe (Aebi et al., 2022: Table B and table 3), the Netherlands has a "very low" prison rate for adults with a prison population ratio of 53.9 per 100,000 inhabitants in January 2021.[1] After a strong increase between 1990 and 2005, the prison population has been declining until 2016, and has been on a (slight) rise again since (see Figure 8.1). In September 2021, prison population was 9,329 (Meijer et al., 2022). The percentage of foreign inmates in the prison population (23.3%) is considered to be "very high" in the SPACE statistics (Aebi et al., 2022: Table B, Table 13). This percentage also indicates that foreigners are overrepresented in prisons, as 7.1% of Dutch population does not have the Dutch nationality (CBS, 2022). According to a recent quantitative study of 10% of all criminal cases referred to the Public Prosecutor's Office in 2012 (N = 18,274), foreign nationals were 1.7–2 times more likely to be in pre-trial detention than Dutch citizens when all measured, legally relevant variables were taken into account (Wermink et al., 2022).

The rate of pre-trial detainees in absolute terms is 24.4 per 100,000 in January 2021 (Aebi et al., 2022: Tables 3 and 8). However, pre-trial detainees form a significant part (roughly between 40% and 50%) of the total prison population in the past years. The percentage of pre-trial detainees declined from 48.9% in 2012 to 42.1% in 2017 but since then increased to 44.2% in 2019 and 47.3% in 2020, only to decrease to 41.0% in 2021 (Meijer et al.,

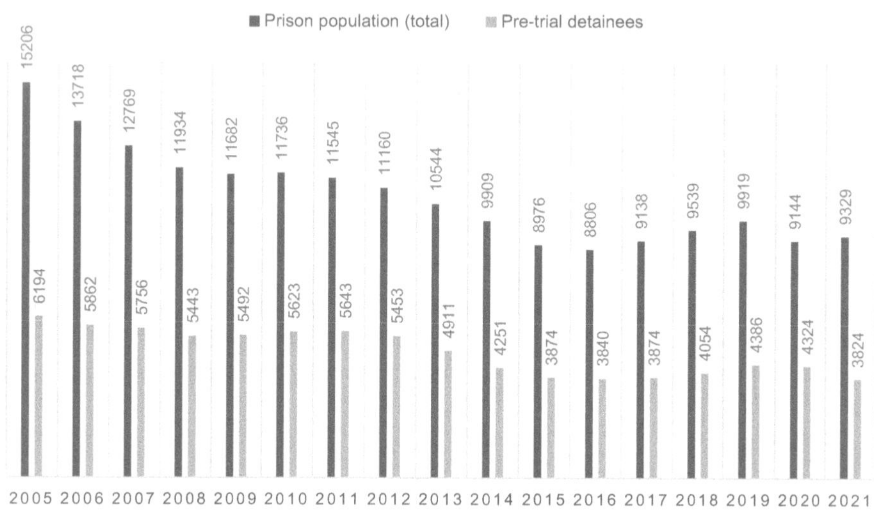

Figure 8.1 Prison population in the Netherlands, 2005–2021.

Source: Meijer et al. (2022).[2]

2022); the lowest percentage in a long time. Also, the absolute number of pre-trial detainees in 2021 (3,824; a significant drop compared to 2020) is the lowest in 15 years. This significant drop could perhaps be attributed to COVID-19, as there has been a drop of 9.1% of suspects in 2020 (Moolenaar and Choenni, 2021), but we are not certain. In sum, absolute numbers of pre-trial detainees have come down (most significantly between 2012 and 2015), but in relative terms, there does not seem to be a significant shift.

Research in 2016 suggested that between 2011 and 2014, a trend became visible in which the number of orders for pre-trial detention went down, the average length of pre-trial detention went down and the number of suspensions went up. Based on those numbers, Berghuis et al. (2016) concluded that judges seemed to have adopted a more cautious approach towards the application of pre-trial detention. Unfortunately, a similar analysis of statistics has not been made since, and the downward trend has come to a halt since 2015.

The percentage of pre-trial detainees related to the total population of prisoners currently is 41%. The relatively short prison sentences in the Netherlands are an important factor contributing to this high percentage. In the SPACE statistics over 2021, this percentage is ranked as "very high" in comparison with other European countries (Aebi et al., 2022: Table B). The Netherlands Court of Audit has expressed reservations regarding the SPACE comparisons, though[3]:

> For a variety of reasons, it is not possible to make a meaningful quantitative international comparison based on the data currently available. The legal systems, definitions and data registration methods used in the various European countries often cannot be compared with each other.
>
> (Algemene Rekenkamer, 2017: 17)

Current discussion and debates

Academics as well as defence lawyers and judges have criticised the extensive use of pre-trial detention in the Netherlands. They argue that pre-trial detention is not applied as an *ultima ratio*, but as a default and automatic measure for people awaiting trial and as a means for premature retribution. Often these critics refer to the high percentage of pre-trial detainees in the Netherlands compared to other European countries and the high number of compensations paid to pre-trial detainees that were acquitted (see Boone et al., 2019, for an extensive list of references).

In 2012, Stevens concluded that pre-trial detention was applied extensively rather than restrictively by judges and that it was used as a means to achieve swift punishment and to protect society against the suspect (Stevens, 2012, 2013). In 2013, three judges qualified Dutch judicial practice in decisions on pre-trial detention as an "efficient cookie-factory", in which pre-trial detention is the rule rather than the exception (Janssen et al., 2013). In 2016, Crijns et al. concluded that the Dutch legislation on pre-trial detention meets the relevant standards of the ECtHR, but that there is indeed reason to criticise the way in which the legal rules on pre-trial detention are applied in practice. They conclude that alternatives to pre-trial detention are underused, especially in the first phase of pre-trial detention and state that "[m]ore research and discussion is necessary to fully develop alternatives in terms of new legislation and better use of existing alternatives such as bail and electronic monitoring" (Crijns et al., 2016: 7–8). In 2017, the Netherlands Institute for Human Rights (College voor de Rechten van de Mens, 2017) examined more than 300 case-files and found that judges often insufficiently substantiate their decisions concerning pre-trial detention. These findings created some awareness in Dutch Parliament[4] and the judiciary introduced so-called professional standards,[5] that underlined the importance of sound substantiation of pre-trial detention decisions. A slight tendency towards improvements has been reported since (Docter and Baar, 2017), but it has also been argued that additional substantiation of pre-trial detention decisions might not change practice a lot, as the real issue is not a lack of substantiation but much more a fundamental disagreement on the extent to which pre-trial detention should be applicable (Robroek, 2017: 65).

Our research for the DETOUR project generated empirical data that mainly confirmed the findings of the research already mentioned earlier and furthermore added perspective and depth to the findings that pre-trial detention is used rather extensively in the Netherlands. We found that this extensive use is mainly based on a legal culture that focuses on prevention and that tries to meet an alleged need for preliminary retribution. An important finding is that, indeed, more thorough reasoning and much more attention for alternatives for pre-trial detention are of pivotal importance. Changes are needed regarding the mindset of the authorities deciding on pre-trial detention as well as regarding the possibilities to uncover information that is relevant for the consideration of alternatives (Boone et al., 2017). We will elaborate on these findings in more detail later.

In other comparative research, Jacobs and Lindeman found that the execution of pre-trial detention led to significant obstacles regarding the exercise of defence rights, both in pre-trial detention proceedings and in the proceedings before the trial judge (Jacobs and Lindeman, 2018; Jacobs and Lindeman, 2019; also see Jacobs et al., 2018 and Suremain et al., 2019).[6] This research questioned the regime for pre-trial detainees, because it is of a stricter nature than the regime for convicted prisoners: pre-trial detainees cannot benefit from the reward system (called promotion and degradation), which means that they are always in the "basic" regime, while convicted prisoners, who are in a prison, can upgrade to a "plus" regime after six weeks of good behaviour (Jacobs and Lindeman, 2018: 5). This regime, that applies to more than 40% of the prison population (see earlier), is at odds with the principle that detainees should not be restricted more than necessary. This principle of minimal restrictions (*minimale beperkingen*) is an important principle in the Dutch Penitentiary Principles Act (*Penitentiaire beginselenwet*), that originally was aimed specifically at pre-trial detainees, but has been made applicable to all detainees in the 1990s (Jacobs and Lindeman, 2019: 8).

A provisional version of a completely modernised Dutch CCP has been published in 2020. Although after a failed attempt for a thorough reform, the system for pre-trial detention will largely remain as it is, the draft of the explanatory memorandum specifically mentions the DETOUR research findings and the recommendations that were made regarding the Dutch situation. The legislator has taken on board some of the DETOUR recommendations and states that

> alternatives to pre-trial detention should be better embedded in both law and policy. The system of suspending pre-trial detention subject to conditions has been improved. In accordance with the recommendations, the judge will be given the legal duty to examine in all cases whether suspension of the pre-trial detention is possible immediately or in due time (Article 2.5.31). Furthermore, also in line with the recommendations, the conditions to be attached to the suspension are laid down by law (Article 2.5.33). Regulation of the conditions for suspension promotes legal certainty and supports the work of the probation service.

In May 2022, the Dutch Council of State advised that, while it endorsed this underlying principle, regulation alone might not be enough: "flanking measures" would be necessary to come to a more restrictive use of pre-trial detention. The definitive legislative proposal is expected to be sent to the parliament in the first half of 2023. Still, we expect that it will take several years before new legislation enters into force.

COVID-19

As stated earlier, we do not have enough data to substantiate the claim that the modest decline in the detention population can be attributed to COVID-19. Especially during the first months of the pandemic, a somewhat more restricted approach to the application of pre-trial detention has been considered possible (Van der Meij, 2020; Rodermond and De Knegt, 2020; De Vocht, 2020), but we have also seen decisions in which fear of COVID-19 was not seen as a reason to decline the request for pre-trial detention or to suspend the order (e.g. Court of Appeal The Hague, 26 March 2020, ECLI:NL:GHDHA:2020:808). Literature suggests that pleas to suspend the pre-trial detention order, that is, because the pandemic would lead to substantial delays in the criminal investigation, had to be thoroughly substantiated to have any chance of success (De Vocht, 2020: 979). All in all, there does not seem to be much evidence for a significant change in decision-making concerning pre-trial detention. At the same time, the procedural safeguards are hampered by restrictions caused by the pandemic: courts aim to do as much hearings as possible by way of videoconferencing and suspects are actively discouraged to appear in person, limiting the right of access to court. Furthermore, the regime in the detention facilities is more restricted to avoid contamination among the detainees (Van der Meij, 2020: 112).

Legal framework

Stages of pre-trial detention

The police can hold the suspect for questioning for a maximum of 18 hours (Article 56a CCP) and can subsequently order police custody (*inverzekeringstelling*) for three days (Article 57 CCP). After that, that the possibility of pre-trial detention (*voorlopige hechtenis*) will be considered: the order of deprivation of liberty by a judge that precedes the trial in criminal procedures. Public prosecutors are the sole party that can request pre-trial detention and they have a wide margin of appreciation in that respect. The three stages of pre-trial detention are as follows:

1. Remand in custody (*inbewaringstelling*)

   The examining judge (*rechter-commissaris*) decides on the request and can grant the order for a maximum period of 14 days (Article 63 and 64 CCP).

2. Detention in custody (*gevangenhouding* or *gevangenneming*)

   After the period of remand in custody, the public prosecutor may request the court in chambers to order the detention in custody for a maximum of 90 days (Article 65 and 66 CCP). Detention can also be ordered if the suspect is at liberty and must be taken into custody to appear before the judge (*gevangenneming*).

3. Detention pending trial (*gevangenneming* or *gevangenhouding*)

   After 104 days (14 days of remand in custody + 90 days detention in custody) the trial will have to start. More complex investigations will not have been finished within 104 days, which leads to so-called *pro forma* hearings, where the trial court will hear the case for no other reason than to decide on the continuation of the pre-trial detention, which it can then extend until the next hearing, that will have to take place within a maximum of three months (Article 66, Section 2 and Article 282 CCP). There is no statutory limit to these extensions, but the so-called anticipation requirement (see next section) can become an important factor.

The time the defendant has spent in pre-trial detention will be deducted from the imposed prison sentence. After an acquittal, defendants may ask for financial compensation for the time spent in pre-trial detention (Article 553 CCP).[7] This provision only applies to time effectively spent in prison. There is no similar legislation (and therefore no financial compensation) regarding alternatives for pre-trial detention, such as electronic monitoring or participation in rehabilitation programmes.

Once the court has come to a verdict, pre-trial detention will automatically continue for another 60 days (Article 66, Section 2, CCP), after which the Court of Appeal is to hear an eventual appeal, again with the possibility of *pro forma* hearings. During an appeal, the pre-trial detention will continue. In most cases, the execution of the detention will be transferred from a remand prison (*huis van bewaring*) to a prison for convicts, which will allow the detainee to participate in the reward system (see the following sections).

Statutory requirements

(1) There must be a "grave suspicion" (*ernstige bezwaren*, Article 67, third section, CCP). This implies that there must be more than the mere suspicion that the suspect has committed the offence.

(2) Following Article 67 CCP, first section, pre-trial detention can only be applied in case of a suspicion of a criminal offence which carries a sentence of imprisonment of four years or more (bar some exceptions). Also, the order can be issued regarding suspects for whom no permanent address or place of residence in the Netherlands can be established and who are suspected of an offence which carries a sentence of imprisonment.

(3) There must be a ground for pre-trial detention (Article 67a CCP):

  (a) The (serious) risk of absconding of the suspect.

  (b) The existence of a serious reason of public safety requiring the immediate deprivation of liberty. This ground has been defined further in Article 67a, Section 2:

    (i) Fear for serious upset to the legal order due to the very serious nature of crimes carrying a sentence of 12 years imprisonment or more (the so-called 12-years/shocked legal order ground).
    (ii) Fear of reoffending.
    (iii) Fear for obstruction of justice.
    (iv) The need to facilitate expedited proceedings against suspects of unsettling crimes in public areas or against public officials (policemen, firemen, and ambulance staff). This last ground is relatively new: it was added in 2015.

(4) The anticipation requirement has to be fulfilled by the judge (Article 67a, third section, CCP).

An order for pre-trial detention should not be issued if it is expected that the pre-trial detention is to exceed the custodial sentence or measure applied by the trial judge.

Basic principles regarding pre-trial detention, derived from the presumption of innocence, and expressed by the ECtHR, are that pre-trial detention should be used restrictively and that suspects should be released whilst awaiting their trial, ECtHR [GC] *Buzadji v. Moldavia* (23755/07, 5 July 2016, §§ 87–89). Dutch legislation aims to reflect these principles and holds several statutory thresholds that are to be met before pre-trial detention can be applied. This shows the *ultima ratio* character of this drastic coercive measure. The grounds for pre-trial detention represent the requirement of proportionality and (to a lesser extent) subsidiarity: detention should be a reasonable means to a reasonable aim and should only be applied when other, less severe measures, are not suitable to fulfil these aims.

From a comparative perspective, the "12-years/shocked legal order ground" may need some more explanation: this ground presupposes that the shock to the legal order that usually goes with grave crimes that carry a maximum sentence of 12 years or more (manslaughter, murder, rape, human trafficking) may constitute the social need for pre-trial detention. The aim of pre-trial detention is, then, to subdue this disturbance of public order (the ECtHR acknowledges that there are circumstances in which the (conditional) release of the suspect could, in itself, cause public disorder (*Geisterfer v. Netherlands*, 15911/08, 9 December 2014; *Hasselbaink v. Netherlands*, 73329/16, 9 February 2021).

The subsidiarity principle requires that the use of fitting alternatives to pre-trial detention should always be considered (Uit Beijerse, 2008, 2009; Boone et al., 2019), but Dutch law doesn't hold an obligation to unequivocally address this in pre-trial detention decisions. We already mentioned earlier that, in the medium-term, new legislation may change that.

Expedited proceedings as a driver for pre-trial detention

Dutch authorities profess a steady belief in a fast-track justice system (also known as "on the spot", *lik op stuk*): an offender-oriented approach in which the authorities provide an "on the spot" reaction to certain crimes (e.g. violence or vandalism in public places and/or against public officials). Criminal policy developed in cooperation with the PPS indicates that certain crimes are preferably dealt by way of expedited proceedings (*snelrecht*). In these proceedings, the trial is to take place while the accused is remanded in custody (so within 14 days). Thus, expedited proceedings preferably go hand in hand with the application of pre-trial detention. Research (Lindeman et al., 2020) has pointed out that, while these expedited proceedings are of course efficient, they are at odds with the presumption of innocence, as implicit assumptions are that the suspect is, indeed, the offender and that society does not accept a release pending trial. Also, the research showed that matters are hardly ever as clear-cut: a lot of cases are difficult to solve on such short notice and suspects often have behavioural problems and/or suffer from addiction, which means that the straightforward mould of expedited proceedings does not fit at all. Currently, expedited proceedings are mostly used in relatively simple cut-and-dried cases (e.g. repeat offenders for shoplifting), but government policy is still striving for a broader use (Lindeman et al., 2020).

Alternatives to pre-trial detention: conditional suspension of the execution

Strictly speaking there are no alternatives to pre-trial detention in the Dutch system: either the suspect awaits the trial in freedom, or pre-trial detention is ordered. The only possibility to replace pre-trial detention with a non-custodial setting is the conditional suspension (*schorsen onder voorwaarden*) of pre-trial detention (Articles 80–86 CCP), constituting a clear example of the substitution model (see Chapter 1). The judge or court ordering pre-trial detention can, straight after the order or later during the execution of the pre-trial detention, decide to suspend the execution (Article 80, Section 1, CCP).

The CCP distinguishes between general and specific conditions. The general conditions attached to a suspension of the pre-trial detention are that suspects will comply with possible future court orders regarding pre-trial detention and will cooperate with the execution of a possible future prison sentence (Article 80, Section 2, CCP). The only specific requirement mentioned in the law is financial bail to guarantee the fulfilment of the conditions of a suspension (Article 80, Section 1, Subsection 3, CCP). The law does not mention any other specific conditions, leaving room for any condition deemed suitable. In practice, a number of specific conditions is used regularly, as will be explained later.

Decision-making

The actors in the decision-making process

The public prosecutor

It is the prerogative of the public prosecutor to request pre-trial detention. Together with the Department of Justice and Security, the PPS develops and executes criminal policy that significantly impacts the selection, evaluation and processing of criminal cases (Holvast and Lindeman, 2020). Specific policy regarding pre-trial detention is scarce, but as we will illustrate later, the legal culture on pre-trial detention plays an important role in the decision-making by the prosecutor (see Boone et al., 2019; Lindeman et al., 2020). Even when there are no legal duties to request pre-trial detention, public expectations regarding such requests can be high and in certain cases, a request for pre-trial detention is the rule rather than the exception, as one of the prosecutors in our research pointed out:

> Looking at commune cases – in particular in the somewhat heavier cases – the prosecutor will always request, although I won't say automatically, remand in custody.
>
> (Boone et al., 2017: 19)

We found that prosecutors do not initiate looking into alternatives for pre-trial detention very often and that it is quite common that they expect the defence lawyers to come up with arguments to substantiate a possible suspension of pre-trial detention.

The judiciary

The first decision on pre-trial detention is taken by an examining judge (*Rechter-Commissaris*). The follow-up of pre-trial detention is decided by the court in chambers (*raadkamer*), consisting of three judges. Very little time is allocated for pre-trial detention hearings, which can lead to judges having to decide on dozens of cases per day. Judges have broad discretionary powers in deciding on pre-trial detention, as there is no legal obligation to grant a request for pre-trial detention, even when all statutory requirements have been met. Most applications are granted, though, and we will demonstrate later that we found that – in line with previous research discussed earlier – the judiciary does not always show much scrutiny in its decisions.

Defence lawyers

Pursuant to the Legal Aid Act (*Wet op de rechtsbijstand*), a lawyer will always be appointed to a suspect in pre-trial proceedings. We found that lawyers play a significant role in these proceedings because public prosecutors and judges are not very likely to actively gather information that is necessary to substantiate the (provisional) release of the suspect. Public prosecutors and judges confirm that lawyers that manage to find relevant information to substantiate a request to suspend pre-trial detention can really make a difference for their client (Boone et al., 2017). That said, lawyers claim that they experience difficulties in fulfilling this task: they have very little time to compile all the information and they often do not get all the documents from the casefile until very shortly before the hearing. This can also hamper their possibilities to challenge incriminating facts and circumstances that substantiate a "grave suspicion". Another handicap is that lawyers cannot directly communicate with the probation service if they wish a report on one of their clients. Lawyers also denounce the often very thin reasoning of the judicial decisions on pre-trial detention: they feel that they can talk until they are blue in the face, but their arguments would be refuted with a fatuous reasoning. Jacobs and Lindeman (2019) found that the financial compensation they receive in many cases is insufficient for the time-consuming work that is needed to really paint a complete picture of the suspect's life. They also found that access to a lawyer for pre-trial detainees can be difficult because of restrictions that go with pre-trial detention (i.e. limited visiting hours, very restricted possibility to use a telephone).

Probation service

The probation service[8] can be ordered to produce a so-called pre-trial assistance report (*vroegrapportage*). As far as the very limited timeframe will allow, it will try and establish whether the release on bail of the suspect would have risks attached to it and, if so, what conditions could be suitable to mitigate that risk. We found that, for a variety of reasons (among others lack of capacity, suspects (allegedly) not cooperating), a pre-trial assistance report is not available for all hearings (see the next section).

The hearing and the decision

First stage: remand in custody

We found that the hearing that precedes the decision-making process of the examining judge usually takes 20–30 minutes. In general (and rather paradoxically), the prosecutor is not present during these hearings, whereas the suspect and the lawyer usually are, but judges told us that they sometimes call the prosecutor during the hearing, should questions arise. The examining judge hears multiple requests in one session and decides on the spot. It is not uncommon that the relevant casefile does not emerge until shortly before the hearing, indicating once more how thin the basis is for this initial decision: after all it has only been a couple of days since the suspect was apprehended so relevant information regarding the charges and information on the personal background is scarce.

Depending on the state of the police enquiries, the fear of obstruction is a relevant ground for pre-trial detention in this stage. As mentioned before, the fear of reoffending is a ground that is used relatively often as is the 12-years/shocked legal order ground (in eligible cases: crimes that carry a maximum of 12 years imprisonment or more). To a lesser extent, fear of absconding is used as a ground for pre-trial detention. Our research confirms that the use of the fear of reoffending and the 12-years/shocked legal order ground go with superficial substantiation. Depending on the nature of the crime and the background of the suspect, even a first offender that has committed a crime can be considered as a potential recidivist:

> [Y]ou may still feel that it's necessary to find out why a suspect may have done what he did. You want to clarify that, or he might do it again tomorrow.
>
> (Boone et al., 2017: 45)

This is why this ground is considered to be the "mother of all grounds" by certain judges (Janssen et al., 2013: 436). Also, shocked legal order can already be considered as manifest when a judge feels that releasing the suspect of a serious crime would be (in his own words) "*hard to explain to my neighbour*".

Because information is scarcely available, there does not seem to be much room for considerations regarding alternatives (the suspension of the pre-trial detention), but there are exceptions. We will elaborate on this later.

Second stage: detention in custody

The hearing before the court in chambers will be in the presence of the suspect, the defence lawyer and the public prosecutor, and the court decides straight away on an eventual order for detention in custody. The court in chambers can order a 90-day term straight away, but it can also initially order a 30- or 60-day term, which implicates that, on the initiative of the public prosecutor, a new hearing will have to take place after the initial term before the order can be renewed for another 30 or 60 days. After these 90 days (so 104 days after the order for remand in custody), the trial against the – by then – defendant will have to start.[9]

The court in chambers deals with dozens of cases in one session and a hearing usually takes no longer than 10 minutes. The time between the order for remand in custody and the hearing before the court in chambers usually is considerably shorter than 14 days, which means that there still is no significant timeframe in which the probation service and/or the lawyer can gather more information to substantiate a request for suspension of the pre-trial detention.

Third stage: continuation of pre-trial detention during the trial phase

More complex investigations cannot be completed within 104 days, which leads to so-called *pro forma* hearings, that serve no other purpose than to extend the pre-trial detention. There is no limit to the number of suspensions of *pro forma* hearings, but of course the anticipation requirement will have a bearing on the decisions of the court regarding pre-trial detention.

Obviously, this is a stage in which the length of pre-trial detention can add up substantially, which can have a bearing on the weighing of personal versus public interests – as we will elaborate on later.

Appealing pre-trial detention

The court in chambers' decisions concerning the detention in remand can by appealed at the regional Court of Appeal. Significant restrictions apply as suspects can only appeal once against an order for (extension of) detention in remand. Similarly, they can only appeal once against the rejection of a request for suspension of the execution of pre-trial detention. Suspects cannot lodge an appeal in cassation at the Supreme Court (*Hoge Raad*) – while in some instances, the prosecution can. This is considered to be a closed system of legal remedies (*gesloten stelsel van rechtsmiddelen*), which means that the trial judge has very little room to address faulty pre-trial detention decisions. The information we gathered in our research on this topic was rather scarce, as we did not speak to appeal judges or advocates-general. Most lawyers agreed that the appeal procedure often was rather frustrating, as, again, the hearings would be very brief, the appeal judges would be very formalistic, and the decisions would hardly contain any substantial reasoning.

Bail and alternative solutions

Common situations in which suspension may be considered

The judge can order pre-trial detention and at the same time suspend the pre-trial detention with conditions, but an immediate suspension is not something that happens on a very regular basis. Especially in the early phase of pre-trial detention, the decision-making process does not lean towards a decision in favour of the release.

A fundamental feature of the Dutch system is that the alternatives are created within the framework of the pre-trial detention itself. This means that, in theory, the use is restricted to cases in which one or more grounds for pre-trial detention exist and that the alternative is a sufficient and necessary means to prevent the risk(s) that, given the ground(s) used, the pre-trial detention aims to prevent (subsidiarity principle). In practice, a much more general criterion is often used: whether the interests of the suspect in suspension of the pre-trial detention outweighs the interests of the criminal procedure in continuation of the pre-trial detention (Crijns et al., 2016: 36–37). The judge weighs the personal interests of the suspect against the interests represented in the legal grounds (interests of the criminal investigation and society in general), before deciding on an eventual suspension of the pre-trial detention. Some of the grounds for pre-trial detention (e.g. the 12 years/shocked legal order ground) may become less compelling with the passing of time.

Arguments that initially could not persuade the examining judge or the court in chambers to release the suspect, may be weighed differently in this stage.

Statistics on the number of suspensions are not readily available. Crijns et al. (2016: 36–37) observed in their study that at the initial review, pre-trial detention was suspended in 16% of the cases. At the court in chambers, pre-trial detention was suspended in 13% of the cases. These figures are in line with those mentioned by the Council for the Administration of Criminal Justice and Youth Protection (Raad voor Strafrechtstoepassing en Jeugdbescherming, 2011: 15), that shows that in 2011 14% of pre-trial detentions were suspended at the initial hearing and 12% at the court in chambers. Berghuis et al. (2016: 80) however, found a substantially higher proportion of suspensions by investigation judges since 2011 (2011: 33.8%; 2012: 35.0%; 2014: 36.4%) which they claim to be a result of the changed attitude of the judges towards pre-trial detention. These numbers have been confirmed by the Netherlands Court of Audit in 2017 which, unfortunately, does not provide more recent statistics (Algemene Rekenkamer, 2017: 24).

We found that, regarding the suspension of pre-trial detention, roughly three situations can be distinguished: (1) cases that are not eligible for suspension; (2) cases that are possibly eligible for suspension and (3) cases in which pre-trial-detention is applied to make it possible to suspend it under conditions ("improper remands").

As to situation (1), we found that two grounds for pre-trial detention do not seem to leave much room for conditional release of the suspect: the shocked legal order/12 years-ground and the fear of collusion. Especially the first ground concerns so-called high impact crimes and the general feeling seems to be that it cannot be explained to the victims and/or society that a suspect is released. As one judge put it:

> If you use alternatives in cases in which pre-trial detention is based on one of these grounds, these grounds are actually substantiated insufficiently.
>
> (Boone et al., 2017:54)

It is, indeed, hard to imagine how conditional release would be an alternative that could still subdue disturbance of public order or prevent collusion that is of such a nature that it necessitates pre-trial detention. A well-substantiated application of (one of) these grounds intrinsically leaves very little room for (conditional) release of the suspect.

In other cases (situation 2), suspension of pre-trial detention can be a viable option. These are often cases where the fear of reoffending plays an important role, as, to a somewhat lesser extent, does the fear of absconding. Despite these grounds, our research showed that prosecutors and judges also still seem to weigh the gravity of the crime and the potential shock of the legal order against the personal circumstances when considering this ground and the options for provisional release. Personal circumstances are of pivotal importance. For example, our research showed that suspects who can substantiate that they have a "wholesome" life (a job, a house, a family, responsibilities as breadwinner) may be eligible for provisional release, which can also partly explain the overrepresentation of foreign nationals in pre-trial detention (more extensively in Chapter 13). The same is less true for repeat offenders, especially when they have a background of addiction and/or mental disorders. They are seen as particularly at risk of reoffending. Still, conditions (such as participating in an addiction programme) may be beneficial to these people, as these conditions can be a start of a treatment process. So, in well-substantiated cases, in which it is clear what kind of treatment would be best *and* that such treatment is readily available, a suspension of pre-trial detention is a possibility. Finally, we found that some of the respondents (especially some of the prosecutors) thought that the residence status of the suspect could be a possible obstacle for suspension of the pre-trial detention. They put forward the view that it seems counterintuitive to use scarce resources available for rehabilitation programmes or probation trajectories if it concerns people who hardly speak Dutch and/or who are irregular migrants that are likely to be deported in due time. These considerations can probably contribute to the overrepresentation of foreign nationals in pre-trial detention as mentioned in the introduction.

The foregoing demonstrates that in a lot of cases, the suspension of pre-trial detention is used as a driver for the rehabilitation of the suspect. Following on a judge we spoke to, we call these "improper remands" (*oneigenlijke bevelen*), because pre-trial detention is applied first and foremost to create a legal framework for (probation) supervision, help or treatment. We learnt that sometimes the assessment of prosecutors and/or judges was that detention of suspects was not in order (for example because of the anticipation requirement as mentioned earlier), but that their release would preferably be conditional. Examples were given regarding repeat offenders (shoplifting, burglaries) or suspects of domestic violence. The strategy that usually requires that both the prosecution and the judiciary agree, is to start probation supervision and/or treatment as early as possible by setting conditions to the suspension of the pre-trial detention. The trial judge can then follow up on the conditional release of the suspect by passing on a conditional sentence with the same conditions. A problem that could arise in this regard is the so-called net-widening effect of alternatives: prosecutors and judges may risk using the framework of pre-trial detention because they want to use the alternatives. Of course, this raises questions in light of the presumption of innocence (hence the judge's use of the word "improper"), but we didn't come across respondents that significantly problematised this practice.

Apart from the "improper" use of the framework for pre-trial detention, another dilemma arises regarding this approach. Most Dutch judges are not very keen on sending defendants to prison who seem to be successfully abiding to the conditions set to the suspension of pre-trial detention. A prosecutor that wants the suspect to serve an unconditional prison sentence is therefore not likely to agree to a framework of conditions for suspension. When an unconditional sentence seems imminent, even defence lawyers seem to agree that "doing time" straight away may be the better option for their clients.

Types of alternatives and the subsidiarity principle

In practice, the following list of conditions are used most often:

- Reporting to the police
- Contact ban
- Electronic monitoring
- Financial guarantee
- Hand in identity papers
- Location order (house arrest)
- Location ban
- Probation supervision (eventually including training orders)
- Treatment (clinical or ambulant)

The lack of regulation and the wide variety of conditions used in practice raise questions regarding the subsidiarity principle: Do the conditions that are attached to the suspension of pre-trial detention contribute to a less intrusive way to the underlying goals of pre-trial detention (Uit Beijerse, 2009: 316)? It follows from this principle that conditions attached to the suspension should contribute to the realisation of the objective on which pre-trial detention it is based. However, regarding these grounds, the fundamental problem is that they are so widely interpreted (and scarcely substantiated) that it is difficult to judge if an alternative for detention really meets the subsidiarity principle or not. To really answer the question if a condition is in accordance with the subsidiarity principle, it would be necessary that judges clarify in every individual case which exact aims they want to serve with the pre-trial detention and, when these aims are compatible with the legal grounds for pre-trial detention, whether the conditions attached to a suspension are suitable to serve those particular aims.

The (lack of) use of alternatives in practice

Several practical issues stand in the way of a broad use of alternatives. We found that judges only consider alternatives if they have concrete information on the availability of valid options as well as guarantees that the conditions attached to the release provide a solid alternative related to the ground of the pre-trial detention (such as preventing recidivism). This information, however, is often difficult to get in an early stage of the investigation. A sufficiently conclusive (preliminary) probation report is not always available at the hearing before the investigation judge (Lindeman, 2018). Consequently, information that is much needed for a well-informed judicial decision in the early stage of pre-trial detention is not or hardly available. Defence lawyers often try to fill this gap. Due to time constraints and insufficient renumeration, however, their resources are limited (Jacobs and Lindeman, 2018, 2019). Furthermore, they cannot directly contact the probation office and ask them to gather certain information. The public prosecutor is in the lead in this regard, and we found that not all prosecutors are equally willing to pass on requests by the defence lawyer to the probation office.

In short: lack of time, capacity and information are three interrelated obstacles to the realisation of alternatives for pre-trial detention. These obstacles affect foreign nationals even harder, in particular because of a (perceived) lack of residence in the Netherlands (Boone et al., 2017: 54; Wermink et al., 2022, see also chapter 13). Many practical issues are mentioned: unwillingness of suspects to reveal information to lawyers they hardly know; privacy issues preventing social workers or therapists from sharing information, inability to cover costs that come with them advising, or capacity issues in case of more intensive behavioural intervention or treatment (waiting lists were often mentioned as an impediment, Boone et al., 2017).

This leads to rather scarce use of some relevant options. Electronic monitoring (EM) is only used in the context of pre-trial detention in exceptional cases. We found that lack of knowledge and initiative at the Prosecution Service, limited capacity and time-consuming feasibility assessments are reasons for the limited use of EM, especially in the first two stages of pre-trial detention. Financial bail is another example of an alternative that is almost never used, for a variety of reasons – such as lack of knowledge and initiative, a fear for class justice or fear of laundering of criminal assets (Boone et al., 2017: 63–64; Polman, 2015; Crijns et al., 2016: 37).

In those cases where alternatives are being used, the impression that we got from our research was that conditions were not always monitored very intensively. Violations happen and can result in a termination of the suspension order, so much is clear. But respondents also gave examples of cases in which a violation of the conditions resulted in an alteration of the suspension order (Article 81 CCP) or simply a continuation of the suspension order.

European aspects

ECtHR case law and EU directives on procedural rights

After a long period in which the Dutch practice did not seem to raise eyebrows in Strasbourg, the ECtHR has recently found violations against the Netherlands in relation to pre-trial detention. The first of these recent violations was found in 2014, in *Geisterfer v. The Netherlands* (15911/08, 9 December 2014). The Court found that the "shocked legal order/12 years-ground", while generally acceptable, was insufficiently substantiated, because the Dutch judges had not given a reasoning capable of showing that the accused's release would actually disturb the legal order. The details of that case were very specific, because pre-trial detention had already been conditionally suspended and the accompanying release of the accused had not led to any unrest. Therefore, it was indeed implausible that the ground was still relevant. Even when the judgment contained important general principles (especially in § 39), it did not lead to the sentiment that important changes in the assessment of pre-trial detention were necessary.

On 9 February 2021, the ECtHR delivered three more judgments on Dutch pre-trial detention cases and in all three judgments the court unanimously held violations of Article 5 (*Hasselbaink v. Netherlands* 73329/16; *Zohlandt v. Netherlands* 69491/16, and *Maassen v. Netherlands*, 10982/15). Again, the superficial substantiation of grounds for pre-trial detention (not only the shocked legal order, but also fear of absconding and fear of collusion) was denounced. The Court not only referred to its own case-law, but also to the earlier mentioned third-party intervention by the Netherlands Institute for Human Rights (*College voor de Rechten van de Mens*), that had already identified the lack of (sound) argumentation in pre-trial decisions in 2016. At the moment of the writing of this chapter, it is too early to measure the impact of the judgments.

The EU-directives on procedural rights (Asselineau, 2018; Costa Ramos et al., 2020) also hold relevant provisions that relate to some of the shortcomings in Dutch practice. In this chapter, we specifically address Article 7 of Directive 2013/12/EU on the right to information in criminal proceedings, that aims to secure the right of access of the material of the case, also specifically in the pre-trial detention stage, in order to effectively challenge the lawfulness of the arrest or detention and to allow the effective exercise of the rights of the defence (Pivaty and Soo, 2019). We found that access to relevant information in the pre-trial detention phase is very limited and that lawyers often are empty-handed when it comes to substantiating requests for (provisional) release. In other comparative research, Jacobs and Lindeman (2019) found that the execution of pre-trial detention led to significant obstacles regarding the exercise of defence rights.

European Supervision Order (ESO)

The European Supervision Order (ESO; see Chapter 14) has been implemented in Article 5.7.1 et seq. of the Dutch CCP). The Public Prosecution Service has been appointed as the competent authority (Article 6 framework decision: Article 5.7.4 CCP). Within the Public Prosecution Service, the Centre for International Legal Assistance in Criminal Matters – Noord Holland (CILA, *Internationaal Rechthulp Centrum (IRC) Noord-Holland, department WETS-ETM*) has been appointed as the central authority concerning the ESO.[10] The CILA processes all incoming and outgoing requests based on this mechanism and it decides independently on the incoming requests. Our DETOUR research showed that, while the PPS has made considerable effort to facilitate the ESO, it is not being used much. A lack of knowledge, the bureaucracy involved, and the length of the proceedings seem to stand in the way of a widespread use of the ESO (Lindeman et al., 2018).

Concluding remarks and suggestions for reform

In this chapter, we have demonstrated that decision-making in pre-trial detention cases in the Netherlands is driven by a couple of important factors: legal culture, time constraints, case load, limited safeguarding of procedural rights, lack of effective remedies and a reluctance to use alternatives.

Legal culture and criminal policy have culminated in certain conventions towards pre-trial detention. A preventive approach is leading, based on assumptions about the societal impact of the release of the suspect. Government policy is aimed at an "on-the-spot" approach and the mantra is being "tough on crime". This causes a climate in which the provisional release of suspects of so-called high impact crimes or repeat offenders is an exception. This legal culture, that is manifest in the policy on the expedited proceedings as well, seems to be deeply institutionalised and has led to a very extensive interpretation of the statutory grounds for pre-trial detention.

Time constraints lead to very little information being available in the first stage of pre-trial detention: the police have very little time to compile a comprehensive casefile and the probation office has very little time to provide relevant information on the personal circumstances of the suspect. The lawyer therefore has very limited opportunities to thoroughly substantiate a plea for alternatives.

The caseload for examining judges and courts in chambers is very high, which stands in the way of thorough deliberation. In more recent years, the introduction of so-called professional standards does not seem to have had a significant impact (Boone et al., 2019: 177).

Furthermore, procedural safeguards are far from ideal. As said, lawyers have little time to prepare the case and with a fixed (and not very generous) remuneration only limited resources are available. Access to the casefile is often problematic, as the file is often provided on very short notice and contains ample relevant information. Access to the suspect can also be problematic. This is all the more cogent when we bear in mind that in most cases it is only after considerable efforts by the lawyer that a suspect may face suspension of pre-trial detention.

Legal remedies for the suspect are limited and not very effective. Appeal in cassation at the Supreme Court is not possible, whereas the hearing before the trial court also leaves no room to address earlier faulty pre-trial detention decisions. Consequently, faulty or ill-substantiated decisions often remain without consequence. No significant legal development exists, even when the ECtHR has repeatedly found a violation of Article 5 ECHR in Dutch cases in recent years. All in all, there is little incentive for the judiciary to change its attitude towards pre-trial detention.

Earlier we mentioned the current proposal for a new CCP, that also addresses pre-trial detention and aims for a legal duty for judges to examine the possibility of alternatives. This proposal explicitly follows some of the recommendations that were given in our DETOUR-report on the Netherlands. However, we feel that that it is not necessary to wait for a change in legislation. To reduce the use of remand detention, the question that should be considered in the pre-trial stage is not if detention should be applied or not, but what restrictions of liberty are necessary to fulfil the aims that are at stake in this stage of the criminal justice process.

Notes

1 Compared to most northern, western and southern European countries with more than one million inhabitants (Aebi et al., 2022, table B). For an elaboration on the reasons for this low prison rate, see Boone et al. (2022).
2 These numbers are based on an annual count in September of each year. It includes not only adult prisoners who are detained within a penitentiary institution, but also prisoners who are placed in special healthcare institutions used for those who are particularly vulnerable and persons who follow a penitentiary programme outside prison.
3 Quote taken from a press release in English, at https://english.rekenkamer.nl/publications/reports/2017/11/14/pre-trial-detention-suspects-in-the-cells (accessed 10 January 2023).
4 Answers to Parliamentary questions by the member Van Nispen (SP) to the Minister of Justice and Security, *Aanhangsel Handelingen II* 2016/17, 1848.
5 www.rechtspraak.nl/SiteCollectionDocuments/professionele-standaarden-strafrecht.pdf (accessed 10 January 2023).
6 This research was carried out for the EUPRETRIALRIGHTS project. See www.prisonlitigation.org/eupretrialrights/?lang=en (accessed 10 January 2023).
7 Until 1 January 2020, this was Article 89 CCP.
8 There are three Dutch probation organisations ("3 Reclasseringsorganisaties (3RO)"), of which the Dutch probation service (Reclassering Nederland) is the largest.
9 An important exception in this regard is made for cases in which there is a suspicion for terrorist crimes: after the first 90 days, the court in chambers can extend the pre-trial detention during two years, with a maximum of 90 days at a time.
10 In addition to mutual recognition of judgments in criminal matters imposing custodial sentences or measures involving deprivation of liberty (Framework Decision 2008/909/JHA).

References

Aebi, M.F., Cocco, E., Molnar, L. and Tiago, M.M. (2022) *SPACE I – 2021 – Council of Europe Annual Penal Statistics: Prison Populations*, Strasbourg: Council of Europe.

Algemene Rekenkamer (2017) *Voorarrest: verdachten in de cel. Een kwantitatieve analyse van inverzekeringstelling en voorlopige hechtenis*, The Hague: Algemene Rekenkamer.

Asselineau, V. (2018) 'Agenda 2020: A new Roadmap on minimum standards of certain pro-cedural safeguards', *New Journal of European Criminal Law*, 9(2): 184–190.

Berghuis, B., Linckens, P. and Aanstoot, A. (2016) 'De voorlopige hechtenis een halt toegeroepen?', *Trema*, 3: 76–81.

Boone, M.M., Jacobs, P. and Lindeman, J.M.W. (2017) *DETOUR. Towards Pre-trial Detention as Ultima Ratio – 2nd Dutch National Report on Expert Interviews*, Vienna: Institute for the Sociology of Law and Criminology, at www.uibk.ac.at/irks/projekte/detour.html [accessed 10 January 2023].

Boone, M.M., Jacobs, P. and Lindeman, J.M.W. (2019) 'Alternatieven voor voorlopige hechtenis in Europa en Nederland: de advocaat als onterechte sleutelhouder', *Delikt & Delinkwent*, 3: 170–187.

Boone, M.M., Pakes, F. and Wingerden, S.G.C. van (2022) 'Explaining the collapse of the prison population in the Netherlands: Testing the theories', *European Journal of Criminology*, 19(4), 488–505.

Brinkhoff, S., Bemelmans, J.H.B. and Kuipers, M. (2019) 'Criminal Procedure Law', in P.H. van Kempen, M. Krabbe and S. Brinkhoff (eds) *The Criminal Justice System of the Netherlands. Organization, Substantive Criminal Law, Criminal Procedure and Sanctions*, Antwerp: Intersentia: 97–134.

CBS (2022) *Statistics Netherlands Database* at https://opendata.cbs.nl/statline/#/CBS/nl/dataset/03743/table?dl=72EFD [accessed 10 January 2023].

College voor de Rechten van de Mens (2017) *Tekst en uitleg. Onderzoek naar de motivering van voorlopige hechtenis. Utrecht: College voor de Rechten van de Mens* at https://publicaties.mensenrechten.nl/publicaties [accessed 10 January 2023].

Costa Ramos, V., Luchtman, M. and Munteanu, G. (2020) 'Improving defence rights including available remedies in and (or as a consequence of) cross-border criminal proceedings', *Eucrim*, 3: 230–245.

Crijns, J.H., Leeuw, B.J.G. and Wermink, H.T. (2016) *Pre-trial Detention in the Netherlands: Legal Principles Versus Practical Reality*, The Hague: Eleven International Publishing.

De Suremain, H., Fischer, N., Boe, C., et al. (2019) *Bringing Justice into Prison: For a Common European Approach. White Paper on Access to Justice for Pretrial Detainees. A Report Based on Comparative Analysis and Empirical Studies in Nine EU Countries by the Research Project EUPRETRIALRIGHTS*, Paris: European Prison Litigation Network at www.prisonlitigation.org/white-paper-pretrial/ and www.prisonlitigation.org/wp-content/uploads/2021/04/WHITE-PAPER-final-ENG.pdf [accessed 10 January 2023].

De Vocht, D. (2020) 'Van hoesters en spugers tot ingetrokken verloven. De impact van corona op de Nederlandse strafrechtspleging', *Nederlands Juristenblad*, 14: 977–979.

Docter, M.A. and Baar, J.L. (2017) 'De motivering van voorlopige hechtenis schiet tekort. De gronden die tot eerdere artikelen en commentaren hebben geleid, zijn nog onverkort aanwezig', *TPWS*, 24: 178–184.

Fedorova, M.I. (2019) 'The Main Organs of the Criminal Justice System', in P.H. van Kempen, M. Krabbe and S. Brinkhoff (eds) *The Criminal Justice System of the Netherlands. Organization, Substantive Criminal Law, Criminal Procedure and Sanctions*, Antwerp: Intersentia: 9–35.

Holvast, N.L. and Lindeman, J.M.W. (2020) 'An inquiry into the blurring boundaries between professionals and paraprofessionals in Dutch Courts and the public prosecution service', *International Journal of Law in Context*, 16(4): 371–389.

Jacobs, P. and Lindeman, J.M.W. (2018) *Analysis of National Law: National Norms as Regard to Access of Detained Persons to the Law and to Court: Report on the Netherlands for the EUPRE-TRIALRIGHTS Research Project*, Utrecht and Paris: Universiteit Utrecht/European Prison Litigation Project at https://library.prisonlitigation.org/nl/items/36 [accessed 10 January 2023].

Jacobs, P. and Lindeman, J.M.W. (2019) 'De tenuitvoerlegging van de voorlopige hechtenis. Belemmerend voor of juist in dienst van de voorbereiding van de strafzaak?', *Strafblad*, 2: 6–14.

Jacobs, P., Van Kalmthout, A. and Lindeman, J.M.W. (2018) *Empirical Study: The Actors of Legal Protection, Their Professional Practices and the Use of Law in Detention: Report on the Netherlands for the EUPRETRIALRIGHTS Research Project*, Utrecht and Paris: Universiteit Utrecht/European Prison Litigation Project at https://library.prisonlitigation.org/nl/items/45 [accessed 10 January 2023].

Janssen, J.H., Van den Emster, F.W.H. and Trotman, T.B. (2013) 'Strafrechters over de praktijk van de voorlopige hechtenis. Een oordeel van de werkvloer!', *Strafblad*, 6: 430–444.

Lindeman, J.M.W. (2018) 'De hulpofficier van justitie "nieuwe stijl" en de modernisering van het Wetboek van Strafvordering', *Tijdschrift Modernisering Strafvordering*, 1(1): 29–40.

Lindeman, J.M.W., Jacobs, P. and Boone, M.M. (2018) 'De praktijk van de Europese toezichtmaatregel: begin van een meeromvattende invloed van de EU op de voorlopige hechtenis?', *Strafblad*, 6: 30–34.

Lindeman, J.M.W., Van Lent, L., Van der Vorm, B. and Smits, I. (2020) *Wie past de schoen? De snelrechtgrond in de praktijk. Evaluatie van de Wet uitbreiding gronden voorlopige hechtenis*, Utrecht and Den Haag: Montaigne Centrum/WODC at https://repository.wodc.nl/handle/20.500.12832/2457 [accessed 10 January 2023].

Meijer, R.F., Moolenaar, D.E.G., Choenni, R. and Van den Braak, S.W. (eds) (2022) *Criminaliteit en rechtshandhaving 2021. Ontwikkelingen en samenhangen*, The Hague: WODC.

Moolenaar, D. and Choenni, S. (2021) *Effect van COVID-19 op de strafrechtketen (WODC Memorandum 2021–3)*, Den Haag, WODC at https://repository.wodc.nl/handle/20.500.12832/3113 [accessed 10 January 2023].

Pivaty, A. and Soo, A. (2019) 'Article 7 of the directive 2012/13/EU on the right to information in criminal proceedings: A missed opportunity to ensure equality of arms in pre-trial proceedings?', *European Journal of Crime, Criminal Law and Criminal Justice*, 27(2): 126–154.

Polman, B.J. (2015) 'Het instituut van de borgsom in het Nederlandse strafprocesrecht. De voor- en nadelen in nationaal perspectief', *Ars Aequi*, 6: 437–447.

Raad voor Strafrechtstoepassing en Jeugdbescherming (2011) *Voorlopige hechtenis – maar dan anders. Verkenning van alternatieven in het kader van schorsing en tenuitvoerlegging. Advies van 4 juli 2011*, The Hague: RSJ at www.rsj.nl/adviezen/ [accessed 10 January 2023].

Robroek, R. (2017) 'De motivering van de voorlopige hechtenis in Nederland en het EVRM', *Delikt en Delinkwent*, 1: 43–56.
Rodermond, E. and De Knegt, M.A. (2020) 'Detentie en re-integratie ten tijde van corona', *Sancties*, 3: 183–186.
Stevens, L. (2012) 'Incapacitation by pre-trial detention', in M. Malsch and M.J.A. Duker (eds) *Incapacitation: Trends and New Perspectives*, London: Ashgate Publishing: 97–108.
Stevens, L. (2013) 'The meaning of the presumption of innocence for pre-trial detention. An empirical approach', *Netherlands Journal of Legal Philosophy*, 42(3): 239–248.
Toor, D. van (2020) 'The Dutch pre-trial procedure', in E. Johnston et al. (eds) *A Comparative Analysis of Pre-trial Procedure in Europe: The Search for an Ideal Model*, Istanbul: Istanbul University Press: 41–67.
Uit Beijerse, J. (2008) 'Naar een bij onschuldpresumptie passend systeem van voorlopige hechtenis. De lessen van Europa en van de klassieke rechtsgeleerden', *Strafblad*, 5: 465–487.
Uit Beijerse, J. (2009) 'De nieuwe regeling van de schorsing van de voorlopige hechtenis bij jeugdigen in het licht van de onschuldconsumptie', *Proces*, 6: 314–325.
Van der Meij, P.P.J. (2020) 'COVID-19/CATCH-22. Besmettingsgevaar en voorlopige hechtenis', *Boom Strafblad*, 2.
Wermink, H., Light, M.T. and Krubnik, A.P. (2022) 'Pre-trial detention and incarceration-decisions for Foreign Nationals, a mixed-method approach', *European Journal on Criminal Policy and Research*, first published, 28(3): 367–380.

Chapter 9

Pre-trial detention in Romanian: improvements and shortcomings

Ioan Durnescu and Gabriel Oancea

Introduction

Romania is a country situated in Eastern Europe which therefore was placed under Soviet influence for a large part of the last century (1948–1989). This type of political influence came also with certain social, cultural and legal pressures. As far as the criminal justice system is concerned, the communist fingerprint includes a prison-centric view on the sanctioning system, an excessive power of the prosecution, an overuse of pre-trial detention and frequent use of pardons.

Although the Romanian Penal Code and the Penal Procedure Code have been amended several times since 1989, the fundamental philosophy behind them remained to be the one instilled in the former acts of 1968. A new Penal Code and Penal Procedure Code were adopted in 2009 and entered into force on 1 February 2014. As announced in the Explanatory Notes, these regulations aim at creating a coherent legislative framework in line with the new Constitution (adopted in 1991) and the European standards. Literature on these reforms has mainly taken a descriptive approach. For example, Tuculeanu and Sima (2015) were very focused on the procedure that the judiciary must follow to impose pre-trial detention, while Potrivitu (2015) was more interested in the use of judicial control and judicial control on bail.

A handful of scholars analysed the new pre-trial measures against the European Court of Human Rights (ECtHR) standards and concluded that much is still to be done to ensure that Romanian practice follows the European Convention on Human Rights (ECHR) jurisprudence (Ivan and Ivan, 2016; Tomulet, 2016). Special attention was given to applying the reasons to impose pre-trial detention in specific cases using concrete and case-specific arguments, as suggested in ECtHR case law. The same requirement to carefully apply pre-trial detention using concrete arguments and not generic ones was mentioned in research about the proportionality principle in pre-trial detention practice (Grigorie, 2015).

Human rights in case of pre-trial detention have also been the focus of some researchers. Doseanu (2015), for example, analyses the practice of

DOI: 10.4324/9781003159254-9

pre-trial detention in relation to prison overcrowding, poor material conditions and proportionality, concluding that the Romanian courts should pay much more attention to the alternatives. The same conclusion was emphasised by Doseanu and Doseanu (2015) who noted that while the procedure on pre-trial detention is very elaborate in the Criminal Procedure Code, the same cannot be said on the procedure regarding judicial control on bail. In their opinion, the lack of clarity in the procedure may impact on the infrequent application of this type of alternative measure. However, as one can see in the following graphs, the number of defendants under pre-trial detention is decreasing each year, at least in the investigation stage.

However, the aforementioned research has a rather theoretical and general character. We have not identified empirical studies focusing on an analysis of the practice of pre-trial detention, which would capture the perceptions of the main "actors", that is, judges, prosecutors, or lawyers. An empirical study on pre-trial decision-making, carried out in 2015 by the Association for the Defence of Human Rights in Romania – the Helsinki Committee, APADOR-CH – however, summarised the main practical problems:

- The short periods of time provided by the criminal procedure for the resolution of prosecutors' requests for the application of the pre-trial detention measure.
- The lack of secondary legislation allowing for a uniform application of the legal provisions relating to alternative measures.
- The lack of resources to contribute to greater application of these alternatives.
- The lack of available tools for the judges to assess the risk of defendants.

Thus, the report pointed out that the main effects of the celerity imposed by the procedural rules were to adversely affect both the quality of the defence and the decisions of the judges, most often to the disadvantage of the defendant. It was also pointed out that another factor likely to affect the quality of defence was the reduced amount of fees for public defenders. The report also highlighted the role the Superior Council of Magistracy has in establishing a uniform practice, and it proposed the publishing of different guides on the criteria and practical conditions for the application of preventive measures as an alternative to pre-trial detention, ways of determining the amount of bail, etc. The report stressed that the lack of coherence in the application of preventive measures is likely to undermine their credibility, especially since public opinion is sometimes interested in the way in which the courts apply preventive measures. Finally, the report stated that an extensive application of alternatives to pre-trial detention was conditional on the allocation of material and human resources to make them more efficient and the level of confidence, mainly of the judges, in the implementation of these measures (for example, the need to introduce electronic monitoring, as provided for in the Code of Criminal Procedure).

In the practice of pre-trial detention in Romania, this measure is carried out both within facilities at the level of police stations and within the penitentiary units under the supervision of the National Administration of Penitentiaries. Figure 9.1 shows the annual evolution regarding the number of people on pre-trial detention held in police stations, while Figure 9.2 shows the number of people under pre-trial detention held in prisons subordinated to the National Penitentiary Administration.

As a rule, at the end of the investigation and prosecution stage, those who are under pre-trial detention are transferred from police station arrest

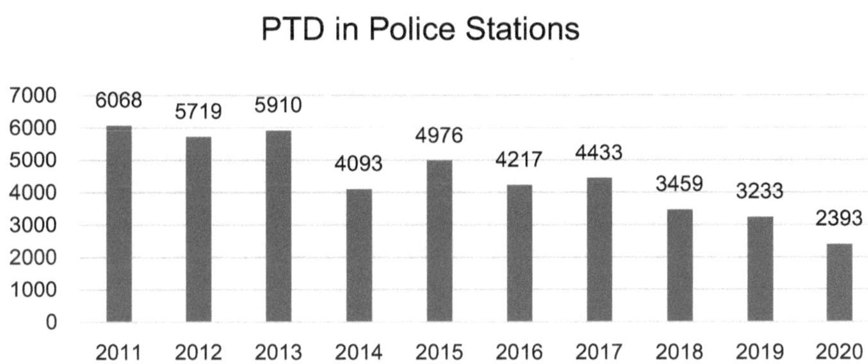

Figure 9.1 The number of defendants under pre-trial detention in police centres (at 31 December).

Source: National Inspectorate of Police.

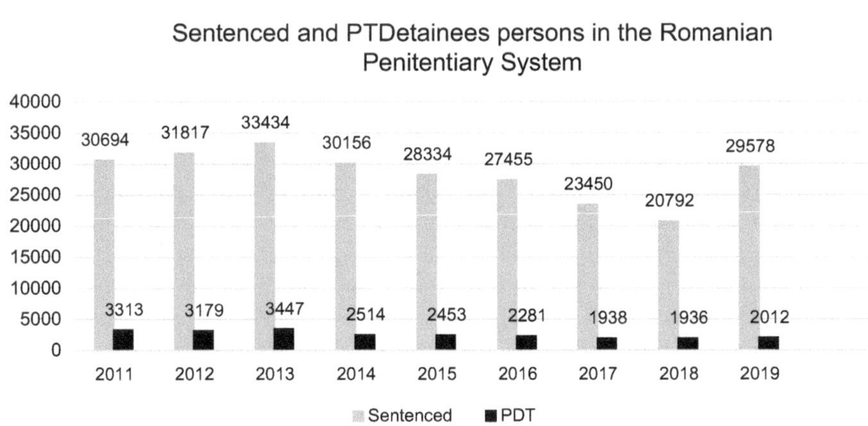

Figure 9.2 The number of pre-trial detainees during the trial stage (at 31 December).

Source: National Administration of Penitentiaries.

facilities to prisons. Their number is lower compared with that in Figure 9.1 because during the prosecution in some cases pre-trial detention is no longer maintained, either being repealed or replaced by other measures.

As explained earlier, pre-trial detention is normally carried out in police stations in the case of defendants against whom the prosecution is being carried out, and when the case is sent to trial, they will be transferred to prison units. The justification for this practice lies mainly in the fact that during investigation and prosecution, in view of the speed with which the proceedings are carried out, a more active participation of the defendant is required, and the police escort services show more flexibility as compared to those of the National Administration of Penitentiaries. We must also consider the fact that, in many cases, the prosecution is carried out directly by police officers belonging to the judicial police, under the supervision of a prosecutor. Once the case is brought to trial, the situations involving the transport of the person remanded in custody are considerably reduced, and it is necessary to participate almost exclusively in the trial of the case or in the resolution of requests for an extension of pre-trial detention. This solution is also likely to contribute to maintaining under some control the number of pre-trial arrestees kept in detention and pre-trial detention centres in police stations, where the Committee on the Prevention of Torture has repeatedly observed their precariousness in relation to those in prison units.[1]

Regarding the developments which the two figures indicate, it should be noted that they cover a period during which the provisions of two codes of criminal procedure have been applied, the one adopted in 1968 and which, with some amendments, was in force until 1 February 2014; and the new code of criminal procedure respectively (Law No. 135/2010). As far as we are concerned, we consider that this succession of criminal procedural codes is likely to explain the downward trend that can be noted after 2014. Thus, in 2009 there were several legislative changes which provided for restricted time limits for sentences, which also led to an increase in the number of defendants remanded in custody. This is because, according to the provisions of Article 148 para. 2 of the former Code of Criminal Procedure, the measure of pre-trial detention of the accused could only be taken if the penalty provided for by law was life imprisonment or imprisonment of more than four years. The new criminal regulations that came into force on 1 February 2014 had introduced a reduction in the limits of penalties but also a much more precise regulation of the pre-trial detention. Another factor which was likely to contribute to this downward trend was ECtHR jurisprudence in the field of pre-trial detention and of the conditions of detention, which acted as a pressure factor in limiting the application of pre-trial detention. The decisions against Romania made by the Court covered a wide-ranging issue, starting with the violation of the presumption of innocence by taking the measure of pre-trial detention (*Hamvas v. Romania*, 6025/05, 9 July 2013), the fact that the pre-trial detention was ordered for an unreasonably long period (*Rupa and Tsompi v. Romania*, 60272/09, 2 May 2017) or the precarious conditions in the detention facilities of persons remanded in custody (*Casuneanu v. Romania*, 22018/10, 7 June 2011).

Looking at statistics, one can note a steep decrease of the proportion of pre-trial detainees from 10% in 2018 to 6.8% in 2019. One possible explanation for this blatant difference is that, according to the Criminal Procedure Code, the maximum duration of pre-trial detention during the investigation stage is 180 days while the upper limit for the trial stage is half of the maximum of prison sentence applicable in that case, which can be measured in years. This difference in regulating pre-trial detention at different stages of the criminal procedure may imply that this measure could be shorter for the trial stage compared to the investigation one.

In this chapter, we argue that the most important changes in the practice around pre-trial detention in Romania were the Revolution (1989) and the adoption of the new democratic Constitution (1991), followed quite some time later by the new Penal and Penal Procedure Code (2009/2014). Another significant steppingstone in the process of modernisation and democratisation was the ratification of the European Convention on Human Rights (20 June 1994) that brought with it a positive pressure on the Romanian law and practice to align to European standards – expressed both in the Convention and in the ECtHR jurisprudence.

In the next sections, we will describe the legal framework that regulates pre-trial measures while comparing it with the judiciary's perceptions on their own practice related to this part of penal procedure. To capture these perceptions, nine judges, six prosecutors and four defence lawyers were interviewed as part of the EU-funded DETOUR project (see Chapter 1). Judges and prosecutors were selected from different levels of the judiciary hierarchy, including the High Court of Cassation and Justice.

Legal framework

Relevant constitutional requirements regarding preventive measures

Romania belongs to the civil law tradition. Therefore, the Constitution and other legal texts are essential in shaping the pre-trial detention practice. One of the first legislative reforms that took place after the Revolution was the creation of the new Constitution which entered into force in 1991 and provides guarantees for all democratic rights, such as the right to life, individual freedom, right to defence, and so on. The right to a legal defence, for example, stipulates that all citizens have the right to a fair trial where the suspected or accused are to be informed about the charges against them and have the right to a defence counsel. Some of the new principles introduced have an important impact on pre-trial detention practice: the principle of humanism, the principle of innocence until proven guilty, the principle of finding the truth (the obligation for the investigation body to find evidence both in favour or against the suspect or defendant), the principle of ne bis in idem, the principle of a fair and reasonable period of trial, etc. Also, the Constitution provides that the person under pre-trial detention is entitled to apply for provisional release, under judicial control or judicial control on bail. Another important provision of this text is that in case of conflict between the national and international regulations, as far as human rights are concerned, the international ones prevail. Therefore, domestic human rights shall be interpreted and enforced in line with the Universal Declaration of Human Rights and other conventions and treaties that Romania has signed up to. Once Romania ratified the European Convention of Human Rights a new set of standards became essential for the Romanian courts in respect to pre-trial detention practice and the European Court of Human Rights plays an important role in promoting moderation in the use of pre-trial detention in Romania.

Article 23 of the Constitution provides that individual freedom and security are inviolable. The search, detention or arrest of a person shall be allowed only in cases stated in the law and under a strict procedure.

Pre-trial detention shall be ordered by a judge and only during criminal proceedings (para. 3). During the criminal investigation stage, pre-trial detention can be ordered for maximum of 30 days and extended for another 30 days, without the overall length to exceed a reasonable term and no longer than 180 days (para. 5). During the trial stage, the grounds for pre-trial detention must be checked regularly by the judge and, if the grounds for applying it cease to exist, the court must order the release of the defendant (para. 6). As in the criminal investigation stage, pre-trial detention can be applied for 30 days and extended for another 30 days but the overall length of it shall never exceed half of the maximum penalty provided by the law for the indicted offence (Article 239 Criminal Procedure Code). For example, if the maximum penalty for theft is 7 years, the maximum length allowed by the law for pre-trial detention in the trial stage cannot exceed 3.5 years. Furthermore, the same article (Article 239 para 1 Criminal Procedure Code) provides that the length of the pre-trial detention shall not exceed five years in the first instance.

Relevant provisions from the Criminal Procedure Code regarding preventive measures

As noted earlier, different procedures apply depending on the criminal procedure stage. According to the Criminal Procedure Code, four stages exist: criminal investigation; preliminary chamber's judgment; the trial; and the enforcement of the court decision.

The criminal procedure starts with a document called an ordinance issued by the judiciary police and confirmed by the prosecutor. In some special cases, the ordinance is issued directly by the prosecutor. After the investigation, the prosecutor may decide on one of the following solutions: dismissal of the case, waiving prosecution or indictment, when the prosecutor decides to take the case to the court.

Based on these principles, the Penal Procedure Code stipulates that during trial every person has the right of freedom and safety guaranteed. Any restriction of freedom is exceptional and must be based on the law. In case of pre-trial detention, every person must be informed about the charges as soon as possible and in a language that s/he understands. Furthermore, the person has the right to file an appeal against the measure. In case of unlawful deprivation of liberty, the person has the right to compensation or repair for the damage.

The new Penal Procedure Code provides for the right of the person to remain silent and for the right to defence (Article 10). During the investigation and the trial stage, the suspected or the defendants have the right to defend themselves and to be assisted by a lawyer. Assistance from a lawyer is obligatory and therefore can be covered by an *ex officio* lawyer in the following cases:

- For juveniles, for students at military schools and for military personnel
- In case the indicted offence is punishable with life imprisonment or a penalty higher than five years of imprisonment
- When the investigative body evaluate that the defendant cannot defend himself/herself

Preventive measures

The Penal Procedure Code (PPC, adopted by Law No. 135/2010) regulates all the preventive measures that can be ordered in the criminal trial, such as detention, judicial control, judicial control on bail, house arrest and pre-trial detention.

The general principle underlying such measures is mentioned in Article 202 para. 1, according to which

> preventive measures may be ordered if there is solid evidence or indications underpinning reasonable suspicion that a person has committed an offence, and if they are necessary to ensure the proper conduct of the criminal trial, to prevent the suspect or the defendant from evading criminal prosecution or trial, or to prevent another criminal offence from being committed.

Additionally, para. 3 of the same article introduces the criteria of proportionality and of the necessity of preventive measures, providing that the preventive measure taken must be *proportionate* to the gravity of the accusation brought against the person against whom it is taken, and it must also be *necessary* for the attainment of the aim pursued by its disposition.

Taking a person into custody (Articles 209–210 PPC)

"Taking into custody", it is the easiest of the preventive measures depriving of liberty, which can be taken for a period of not more than 24 hours, by the prosecutor or by the criminal investigation body (also being the only preventive measure depriving of liberty that the criminal investigation body can take). The law stipulates that this measure can only be taken during criminal prosecution and not during the trial phase. It is also the only measure that can be taken against a suspect, that is, the person against whom the existing evidence gives rise to a reasonable suspicion that they have committed an act that infringes a provision of criminal law. This measure can be applied even before the person is formally charged yet.

The conditions necessary for the disposition of detention:

1 The general condition provided for in Article 202 para. 1 PPC.
2 A preliminary hearing of the suspect/defendant by the judicial body *(judge) taking* the measure. This shall be done only in the presence of a lawyer who was chosen or appointed *ex officio* (legal aid).

The act ordering detention is represented by a reasoned ordinance in which, in addition to the reasons for taking the measure, the day and time on which the detention begins and ends must be stated. Furthermore, the measure of taking in custody cannot be extended.

Judicial control (Articles 211–215 PPC)

Judicial control is an alternative to pre-trial detention and can be taken at each stage of the criminal trial by the magistrate investigating the case at that stage (prosecutor or judge). Judicial control may therefore be ordered by the prosecutor, the court, the judge of rights and liberties[2] and the judge of the preliminary chamber.[3] This measure may be taken by the prosecutor to achieve the purpose set out in Article 202 PPC. As regards the judge of rights and liberties, s/he may order the application of the measure of judicial control if s/he substitutes pre-trial detention or house arrest.

During the criminal prosecution, the measure of judicial control may be ordered by the prosecutor or the judge of rights and liberties for a maximum period of 60 days. This period may be extended by the prosecutor if the grounds for taking the measure are maintained or new grounds have emerged justifying its extension, each extension not exceeding 60 days.

During the investigation stage, the duration of the judicial control measure may not exceed one year if the penalty provided for by law is a fine or imprisonment of no more than five years, or two years if the penalty provided for by law is life imprisonment or imprisonment of more than five years. During the trial stage, the total duration of the judicial control may not exceed a reasonable period and, in all cases, may not exceed five years from the time of referral for trial. Upon expiry of the time limits, the court may order another preventive measure, in accordance with the law.

If the measure is ordered by the prosecutor, during the criminal investigation, it will be done after the hearing of the defendant, in the presence of the lawyer chosen or appointed ex officio. The prosecutor orders the judicial control measure to be taken through a reasoned ordinance, which is communicated to the defendant. The defendant can file a complaint against the prosecutor's order establishing judicial control within 48 hours

While under judicial control, the defendant *must* comply with the following obligations:

- To appear before the criminal prosecuting body, the preliminary chamber judge or the court whenever called upon
- To immediately inform the judicial body which ordered the measure or before which the case is located of a change of residence
- To appear before the police station designated with the supervision by the judicial body which ordered the measure, in accordance with the surveillance programme drawn up by the police body or whenever called upon

In addition, the judicial body which ordered the measure, can require the defendant, during the judicial control, to comply with one or more of the following obligations:

- Not to exceed a certain territorial limit, set by the judicial body, except with the latter's prior approval (not to visit certain places without prior approval)
- Not to travel to specific places established by the judicial body or to move only to places established by the latter
- To wear an electronic surveillance system at all times
- Not to return to the family home, to not approach the injured person or the latter's family members, other participants in the commission of the crime, witnesses or experts or other persons designated by the judicial body and to not communicate with them directly or indirectly through any means
- Not to practice their profession or job or to carry out the activity in which they committed the criminal act
- To periodically communicate relevant information about their means of subsistence

- To undergo control measures, medical care or treatment, in particular for the purpose of detoxification
- Not to participate in sporting or cultural events or other public gatherings
- Not to drive specific vehicles as established by the judicial body
- Not to possess, not to use and not to carry weapons
- Not to issue checks (bank checks or other financial orders)

The manner of exercising judicial review is regulated by Law No. 253/2013 (Article 83), but also through a series of regulations/instructions issued by the General Inspectorate of the Romanian Police. Judicial review mainly involves regular reporting by the defendant to the police station according to an established schedule. In the context of judicial review, the police also exercise control over the way the defendant complies with the imposed obligations. For example, the supervising police officer contacts the medical unit in which medical treatment is provided to obtain the necessary information for surveillance. In the case of a defendant who has been required not to approach the injured person or her/his family members, the accused will contact these persons and provide them with his contact details and the concrete ways in which the police can be referred in case of non-compliance with the obligation.

Regarding the obligation to provide for the possibility of the defendant always wearing an electronic surveillance system, it should be noted that the system ensuring the application of that obligation is not fully operationalised. Implementation of the electronic monitoring (EM) system started in October 2022 and the system is expected to be operational nationwide in 2025. Nowadays, EM is applied as an experiment for domestic violence cases when the restriction order is applied to protect the victim.

Judicial control on bail (Articles 216–217 PPC)

As a regulatory method, the measure of judicial control on bail is like that of the judicial control. The notable difference is that its application is conditional to the defendant submitting financial bail, through depositing a specified amount of money at the disposal of the judicial body, or by lodging a warranty or guarantee, concerning movable or immovable property, within a specified amount of money, in favour of the same judicial body.

As for financial bail, the Criminal Procedure Code provides only the minimum amount that can be deposited, namely 1,000 lei (€200). The precise amount in a given case is determined by the judicial body in relation to the gravity of the accusation brought against the defendant, the latter's economic situation and their legal obligations. Furthermore, the regime of time limits and obligations which may be imposed on the defendant against whom the judicial control measure has been applied is also applicable to the defendants on whom judicial control on bail has been imposed.

If during the period of the judicial control on bail, defendants breach their obligations in bad faith or there is reasonable suspicion that they have intentionally committed a new offence for which criminal proceedings against them have been ordered, the judge of rights and liberties, the judge of the preliminary chamber or the court, at the reasoned request of the prosecutor or ex officio, can order the replacement of this measure with the measure of house arrest or preventive arrest, under the conditions laid down by law as well as the confiscation of bail (Article 217 para. 9 CPC).

House arrest (Articles 218–222 PPC)

House arrest or home detention is a preventive measure involving the deprivation of liberty and consisting of the obligation imposed on defendants, for a specified period, not to leave the premises where they live, without the permission of the judicial body which ordered the measure or before which the case is tried, and to submit to restrictions laid down by the latter, for the purpose of proper conduct of the criminal trial.

The Penal Procedure Code does not allow the enforcement of this measure in the case of defendants against whom there is reasonable suspicion that they have committed an offence against a family member, nor in the case of a defendant who has previously been convicted for escape. During the criminal prosecution, the measure is ordered by the judge at the proposal of the prosecutor.

During house arrest, the defendant must comply with the following obligations:

- To appear before the criminal prosecuting body, the judge of rights and liberties, the judge of the preliminary chamber or the court whenever called upon
- Not to communicate with the injured person or the latter's family members, other participants in the commission of the offence, witnesses or experts and any other persons who do not normally live with them or are not in their care

Leaving the premises where the measure is being carried out is permitted to appear before the judicial bodies at their request. Furthermore, at the reasoned request of the defendant, the court may allow them to leave the premises to attend work, training courses or similar activities or for acquiring means of subsistence, as well as in other duly justified situations, for a specified period, if this is necessary for the realisation of the defendant's legitimate rights or interests. In case of emergency, for valid reasons, the defendant may leave the building without permission immediately informing the institution, body or authority designated with their supervision and the competent judicial body (Article 221 para. 7 CPC).

Verifying the way the defendant complies with the measure is mainly the responsibility of the police authorities who may enter the building where the measure is carried out, without the agreement of the defendant or of the persons living with the latter.

During the criminal prosecution, house arrest may be imposed for a maximum period of 30 days and may be extended only if necessary, if the grounds for taking the measure are maintained or new grounds have arisen, each extension not exceeding 30 days. The maximum duration for which it can be granted at this procedural stage is 180 days.

If the defendant is ultimately given a custodial sentence, the period of house arrest shall be deducted from the sentence imposed by equating one day of pre-trial house arrest to one day of the sentence.

Pre-trial detention (Articles 223–240 PPC)

Pre-trial detention is the most severe preventive measure and, according to the Penal Procedure Code, it can only be ordered by the court if the evidence gives rise to reasonable suspicion that the defendant has committed an offence and there is one of the following situations:

1 The defendant fled or hid in order to evade criminal prosecution or trial, or made preparations of any kind for such acts.
2 The defendant attempts to influence another participant in the commission of the offence, a witness or an expert, or to destroy, alter, conceal or steal material evidence or cause another person to engage in such conduct.
3 The defendant puts pressure on the injured party or tries to make a fraudulent arrangement with the latter.
4 There is reasonable suspicion that, after the criminal proceedings against him have been initiated, the defendant has intentionally committed a new offence or is preparing to commit a new offence.

First of all, irrespective of the aforementioned reasons, the measure may also be taken if the evidence gives rise to reasonable suspicion that the defendant has committed an intentional offence against life, an offence which caused personal injury or the death of a person, an offence against national security provided for in the Criminal Procedure Code and other special laws, an offence of drug trafficking, arms trafficking, human trafficking, acts of terrorism, money laundering, counterfeiting of coins or other values, blackmail, rape, deprivation of liberty, tax evasion, assault, judicial assault, a corruption offence, an offence committed by means of electronic communication or another offence for which the law provides for a prison sentence of five years or more. Subsequently, on the basis of assessing the gravity of the act, the manner and circumstances of its commission, the entourage/peer-group and the environment from which it originates, the criminal history and other circumstances concerning the person, it is found that the latter's deprivation of liberty is necessary in order to remove the danger for the public order.

The defendant's pre-trial detention may be ordered for a period of up to 30 days.

During the criminal prosecution, pre-trial detention may be extended if the grounds for the initial arrest still require the deprivation of liberty of the accused or there are new grounds justifying the extension of the measure. The extension may be granted for a maximum period of 30 days and the total duration of the defendant's preventive arrest during the criminal prosecution may not exceed a reasonable period and may not exceed 180 days.

If the court considers that the conditions laid down by law for prolonging the preventive arrest of the defendant are not met, it will reject the prosecutor's proposal and order the replacement of the preventive arrest with the measure of judicial control, judicial control on bail or house arrest.

During trial, the total duration of the defendant's pre-trial detention may not exceed a reasonable period and may not exceed half the special maximum laid down by law for the offence which is the subject of referral to the court. In all cases, the duration of preventive arrest in the first instance may not exceed five years. In practice, there are no guidelines (elaborated by Superior Council of Magistracy or National Institute for Magistracy) regarding the concept of reasonable period. Judges correlate this concept with aspects such complexity of the case or the attitude of the defendant during prosecution.

Decision-making: the role of judges, public prosecution/police and the position of the suspect

As mentioned earlier, Romania belongs to the civil law tradition and therefore all procedural steps must be grounded on legal texts. Article 202 of the Penal Procedure Code stipulates that preventive measures may be imposed if there are evidence or solid indices that can lead to a reasonable suspicion that a certain person has committed a crime and if these measures are needed to ensure the good management of the trial, or to prevent flight or a new crime. Later, the same article stipulates that any preventive measure must be proportionate to the seriousness of the crime and necessary to the aims mentioned earlier.

In this section, we will elaborate further on the procedural aspects concerning the use of pre-trial detention and alternatives, aiming to capture the mental steps that all those involved are taking to reach a decision related to a preventive measure, and the factors which influence these internal processes.

Interviews conducted during the DETOUR study (see Chapter 1) highlighted that the decisions ordering the measure of pre-trial detention are usually appealed by the defendant. In cases where an alternative preventive measure is ordered instead of pre-trial detention, the appeal is exercised by the prosecutor.

In general, the judges and prosecutors we have interviewed consider that the practice around pre-trial detention has evolved in recent years, and is now much more balanced, which confirms the statistical data presented at the beginning of this chapter:

> The practice has evolved recently. First, PTD was imposed by the prosecutors, now we have the judges applying it. Later the ECtHR jurisprudence became more important. Of course, the first steps were a little insecure but now I think it is balanced.
>
> (Judge 3)

Or

> I think nowadays the PTD is an exceptional measure. Every measure is analyzed and alternatives are considered.
>
> (Judge 2)

On the other side, lawyers seem to think that some personal factors related to the defendant are not taken seriously when imposing the measure:

> [...] when the offence was committed, previous history, specialization etc. The courts do not pay enough importance to these issues.
>
> (Lawyer 1)

In this case, the lawyers are in favour of introducing a new report from the probation service that can provide more accurate and objective information about the defendant's personal circumstances that should be considered by the judge when imposing preventive measures.

Based on the interviews with the judges and prosecutors, it seems that the decision-making process follows a two-step procedure. In the first stage, the judges seem to evaluate the offence and the person. In this respect, the following factors seem to be considered: the seriousness of the offence, the offence circumstances, the personal circumstances, and the way the crime was committed.

In most of the cases, the seriousness of the offence seems to play a key role:

> If I refer only to my own activity because I work with cases of violence, homicide and attempted murder, I can almost say that preventive arrest is a rule. But this is the nature of the offenses I work with; they are violent crimes, most of them against life. The automatic rule in these crimes is to impose PTD. As a rule, if we look to all the prosecution practice, PTD is an exception.
>
> (Prosecutor 1)

Another stated:

> For violent offenses, such as crimes against life, PTD is applied for almost all cases. The same goes, for example, in case of murder or attempted murder, battery resulting in death, rape and so on. Regarding robbery offenses, which also involve an element of violence, the practice is much more diverse as we have different forms of robbery: robbery under threat, robbery with guns, robbery by snatch or robbery through simple violence.
>
> (Judge 8)

In terms of influential factors, following the seriousness of the offence is the risk of reoffending and the attitude of the offender during the investigation and the hearings. In this evaluation, judges mentioned several times that more reliable information on the personal circumstances of the defendant could make a difference in using the alternatives.

The second step of the reasoning is the evaluation of the risk of absconding, influencing the witnesses or tampering with the evidence. In this analysis it seems that prosecutors and judges do not have any coherent guideline. In most cases they seem to count on their instinct and on the defendant previous behaviour.

In terms of decision-making, most stakeholders emphasised the complexity and the dynamic nature of the process. It is almost impossible to say *de plano* which is the most important factor in the decision-making process. What matters is how they interrelate and how the whole picture is taken into account:

> Even in sexual offences where the probability of pre-trial detention is high or when dealing with homeless people, the decision is corroborated with many other factors. Are they employed, is there a fixed address, what is the criminal history of the person, what about the substance abuse etc.? I would not be able to say: only one factor – let's say the lack of a fixed address – could lead automatically to the PTD decision. It is rather a corroborated decision where the whole ensemble is taken into account.
>
> (Judge 1)

Overall, judges and prosecutors stated they have enough resources of time and staff to make high quality decisions. However, more reliable information on the personal circumstances of the defendant may further enhance the quality of decision.

Bail and other alternatives

The previous sections examined the legal framework and the procedure around the use of preventive measures. In this section, we will refer to the alternatives to pre-trial detention and the stakeholder's perceptions regarding their use. In other words, we will look at how judges, prosecutors and lawyers evaluate the use of alternatives to pre-trial detention in Romania. When we talk about the alternatives to pre-trial detention in Romania, we mean judicial control, judicial control on bail and house arrest.

Regarding the use of alternatives in Romania, it seems to be a consensus among the stakeholders that there is a significant progress in the recent years. This progress seems to be supported by many factors, such as: the new Penal Procedure Code, the European Court of Human Rights jurisprudence but also changes in mentality:

> I think the vision regarding the alternatives has changed as well. It is a matter of mentality that not all the offenders should go to pre-trial detention. There are other measures that the prosecutor could impose. They have noted that these alternatives work and maybe they do not ask for PTD if not necessary.
>
> (Judge 4)

Training provided in the National Institute of Magistracy (NIM) seems to also influence the new approach:

> There are new generations now. There are prosecutors that entered the system in the last 3–4 years and they come with a different vision. I have seen this also among the new judges. The new ones seem to be more open to use alternative measures . . . they seem to start the analysis from the alternatives and not from the PTD.
>
> (Judge 1)

or

> The new magistrates are now called "human rights activists" as the training in NIM is very much based on human rights and ECHR jurisprudence.
>
> (Judge 3)

The most popular alternative to pre-trial detention seems to be judicial control. It appears that judges and prosecutors have confidence in this measure to ensure the good management of the trial while protecting the rights of the defendant:

> Judicial control allows the person's mobility. . . . It allows the supervision of not leaving the country or a locality. Yet, he may go to work, school, etc. He is permitted also to appear before the court or criminal prosecution body when asked to do so.
>
> (Judge 5)

However, the participants in the study argued also that sometimes this measure is overused and almost automatically prolonged. Unfortunately, there is no statistical data available to support this observation.

Another criticism was that sometimes the police capacity of monitor a large number of defendants is in doubt. In this direction, most judges stated that they would feel more confident in this measure if electronic monitoring infrastructure would exist and would allow real time surveillance of those under judicial control or house arrest.

Judicial control on bail seems to be quite rarely used due to its deficits in the law. In this case many judges complained about the lack of clarity:

> It is a rather ineffective measure because the steps that need to be taken are not clearly regulated. Some (judges n.red.) say there are two steps. As a first step, you notify him of his duty to plan to pay a bail, and after he pays, you install the measure of control. Here, the regulation in the Criminal Procedure Code is to be improved.
>
> (Judge 5)

Or the lack of capacity to pay the bail:

> And we still have to consider the reduced financial possibilities and a certain kind of mentality that some prefer to stay behind bars rather than pay.
>
> (Judge 5)

The lack of guidance on how to set the amount of bail is another difficulty that makes judicial control on bail a rather *rara avis* among the alternatives used in practice.

House arrest is evaluated by most respondents as an effective alternative to pre-trial detention. In many cases it is used after pre-trial detention to ease the severity of the preventive measure. Although it is quite popular among judges, there are at least two limitations that were mentioned during the interviews. The first one is that house arrest is deducted from the prison term exactly like in the pre-trial detention case. This was perceived by some respondents as unfair as conditions of pre-trial detention and house arrest differ significantly:

> We have had some objection in taking the HA measure because there is a rule that the time on HA is deduced from the length of the punishment applied at the end of the trial. This aspect did not seem quite fair or equitable at least to the person in PTD. Many defendants are on HA, sometimes for a long period of time, and they deduct the same days, as the defendants who were on PTD. From this point of view, we have had some reservations.
>
> (Judge 4)

Another criticism is that police has limited capacity to oversee these measures. Again, electronic monitoring was seen as an effective solution to strengthen this measure:

> So, my personal point of view is to introduce an automatic system, such as the monitoring bracelets, to render these measures efficient. Of course, it is not infallible, but it is much better than what we have now, that is to have the policeman call him up from time to time or to call on his home and to make a visit when he is around.
>
> (Judge 6)

European aspects

One of the most important moment in the transformation of pre-trial detention in Romania was the ratification of the European Convention of Human Rights (1994). Besides the human rights standards that became a sort of mantra in the coming years, the Convention also acknowledged the jurisprudence of the European Court of Human Rights (ECtHR) in matters related to human rights.

In this respect, Romania was affected by many ECtHR decisions related to the excessive use of pre-trial detention. In cases such as *Creanga v. Romania* (23 February 2012, 29226/03) or *Tase v. Romania* (10 September 2008, 29761/02), Romania was encouraged to apply pre-trial detention with moderation and only after considering concrete factors in each case. These cases are now part of the training provided by the National Institute of Magistracy and contribute to the shaping of the new approach on pre-trial detention.

Another important development in the European law that has the potential to influence the pre-trial detention practice in Romania is the transposition of the Framework Decision No. 2009/829 on the European Supervision Order (see also chapter 14).

According to the Romanian transposition law, all prosecutors and all judges dealing with alternatives to pre-trial detention, may issue certificates under the FD 2009/829. As an Executing State, the central authority for the implementation of this FD are the Prosecution Office of the High Court of Cassation and Justice (during the investigation phase) and the Ministry of Justice (during the trial stage). After performing an administrative check, the certificates are sent to the territorial prosecution office or the district court, depending on the procedural stage.

In the last two years (2018–2020), the FD 2009/829 was used only in 25 incoming cases – 21 during in the investigation phase and four in the trial stage. The main reasons behind this underuse, as mentioned by the Romanian prosecutors and judges involved in the study, were the time-consuming nature of the procedure, the bureaucratic burden that comes with it and the low number of cases where the procedure seems necessary.

Concluding remarks and suggestions

Despite the significant reforms in the use of pre-trial detention and its alternatives in the recent years, more changes could be implemented to improve the position of defendants in the procedure and in a responsible use of pre-trial detention alternatives. One of the first measures we think could be useful would be an in-depth analysis of the use of judicial control. Unfortunately, this study was not able to use relevant statistics (the main reason being that the institutions involved do not have an integrated system regarding preventive measures), but based on the judiciary's accounts we may suspect a net-widening effect in its use. We are not sure that, in the absence of judicial control, the defendants would be under pre-trial detention. There is a real risk that judicial control may be used instead of complete freedom while under investigation and trial.

The second important change that could reinforce the alternatives could be the development of an electronic monitoring infrastructure and a responsible use of it. It is possible that such a reform could strengthen judicial control and house arrest and therefore diminish the use of pre-trial detention.

We appreciate that there are premises for an extensive application of alternative measures represented by a more precise regulation of their framework in the Code of Criminal Procedure, ECtHR jurisprudence that emphasises the priority of these measures (especially given the existing problems at the level of detention facilities) and a training of judges in which the importance of alternatives is emphasised.

Notes

1 Council of Europe at https://rm.coe.int/16809390a6 (accessed 13 February 2023).
2 According to the provisions of Article 53 of the Code of Criminal Procedure, the judge of rights and freedoms is the judge that, during criminal investigation, decides upon applications, proposals, complaints, challenges or any other motions referring to preventive measures; asset freezing; temporary safety measures or acts performed by prosecutors, in cases explicitly stipulated by law.
3 According to the provisions of Article 54 of the Code of Criminal Procedure, a Preliminary Chamber Judge is a judge who, in court, according to its jurisdiction, verifies the lawfulness of the prosecutions ordered by prosecutors; verifies the lawfulness of evidence production and of the performance of process acts by criminal investigation bodies; rules on challenges against decisions to not initiate a criminal investigation or to drop charges; rules on other situations explicitly stipulated by law.

References

APADOR-CH (2015) *Is Pre-trial Detention Used as Last Resort Measure in Romania?* – Research Report at www.fairtrials.org/app/uploads/2022/01/Pre-trial-detention-in-Romania-by-APADOR-CH.pdf [accessed 3 January 2023].

Doseanu, R.-V. (2015) 'Omisiunea audierii in calitate de inculpat urmată de formularea unei propuneri de arestare preventivă (Hearing failure as a defendant putting

forward followed by arrest)', *Impactul transformărilor socio-economice şi tehnologice la nivel national, european si mondial*, 6: 42–48.
Doseanu, R.-V. and Doseanu, L.-S. (2015) 'Aspecte practice privind înlocuirea masurii arestarii preventive cu masura controlului judiciar pe cautiune', *Dreptul*, 6: 181–190.
Grigorie, I. (2015) 'Scurte consideraţii privind măsurile preventive privative de libertate în reglementarea noului cod de procedură penală', *Revista de Stiinte Juridice*, 29(2): 263–272.
Ivan, M.-C. and Ivan, G. (2016) 'Solutionarea propunerii de arestare preventiva a inculpatului în cursul urmaririi penale', *Dreptul*, 3: 158–180.
Potrivitu, G. (2015) 'Unele consideraţii teoretice şi practice referitoare la controlul judiciar şi controlul judiciar pe cauţiune', *Dreptul*, 1: 174–178.
Tomuleţ, C. (2016) 'Interese contradictorii în materia arestării preventive', *Caiete de drept penal*, 12(1): 72–103.
Tuculeanu, A. and Sima, C. 'Temeiurile retinerii si ale arestarii preventive in reglementarea Noului Cod de Procedura Penala' *Curierul Judiciar*, 2: 95–101.

Chapter 10

The basis for decision-making

Legal grounds, factual motives and influential factors

Walter Hammerschick and Skirmantas Bikelis

Introduction

The descriptions of the fundamental legal regulations with respect to PTD in jurisdictions represented in this book indicate that the basic principles are quite similar and respect the standards set by the ECHR and the jurisprudence of the ECtHR with regard to Article 5(1) and (3). The following principles can be viewed as common across the countries. A person may only be remanded in custody if the following conditions are satisfied:

- There is a reasonable suspicion that s/he committed an offence and a reasonable likelihood that s/he will face conviction and prison sentence if found guilty.
- There are substantial reasons to believe that, if released, he or she would either
  - try to avoid criminal investigations, trial and punishment;
  - interfere with the course of justice for instance by tampering with evidence or by influencing witnesses; or
  - commit (a) serious offence(s).[1]
- In view of both the presumption of innocence and the presumption in favour of liberty PTD of persons suspected of offences shall be the exception.
- The proportionality principle in criminal matters requires that coercive measures are only used when this is proportionate, considering the offence as well as the expected sentence and only for as long as required.
- Remand in custody shall only be used as a measure of last resort when less severe alternatives are insufficient to exercise needed control over the suspect and to guarantee his or her presence at trial.

From these starting points, this chapter explores in more detail the grounds and the motives for the imposition of PTD in practice, as well as other factors reported to be influential in the decision-making process.

DOI: 10.4324/9781003159254-10

The legally defined grounds for pre-trial detention in practice

The risk of absconding and preventive grounds

Looking at the use of the grounds for detention in practice, the countries represented in this study, at first sight, appear divided in two groups: on the one hand countries in which PTD is mostly grounded on the assumption that suspects will try to avoid criminal procedures, convictions and punishment; while on the other, countries which place more emphasis on the risk of offending ground. The responses of participants in the research presented in this work (see Chapter 1 for further details on the research designs) along with available data indicate that this first group includes Germany, Ireland and Lithuania.[2] Besides the risk of interfering with the course of justice, the grounds for detention which focus on securing the proceedings can be viewed as the "classic" or traditional bases for PTD. The term "classic" refers to the fact that these grounds are directed at securing the criminal investigations, the criminal proceedings, verdicts and finally the execution of sentences, which are, taken together, the motivations historically central to how most legal systems have used PTD proceedings (e.g. Morgenstern, 2018). Risks with respect to interfering with the course of justice only play a minor role in all countries observed – such applications primarily concern the early stages of the proceedings and, mostly, cases involving several suspects. Only in Belgium was the risk of collusion reported to be applied quite frequently in the early stages of the investigations, and notably in drug related crimes.

In Austria, Belgium and the Netherlands it is mainly preventive reasons which are most often employed as a basis for PTD. Interestingly, for instance, Austria and Germany the two neighbouring countries with very similar legal traditions appear to be in contrast with each other in this respect. While in Austria available data shows that the risk of reoffending is applied in about 90% of all PTD-cases (Birklbauer et al., 2011), it is the opposite in Germany with more than 90% of all PTD-cases based on a risk of absconding (Chapter 5). With an estimated rate of applications in about 60% of all PTD cases, the risk of absconding is also often applied in Austria, while in Germany the risk of reoffending was explained to play a minor role being only applied in about 6% of all PTD cases (ibid). The dominance of the risk of reoffending in Austrian PTD-practice appears, not least, due to very detailed regulations with respect to this ground for detention which allow for diverse options to apply it.[3] These regulations were reported to have been introduced in 1993 not least in order to reduce the frequent application of this ground at that time (Hammerschick and Reidinger, 2017). This obviously has not worked, providing an example of the difficulty in regulating and reducing PTD via legal changes. The legal requirements for the risk of absconding in order to justify PTD were explained by Austrian participants as being more difficult to be fulfilled. In contrast the risk of reoffending was repeatedly referred to as the ground for detention one would prefer, because it is a strong ground rather easily applied in many cases (Chapter 2). The broad scope of application of this ground is also emphasised by the fact that it is often applied in rather minor cases involving so-called criminal tourists who are, for instance, accused of engaging in multiple property offences (primarily shop-lifting) as a source of regular income, and who travel into Austria for this purpose. The outcomes of the German research, on the contrary, indicate that the risk of absconding is the ground for detention applied most easily, which can be explained by reference to the legal requirements (Morgenstern, 2018 and chapter 5). In this jurisdiction, the risk of reoffending is defined as a subsidiary ground for detention only applicable if none of the other grounds apply and it depends on additional criteria; for example, that the alleged offence must be committed "repeatedly or continually".

According to estimates in Lithuania, the risk of absconding is applied in 80 to 90% of all PTD-cases, mostly in combination, and frequently together with a risk of reoffending (about 50% of all PTD cases – Chapter 7). As in Germany, here the risk of absconding is described as being applicable without particular restrictions. Despite there being references to the regular use of the risk of reoffending as a ground for PTD in Romania as well, securing the criminal investigation, the trial and punishment were reported as the primary motivation.

A critique discussed with respect to the risk of reoffending as a ground for detention refers to the combination of motivations associated with criminal prosecution and the objectives of crime prevention (Morgenstern, 2018). Detaining a person at the pre-trial stage on the basis of a risk of offending blurs the distinction between the prosecution of an offence which is the trigger for the PTD proceedings and managing contemplated future offences. This ground poses the greatest challenges for the presumption of innocence. Ireland only introduced this ground for detention in 1997 with a new Article (40.4.6) to the Irish Constitution. In doing so a ruling of the Supreme Court was overturned, which had denied this ground for detention because it would allow for a preventive justice (*People [Attorney General] v. O'Callaghan [1966] I.R. 501*); this ruling held that detention for preventive reasons would not be compatible with the key rationale of bail being a measure to secure the proceedings. Despite the risk of reoffending now having been an option to justify detention for more than 20 years the legal culture expressed by the Supreme Court ruling appears still enduring and influential (Rogan, 2022). This demonstrates how important and persistent legal traditions and legal culture are for actual practice. The "new" ground, which asks for rather concrete evidence for the risk of committing mostly relatively serious offences, indeed is applied, mostly in combination with other grounds. The risk of absconding or of otherwise evading justice by failing to appear at the court, however, remains the ground for detention most often applied in Ireland (Chapter 6).

As in the other countries, prior record, expected sentences, residential status/regular place of living, social ties (e.g. family, employment) in the country are criteria employed to substantiate the grounds in Bail-/PTD-decisions. Because of the practical importance of the risk of failing to appear at the court the bail-history of a suspect plays a central role in Ireland, with prior violations increasing the likelihood of PTD considerably (ibid). In the other countries, this aspect was hardly addressed. This may be partially explained by the limited use of alternatives to PTD in some countries (e.g. Germany, Austria), which also limits the possibility of failures, or by high numbers of foreign nationals, who often don't have records in the country of the proceedings (e.g. Belgium). All in all, the focus on the likelihood of the proceedings going ahead versus an emphasis on the person's likelihood of committing offences seems to make an important difference to outcomes in the countries studied here.

An interesting aspect of the assessment of a risk of absconding was stressed in Lithuania: against the background of many Lithuanians leaving the country for economic reasons, attention is paid to their contacts and social ties outside the country, with the assumption being that there are higher risks of absconding in such cases. Social ties with other countries are also considered in the assessment of risks of flight in the other countries studied, however mainly with respect to non-nationals lacking ties to the country where the criminal procedures take place.

Looking again at the dominance of preventive grounds, Belgium and the Netherlands seem to represent this position most sharply. Similar to Austria, in both countries the legal possibilities for an assumption of a risk of reoffending appear rather broad and practitioners there also described this ground as being one which can be justified quite easily (Chapters 8 and 12). In both countries it was also explained by practitioners that the assumption of a risk of reoffending does not necessarily require a prior record of offending, and that social conditions and personal problems (e.g. substance dependency, financial problems, aggression, etc.) may suffice to justify this ground for detention (Boone et al., 2017; Maes et al., 2017). In these countries, the legal concept and rationales behind the dominance of preventive considerations appear to be broader than in Austria. Central to the legal provisions for PTD in Belgium and in the Netherlands, is the notion of "public security". In Belgium a warrant is only possible when it is absolutely necessary for public security. In the view of practitioners, however, this criterion appears to be fulfilled rather easily, and does not require detailed substantiation. Besides applying broad definitions of risks with respect to security aspects (e.g. the security of the state), in the Netherlands, there is also a specific ground requiring PTD in circumstances where it is argued there is a need to facilitate expedited proceedings against people suspected of unsettling crimes in public areas, (what we might also call disturbing the peace) or against public officials (policemen, firemen and ambulance staff). An aspect possibly explaining part of the lesser use of the risk of absconding to justify PTD is the fact that Belgium[4] and the Netherlands also allow for trials and verdicts in the absence of the suspect, while this is for instance not permissible in Germany. In Austria, proceeding in the absence of the suspect is also possible, but is rarely done according to the judges interviewed, probably because of the rather narrowly defined conditions which have to be fulfilled.[5] The option to have trials *in absentia* appears to reduce further the application of the risk of absconding ground.

Statistics on the number of pre-trial detainees per 100,000 of the population (PTD rate) in our country sample (Figure 1.1) suggest that the countries focusing on preventive aspects in PTD decisions in the tendency have higher pre-trial detainee rates than those focusing primarily on securing the criminal investigation, the trial and punishment (ibid, see also Rogan, 2022). The rather high detention rate of Lithuania seemingly does not support this hypothesis, but must be explained in a historical-political context: Lithuania underwent far reaching political, legal and societal changes in the recent past which already lead to considerable declines in the numbers of detainees. Considering the political past and also the relatively high overall prisoner rate (Figure 1.1), Romania meanwhile managed to have a surprisingly low rate of PTD.

The seriousness of offences and decisions on pre-trial detention

The seriousness of the alleged offences is an aspect considered in all countries in decision-making on PTD (or release). Not least the seriousness of the offence is also an aspect highly relevant for the assessment of the proportionality of PTD. Interestingly, the issue of proportionality was rarely addressed by practitioners in the DETOUR study. While occasionally practitioners in Germany spoke of PTD as disproportionate for minor offences, some judges and prosecutors in Austria and Belgium explained the proportionality principle to be fulfilled easily, considering the sentences expected in these cases. Not very surprisingly, some defence lawyers had a different perspective (e.g. in Austria and Belgium). In fact, the assessment of the seriousness of offences appears to be subject to a wide margin of discretion in all countries observed in this study. The research indicated, however, that there were quite diverse definitions or assessments even within the jurisdictions on this issue, which makes comparisons between the countries unfeasible. The research on Germany presented here (Chapter 5) for instance shows a remarkable variation within the sample and even among practitioners of the same profession. When asked about detention thresholds, some interview partners referred to minimum thresholds and explained that in some cases PTD was acceptable for crimes where a sentence of six months to one year of imprisonment can be expected. Others referred to higher thresholds, explaining that it was only for crimes carrying a minimum of five years of imprisonment that PTD was almost unavoidable (Chapter 5). While the expected sentence played a significant role in the interviews in all countries where empirical research was conducted, decisions on PTD generally will not exclusively be based on the seriousness of the alleged offence. At the very least, judges and prosecutors interviewed in the DETOUR project countries regularly explained that they look at a multitude of factors in their decisions.

The case of Germany shows, that in the most serious cases, mainly murder cases, the need is felt to detain suspects. The law therefore foresees the seriousness of the alleged offence in these cases as stand-alone ground. It was, however, not accepted as constitutional by the German Federal Constitutional Court and may be applied only in conjunction with one of the other grounds, namely, when a risk of flight cannot be excluded. The motivation behind this ground is the impact of such crimes on the public (Morgenstern, 2018 and Chapter 5). Similarly, in the Netherlands there is also a ground requiring PTD if someone is suspected of an offence subject to a sentence of 12 years or more in circumstances which give rise to serious indications that this will cause serious upset to the legal order, society, respectively (Chapter 8). Practitioners indicated that in practice this ground is mostly applied in a way which focuses on the severity of the offence and often lacks detail regarding the grounds giving rise to the alleged serious upset to the legal order; this was also of concern in recent decisions by the European Court of Human Rights (ibid). In Austria, the law requires PTD for offences subject to sentences of at least ten years, unless there are reasons to assume that all grounds for detention defined by law can be excluded (Chapter 2). In practice, offenders accused of such offences are always detained, giving rise to the assumption that the impact of homicide crimes on the public plays a role here as well. Homicide offences will lead to PTD in most countries, while this is not necessarily true for Ireland. Although it was reported that the seriousness of offences such as homicide or murder is a crucial factor regularly resulting in objections to bail, it was also reported that even in murder cases judges would not always deny bail (Rogan and Perry, 2017). Even more surprising are reported examples from Lithuania, suggesting that there, too, the most severe offences (like murder or drug trafficking) do not always mean PTD (Chapter 7).

There are some kinds of offences which have been reported to have a rather high likelihood of PTD in general, such as sexual offences, severe violence, human trafficking or drug related crimes. In the Netherlands "high impact crimes", which are considered to have high impact on the general perception of safety and high rates of recidivism such as robbery and burglary were reported to almost automatically lead to PTD. From Austria, Belgium, Ireland and the Netherlands it was also reported that domestic violence would particularly often justify PTD. Some respondents from Austria and Ireland noted difficulties in assessing such cases.[6]

Additionally, in all countries, the seriousness of the alleged offence is a factor considered in the assessment of the risk of absconding because the length of the expected sentence is considered to be a motivating factor for flight. In some countries the seriousness of the alleged offence also influences decisions with respect to the risk of reoffending, for example, in Austria and the Netherlands there is, among other things, a definition of a risk of reoffending based on the seriousness of the offence. In Ireland, the risk of reoffending ground may only be used where certain offences are being prosecuted.

Substantiating the grounds

Time pressure and personal and social information on the suspects

The decisions on PTD or release with or without conditions are often defined by the little time available to prepare them (Chapter 11). Prosecutors and judges in the country case studies refer to the time pressure and some of them explain that the information available is often very restricted, but, generally, these actors do not complain about this situation. On the contrary, judges and prosecutors often explicitly thought of the available time and information as sufficient. Across the countries they apparently have arranged their practice accordingly and learned to deal with this situation. Concerning personal and social information on the suspects many practitioners report that there is often a lack of this kind of information (see also Hammerschick et al., 2021b). On the other hand, this kind of information is considered important and helpful for the decisions in general and particularly for the application of less severe measures or for release without conditions. Only in Romania do we see that rather little attention is paid to these aspects in the decision-making. In practice, this kind of information is mostly provided by the suspects themselves and/or is expected from the defence lawyer.

Social work support can play an important role in this respect. Apart from the support for the decision-makers and the decisions, the involvement of practical social work can actually also support the defendants to organise measures themselves that would allow the application of less severe measures (e.g. to find housing, possibly treatment or employment, etc.). In Germany the existing court aid for adults could be involved in this, but in practice never is, although its counterpart in the juvenile justice system is available and seen as doing useful work (Morgenstern, 2018). The juvenile justice court aid (Jugendgerichtshilfe) is also regularly employed in juvenile cases as in Austria, where this option is very well received, though it does not exist for adults (see also Hammerschick et al., 2021a). In the Netherlands, experiences with the option to involve the probation services are mixed, however participants gave positive evaluations of this system where sufficient resources were reported to be in place (Boone et al., 2017). In Belgium, probation officers can also be asked for reports, which is seldom done, however, due to time restraints (Chapter 3). Asked about this kind of support, prosecutors and judges in the DETOUR study responded very differently, some were in favour, others sceptical or opposed. Often, there is little time available for such involvement, which would also restrict the possibilities for social inquiries. The reluctance to support the possibility of social inquiries among practitioners appears hard to understand. Even though it is true that the little time available is a difficulty and even if the information might not be available in time for the first decision it still can be valuable for the following hearings and decisions (see also Hammerschick et al., 2022).

Decision-making and discretion

Looking at the main criteria considered in the assessment of the grounds for detention it appears that, to a large extent, these aspects are the same for the risk of absconding as well as for the risk of reoffending: Prior criminal records, seriousness of the charge, expected sentence, employment situation, (lack of) income, (lack of) social and/or family ties and even a lack of residency may not only be used to substantiate the risk of absconding but also for assessing the risk of reoffending.

One of the particularly interesting findings of this comparative study, therefore, is that the grounds for detention to some extent seem interchangeable, though much less so in England, Wales and Ireland, though, even there, when prosecutors are especially keen to advocate for PTD, both sets of grounds may be used as a kind of "back up" approach in the event that one ground fails. Our research also indicates that the grounds for detention applied are not necessarily the ones considered most relevant in individual cases. In Austria for instance, we see cases in which a central factual motivation for PTD was to avoid absconding, while a risk of reoffending is central to the formal motivation of detention. This was explained by the risk of reoffending being the ground which was easier to substantiate and because using such a ground would make it more certain that a suspect will remain in detention (Hammerschick and Reidinger, 2017). In Germany it was explained the other way around: there were indications that the ground of a risk of absconding may be applied in cases in which a risk of reoffending is, in fact, essential to the actual motivation for PTD (Morgenstern, 2018). As mentioned before, here the risk of absconding is considered the stronger ground and easier to apply. This gives rise to the impression that the normative framework for the legal grounds may be of lesser importance once decision-makers are convinced that PTD is necessary and are able to interpret the grounds in a way that fit to the factual risks (mainly posed by suspects in difficult social circumstances). Regarding the Netherlands, the DETOUR study and other research confirmed this assumption (Chapter 8). After having determined whether there is a case for PTD and a grave suspicion, judges will firstly see if they want the suspect remanded in custody or not.

Only then do they choose the right grounds on which to base their decision, most often the risk of reoffending, because of its broad definition. The actual motivation behind PTD may, in fact, differ and can be based on prevention, considerations of security, retribution/punishment and anticipation of the expected sentence, etc.

A critique reported from most countries refers to a prevailing practice of justifying PTD on the bases of rather general assumptions about the suspect accompanied by a lack of thorough assessment of the risk. In Germany the difficulty was expressed with regard to risk prognoses (Morgenstern, 2018). It is the case that such prognoses can be difficult, but we can assume that the quality of assessments benefits from broad information about the person and their social conditions. This situation again may therefore recommend institutional support to the courts concerning background or social inquiries. With respect to the risk of absconding, evidence from Germany and from Lithuania for instance suggests that practitioners feel such risk would be overstated regularly (ibid, and Chapter 7). A high risk of absconding is often not considered to be realistic or likely to transpire, as evading justice, and the consequent forfeiture of financial guarantees or sureties brings a huge burden and requires financial means which most suspects do not have. On the other hand, the Austrian, Dutch and Belgian studies feed the suspicion that the risk of reoffending may not only be assumed for the (rather short) time of the criminal proceedings but that practitioners in these jurisdictions consider risks beyond this timeframe.

The findings represented in this study suggest that much depends on the approaches and the personal attitudes of the individual decision-makers. Their discretionary power seems to be quite extensive and is hardly constrained by legal provisions such as explicit thresholds. This becomes, for instance, visible in the differing PTD practice in the east (rather extensive PTD) and in the west (less PTD) of Austria and significant regional differences between the Federal States in Germany (Morgenstern and Kromrey, 2016). Interestingly, judges and prosecutors often reported having little knowledge about the generally prevailing practice with respect to PTD and alternatives, which suggests rather limited reflection on their individual practice. Decisions on PTD require, of course, the exercise of discretion, and the limited time and information available for making such decisions must be taken into account, along with the complexity of cases. At the same time, however, considerable attention ought to be paid to the procedural and legal safeguards which protect of the rights of the suspects. In most of the countries in our study, the fact that judges rarely deny applications for PTD brought forward by the prosecution was criticised. Of course, the selection or filtering processes by the prosecutors have to be taken into account in understanding pre-trial detention practice. The very high rates of acceptance of applications reported (see also the results in Fair Trials, 2017) at least remind us of the need for critical assessments of such applications. Among the jurisdictions represented in the DETOUR study, Ireland stands out for its practice of it being unremarkable for applications for PTD to be denied, or, more precisely, for objections to bail not being upheld. In England and Wales, too, it cannot be said that a prosecution's application for PTD will be inevitably or routinely granted (Chapter 4).

Hidden and extra-legal grounds for pre-trial detention and motivations

Procedural economics, foreign nationals and general prevention

PTD appears sometimes motivated by the fact that it is the easiest way to secure the proceedings and to promote the investigations. There is an imminent danger that "procedural economics" as we may call them, may prevail over the ultima ratio principle. Legally, a permanent residence status within the European Union for instance is supposed to be treated as permanent residence within the country in which the proceedings are taking place (Chapter 14).[7] In interviews, for instance in Austria and in Belgium, but also in Germany, practitioners nevertheless express the view that European residency may not necessarily suffice to exclude an assumption of a risk of absconding. Practitioners explained this by reference to problems in verifying places of residence and addresses in other countries and to worries about apprehending suspects when abroad. Although the European Arrest Warrant was described in all countries as a tool functioning mostly well, some participants indicated worries about delays and bureaucratic hassle. In view of delays in the proceedings and of administrative difficulties participants reported that it may be tempting to keep the suspect in custody and at one's disposal rather than rely on a European Arrest Warrant in the future (see also Chapter 14).

In some of the project countries more than 50% of the pre-trial detainees are foreigners. (Austria, Belgium and Germany; see Chapter 13, Table 13.1). The frequent use of PTD for foreigners feeds the worry that foreigners may not be treated equally to nationals. The outcomes of our research do not imply that foreign nationals have a higher risk of detention per se. There are however certain groups of foreigners who definitely appear to have a higher risk than others, particularly "mobile offenders" also described by some as "criminal tourists" as well as, more generally, foreigners who lack social ties and proven residency, along with foreign nationals suspected to be involved in drug dealing. We can assume that for the majority of these groups the categorisation of having "precarious social conditions" applies to them. Suspects who are socially integrated have a better chance of avoiding PTD while others living in vulnerable conditions, and engaging in criminal activities for reasons related to poverty and marginality, are increasingly those in detention, often because of rather minor offences. States and societies are understandably anxious to prevent such offences, PTD, however, cannot be the tool to tackle this problem. Moreover, the situation of such individuals is compounded by the fact that the social conditions of the suspects often make it rather easy to substantiate grounds for detention.

In this context, on the one hand the question is whether the principle of proportionality and the risks assumed are always assessed adequately. On the other hand, it seems that general preventive considerations may influence the decisions made in this area. A few Austrian judges and prosecutors explicitly said that PTD for "criminal tourists" may sometimes also aim at deterring others, a view occasionally also presented in interviews conducted in Germany. In any case, we can suggest that the risks described are attributed in a blanket way to all members belonging to a certain group, rather than being sufficiently individually assessed in concrete cases.

Pre-sentence motivations

The notion that PTD may teach the suspect a lesson seems to be widespread. There is some room for interpretation, but this is at least close to what can be described as a "pre-sentencing motivation" that is, a desire to ensure the person spends some time in prison. In a powerful leading judgement, the Irish Supreme Court considered it an improper use of detention to "*. . . refuse bail to an unconvicted person for the purpose of giving him a taste of imprisonment*" (*People [Attorney General] v. O'Callaghan* [1966] I.R. 501 at 517). This statement of principle, however, is not being observed everywhere in the countries studied here. Some observations from research partners in the DETOUR project express motives which are quite clearly of a pre-sentencing nature. In the Netherlands and in Belgium we see, for example, participants reporting that judges in charge of PTD decisions may order detention because they are afraid that suspects may be able to fully avoid prison – in Belgium because of the fact that short term sentences are regularly substituted by non-custodial alternatives, in the Netherlands because the trial judges may be reluctant to send a suspect released from PTD back to prison (Maes et al., 2017; Chapter 8 and Boone et al., 2017). Closely connected to this, evidence from the Netherlands shows that decisions may be made to impose PTD because decision-makers fear being unable to explain to the public or to victims of serious crimes that a person who had just committed a serious crime would be released quickly (Boone et al., 2017).

Decisions in favour of PTD sometimes also appear to be promoted by the view that a suspect will face an unconditional prison sentence anyway. Since the time in PTD will be deducted from the sentence in all jurisdictions represented in this volume, this practice is explained as being for the benefit of the suspect, who can complete the prison term quickly rather than going back to prison after release. Leaving the presumption of innocence aside, this reasoning is nevertheless wrong: the conditions in PTD are often worse than in prison in general and the situation for the suspect is particularly difficult because of the many uncertainties he/she is confronted with. Release from PTD may also have favourable effects on the ability to prepare for a case, and to the eventual sentence, while detention may have a negative impact when it comes to the decision of suspending a prison sentence or not (indicated, for example in interviews with German defence lawyers and judges; Morgenstern, 2017).

Public perceptions and discussions and their influence on decision-makers

Judges and prosecutors in most countries regularly deny that the following matters influence their PTD- and bail-decisions: the media; political groups; public discussions about security in general and event-based ones in particular (Hammerschick et al., 2017). Responses, however, in all project countries indicate that such influences can indeed play a role. Even in Ireland where defence lawyers largely agreed with judges and prosecutors that there is no such influence in general, defence lawyers said that the prosecution might be more reluctant to consent to bail where sensitive features of a case might trigger negative media commentary. In Romania for instance public pressure appears to be regularly directed towards PTD in cases of public officials suspected of corruption. The Netherlands seems to be the only country represented in this study where public expectations and perceptions with respect to feelings of safety appear to be quite explicitly and largely undisputed considered factors relevant in decisions on PTD. This is also expressed by the fact that there is a ground for detention on the basis of indications that an offence will cause serious upset to the legal order (see earlier). The Dutch chapter, referring to wider research findings, further explained that judges not least aim at a feeling of safety amongst victim(s) and others affected by offences (Chapter 8).

Conclusions

The legal regulations and definitions concerning pre-trial detention provide a framework for the practical implementation of course directing the practice, but only to some extent. The actual practice appears particularly determined by the prevalent legal culture, a wide margin of discretion afforded to decision-makers and also societal developments and concerns. Considering the observation that countries which focus primarily on preventive aspects in their PTD practice tend to have rather high rates of PTD there seems to be some risk that PTD rates may rather rise than decline in the future. We further observe social changes accompanied by decreasing perceptions of safety, which are taken advantage of by political parties and groups to call for increased or more extensive mechanisms of control. This gives rise to concerns that preventive motives may generally gain more importance in PTD practice and that thereby detention rates may increase. Even in Ireland where risks of reoffending are still reported to be of subordinated relevance there were indications that this ground is becoming more significant and more likely to be used.

Considering the requirement/imperative that PTD is an exception and a measure of last resort, strategies employing PTD as a tool for prevention are the most critical to examine and to tackle. In view of the scenarios addressed earlier, it seems of utmost importance to work on and strengthen the understanding of prosecutors and judges about PTD being the ultima ratio. The legal culture in Ireland – rejecting strong preventive notions with regard to PTD – up to now persists and has not led to a breakdown of the criminal justice system or crime rates going astray. Apart from the different legal traditions, a different attitude has been expressed by all the key actors in Ireland which allows for the presumption in favour of bail to guide the practice in real terms.

We found a certain degree of interchangeability between the grounds for detention and the justifications provided for them respectively. Our research shows that, besides the official grounds for detention, there are also often hidden and extra-legal motives influencing the decisions. Additionally, some reports also referred to weak substantiation for the grounds applied. PTD practice across most countries therefore appears to be applied too easily, not sufficiently paying attention to the ultima ratio principle and the drastic infringement PTD means for personal rights. Understanding how persistent practice and culture can be, we do not assume this situation can be adequately improved by relying only on directives or legal changes. This scenario calls for continuing efforts with respect to awareness raising and training for prosecutor and judges. Building on reflections about the practice, such training should be directed at pushing back hidden motivations, adequately operationalising the principle of proportionality and paying attention to the assessment of the factual risks.

There are groups which can be observed as being particularly at risk of PTD. Foreign nationals do not have a higher risk of detention per se. There are however certain groups of foreign nationals who have a higher risk than others not least because of their "precarious living conditions" providing justifications for PTD. Criminal law cannot solve social inequalities. Its application however should try to avoid aggravating them.

Notes

1 In exceptional cases, a "shocked legal order" can also be the ground to order PTD (see later and Chapter 8).
2 In addition, England and Wales which has not been part of the original DETOUR project (see Chapter 4).
3 According to Section 173(2)(3) of the Code of Criminal Procedure, the ground for detention shall exist if, on the basis of certain facts, there is a risk that the accused,

while at liberty and notwithstanding the criminal proceedings against him for a criminal offence punishable by more than six months' imprisonment (a) will commit a punishable act with serious consequences directed against the same legal values as the punishable act with serious consequences with which he is charged, (b) will commit a punishable act with not merely minor consequences directed against the same legal values as the punishable act with serious consequences with which he is charged, if he has either already been convicted of such an offense or if he is now charged with repeated or continuing acts, (c) will commit an offence punishable by more than six months' imprisonment which, like the offence with which he is charged, is directed against the same legal values as the offences for which he has already been convicted twice; or (d) will carry out the attempted or threatened offense with which he is charged.

4 It should be noted that the risk of absconding is nevertheless also often applied with foreign nationals without residency in Belgium (see Chapter 2).

5 In cases with possible sentences of up to three years, if the suspect has already been interrogated with respect to the suspicion and if there is a registered address where summons can be delivered.

6 Mostly because of regularly contradicting statements of suspects and victims.

7 See, for instance, also ruling of the Austrian Supreme Court 11 Os 31/08f, 27 February 2008.

References

Birklbauer, A., et al. (2011) *Die Rechtspraxis des Ermittlungsverfahrens nach der Strafprozessreform – eine rechtstatsächliche Untersuchung*, Wien: Neuer Wissenschaftlicher Verlag.

Boone, M., Jacobs, P. and Lindeman, J. (2017) *Towards Pre-trial Detention as Ultima Ratio – 2nd Dutch National Report on Expert Interviews*, Utrecht at Microsoft Word – Final version_Netherlands_for_Web.docx (uibk.ac.at) [accessed 10 February 2023].

Fair Trials (2017) *A Measure of Last Resort? The Practice of Pre-trial Detention Decision Making in the EU* at www.fairtrials.org/wp-content/uploads/A-Measure-of-Last-Resort-Full-Version.pdf [accessed 10 February 2023].

Hammerschick, W. and Reidinger, V. (2017) *DETOUR – Towards Pre-trial Detention as Ultima Ratio – 2nd Austrian National Report on Expert Interviews*, Wien at Microsoft Word – 2nd Nat Report-Part AT corr fin221217.docx (uibk.ac.at) [accessed 10 February 2023].

Hammerschick, W., et al. (2017) *DETOUR – Towards Pre-trial Detention as Ultima Ratio – Comparative Report, Vienna at* Microsoft Word – Comparative report master fin.docx (uibk.ac.at) [accessed 10 February 2023].

Hammerschick, W., et al. (2021a) *Pre-triad Project – Alternative Pre-trial Detention Measures – D2.2 – Pre-trial Detention Alternatives: Best Practices* at d2.2.-pre-trial-detention-alternatives-best-practices.pdf (uibk.ac.at) [accessed 10 February 2023].

Hammerschick, W., et al. (2021b) *PRE-TRIAD Project – Alternative Pre-trial Detention Measures – D2.4 Interviews Report* at Microsoft Word – D2.4. Interviews Report.docx (uibk.ac.at) [accessed 10 February 2023].

Hammerschick, W., et al. (2022) *Pre-triad Project – Alternative Pre-trial Detention Measures – D3.1 Recommendation Paper on Pre-trial Detention National Application* at www.pretrial-detention.org/uploads/1/3/0/4/130474014/d3.1_-_recommendation_paper_on_pre-trial_detention_national_application.pdf [accessed 10 February 2023].

Maes, E., Jonckheere, A. and Deblock, M. (2017) *Towards Pre-trial Detention as Ultima Ratio – 2nd Belgian National Report on Expert Interviews* at 2nd Belgian National Report_Frontpage_DEF_v2017_12_19.pdf (uibk.ac.at) [accessed 10 February 2023].

Morgenstern, C. (2018) *Die Untersuchungshaft. Eine Untersuchung unter rechtsdogmatischen, kriminologischen, rechtsvergleichenden und europarechtlichen Aspekten*, Baden-Baden: Nomos.

Morgenstern, C. (2017) *DETOUR – Towards Pre-trial Detention as Ultima Ratio – 2nd German National Report on Expert Interviews*, Greifswald at 2nd-german-report_interview.pdf (uibk.ac.at) [accessed 10 February 2023].

Morgenstern, C. and Kromrey, H. (2016) *DETOUR – Towards Pre-trial Detention as Ultima Ratio – 1st National Report on Germany* at 1st-german-report.pdf (uibk.ac.at) [accessed 10 February 2023].

Rogan, M. (2022) 'Examining the role of legal culture as a protective factor against high rates of pre-trial detention: The case of Ireland', *European Journal on Criminal Policy and Research*, 28(3), 425–433.

Rogan, M. and Perry, D. (2017) *DETOUR – Towards Pre-trial Detention as Ultima Ratio – 2nd German National Report on Expert Interviews*, Dublin at 2nd-irish-report_interviews.pdf (uibk.ac.at) [accessed 10 February 2023].

Chapter 11

Actors, roles and responsibilities in the pre-trial detention decision-making process

Mary Rogan and Joep Lindeman

Introduction

This chapter will examine the key players in pre-trial detention proceedings: the prosecution; the defence; the judiciary; and the probation service, where this body is involved. It is based on the country chapters in this volume and findings from the DETOUR study (see Chapter 1). While many differences exist in practice across jurisdictions, and even within jurisdictions, it is notable that, across all countries included in this research, the position of the prosecution can be pivotal in terms of the practices implemented regarding pre-trial detention decision-making, as well as the culture which surrounds it. The relationship between judges and prosecutors is also a key influence in how pre-trial detention is used, where this relationship is close, there seems to be a higher use of pre-trial detention. As for defence lawyers, their role and influence can vary widely across countries, but where they are active and well resourced, they can contribute to an increased application of alternatives. The involvement of the probation service is also not consistent across countries.

The chapter will first outline the roles of the various players in the pre-trial detention decision-making process. It will then focus on the particular role of the prosecution. We will then explore the position of defence lawyers, and the common challenges they face across jurisdictions. We then assess the relative positions and influences of these actors and the dynamic between them, before examining the legal and social cultures which influence these relationships. Finally, we examine the position of the probation service, before concluding with some reflections on the lessons learned from our cross-jurisdictional assessment, and policy recommendations.

The key players

Across all countries included in this collection, it was clear that the dynamic between, and relative influence of, the prosecution, defence lawyers and the

DOI: 10.4324/9781003159254-11

judiciary were critical influences on pre-trial decision-making processes and outcomes. The role of the probation service is variable, and some actors in some countries question whether the probation service should be involved in PTD proceedings.

The prosecution

Across the countries explored in this collection, the initiative for pre-trial proceedings, or at least the initiative to seek pre-trial detention, lies with the prosecution. The prosecution often also leads the police investigation, and, in these cases, is the party with the most relevant information and evidence on the questions before the court. While the prosecution has a major influence across all countries in this collection, there are big differences across jurisdictions when it comes to the position of the prosecutor in the legal system, with some prosecutors having more autonomy than others, and some having a closer relationship with political actors than others. For example, in Germany, the head of the public prosecution authority in each Federal State (*Bundesland*) has a post that may be politically influenced since the respective Minister of Justice can issue orders to him or her and usually also influences the decision on who is appointed (Morgenstern, 2017).

Prosecutors play an important "filtering" role. Their decisions as to when and whether to instigate applications for pre-trial detention are of central importance to the process. In Germany, for example, falling numbers in PTD have been attributed at least in part to a more cautious practice by public prosecutors when requesting PTD, while in Ireland, as will be described further later, a certain self-restraint amongst prosecutors is viewed as a reason behind lower rates of PTD there.

Across all countries examined in this volume, there was little evidence of the prosecution actively seeking alternatives to PTD. However, we see variation in the powers which prosecutors have themselves to apply less severe sanctions outside of the formal PTD legal frameworks. For example, in Lithuania and Austria, prosecutors can and should apply less intrusive provisional measures, whereas, at least in Austria, these options are almost never used. In Lithuania, by contrast, the prosecution is somewhat zealous in applying alternatives, which can have the result that defendant may be in the net of increased conditions, when they might otherwise simply be at liberty.

Prosecutors in the Netherlands have very limited legal options to seek alternatives straightaway: most conditions for release can only be set *after* a judicial order for PTD. This means the prosecutor should apply for PTD first, before an eventual suspension of PTD with conditions can be considered. While legislation permits the prosecution to order PTD and ask for conditional suspension in the same application, this is not common practice. Proposals for a new Dutch code of criminal procedure hold a legal obligation for the judge to consider alternatives before ordering actual detention, but this provision is not yet in force. This situation already pertains in Germany. Notably, in Ireland as well as in England and Wales, the prosecution does not initiate an application for PTD, but rather resists or opposes an application for release, a difference which seems to play a large role in the development of a legal culture which looks at the application as one which starts with the position that there must be arguments for why the person should be detained, rather than arguments for why they should be released.

In countries where the prosecution can seek alternatives to PTD, in practice, these jurisdictions reported that such applications were constrained by the reality that finding suitable alternatives to PTD takes time and requires evidence and information which may not be readily available. As such, the administrative burden involved in seeking alternatives prevents prosecutors from doing so, with prosecutors in civil law jurisdictions described here reporting that a straightforward application for PTD is often the easiest option. This position is compounded by the fact that there is little societal encouragement for a broader use of alternatives – and sometimes even possible political encouragement *against* such use. As such, this approach seems unlikely to change in the current climate of criminal law enforcement.

A further feature of prosecution practice is also noteworthy. In the Netherlands, Germany and Belgium the prosecution is usually not present during the first judicial hearing concerning PTD, with prosecutors reporting that they do not have time to attend all these hearings. This also seems to set a lower threshold for the implementation of PTD, as prosecutors expressed a feeling that seeking PTD is a safer course of action, and that the case is in good hands with the judge, the defence lawyers and the suspect. In England and Wales, and indeed in Ireland, pre-trial detention hearings are adversarial. In England and Wales, for example, the prosecution is required to prove that the defendant poses a substantial bail risk and the right to unconditional bail should be rebutted (Chapter 4). Framing proceedings in this way seems to establish liberty as a starting point, placing a key obligation on the prosecution to place arguments before the court as to why a person must not be at liberty, rather than the defence having the burden of showing why the person should not be in detention, though the defence must provide arguments to support why bail should be granted. The difference in emphasis, perspective and perhaps role of the prosecution between England and Wales, and in Ireland, compared to continental European countries in this volume is also found in the practice of "consent to bail". As Hucklesby (Chapter 4) writes, the majority of bail hearings are not contested in England and Wales, even in cases where the prosecution had been requesting detention. While a consequence of this is that decisions must be taken on limited information in light of the early stage of the proceedings, it does have the effect of ensuring that the proceedings move, relatively, speedily.

The defence

The importance of the role of the defence lawyer in pre-trial proceedings can hardly be overrated. Their importance has been recognised in the creation of Council of Europe and European Union legal instruments on the tasks of defence lawyers in criminal proceedings (see also Chapter 14). The European Court of Human Rights (ECtHR) has emphasised that the defence plays a key role right from the moment a criminal charge exists (*Imbrioscia v. Switzerland*, 13972/88, 24 November 1993). In the past decade, since the Salduz judgment (*Salduz v. Turkey*, 36391/02, 27 November 2008), assistance from a lawyer in the earliest phase of the investigation has become be the norm, while in the Dayanan judgment (*Dayanan v. Turkey*, 7377/03, 13 October 2009), the court made clear that the term "assistance" refers to the whole range of services specifically associated with legal assistance which should be available to the suspect. Particularly focusing on PTD proceedings, the ECtHR held that in view of the dramatic impact of deprivation of liberty on the fundamental rights of the person concerned, PTD proceedings must in principle also meet – to the largest extent possible under the circumstances of an ongoing investigation – the basic requirements of a fair trial as guaranteed by Article 6 of the convention. This requires the equality of arms, and more specifically the disclosure of relevant documents and files (ECtHR, *Schöps v. Germany*, 25116/94; *Lietzow v. Germany*, 24479/94; *Garcia Alva v. Germany*, 23541/94; all 13 February 2001). In the meantime, the European Union has issued several relevant instruments, such as directives as well as a green paper and an impact assessment (see Chapter 14). All this makes clear that legal aid to remand prisoners is one of the core defence rights.

Across all the jurisdictions examined in this volume, defence lawyers feel that they play an important role and contribute significantly to the fairness of proceedings, as well as limiting the use of PTD. In Belgium, the Netherlands and Germany, defence lawyers emphasise that, if it wasn't for their input, alternatives to PTD would hardly be considered at all. In all countries, defence lawyers are found to be the parties pushing for alternatives to PTD.

Access to defence lawyers may be limited, however, by practical and cultural barriers, explored in more detail later. While funded legal aid is available for defence layers' participation in many countries, defence lawyers in Romania and Lithuania consider that state paid defence lawyers are not able to provide an adequate standard of representation, while in Austria, the manner in which the legal aid scheme is organised means that inexperienced lawyers are required to represent suspects. Inadequate funding has also been the subject of complaint in the Netherlands.

The desire for release, which defence lawyers may understandably possess, may give rise to potential net-widening concerns. Prosecutors may press for an alternative to PTD, or for the application of conditions on release, even in cases where PTD might be rejected by the judge outright. Defence lawyers may not always contest conditions, feeling that this might jeopardise the ultimate prize: release. Indeed, in Belgium and Germany, defence lawyers report concerns that lawyers may feel pressure to steer the proceedings towards the application of an alternative measure rather than risk the request for unconditional release being denied. In Ireland, too, defence lawyers reporting needing to be vigilant, as their clients may agree to any condition if it means avoiding PTD.

Judges

In accordance with Article 5 ECHR, in all countries represented in this volume, the judge is the final decision-maker concerning the use of PTD and therefore plays a decisive role. However, it is also clear that the dynamics between the different players can act to ensure that the judge does not take the decision in a vacuum. The decision is influenced by not only the facts of the case and the arguments presented, but also by the legal culture and relative positions of the prosecution and defence. As described further in the following, a particularly important relationship is the one between prosecution and judge, with civil law countries represented in this volume reporting that judges and prosecutors have shared views and understandings of the legal culture surrounding PTD. Informal communications between judges and prosecutors are also a feature of some countries, though not in Lithuania or Ireland, where such discussions would be considered irregular.

There was no strong sense in any of the countries represented here that the discretion afforded to judges was problematic. However, the level of proactivity of the judge regarding the pursuit of alternatives has been described as highly variable. In the Netherlands, for example, we see the attitude of the judge described as "passive" in this respect (Boone et al., 2017: 50). However, in Austria, judges do play a stronger role than prosecutors in putting forth the possibility of the use of an alternative. For Ireland, it was felt that judges were, on the whole, unlikely to rule that bail should not be granted when the prosecution was consenting to it, but that there may be situations where judges would question such an agreement.

Across many countries, we see concerns about a lack of time given to judges to prepare to hear applications for PTD. This can be a serious problem, which participants reported as leading to more use of PTD simply because of a lack of time to hear a matter fully. For example in Germany, we find that the decision had to be made within a relatively short period of time and on quite limited information, and in Austria, a heavy workload for judges has been described as being a possible restraint on the use of alternatives to detention, as it could be viewed as more efficient for the investigation to have the person in PTD (Hammerschick and Reidinger, 2017).

The particular role of the prosecution

As highlighted earlier, research from several countries indicates the central role which the prosecution plays in PTD decision-making and outcomes. In addition to the decisive influence prosecutors can have themselves, the relationship between judges and prosecutors is also a highly consequential factor which shapes the use of PTD. As such, it is worth dwelling on this position in a little more detail.

One of the most important ways in which prosecutors influence PTD practice is in the "filtering" role they play. The initiative for pre-trial proceedings or at least seeking PTD lies with the prosecution and as the prosecution often is also leading the police-investigation – and therefore is the party with the most relevant information on the suspect – their influence can hardly be exaggerated. In many of the countries explored here, the prosecution view was seen as being highly influential in the ultimate decision as to whether PTD will be ordered by a judge. In Germany, it was clear that the judicial decision to order PTD was based to a considerable degree on the submissions of the public prosecutor. Strikingly, some prosecutors in Germany therefore felt that they were the dominant players in the process, with the judge felt to be relying primarily on what they presented, and a few judges agreed on that. Other judges, however, insisted they were dominating the decision-making process or at least at having the last and decisive word (Morgenstern, 2017). Similar views were expressed in Lithuania, where it was found that a judge was very likely to approve a prosecutor's request for PTD. The prosecutor was also seen as highly influential in the proceedings, as the actor which ultimately decides whether a case for PTD should be put forward or not (Bikelis and Pajaujis, 2017). In the Netherlands, too, the power of the prosecutor was significant, with refusals of requests for PTD by the prosecutor being rare (Boone et al., 2017). In Austria, this filtering role was explicitly recognised by prosecutors, with one describing their role as being the second "filter", with the first being the police (Hammerschick and Reidinger, 2017: 57). There, the focus of the prosecution can be seen as being on the imposition or extension of PTD rather than the pursuit of alternatives, a view expressed also by judges. As a judge explained:

> If there are any requests (by the prosecution), then they usually request the imposition of PTD.
>
> (Hammerschick and Reidinger, 2017: 61)

Part of the reasons provided for this was prosecutorial risk-avoidance. On the other hand, in Ireland, the prosecution exhibited a degree of self-restraint, which resulted in PTD being requested less frequently than might otherwise be the case. The prosecutorial "self-restraint" noted there may be an important factor influencing the comparatively lower rates of PTD.

In some countries, prosecutors indicate that they anticipate the assessment of the case by the judiciary: established practice towards certain types of suspects or certain types of crimes would be taken into consideration regarding the decision to apply for PTD or not (Hammerschick and Reidinger, 2017). While this is in itself may not really be that surprising – it is common sense and professional to abide to established practice – it may become problematic when the person of the judge dealing with the application is a determinative factor in the decision-making process. This may be the case in the French-speaking part of Belgium, where prosecutors may choose to not refer the case to the investigation judge because they know that the judge in question will likely not provide an outcome they favour.

Challenges faced by defence lawyers

Defence lawyers play a critical role in the fairness of all criminal proceedings. Across many countries, defence lawyers report being underfunded, overstretched and at a disadvantage to the prosecution in terms of resources, but, in some cases, because of a shared culture and understanding between the prosecution and judiciary (Fair Trials International, 2017; De Suremain et al., 2019). While that is so, defence lawyers in most countries explored in this collection, consider themselves to play an important role, contributing to fair proceedings and in limiting the use of PTD. In some countries, particularly Belgium, the Netherlands and Germany, defence lawyers emphasise that, without their input, alternatives to PTD would hardly be considered at all as options. At the same time, almost all lawyers stress the limitations they encounter, especially at the very beginning of PTD: the very short time-span between the moment of their involvement and the first hearing simply doesn't allow for much thorough research or scrutiny. It seems that in some of the countries lawyers simply take this for granted, whereas in other countries, lawyers can be quite frustrated. Romanian lawyers, for example, seem to have the impression that they do not have an equal position compared to the prosecutors, as one lawyer stated:

> I have not seen yet in Bucharest a courthouse where the prosecutor stands face to face with the lawyer.
>
> (Lawyer 3, Oancea and Durnescu, 2017: 24)

Time, therefore, or the lack thereof, is a clear theme for the vast majority of defence layers. Limited access to lawyers is simply caused in many situations by organisational problems: sometimes there are too many suspects in the same case and not enough different lawyers (Maes et al., 2017, for the French speaking part of Belgium). The lack of time can also result simply from the pressures of workload and the immediacy of the short time allocated before the defence lawyer must become involved, but, in some cases, we see a view amongst defence lawyers that there are reservations from prosecutors and judges regarding early representation from the defence: they feel that lawyers could hamper the investigation by urging their clients to remain silent (Hammerschick and Reidinger, 2017). Similarly, access to case files and evidence is of the utmost importance in PTD cases. Yet access is cited in some countries, notably the Netherlands, as a barrier for defence lawyers on a regular basis. This may often be due to logistical issues and deliberate non-disclosure of parts of the case file doesn't seem to occur very regularly. Still the prosecution can "play for time" quite a bit without having to admit that they rather not share certain information yet. Access was not reported as being an issue elsewhere, however, such as in Germany (Chapter 5), with a relative happiness with the implementation of the principle of equality of arms also expressed in Ireland (Chapter 6).

A critical concern across many countries is that of the availability of legal aid and its sufficiency. In some countries state paid lawyers do not seem to provide legal aid that meets the standard (Lithuania, Romania). In other countries, no measurable differences between legal aid scheme lawyers and private lawyers were reported, notably in Ireland and Germany. Austria can also be regarded as one of those countries, although at the same time Austria seems to have problems with the fact that their legal aid scheme is organised in such a way that inexperienced lawyers are obliged to represent suspects (Hammerschick and Reidinger, 2017). Lawyers in the Netherlands have been fiercely campaigning in recent years for a considerable extension of the budget available for legal aid schemes, with some success in 2021. Comparative research (funded by the European Commission) on legal aid to remand prisoners, conducted shortly after the DETOUR project, showed findings similar to ours and made clear that pre-trial detention can effectively complicate legal aid, for example due to limitations regarding visits to clients in detention facilities (De Suremain et al., 2019).

Defence lawyers evidently play a crucial role in advocating for alternatives to PTD. In some countries, practitioners feel that defence lawyers could be more proactive in their efforts to support the application of alternatives. In Austria for instance lawyers are the ones most often initiating and promoting the use of alternatives. Still some Austrian practitioners see room for more creativity. In Ireland, where defence lawyers are particularly active, some judges still find that lawyers should be more specific and do more than suggest "some kind of bail". Yet this is easier said than done, as finding the right information within a short amount of time is hard, especially when the information needs to be obtained through semi-official channels which means that the defence lawyer is dependent on those channels. For example, in the Netherlands, lawyers can not directly ask the probation service for information: this will have to go through the public prosecutor. And then of course in some countries there is no involvement of the probation service at all.

Defence lawyers also bear a burden in the form of being in the very difficult position of resisting net-widening. Prosecutors and judges may press for an alternative and seek some restriction on liberty, even in cases where PTD might be rejected altogether. Defence lawyers report that they may not always contest these unnecessary conditions, for them, it may not matter how they get their client out of prison, and, indeed, this is the highest priority for most defendants. Defence lawyers may be instructed by their clients not to contest conditions or try to steer the proceedings towards the application of an alternative rather than risk the request for unconditional release to be denied outright (Morgenstern, 2017, for Germany and Maes et al., 2017, for Belgium).

The relative positions and influences of these actors

In addition to the individual challenges posed for the work of each of the legal actors in PTD decision-making, a critical influence on the proceedings is the dynamic between them. Where there is a reported feeling of equality between prosecution and defence, and a neutral judge deciding, participants in the process tend to report greater feelings of fairness about the proceedings, and a less automatic application of PTD. Where participants identified a shared culture or sense of closeness between prosecutors and judges, PTD seems to be more likely to be imposed, in the view of the actors. In general, a common theme to emerge across the countries considered in this volume was that prosecutors were generally viewed by judges as responsible and careful, and this could mean that judges were inclined to follow their view (for example, in Germany, Morgenstern, 2017: 67, and chapter 5). In Lithuania, too, participants felt that the requests made by prosecutors were of high quality and this was the reason why they were so likely to be accepted. In Romania, prosecutors felt that judges tended to follow their applications because they applied only when the likelihood of success was high (Oancea and Durnescu, 2017: 25, and chapter 9).

Informal communications between judges and prosecutors on the case were reported in most countries with the exception of Ireland and Lithuania, where such discussions would be considered irregular. In some of the countries (Romania, Belgium, Austria) the relation between the prosecutors and the judges were mentioned as potentially prejudicial of the outcome of the case. The fact that these actors work in the same building, use the same canteen and enter the court room through the same door is, in the perception of lawyers, an indication that there are possibilities for the prosecution to influence the decision-making by the judge. Defence lawyers expressed concern about this closeness and felt that it could weaken the procedural safeguards in place to protect the accused person and the administration of justice. By contrast, Belgian judges reported that they were not constrained by the decisions or views of the public prosecutor, and some even reported frustration with public prosecutors seeking detention too frequently (for both the Dutch speaking and the French speaking part of Belgium, Maes et al., 2017). Informal connections and discussions between prosecutors and judges were also, however, reported here.

In Ireland, most participants felt that there was generally "equality of arms" between prosecutors and defence lawyers, with prosecutors having some more access to resources. It was not felt by participants that there was a particular closeness between judges and prosecutors, nor that prosecutors' arguments were afforded a special status. At the barrister level, it is quite common for practitioners to appear regularly both for the prosecution and the defence, swopping roles regularly over the course of a single day. However, the opinion of the prosecutor could be determinative in situations where the prosecution was not seeking PTD.

At the same time, however, in the Netherlands, the prosecution is not always present at the initial hearing before the first order of PTD is made. Even when not present, however, the approach and values of the prosecution may permeate the proceedings. Until the last decade or so, prosecutors and judges had the same training programme; the shared legal culture between them seems to influence how the proceedings are run, in this case, with a more prosecution-focused mind-set. As written about elsewhere (Rogan, 2022), a shared legal culture between all players: prosecution, defence and judges (shaped by both constitutional doctrine and a common experience of legal practice) which tends to favour liberty may partly explain the lower rates of PTD there (see also Chapter 4 for England and Wales).

The role of the probation service

There is considerable variation across Europe regarding the involvement of the probation service in PTD proceedings. Some countries have quite extensive and intensive involvement by probation staff in the decision-making process, where in others they are not formally involved at all.

Probation officers do not play a role in pre-trial decision-making in Germany, nor do any other criminal justice social work institutions deal with adults during this phase. There is no role for probation staff or social services in Lithuania either. Romania, similarly, has no role for probation staff in the decision-making process. In Ireland, there is no formal role for probation staff, who begin their work after the sentencing process has concluded. However, probation staff could be involved on an informal basis, for example where a person was under the supervision of the probation service for a different matter.

By contrast, in Belgium, probation officers may be involved in the process, but, in practice, they are rarely asked to produce social inquiry reports by an investigating judge (Maes et al., 2017). In the French-speaking part of Belgium, the investigating judge tends to attribute a role to the probation staff only after a decision to release under conditions has been made, with probation staff working mainly on the monitoring and enforcement of conditions (ibid.). The Netherlands has an active role for the probation service, which can be involved at the early stages. Probation staff are also involved in Austria, where, similar to the Netherlands, preliminary probation can be ordered as an alternative to PTD. In Austria, however, the probation service is not engaged in social inquiries and in the decision-making process. The potential advantages and disadvantages of the involvement of probation services are explored further in the following.

Whether probation staff were involved or not at the pre-trial stage, similar themes emerged concerning their work. A recurring concern was that of time pressure on probation staff and high workloads.

In Germany, there were mixed views about a greater role for probation staff. Defence lawyers generally felt that their support and involvement for the accused person was sufficient. Several interview partners indicated that it would be unwise to involve the probation staff as they are already very overburdened (Morgenstern, 2017: 61). The time pressure involved in decision-making was also a factor behind the limited involvement of probation staff in the Dutch-speaking part of Belgium, with a heavy workload also cited in the French-speaking part (Maes et al., 2017: Part II: 27 and 38). In the latter case, the investigating judge tends to attribute a role to the probation staff only after a decision to release under conditions has been made, with probation staff working mainly on the monitoring and enforcement of conditions, though this work was generally favourably viewed. For the Netherlands, the pressure of time in the proceedings was also cited as a factor which can lead to reports which are of insufficient quality (Boone et al., 2017: 50). The problem of workload amongst probation staff was also cited as a reason against the introduction of more probation involvement in Romania (Oancea and Durnescu, 2017: 49). Austrian respondents considered judges were reluctant to use preliminary probation with adults, especially at the early stages, because of the time it takes for probation staff to be appointed (Hammerschick and Reidinger, 2017: 44). Irish participants also felt that it would be unfeasible for the probation service to be involved as they did not have the resources to be involved at present (Perry and Rogan, 2017: 73).

A further recurring issue was the possible effect of probation involvement on the presumption of innocence. In the Netherlands, which has a lot of experience of probation involvement at the pre-trial stage, some participants noted that they cannot do meaningful work with a person who refuses to give any insight into the circumstances surrounding the alleged crime (a reasonable position should the person be contending they are innocent). There was also concern amongst defence lawyers about infringing the presumption of innocence through such engagement, and it was reported that some suspects were wary of speaking to probation staff as they are seen as part of the "system" (Boone et al., 2017: 50). Defence lawyers in Germany also reported concerns that the probation staff does not act under confidentiality and that probation staff also have to provide all information they get from the suspect to the courts (Morgenstern, 2017: 61). Similarly, a possible effect on the presumption of innocence was cited in Ireland, where it was also felt that adding in probation involvement could lead to net-widening (Perry and Rogan, 2017: 73).

Another problem reported concerning probation involvement came from the Netherlands, where the prosecutor must agree to a probation report being ordered before it can be made. Agreement was usually forthcoming, but not always, as the prosecutor may believe it unlikely a person who has, for example, remained silent in the proceedings, will talk to a member of the probation staff. In the Netherlands, however, it was felt strongly that the probation service plays an important role in advocating for alternatives to PTD, with almost all successful requests for suspension of PTD following a positive report by the probation service. However, the Dutch DETOUR report also mentions that the availability of such a report can depend on very arbitrary grounds (Boone et al., 2017: 13).

While there was no clear consensus about the benefits of involving probation staff formally amongst the countries and within the countries, participants generally agreed that there was a need for more social work strategies and support for at least some groups facing PTD. The use of bail support and information schemes deserve special mention in this respect. As Hucklesby (Chapter 4) writes, though sadly in very serious decline, bail information schemes which are operated by probation or prison staff or NGOs provide collated and relevant information for the courts which may support a decision to release. Such information could include details of the person's address and employment status. These schemes also offer support in accessing accommodation and other important services. They provide a structured and effective way to provide reassurance to the court about the veracity of information which can support the decision to release. This type of intervention does not impinge on the presumption of innocence, but provides information which is often difficult to obtain in a timely way, but which can provide great assistance to a court. Practitioners have argued for the need for such information, regardless of its source. For example, defence lawyers in Romania considered, that an evaluation by probation staff would be helpful to provide reliable information about the social background of the accused person and support better decision-making, though prosecutors and judges did not feel this would be helpful (Oancea and Durnescu, 2017: 9 and 16). A recurring concern was the prevalence of drug use and housing problems amongst suspects, and it was clear participants felt that some support mechanisms were needed to address these issues.

Conclusion

The individual actions of each of the actors in the PTD decision-making process are clearly influential on how PTD is used. Prosecutors have a central role in making an application for PTD. Their views are taken seriously by judges, and decisions prosecutors make, about whether to apply for PTD, or to agree to an alternative have a key influence. Defence lawyers are essential for the application of the rule of law, the fairness of the proceedings, and the likelihood of the implementation of alternatives. Where defence lawyers have equal status in proceedings, and adequate resources and legal aid funding, they can be essential components in regimes where PTD is less frequently applied. Judges, of course, are determinative, and pressures on them in terms of time and ability to prepare are frequently a problem. The dynamics between these three sets of actors are profoundly important to PTD rates in countries. Further analysis of how these complex relationships play out can tell us much about how to reform PTD decision-making process and, ultimately, to reduce the use of PTD.

References

Bikelis, S. and Pajaujis, V. (2017) *Second Lithuanian National Report on Expert Interviews*, DETOUR at www.uibk.ac.at/irks/publikationen/detour-publikationen/2nd-lithuanian-report_interviews.pdf [accessed 6 February 2023].

Boone, M., Jacobs, P. and Lindeman, J. (2017) *Second Dutch National Report on Expert Interviews*, DETOUR at www.uibk.ac.at/irks/publikationen/detour-publikationen/2nd-dutch-report_interview.pdf [accessed 3 January 2023].

De Suremain, H., Fischer, N. and Boe, C. (2019) *Bringing Justice into Prison: For a Common European Approach. White Paper on Access to Justice for Pre-trial Detainees. A Report Based on Comparative Analysis and Empirical Studies in Nine EU Countries by the Research Project EUPRETRIALRIGHTS*, Paris: European Prison Litigation Network at www.prisonlitigation.org/wp-content/uploads/2021/04/WHITE-PAPER-final-ENG.pdf [accessed 10 January 2023].

Fair Trials International (2017) *A Measure of Last Resort? The Practice of Pre-trial Detention Decision Making in the EU* at www.fairtrials.org/wp-content/uploads/A-Measure-of-Last-Resort-Full-Version.pdf [accessed 24 May 2023].

Hammerschick, W. and Reidinger, V. (2017) *Second Austrian National Report on Expert Interviews*, DETOUR at www.uibk.ac.at/irks/publikationen/detour-publikationen/2nd-austrian-repor_interviews.pdf [accessed 6 February 2023].

Maes, E., Jockheere, A. and Deblock, M. (2017) *Second Belgian National Report on Expert Interviews (Part I: Report on Dutch-speaking Expert Interviews [Flanders]; Part II: Report on French-speaking Expert Interviews; Part III: Integrated Conclusions and Recommendations)*, DETOUR at www.uibk.ac.at/irks/publikationen/detour-publikationen/2nd-belgian-report_interviews.pdf [accessed 6 February 2023].

Morgenstern, C. (2017) *Second German National Report on Expert Interviews*, DETOUR (assisted by Eva Tanz) at www.uibk.ac.at/irks/publikationen/detour-publikationen/2nd-german-report_interview.pdf [accessed 6 February 2023].

Oancea, G. and Durnescu, I. (2017) *Second Romanian National Report on Expert Interviews*, DETOUR at www.uibk.ac.at/irks/publikationen/detour-publikationen/2nd-romanian-report_interview.pdf [accessed 6 February 2023].

Perry, D. and Rogan, M. (2017) *Second National Report on Expert Interviews for Ireland*, DETOUR at www.uibk.ac.at/irks/publikationen/detour-publikationen/2nscud-irish-report_interviews.pdf [accessed 6 February 2023].

Rogan, M. (2022) 'Examining the role of legal culture as a protective factor against high rates of pre-trial detention: The case of Ireland', *European Journal on Criminal Policy and Research*, 28: 425–433.

Chapter 12

Dilemmas in the use of alternatives to pre-trial detention in prison

Alexia Jonckheere and Eric Maes

Introduction

Comparative research (Hammerschick et al., 2017; Fair Trials International, 2017; Morgenstern, 2017) has shown diverse concepts of what is the norm and what is the alternative when it comes to pre-trial measures that aim at securing the defendant's presence in criminal court and the prevention of new offences. "Alternatives" here serve as generic term that covers both Continental European models of "milder measures" as opposed to pre-trial detention and "bail models" as, for example, in Ireland (see Chapter 6) or England and Wales (see Chapter 4). Independent of their conceptual and legal framework, in many European countries, classically, several types of alternative measures to pre-trial detention in prison exist: judicial supervision with conditions, financial bail to guarantee compliance with the procedure (in particular, appearing in court) and house arrest and electronic monitoring. After giving a brief introductory overview over the context and variety of issues of alternatives to pre-trial detention in European Criminal Justice systems, we will focus on these different types. In this chapter, we will only consider the alternative measures that are specifically designed to avoid detention in prison, excluding therefore *diversion measures* which prevent both pre-trial detention and alternative measures. This concerns the measures that could precede the decision on pre-trial detention, for example, the use – in Belgium – of an accelerated procedure ("speedy procedure") instead of an investigative procedure or the behaviour order and the ZSM-procedure[1] and alternatives offered by the probation service in the Netherlands. We will draw on empirical research and the comparative analysis carried out in the framework of the DETOUR project (see Chapter 1) and updated information from the country chapters in this volume.[2]

The legal framework for these alternatives is quite diverse, with significant differences from country to country. In the Dutch and German system, for instance, there are – strictly speaking – no alternatives to pre-trial detention, only the possibility for the judge or court to suspend the execution of the pre-trial detention under conditions. In other countries, some of the alternatives do not exist or are not used, for example in Germany where electronic monitoring is hardly applied in the pre-trial stage. Moreover, the alternatives can be applied

DOI: 10.4324/9781003159254-12

by different authorities: judges and/or courts but also, for certain measures, public prosecutors (in Austria, Lithuania and Romania), even the police (in Ireland and Lithuania) (Hammerschick et al., 2017). While the decision to order alternative measures can be made throughout the procedure but in practice, in some countries, this type of decision is taken more at the beginning of the procedure while in others it is rarely taken immediately but more generally after a few weeks. This explains why alternatives allow for reducing time spent in prison rather than avoiding incarceration from the beginning.

There are almost no statistics allowing for the cross-national comparison of the use of these alternative measures and their evaluation of their impact on the use of pre-trial detention (see nevertheless SPACE II[3] for some indications). However, various research studies (van Kempen, 2012: 45; Jonckheere and Maes, 2019a: 9) show diversity in the use of alternatives as they play a minor role in certain countries but are quite popular in others. This popularity can be explained by different traditions and culture. Equally, the consequences of the use of alternatives are different: in some countries where alternative measures are quite popular – bail serves as the default option in pre-trial procedures – we observe a relatively low use of pre-trial detention (e.g. in Ireland and England and Wales, see Chapters 4 and 6, respectively) while in other countries, pre-trial detention remains quite popular despite their frequent use (e.g. in Belgium). Available statistics suggest, at least for Belgium, a net-widening effect of the use of alternatives: while crime rates remain in general stable (Aebi et al., 2015: 575), the overall population under judicial control[4] in Belgium has tripled since 1980, due to an increase of pre-trial detention (in prison, or outside under electronic monitoring) as well as of the alternative of release under conditions (Jonckheere and Maes, 2019b). In addition, for suspects released under conditions, not only the duration of supervision, but also the number of conditions imposed increased (Maes and Jonckheere, 2017). In other countries however, the use of alternatives seems to remain relatively moderate, even if an increase is observable (Hammerschick et al., 2017: 39). The promotion of alternatives thus calls for vigilance regarding possible unintended effects, such as the extension of the number of people under judicial control, in- or outside prison. This is a first and probably the most important dilemma in the use of alternatives to pre-trial detention to be mentioned. This contribution highlights more such dilemmas relating to different types of alternatives: judicial supervision with conditions as the most common option, financial bail,[5] and house arrest and electronic monitoring.

Judicial supervision with conditions

Decision-making

Less severe measures, other than financial bail and house arrest/electronic monitoring (see the following text), are quite diverse, but they all comprise, at their core, of allowing the suspect to remain at liberty or to be released, with the obligation to respect one or more, more or less intrusive, conditions. This approach exists throughout Europe and can be summarised as "judicial supervision with conditions". In most countries, national laws do not provide for exhaustive lists of conditions. Therefore, in these countries both the choice of conditions and the number thereof is left to the discretion of the authorities. In some countries, the conditions imposed can be significant both with regard to their number and their "depth", that is, their intrusiveness (in Belgium and in Ireland for instance, the condition to follow treatment in a specialised residential care facility).

While, under the *ultima ratio*-principle, the deciding authorities, that is, judges, are responsible to avoid pre-trial detention as far as possible, defence lawyers have an important role in preparing, organising and suggesting liberty/release under conditions. In the Netherlands the magistrates consider that these lawyers can really make a difference for their clients (Chapter 8). In most cases, they are the ones who start the discussion about the alternatives. Similarly, a German judge interviewed for the DETOUR project explained that, according to his estimates, 90% of all initiatives are those of defence lawyers; this assessment was shared by other practitioners (Morgenstern, 2017: 53, and chapter 5). If they do not, often no alternative will be granted. Belgian lawyers highlighted what can be described as a true "dilemma" for them – because of the risk of detention pending, they do not "dare" to apply for release without conditions, potentially attracting a negative decision by the judge (Jonckheere and Maes, 2020). To avoid prison for their client and to convince the judge, they often prefer to ask for electronic monitoring or a release with conditions. A form of negotiation of measures by lawyers is observed in several countries, as they try to obtain a compromise and accept a restriction of the suspect's liberty, as long as detention is avoided and especially when the restriction is fairly lenient. This process of anticipation, by evaluating consciously or unconsciously the decision that will be taken by the next practitioner, is also seen in the practice of some public prosecutors: they will apply for pre-trial detention mainly when they know that they might have good chances of success. In Romania, for example, a prosecutor stated:

> We tend to apply for PTD when we know this is the case, when we know that the court practice is as such. Where we have doubts, we do not apply for PTD.
>
> (Oancea and Durnescu, 2017: 24)

The actors involved in the process accept the strong position of lawyers: judges expect lawyers to take the initiative in terms of alternatives and public prosecutors sometimes indicate in advance that they will not oppose such measures. Information is sometimes also provided by the probation services.

In some countries (such as Austria, Belgium, the Netherlands), preparatory inquiries by probation services can be ordered but this is a rarely used possibility. There is a new dilemma here: during the time of the social enquiry, the suspect often remains in prison, so requesting this enquiry runs the risk of a longer stay in detention. Probation services are only involved in these countries if the service has received a formal assignment of the competent authority. Their role is quite diverse: support on all relevant issues and control (Austria)[6] or support only in the framework of the conditions and control with the police (Belgium). The particularity of the probation services is that they have at the same time to help the suspect to comply with the conditions imposed, but also to control if the conditions are respected.

Conditions and duration

A wide variety of conditions exists in many countries: standard conditions, imposed in a *pro forma* manner, but also tailored conditions. Standard conditions include the duty to report to the police (the most frequent form of condition in Germany, usually on a weekly basis; also considered to be "good tool" by some practitioners in Austria) or to the probation officer; the obligation to have a fixed residence and/or to inform the authorities of any change of address; the prohibition on committing new offences; the seizure of documents; the obligation to appear before an authority on demand or to be reachable at all times by phone. The problem of the homeless has been mentioned in many countries. It seems that practical solutions are sometimes found (e.g. the use of hostels in Ireland), especially at the initiative of defence lawyers, but this situation is potentially a source of discrimination between suspects.

Tailored conditions are dependent on the suspect's situation and include diverse categories:

- Restriction on movement: not to leave the country (with or without the seizure of documents such as a passport), not to visit bars or coffee shops, not to leave the residence during the night (curfew), etc.
- Communication restrictions: for instance, the prohibition to have contact with other suspects or with the victim.
- Other restrictions: not to practice a profession or activity associated to the offence committed, not to take part in sports or cultural events, not to issue cheques, not to use the internet, etc.
- Daily occupation: to seek actively for employment, to follow training, etc.
- Psycho-medico-social guidance: medical treatment, psychological follow-up. This implies in some countries (e.g. the Netherlands) that the problem is recognised and that a competent authority has made a diagnosis. Consent of the suspect with the conditions is not always legally required (e.g. in Belgium) with may pose problems for the practical implementation of the conditions (see Jonckheere, 2011: 16–17).

- Medical test: for instance, blood test for drugs users. A major problem is that these tests are expensive and have to be paid by the suspects themselves in some countries.
- Formal pledges: in Austria (e.g. to refrain from any contact with the victim); this kind of condition often seems to be considered as a rather symbolic one, with rather little impact, in Ireland "to keep the peace".

Other conditions may even include to go regularly to a fitness centre or to go running in the park, to "be polite" and appear to be very "weak" in view of investigative needs and the presumption of innocence. They are sometimes considered by practitioners themselves as unnecessary and disproportionate, as the remark of an Irish prosecution officer shows:

> I have no difficulty saying that some of the conditions are just put there, sometimes there's no real reason for them you know.
>
> (Perry and Rogan, 2017: 47)

Irish defence practitioners have noted also that conditions like staying sober or being polite were "not feasible" and "just ludicrous" (Perry and Rogan, 2017: 50).

A further dilemma exists with respect to the position of foreign nationals. In certain countries (e.g. Austria, Belgium and Germany, see the respective country chapters in this volume), foreign nationals are overrepresented in the pre-trial detention population but underrepresented among those on release under conditions. It can be assumed that being a foreign national makes it more likely to obtain less severe measures instead of pre-trial detention. Elsewhere, there is an impression that they are not treated differently (e.g. Romania) or at least not as long as they are from within the EU (Ireland). This shows that distinctions can be made between different subgroups of foreigners. An essential criterion is the status of residence: do they have a permanent address or a regular residence permit in the country? Other essential criteria are financial resources and family bonds. If one or more of these factors are lacking, pre-trial detention is viewed as the only answer because of a perceived high risk of recidivism or absconding. In Austria, one of the prosecutors interviewed said:

> A central problem is poverty (Authors note: with respect to reoffending). Romanians for instance who commit burglaries here sometimes admit this quite honestly. In such cases it is hard to avoid detention.
>
> (Hammerschick and Reidinger, 2017: 23)

Other factors may also affect the use of lenient measures, for example, language barriers, personal attitude of suspects during interrogations. A particular category that is also distinguished in certain countries (such as in Austria and Germany) are refugees and asylum seekers (e.g. arising out of some major incidents which received international media-coverage were reported in these countries). Finally, a particular problem is often mentioned by practitioners in some countries regarding so-called mobile offenders (Austria, Belgium and Germany) who often come from other EU member states. Judges often feel that they have no other choice than issuing an arrest warrant and order pre-trial detention because these suspects generally do not give an address where they can be reached reliably, and/or because of an assumed risk of reoffending. For this group, the risk of flight seems to be the most important ground for detention (see Chapter 1) and practitioners are not willing to take the risk of alternative options even in relatively minor cases.

Also, some other types of suspects – suspects with a particular profile – face more difficulties to get less severe measures: drug addicts, sex offenders, suspects with alcohol problems and those requiring psychiatric care. For drug addicts, different reasons may explain why there is little use of alternative measures for them: the assumption that an addict person is not reliable and a lack of institutions accepting to take charge of those suspects (long waiting lists). In Belgium, for example, only one institution in the French part of the country accepts to meet drug addicted suspects in prison to organise possible accommodation in a residential service if they are released under conditions. Because of this situation, a judge considered that "*we are almost forced to keep certain people in pre-trial detention*" (Jonckheere, 2017: 26–27). This seems to depend on existing local cultures, as explained for Germany, where sometimes established structures enable defence lawyers to find places for their drug addicted clients more easily than elsewhere (Morgenstern, 2017). Costs related to the regular purchase of drugs can also be perceived as increasing the risk of reoffending. For sex offenders, suspects with alcohol problems and people requiring psychiatric care, practitioners appear to be uninformed about alternative measures that could be adequately proposed, in particular because of a lack of adequate institutions. For England and Wales, Hucklesby (Chapter 4) points to the problem of bail support services. They may help to tackle drug or housing problems and thus to avoid pre-trial detention but intervene with the live of defendants in a way that resembles post-conviction measures, and are thus problematic with respect to the presumption of innocence. In general, treatment is sometimes difficult to implement regarding the limited timeframe within the pre-trial proceedings, questions of consent, and furthermore because the treatment itself takes time.

Even if alternative measures are less intrusive than pre-trial detention, they put a burden on the defendant and should last, under proportionality considerations, as short as possible. In addition, the principle of a speedy procedure applies. There are clear indications, however, that it is taken far less seriously than in the case of pre-trial detention. Some national laws do not provide for any overall time limit for alternative measures (e.g. Austria, the Netherlands) while other legislation partially provides for maximum periods:

three months, renewable for release under conditions in Belgium (except for release under financial bail: no time limits); six months, renewable for intense supervision and house arrest in Lithuania (for other measures, no time limit exists). Separate maximum durations for each phase of the procedure exist, for instance, in Romania (during the criminal prosecution, during the investigation stage and during the trial stage; in the latter phase, the duration must be reasonable and may in any case not exceed five years). However, it seems that, within legal limits, the duration of the measures is sometimes automatically prolonged. A similar tendency can also be observed in Belgium.

Control and consequences

In most countries problems arise with the control of compliance with conditions and the effectiveness of the control. This seems to be one of the particularly weak points of alternative measures: more possibilities to monitor and control compliance and more information on the control of suspects could probably increase the trust of the actors in such measures. An Austrian judge stated for instance:

> If the suspect is detained, I can easily control it . . . but when I release him . . . I have no influence anymore.
>
> (Hammerschick and Reidinger, 2017: 49)

On the other hand, German judges acknowledged across the board that defendants who were conditionally released usually showed up for their trials (Chapter 5). In this regard, it would be relevant to acquire better understanding of judges' expectations: is the imposition of the measure in itself sufficient to them (the measure would then be pure symbolic, see, e.g., the formal pledges in Austria mentioned before, with little interest in compliance with the conditions) or do they desire certain effects that can be controlled? Under this hypothesis, the question arises: what feedback do judges need about compliance? The DETOUR research showed that judges, who usually are not involved in the trial later, have no and seek no feedback of the compliance of those released under conditions (Hammerschick et al., 2017). A particular problem arises when conditions are not clearly defined (e.g. to get help or assistance in order to de-radicalise) and are difficult to comply with (e.g. to look for work while the suspect does not have a work permit in the country). Compliance and its control or enforcement may be especially difficult in these circumstances. Another problem also emerges: the excessive use of less severe measures could impact upon the effectiveness of the control. In Lithuania for example, it was mentioned that this excessive use may provoke weaker control and more tolerance in case of breach of conditions (Chapter 7).

While it is by no means clear what the rates of compliance are, with concerns that compliance may not always be closely monitored (e.g. Ireland), very low (official) revocation rates can be observed for example in Belgium. There, as far as practitioners can assess, conditions can be and are effectively controlled or enforced, and it is experienced that the vast majority of suspects complies with the conditions. The reaction to incidences of breach differs between national systems and is either provided for in the law or left to the discretion of the authorities. Usually, not automatic or mandatory revocations is foreseen and such discretionary power is often judged positively by most actors because it leaves the possibility that minor non-compliance with conditions may not have severe consequences such as issuing an arrest warrant. It is indeed, according to a Belgian investigating judge, a matter of "*being consequent but also flexible*" (Maes and Deblock, 2017: 44).

In Belgium, it is observed that, in some cases, if the suspect complies with the conditions, judges tend to prolong the measure because things are going well. For example, psychiatric treatment will be prolonged if it has a beneficial effect on the suspect. In such a situation, alternative measures can be and are being used as instruments of social policy rather than criminal policies and may amount to an anticipated punishment, even with a rehabilitative focus. Finally, it must also be noted that a breach of conditions does not necessarily lead to a quick, or immediate, reaction (e.g. by re-arresting the suspect). However, if a suspect did not comply with his conditions previously, s/he will no longer benefit from alternative measures in the future or will be sentenced more severely (i.e. that the sentencing court will not grant a community sanction, such as a probationary supervision order).

The existence of different types of measures, with different levels of intrusiveness and restriction, may result in a preference for what might be termed "gradual release". For Belgium, at least, a progressive scale for pre-trial measures emerges: after a period of pre-trial detention in prison, certain suspects will first be released at home under electronic monitoring, and then, under conditions, before finally being released unconditionally. A similar observation is made in Romania, where judges hinted at a "*pattern whereby PTD* [pre-trial detention] *is replaced after 2–3 months with house arrest which is latter replaced with judicial control*" (Oancea and Durnescu, 2017: 20). This practice may contribute to a net-widening effect. Such practices risk imposing alternative measures automatically rather than in a way that is justified and warranted in the circumstances. There are indications that alternative measures are imposed too easily, despite the significant impact they can have on the lives of suspects and their families. This is worrisome in particular when judges do not consider them effective or useful. Once again, we see a factor displayed that contributes to possible net-widening effects.

Financial bail

The possibility of ordering release upon payment of a financial bail or bond exists throughout Europe. Its popularity, however, varies greatly. Among the systems represented in this volume, this measure is popular in Ireland and England and Wales, being embedded in a long cultural tradition, and being viewed as highly convincing. One reason identified is that financial bail is viewed as a mechanism for using family support as a factor in granting bail. According to an Irish prosecution officer:

> [F]or serious offences, the court might want to see if there's family support and that's why an independent surety might be imposed. The surety's job is not only just to lodge money, but it's to make sure that they have an obligation that a person turns up to court.
>
> (Perry and Rogan, 2017: 47)

That this, in principle, seems to be a strong argument elsewhere, too. In Germany, the same argument was made by a judge. Here, however, financial bail is hardly ever used (Chapter 5).

National laws provide for different forms of financial bail: the payment in advance, cash and in full, by the suspect or by a third person (e.g. in Belgium and Germany); the availability of a certain amount of money, securities (in Austria for instance); or, a material guarantee concerning movable or immovable property (e.g. Romania). The Irish system provides for three forms: an "own bond" monetary amount, a cash lodgement and an independent surety. The bail can be applied solely, or in combination with each other, or combined with other conditions.

The determination of the amount of the deposit is left to the discretion of the actors, legislation providing rarely a minimum amount (in Lithuania, a recommendation of the Prosecutor General establishes an amount of minimum €1,500, whereas in Romania the law sets a much lower amount) nor a maximum amount. In practice, the requested amount can vary significantly and depends on the financial means of the suspect as well as the assessment of the risk of a person not showing up for trial, the sentence that can be expected and therefore also the gravity of the offence (see, e.g., Morgenstern, 2017 for Germany).

In general, the money will be lost if the accused person fails to turn up for trial, except for example in Lithuania where the financial bail has to be forfeited also in case of the commission of a new offence. In Ireland and in Romania, a breach of any bail condition can also give rise to a revocation of bail.

Under fair trial deliberations it is required that judges set the financial bail at a level which is not excessive compared to the person's means. Despite these considerations, financial bail, in combination with another alternative measure or not, is also used only to a very limited extent in many other European countries as the DETOUR study shows. Not only scholars, but also many practitioners interviewed rejected this option often as a question of principle (freedom and absolute necessity for security cannot be bought), perceived inequality of the measure (privilege for the rich, rejection of a "class justice"), poverty of suspects, its irrelevance to the risk of absconding, doubt about the legality of the funds (and consequently, fear that authorities would be laundering criminal proceeds) or unfamiliarity with the applicable procedures. The empirical research shows a wider variety of opinions within national systems that may explain the reluctant use: in Lithuania, for example, practitioners evaluate financial bail very positively; yet available statistics show that the use of financial bail is quite rare in this country, probably due to the poor financial situation of suspects as one prosecutor suggests "*people here in the province do not have money*" (Bikelis and Pajaujis, 2017: 22). Given the lack of knowledge about the use and practice of bail in Europe, there is a need for more research, including statistical material.

House arrest and electronic monitoring

While the legislation of some countries does not mention house arrest as alternative to pre-trial detention (Belgium, Germany, Ireland), the measure is provided for in other legislations (e.g. in Romania). In Romania, the obligation to stay at home (except in a situation where this requirement has been dispensed with, for instance to allow a person to go to work or to engage in training) is combined with other obligations, namely to appear before the prosecutor, the judge or the court when required, and not to communicate with the injured person or other specified persons. The possibility of wearing an electronic monitoring device (as an obligation to judicial control or house arrest) is not currently (technically) available. The measure of house arrest is limited in time and leads, in the event of a final conviction, to a deduction of time to be served following sentencing for time spent under house arrest.

With respect to electronic monitoring (EM) it can be observed that many European countries have legal regulations governing or otherwise provide for a legal basis for the application of electronic monitoring as a pre-sentence measure.[7] While in Germany and the Netherlands, for instance, electronic monitoring is not mentioned in the law explicitly, it is considered as an "other suitable measure" among the obligations or conditions that can be imposed to a suspended arrest warrant in Germany. In the Netherlands the use of EM is dealt with under the general provision for adding requirements to a suspension of the pre-trial detention. In other jurisdictions, legislation explicitly refers to electronic monitoring as a possible measure. In Ireland, the possibility of applying EM has been introduced in legislation, but this legal provision has not yet come into force for pre-trial detention.

Often, electronic monitoring is (legally) conceived of as an "alternative" measure (for instance, in Romania, Lithuania: "intense supervision"), a bail condition (Ireland), or a condition attached to a suspension of an arrest warrant (e.g. Germany, the Netherlands). This is different however, in Austria and Belgium, where electronic monitoring constitutes a "modality of execution of an arrest warrant". Being considered as a "modality of execution" (rather than an "alternative" or specific condition) has some important consequences for the defendant because the same strict rules as for pre-trial detention apply: time spent under electronic monitoring is deducted from the final prison sentence, inappropriate EM-detention can lead to financial compensation, and – at least in Belgium – the measure of electronic monitoring is subject to automatic periodic review by judicial bodies. In countries where electronic monitoring is a condition/alternative, these rules do not apply.

Although the public prosecution service plays an important decision-making role with respect to alternative measures in Lithuania (and in Romania in the case of "judicial control"), this role most often only concerns less severe measures, and not the most severe alternative measures like electronic monitoring. More frequently it is ultimately for a judge/court to decide on the application of electronic monitoring. While it is possible to apply electronic monitoring immediately, complicated procedures (cf. the Netherlands, Lithuania) most often result in an application for electronic monitoring after an initial arrest warrant has been issued and executed (i.e. after some time spent in pre-trial detention). In general, there is no "absolute" legal maximum duration of electronic monitoring, although – as mentioned earlier – for instance in Austria pre-trial detention rules, including time limits, apply and, where time limits are mentioned, extensions are possible (e.g. Lithuania).

The technologies used and content of the EM-measure differ between countries. Belgium has a very strict regime of electronic monitoring; only a very limited number of movements outside the assigned place of residence can be authorised (for reasons connected to the criminal investigative proceedings, medical reasons, force majeure). There, the technology used within the pre-trial phase is GPS-tracking. In other countries, for example England and Wales, the suspect is (or can be) allowed to leave the assigned place of residence (within specific time frames), for example, for work, educational reasons, therapy, and the most common technology is radio frequency (RF). However, in some countries, GPS-tracking is possible, but not necessarily known by judicial actors (e.g. in Austria), is becoming used more frequently (e.g. Lithuania), or it is used in specific cases, for example, in the Netherlands in case of "location bans", whether or not these are combined with a location order (movement restriction).

Many European jurisdictions thus have a legal basis for the application of electronic monitoring in the pre-trial stage, but significant differences exist regarding its use in practice. In Romania, electronic monitoring is not used, due to lack of infrastructure, in Austria it is practised only in very small number of cases, in Germany only infrequently in single regions. In contrast, in Belgium, electronic monitoring is – comparatively speaking – much more frequently applied (1,821 EM-placements in Belgium in 2020, in part also caused by the COVID-19-crisis). However, the application of electronic monitoring in Belgium, some time ago, has been qualified as "peanuts", by a member of Parliament (Lahaye-Battheu, 2017), that is, in comparison to its expanded use within other stages of the criminal justice system (in particular, the execution of prison sentences); also the comparison with the yearly number of committals to prison in the pre-trial stage (more than 10,000) is still striking. In addition, big variations exist between judicial districts in their practical use of electronic monitoring; as such, in some districts electronic monitoring is not much or (almost) never used.

We therefore find a particularly mixed picture regarding electronic monitoring in the pre-trial stage within Europe. Practitioners and researchers from different European countries often discussed this option with similar – favourable or critical – approaches. Interestingly, supporters and critics were found alike in the different professional groups. Some defence practitioners, for example, support the use of electronic monitoring for example in cases of economic crimes (for example in Germany, see Chapter 5), while others fear that it would probably replace milder measures or unconditional release. Possible benefits of electronic monitoring mentioned by (legal) practitioners are, for example, the following:

- Alternatives could be applied more often (in some countries it is considered that GPS could be a good alternative, e.g., to define ban areas) if decision-makers had more confidence to avoid pre-trial detention with such a kind of additional "electronic" control. Such confidence depends on actors being sufficiently informed about technological possibilities, which seems not always to be the case.
- Electronic monitoring could possibly enhance better compliance of the suspect with other conditions imposed.
- Electronic monitoring could result in less administrative burden for other institutions currently supervising compliance with conditions by means of human resources.
- Electronic monitoring could create a greater measure of comfort to the public at large.

However, many concerns are also expressed:

- There may be a fear (and experience) of additional administrative caseloads for judges who have to deal with breaches of EM conditions or with respect to the practical and technical implementation of electronic monitoring more generally.
- Serious doubts arise with respect to EM's ability effectively to prevent risks of recidivism. Such doubts also arise about the ability to prevent absconding (e.g. foreign suspects with no residence), and/or collusion (with prison seen as the most "secure" solution). More generally, the added value of electronic monitoring is questioned.
- Equally, there is fear of non-compliance with the strict conditions of the regime; this is especially the case for offenders with mental health problems.

- Some suspects are/may be excluded from the application of the measure as it only suits "well integrated" suspects; homeless or foreign defendants do not meet the criteria of residence or occupation.
- More specific to the Belgian case, the very strict regime of electronic monitoring (almost comparable to a "24-hour home detention") already does severely limit its scope of application, and leaves no place for individualisation (the same rules apply to all suspects, with almost no possibility to leave the assigned residence).
- Electronic monitoring also includes some discriminatory aspects (cf. differences in material comfort of one's own living spaces or EM-detention places) and has a significant psychological impact on suspects and their families. Electronic monitoring can be considered as a very intrusive measure, while in many occasions the same purposes could probably be served by less severe measures.

While these observations can explain why in certain jurisdictions electronic monitoring is only used in a limited number of cases, the question arises as to whether the use of electronic monitoring should be extended (cf. the phenomena of "net-widening" or "strengthening").[8] It is a concern that electronic monitoring risks not to substitute pre-trial detention but rather to be used in cases where the suspect otherwise would not have been held in custody, or that a certain "progressiveness" in form of a gradual transition (mentioned already for other alternatives) is put in place. The latter is sometimes also seen as an "advantage" to "test" the suspect in a more restricted environment but has nothing to do with the limited legitimate aims of pre-trial measures to ensure the orderly conduct of a criminal process. Furthermore, the principle of expediency may not fully apply which may result in a protracted procedure. Finally, instead of obtaining a greater rate of compliance, electronic monitoring might also result in more breaches of bail.

These concerns are all the more pressing since electronic monitoring resembles a kind of "preliminary probation" (with no differences in treatment between suspects and convicted offenders or even a more "severe" treatment), while often not being deducted from the final (prison or pecuniary) sentence (except, for instance, in Austria and in Belgium). These concerns again raise questions about the application of the presumption of innocence in this context.

Conclusions

Alternatives to pre-trial detention, such as judicial supervision, are not without any criticism, although suspects – after a quick and immediate judicial response to their acts – might be motivated to change their situation, bearing in mind eventually more favourable sentencing outcomes. Doubts exist as to whether the "alternatives" reached their intended effects to reduce the size of the prison population, either general or remand.

In addition, other critical questions about alternatives arise. It is not an exception that a lot of and diverse types of conditions are imposed, and in some jurisdictions, there is a tendency of an "aggravation" of conditions. Not seldom do these conditions have a therapeutic and/or even repressive/punitive intention. Sometimes "alternatives" even resemble "real" probation measures and thus appear to start from the point of view of a "presumption of guilt" rather than a presumption of innocence. Maybe not all, but many, jurisdictions allow that measures such as judicial supervision could be initially imposed for longer periods of time, could be frequently renewed, and, in consequence, on average could last longer than pre-trial detention. This happens most commonly without the period of the "alternative" being deducted from the final (prison) sentence, without regularly reviewing its necessity as it is done with respect to pre-trial detention decisions, and without allowing for compensation in case of inappropriate use (in contrast to "inappropriate detention").

Some scholars (see Boone and Herzog-Evans, 2013: 57–58) argue that alternatives to pre-trial detention can be extremely useful in the stage before trial, as unconvicted prisoners form a large part of the prison population and sometimes even outnumber sentenced prisoners. Their risk of being sentenced to imprisonment grows significantly whereas offenders awaiting trial in a free (community) setting are more likely to receive non-custodial sentences. Therefore, alternatives are often seen as positive measures that can help reducing the number of pre-trial detainees. Nevertheless, fundamental objections can also be raised; they refer most prominently to the possible violation of the presumption of innocence and risks of net-widening. This chapter has shown that there are no easy answers to this dilemma – ultimately, alternatives are acceptable where they serve as such: alternatives to pre-trial detention. Too often, however, they are used as an alternative to pre-trial liberty. Bearing in mind the presumption of innocence and the human rights to liberty, individual freedom and privacy, any "alternative" or "milder" measure that restricts the defendant before and during the criminal proceedings must be an "ultimum remedium".

Notes

1 This ZSM procedure aims at providing prosecutorial decisions as to the further processing of the case, as soon as possible ("*zo snel mogelijk*"), as smart as possible (i.e. well-informed, "*zo slim mogelijk*"), and with a clear aim at society in a multidisciplinary setting ("*zo samen mogelijk*") (Boone et al., 2017: 29).

2 This chapter is mainly based on the comparative analysis carried out in the framework of the DETOUR project (see Chapter 1) and has been updated according to new available information. Where reference is made to national laws and/or practices without specific citation, see Hammerschick et al. (2017).

3 Council of Europe Annual Penal Statistics on non-custodial sanctions and measures, at https://wp.unil.ch/space/space-ii/ (accessed 14 October 2021).

4 The term "judicial control" is used in a broad sense to indicate all kinds of measures that can be taken in the pre-trial phase (including pre-trial detention), whereas

"judicial supervision (with conditions)" refers to specific measures where the suspect is released under conditions, other than financial bail or house arrest and electronic monitoring.

5 We use the term "bail" in this contribution in terms of a financial guarantee. Note, however, that the meaning of bail in common law systems is not restricted to the deposit of an amount of money or property as a guarantee to appear in court and eventually serve the sentence. While bail has a much broader meaning in common law countries, it is typically interpreted in its more limited sense in civil law systems (Boone and Herzog-Evans, 2013: 59; see also Chapter 1).

6 In Austria, an alternative called "preliminary probation" above all plays a more relevant role for young suspects, since probation is seen as an educational measure more appropriate for this age cohort. Within the German juvenile justice system, a comparable situation occurs, with youth court aid managing to avoid pre-trial detention, at least in those regions where it is working effectively.

7 See, with respect to electronic monitoring in some EU countries, also the EMEU project and the respective reports published at http://emeu.leeds.ac.uk/reports/ (accessed 14 October 2021).

8 Comparative European research on electronic monitoring indicates that countries with high rates of prisoners are likely to also have high rates of electronic monitoring (Hucklesby et al., 2016: 9).

References

Aebi, M., Delgrande, N. and Marguet, Y. (2015) 'Have community sanctions and measures widened the net of the European criminal justice systems?', *Punishment & Society*, 17(5): 575–597.

Bikelis, S. and Pajaujis, V. (2017) *DETOUR-Towards Pre-trial Detention as Ultima Ratio. 2nd Lithuanian National Report on Expert Interviews*, Vilnius: Lietuvos, Teisės Institutas at www.uibk.ac.at/irks/publikationen/detour-publikationen/2nd-lithuanian-report_interviews.pdf [accessed 20 December 2022].

Boone, M. and Herzog-Evans, M. (2013) 'Decision-making and offender supervision', in F. McNeill and K. Beyens (eds) *Offender Supervision in Europe*, London: Palgrave Macmillan: 51–96.

Boone, M., Jacobs, P. and Lindeman, J. (2017) *DETOUR-Towards Pre-trial Detention as Ultima Ratio. 2nd Dutch National Report on Expert Interviews*, Utrecht: Universiteit Utrecht, Montaigne Centrum. Onderzoekscentrum voor Rechtspleging en Conflictoplossing at www.uibk.ac.at/irks/publikationen/detour-publikationen/2nd-dutch-report_interview.pdf [accessed 20 December 2022].

Fair Trials International (2017) *A Measure of Last Resort? The Practice of Pre-trial Detention Decision Making in the EU*, London: Fair Trials International.

Hammerschick, W., Morgenstern, C., Bikelis, S., Boone, M., Durnescu, I., Jonckheere, A., Lindeman, J., Maes, E. and Rogan, M. (2017) *DETOUR-Towards Pre-trial Detention as Ultima Ratio. Comparative Report*, Vienna: IRKS at www.uibk.ac.at/irks/publikationen/detour-publikationen/comparative-report_detour.pdf [accessed 20 December 2022].

Hammerschick, W. and Reidinger, V. (2017) *DETOUR-Towards Pre-trial Detention as Ultima Ratio. 2nd Austrian National Report on Expert Interviews*, Vienna: IRKS at www.uibk.ac.at/irks/publikationen/detour-publikationen/2nd-austrian-repor_interviews.pdf [accessed 20 December 2022].

Hucklesby, A., Beyens, B., Boone, M., Dünkel, F., McIvor, G. and Graham, H. (2016) *Creativity and Effectiveness in the Use of Electronic Monitoring: A Case Study of Five Jurisdictions*, Leeds: University of Leeds.

Jonckheere, A. (2011) 'La liberté sous conditions des présumés innocents: enjeux et usages d'une mesure alternative', *Annales de Droit de Louvain*, 71(1): 15–38.

Jonckheere, A. (2017) *DETOUR-Towards Pre-trial Detention as Ultima Ratio. 2nd Belgian National Report on Expert Interviews*, Part II, Brussels: NICC at www.uibk.ac.at/irks/publikationen/detour-publikationen/2nd-belgian-report_interviews.pdf [accessed 20 December 2022].

Jonckheere, A. and Maes, E. (2019a) 'Détention préventive en Europe: quelle crédibilité pour les alternatives?', *Revue Internationale de Criminologie et de Police Technique et Scientifique*, LXXII(1): 6–13.

Jonckheere, A. and Maes, E. (2019b) 'Pre-trial detention and alternatives in Belgium: Standards, practices and research', in Ch. Mincke, D. Brutyn, D. Burssens, A. Lemonne, E. Maes, B. Renard and L. Robert (eds) *20 Years of Criminology at the NICC. A Scientific Journey and its Perspectives*, Oud-Turnhout/'s-Hertogenbosch: Gompel&Svacina: 53–83.

Jonckheere, A. and Maes, E. (2020) 'Les mesures avant jugement en Belgique: une éternelle insatisfaction', *New Journal of Criminology and Crime Policy*, 1(1): 5–11.

Lahaye-Battheu, S. (2017) *Vorig jaar kregen 799 gedetineerden in voorlopige hechtenis een enkelband* at www.sabien-lahaye-battheu.be/nl/nieuws/2800/vorig-jaar-kregen-799-gedetineerden-in-voorlopige-hechtenis-een-enkelband.html [accessed 14 October 2021]

Maes, E. and Deblock, M. (2017) *DETOUR-Towards Pre-trial Detention as Ultima Ratio. 2nd Belgian National Report on Expert Interviews*, Part I, Brussels: NICC at www.uibk.ac.at/irks/publikationen/detour-publikationen/2nd-belgian-report_interviews.pdf [accessed 20 December 2022].

Maes, E. and Jonckheere, A. (2017) 'Quo vadis? Dilemma's rond alternatieven voor voorlopige hechtenis', *Panopticon, Tijdschrift voor strafrecht, criminologie en forensisch welzijnswerk*, 38(6): 401–411.

Morgenstern, C. (2017) *DETOUR-Towards Pre-trial Detention as Ultima Ratio. Second German National Report on Expert Interviews*, Greifswald and Berlin: Ernst Moritz Arndt Universität Greifswald at www.uibk.ac.at/irks/publikationen/detour-publikationen/2nd-german-report_interview.pdf [accessed 20 December 2022].

Oancea, G. and Durnescu, I. (2017) *DETOUR-Towards Pre-trial Detention as Ultima Ratio. 2nd Romanian National Report on Expert Interviews*, Bucharest: ASSWR at www.uibk.ac.at/irks/publikationen/detour-publikationen/2nd-romanian-report_interview.pdf [accessed 20 December 2022].

Perry, D. and Rogan, M. (2017) *DETOUR-Towards Pre-trial Detention as Ultima Ratio. Second National Report. Expert Interviews. Ireland*, Dublin: Trinity College Dublin at www.uibk.ac.at/irks/publikationen/detour-publikationen/2nd-irish-report_interviews.pdf [accessed 20 December 2022].

van Kempen, P.H. (2012) 'Pre-trial detention in national and international law and practice', in P.H.P.H.M.C. van Kempen (ed) *Pre-trial Detention. Human Rights, Criminal Procedural Law and Penitentiary Law, Comparative Law – Détention Avant Jugement. Droits de l'homme, droit de procédure pénale et droit pénitentiaire, droit comparé*, Cambridge: Intersentia: 3–95.

Chapter 13

Foreign nationals in pre-trial detention

A neglected and urgent challenge

Anthea Hucklesby, Miranda Boone and Christine Morgenstern

Introduction

Pre-trial detention rates in Europe, and in most of the World, are too high. International Conventions agree that pre-trial imprisonment should be the exception given that it seriously affects the right to liberty and presumption of innocence, which are cornerstones of democratic societies. The European Union and many of its constituent countries have signalled their desire and intention to reduce pre-trial imprisonment, but with little success to date. One reason for the lack of progress is a failure to acknowledge the number of foreign national prisoners in pre-trial detention. Data demonstrate consistently that a disproportionate number of defendants are held in pre-trial detention in Europe are foreign nationals when compared with sentenced prison populations and general populations. Nearly one third of those detained pre-trial in countries of the European Union listed in Table 13.1 (including the UK) are foreign nationals (Aebi and Tiago, 2021). This figure is only likely to increase given that migration within, and from outside, the European Union is set to continue to rise (UNHCR, 2022). Understanding why foreign nationals are overrepresented in pre-trial populations, and putting measures in place to reduce its use, is vital if countries are going to be successful in bringing down their use of pre-trial detention.

The high number of foreign nationals in pre-trial detention suggest that they receive differential treatment in the pre-trial process compared to those accused of offences who are nationals of the country where they appear in court, but with little indication of why this is the case. There are several possible explanations: foreign national defendants may spend longer awaiting trial; there may be differences in legitimate legal factors which impact upon pre-trial decisions, such as nature of alleged offence; other factors such as poor quality defence and interpretation and lack of legal aid and language skills may disadvantage foreign national defendants; courts may indirectly discriminate against this group because of factors such as residency status and lack of community ties; and/or courts may discriminate directly on the basis of nationality and/or race/ethnicity. As this chapter will demonstrate the

DOI: 10.4324/9781003159254-13

explanation for the disproportionate number of foreign nationals in pre-trial detention in Europe is likely to be a mixture of these factors. Data to investigate the role of different factors is sparse but a common theme from the three case studies presented in this chapter is that some of the disproportionality is explained by how the legal criteria of risk of flight/absconding is applied in cases involving foreign national defendants. Another common theme is the interconnection of criminal justice systems and immigration enforcement.

The introduction to this collection highlighted differences in the make-up of pre-trial populations making cross-country comparisons difficult. This chapter also needs to consider the complicated category of "foreign national". Defining foreign national is a particularly interesting exercise in the European Union which has a policy of free movement of people, resulting in many people living and working (and committing offences) in countries where they were not born and/or are not national citizens, but "EU-citizens". This group are very different from foreign nationals from outside of the European Union, partly because agreements are in place for mutual cooperation, via the European Arrest Warrant (EAW) and the European Supervision Order (ESO) discussed later (Chapter 14). Unfortunately, no comparative data are available on the split of EU nationals and non-EU nationals for pre-trial populations, which is only published for prison populations as a whole (Aebi and Tiago, 2021).

"Foreign national" is a contested term. For the purposes of this chapter, it is defined as individuals who are not citizens of the country where they are accused of committing an offence, that is, they have a passport or identity card from another country, are stateless or are of unknown nationality. This definition includes a wide range of circumstances, including individuals detained at the airports who have never been in the country before; individuals on short-term visits for work or holidays; trafficked individuals made to work in illegal industries often run by organised criminals; and individuals who have lived in the country for years, and who may have children or partners who are citizens of their adopted country. Complex and contested histories of migration in many Northern and Western European countries add to the difficulties of accurately identifying who is and who is not or who has the right to be a citizen. Definitions using citizenship status may be confused with place of birth which is one of the ways migrants are defined (The Migration Observatory, 2022). However, some citizens are born elsewhere, for example, because their parents were working overseas potentially resulting in misidentification. Migrant is another term used in connection with the term "foreign national", but it usually refers to individuals who plan to stay for at least a year in their adopted country so does not include individuals visiting a country for a short period (The Migration Observatory, 2022). Hence, we have settled on the definition of foreign national.

Nationality overlaps with other characteristics, most notably race, ethnicity and religion. Assumptions about nationality can be based on these categories and vice versa. Research has also highlighted how stereotypes about race, ethnicity and religion impact upon decisions in the criminal justice process, resulting in discrimination (Bowling and Phillips, 2002; Lammy, 2017; Light and Wermink, 2021; Oberwittler and Lukas, 2010; Schott, 2004). Some foreign nationals potentially face multiple discrimination because of their nationality and their race, ethnicity and/or religion. Other demographic characteristics including gender may also result in multiple disadvantage (Robson, 2020). Consequently, it is important to be aware that "foreign national" is not a homogenous group. The focus of this chapter is on adults, given that both children and young people have a special status in both criminal and immigration law.

It is also important to recognise that individuals may be assumed to be foreign nationals when they are not. This is particularly the case for migrants who have become citizens or have residency rights in the country in question. The police and courts may make assumptions about their nationality status because they look or sound different (Aliverti, 2018). Another problem is accessing information to verify the identity of individuals and their immigration status which may involve liaison with criminal justice counterparts in other jurisdictions. In the short period of time available to make pre-trial detention decisions, delays in confirming nationality status can mean that some defendants are assumed to be foreign nationals when in fact they are not. Unsurprisingly given the high profile of immigration issues across Europe, the police and courts appear to be reluctant to release, or even consider releasing, individuals until they have confirmation that they are in the country legitimately.

The chapter progresses as follows. The first section provides an overview of available data on the number of foreign nationals in pre-trial detention across Europe. The second section presents case studies from three Western European countries. The final section examines potential measures to reduce the use of pre-trial detention for foreign nationals including possible non-custodial measures.

Statistical evidence: foreign nationals in pre-trial detention

With the necessary caution because of the statistical problems highlighted earlier and in Chapter 1, some observations can be made using the data in Table 13.1. Countries with high percentages of foreign nationals in pre-trial detention fall into two categories. One, relatively prosperous Northern and Western European jurisdictions, such as Austria and Denmark, which are desirable countries for migrants to settle in, including from other countries in the European Union; and Southern European countries, such as Cyprus, Greece, Italy and Spain, which are entry points into the European Union for migrants from outside its border and particularly from Africa and the Middle East. Countries where foreign national prisoners comprise a small proportion of those in pre-trial detention are generally Middle and Eastern European countries whose populations tend to emigrate, for example Bulgaria, Poland and Romania. Citizens from these countries comprise a high proportion of the foreign nationals imprisoned pre-trial in Northern and Western European countries (MoJ, 2022a; Morgenstern, 2018).

There are some interesting exceptions to these trends demonstrating the importance of considering socio-economic, historical and geopolitical factors. For example, two Baltic states, Latvia and Lithuania, have very low populations of foreign nationals in pre-trial detention whereas the reverse is true in Estonia where more than a third of the pre-trial prison population are foreign nationals (see Table 13.1). The most likely explanation is the

Table 13.1 European prison populations by nationality 2020, highest to lowest percentages

	Foreign nationals in pre-trial population		*Foreign nationals in sentenced population*		*Foreign nationals in total prison population*	
	N	%	*N*	%	*N*	%
Luxembourg	275	83	218	67	494	78
Austria	1,349	68	3,533	49	5,119	53
Greece	1,934	68	4,401	54	6,347	58
Slovenia	231	58	185	18	416	29
Cyprus*	118	54	197	42	315	44
Spain	4,493	48	16,418	31	16,418	28
Denmark	649	45	597	22	1,246	31
Estonia**	168	38	648	32	816	33
Italy	6,923	37	12,843	31	19,841	33
Finland	232	34	279	13	511	19
Portugal	650	29	1,321	13	1,971	15
Czech Republic	491	27	1,303	7	1,794	9
Croatia	324	26	157	7	481	14
The Netherlands	1,062	24	1,101	20	2,195	22
Ireland	189	23	411	13	600	15
France	5,998	23	10,153	20	16,151	23
England and Wales***	1,865	20	6,323	8	9,225	11
Poland***	680	8	630	1	1,310	2
Slovak Republic	135	8	121	1	256	2
Lithuania**	50	7	78	1	128	2
Bulgaria	43	5	137	3	180	2
Latvia	31	3	34	1	65	2
Romania	24	1	196	1	220	1

Note: Data sometimes do not add up because in some states prisoners with unknown nationality are missing in the subcategories.

* for 2019, no data for 2020 provided, ** data for 1 January 2020; *** data for 31 December 2019

Source: Aebi and Tiago (2021: Table 12) and own calculations, data for 31 January 2020.

sizeable Russian population residing in Estonia. This group have "grey" or alien passports[1] which means that they have residency rights in Estonia but are stateless, resulting in them being defined as foreign nationals in prison data (Morgenstern, 2009). Similarly, Luxembourg's high non-national population (47%) and Romania's, Poland and Slovakia's very low non-national population (<2%) provide some explanation for the proportion of foreign nationals in their pre-trial populations (UN, 2022).

The second notable trend in the data shown in Table 13.1 is that the proportion of foreign national prisoners in pre-trial detention is greater than in the sentenced population in virtually all countries. In countries with high numbers of foreign nationals in pre-trial detention the differences compared with the sentenced population tend to be greatest, for example in Austria, Croatia, Denmark, Slovenia and Spain, where the percentage of foreign nationals in pre-trial detention is up to 23% higher than that of sentenced prisoners. Although it is difficult to make direct comparisons because not everyone who is detained pre-trial will receive a custodial sentence, the disparity suggests that foreign nationals are disproportionately imprisoned pre-trial compared to their national counterparts.

Three case studies

England and Wales

According to SPACE and national statistics, a fifth (20%) of all remand prisoners in England and Wales (1,865 out of 9,559) were foreign nationals in December 2019 (Aebi and Tiago, 2021; MoJ, 2020a). This represents one of the lowest proportions in Europe (see Table 13.1). However, it is higher than the 14% of the population born outside of the UK and 9% of the general population who are foreign nationals (The Migration Observatory, 2022). Foreign national prisoners were more than twice as likely as British National prisoners to be on remand rather than sentenced. A fifth of all foreign national prisoners were on remand compared to a tenth of British National prisoners (Aebi and Tiago, 2021: Table 12). Consequently, whichever way the data are studied, foreign national prisoners appear to be disproportionately represented in the prison remand population.

Figure 13.1 presents the number of British and foreign national remand prisoners for all years between 2002 and 2020 (MoJ, 2020a). It shows that the population trends are very similar for British and foreign national remand prisoners. However, the decline in the number of remand prisoners after 2015 was greater for British nationals than for foreign nationals. All sections of the remand population have increased since 2019. The number of foreign national remand prisoners rose during the COVID-19 pandemic to 2,636 in March 2022 (MoJ, 2022a). However, they comprised a slightly smaller proportion of the prison remand population (17%) compared to 2020 (MoJ,

2020a). The remand population as a whole rose during the pandemic but the increase was greater for foreign nationals than British nationals (41% compared with 29% (MoJ, 2022a)). The general increase was caused by backlogs in the courts and cases involving foreign nationals are likely to have delayed by difficulties in getting information from overseas.

No further official data are routinely published on the foreign national prison remand population. However, a Freedom of Information Act (FoIA) request provides data on prison remand admissions, that is, the flow into prisons, in 2018 and 2019 (MoJ, 2020b). A fifth of prison remand admissions in 2018 (n = 9,681, 19%) and 2019 (n = 10,028, 20%) were foreign nationals. Foreign nationals accounted for 17% of female admissions compared to a fifth of male admissions in 2018 and 2019 (MoJ, 2020b: Tables 5 and 6).

Comparisons with the proportion of sentenced admissions for the same years suggests that foreign nationals are less likely than British nationals to be received into prison under sentence. In 2018, 12% (n = 7,232) and in 2019, 13% (n = 7,076) of sentenced admissions were foreign nationals (MoJ, 2020b: Tables 1 and 2). Both males and females comprised a smaller proportion of sentenced than remand admissions (MoJ, 2020b: Tables 1 and 2). The disparity is greater for women (9% and 10% in 2018 and 2019, respectively) than men (12% and 13% in 2018 and 2019, respectively). These differences are a cause for concern and need further investigation because it may indicate discriminatory decision-making and that some foreign nationals are remanded into custody unnecessarily. However, there is not a clear linear progression from custodial remand to custodial sentence, although the likelihood of a custodial sentence is a legal consideration in bail decisions. The criteria on which bail decisions are made differs from those applied in sentencing and cases can change significantly from when bail decisions are first made to their conclusion. Even if a custodial sentence is imposed, some offenders will have already served their sentences whilst on remand and will

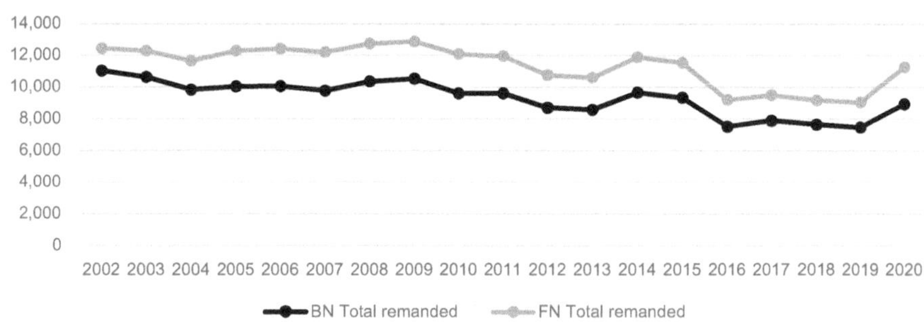

Figure 13.1 British National (BN) and Foreign National (FN) remand prisoners on 30 June 2002–2020 (MoJ, 2020b: Table A1.11).

not appear in the statistics on prison admissions. These and other factors, such as offence types, which are discussed in the following, may explain some of the differences between the proportion of foreign nationals in pre-trial detention and the proportion received into prison under sentence.

The FoIA request (MoJ, 2020b) also provides data on the offences with which defendants in pre-trial detention were charged. Table 13.2. shows differences in profiles of alleged offences of British and foreign national defendants. British nationals were more likely to be accused of violence and motoring offences whereas foreign nationals were more likely to be accused of drugs offences. These variations may explain some of the differences in the number of British and foreign national remand prisoners, but it is difficult to draw conclusions without more detailed information about the offences because the categories are very broad. Of particular note is the much higher proportion of foreign nationals accused of "miscellaneous crimes against society" with a particularly wide disparity for females. This category includes a range of offences with no direct victim, which do not fit into other offence categories including bail offences, offences linked to prostitution and handling stolen goods, many of which are relatively minor (Home Office, 2022b). Foreign nationals are also more likely to have no offence recorded. These data raise a suspicion that the criminal justice system is being utilised for immigration purposes but it may equally be a result of administrative errors. Further research is required to understand how and why this category is used. Offence patterns for sentenced prisoners entering custody are similar to alleged offence patterns of remand prisoners.

No data are published on the country of origin of foreign national remand prisoners. The foreign national prison population as a whole, includes prisoners from 176 countries, with prisoners from Europe comprising the largest group (MoJ, 2022a). The largest single group are Albanians (13%). Notably, the population also includes a relatively high proportion of individuals from Ireland (7%) who have a special immigration status in England and Wales, which means that they are free to enter and leave the UK without a visa or work permit. Unfortunately, no data are published on police or court bail decisions involving foreign national defendants, so we know very little about the processes, which lead to the differences in the prison remand population outlined earlier.

HM Prison Inspectorate, an independent body which inspects conditions in prisons, has largely neglected foreign national remand prisoners. The thematic inspection of foreign national prisoners included remand prisoners as interviewees but then made no separate statements about their experiences, simply conflating them alongside sentenced prisoners (HMIP, 2006). The later thematic inspection of remand prisoners provides evidence for the overrepresentation of foreign nationals in the population using official data but goes no further (HMIP, 2012). Both reports provide ample evidence of the problems faced by both remand and foreign national prisoners, thereby

Table 13.2 Alleged offences of remand prisoners by nationality in 2019 (MoJ, 2020b: Tables 5 and 6)

	Males				*Females*				*Total*			
	BN		*FN*		*BN*		*FN*		*BN*		*FN*	
	N	%	*N*	%	*N*	%	*N*	%	*N*	%	*N*	%
Violence	7,607	21	1,152	12	524	17	64	10	8,131	21	1,216	12
Sexual offences	1,905	5	535	6	21	1	0	0	1,926	5	535	5
Robbery	2,298	6	356	4	204	7	13	2	2,502	6	369	4
Theft	5,475	15	1,070	11	623	20	165	25	6,098	16	1,235	12
Fraud	275	1	203	2	48	2	22	3	323	1	225	2
Property damage	1,836	5	200	2	210	7	15	2	2,046	5	215	2
Drugs offences	4, 695	13	2,063	22	384	12	79	12	5,079	13	2,142	21
Weapons offences	2,644	7	490	5	187	6	17	3	2,831	7	507	5
Public order	1,214	3	132	1	91	3	5	>1	1,305	3	137	1
Miscellaneous crimes against society	1,868	5	1,555	17	219	7	174	27	2,987	8	1,729	17
Motoring	4,997	14	829	9	458	15	56	9	5,455	14	885	9
Offence not recorded	1,206	3	788	8	139	4	45	7	1,345	3	833	8

supporting the argument that foreign national remand prisoners face multiple problems because they fall into both categories. However, foreign national remand prisoners are not a homogenous group. Prisoners who are visibly from minority ethnic groups are likely to face further discrimination (Lammy, 2017). For example, defendants from minority ethnic groups are more likely to be remanded in custody, which is reflected in the high proportion of these groups in the prison remand population (Lammy, 2017; MoJ, 2021). Similarly, prisoners who do not speak English will face more difficulties in court and in prison than those that do (HMIP, 2012).

Explaining the disproportionate number of foreign national remand prisoners

This section discusses some of the factors which are likely to contribute to the disproportionate number of foreign national remand prisoners in England and Wales. There is a lack of research on foreign national prisoners generally, and almost nothing on foreign national remand prisoners, so the evidence base is very limited. Notable exceptions are a recent study which explored bail decision-making in cases involving foreign national women (Robson, 2020) and several reviews undertaken by the Prison Reform Trust, a third sector organisation, again focusing on women (Prison Reform Trust and Hibiscus Initiatives, 2018).

Robson's (2020) study is based on interviews with support workers, lawyers and prosecutors and court observations. It argues that foreign national female defendants are treated as a "suspect population" because of "racialised anxieties around immigration and crime" (Robson, 2020: 5) which lead them to be categorised as high bail risks. Central to this argument is continuing political and media focus on immigration and consistent narratives around "illegal" migrants. This is supported by various policies, which focus on removing the supposed large number of illegal migrants as quickly as possible. To add to the general "hostile environment", that is, a deliberate policy of making migrants lives difficult and uncomfortable, specific legislation and policies have been put in place in relation to foreign national offenders which will inevitability impact upon the whole criminal process (Griffiths and Yeo, 2021; Lousley, 2020). Immigration and criminal justice worlds are so intertwined that criminal justice procedures, including remand, are viewed as an opportunity to identify and detain individuals who are suspected of being in the country illegally (Aliverti and Bosworth, 2017; Lousley, 2020; Robson, 2020). Racialised stereotypes, of manipulative untruthful and untrustworthy migrants from the Global South and Eastern Europe who are abusing the immigration system, are used by legal professionals and the courts to draw conclusions about who is and who is not a foreign national in their submissions and decision-making (Lousley, 2020; Robson, 2020).

Bail research in England and Wales has charted the growing importance of the risk of offending as the primary rationale for pre-trial detention (Chapter 4), although courts often rely on all three exceptions to the presumption of bail (risk of absconding, offending and interference with witnesses). However, for foreign national defendants, risk of absconding has been reported as the pre-eminent exception to bail (Robson, 2020). The risk of absconding is perceived differently for British and foreign nationals. Whereas British nationals simply will not turn up for court, foreign nationals are viewed as likely to leave the country requiring lengthy extradition proceedings or that they may remain out of reach of the justice system entirely. Having "community ties" mitigates against the risk of absconding, but it is more difficult for foreign national defendants to prove they are sufficiently strong. There is no legal definition of community ties, but they generally include stable accommodation, employment, having dependents and other family ties in the UK. Not only do foreign national defendants need to prove they have ties in the UK but, unlike British nationals, they have to satisfy the court that their ties with their "home" countries are not too strong to support them to abscond. Weak or absent community ties in the UK also result from the immigration system which prevents migrants from working, having bank accounts, etc. (Home Office, 2022a). Robson's (2020) research suggests that foreign nationality is used as a proxy for a lack of community ties in the UK. Other explanations for the higher pre-trial detention of foreign nationals include problems with accessing adequate legal advice and interpreters (Aliverti and Seoighe, 2017; Hunter et al., 2022; Prison Reform Trust and Hibiscus Initiatives, 2018; Robson, 2020).

Alternatives to pre-trial detention

The last section of this case study explores some of the issues that foreign national defendants face during the bail process, which when taken together demonstrate that there are significant barriers to being released on bail and may partially explain the higher number of foreign national remand prisoners. A second potential reason for an increased likelihood of being detained in pre-trial detention is that alternatives are not viewed by courts as appropriate. Notably, however, England and Wales has several bail conditions which are specifically targeted at meeting the perceived risk of foreign national defendants absconding.

Both the police and the courts are able to attach conditions to bail (Chapter 4). Although, courts can impose any conditions, the police are not able to impose two conditions, which may be particularly useful to allay concerns about the risk of absconding – electronic monitoring and residing in Community Accommodation Service (CAS) (previously Bail Accommodation and Support Service) (MoJ, 2022b). The inability to impose these conditions, particularly electronic monitoring, may be one reason for defendants being detained by the police prior to their first court appearance, thereby increasing the risk of being remanded in custody by courts (Chapter 4). Other reasons for police detaining suspects for court include a lack of time to collect all the relevant information including immigration status and previous convictions, as this will involve liaising with the border force and police forces overseas. Police reluctance to bail foreign national suspects is also linked to a culture of suspicion of this group and discriminatory decision-making in cases involving defendants from minority ethnic groups (Bowling et al., 2012; Parmar, 2019).

Courts are able to, and do, require defendants who they believe may leave the country to surrender their passports. In addition, courts can require a security or securities to be paid to the court. This requires defendants and/or someone known to them to lodge a sum of money with the court. It differs from sureties, which are also available. Sureties are "trustworthy" individuals known to defendants who agree to forfeit an amount of money to the court if defendants abscond. The issues with both these forms of "money" bail are well known. You need to know someone who can be contacted quickly and who has the financial resources to stand surety or security. In addition, individuals who provide securities need ready access to funds. Individuals who act as sureties or provide securities do not need to be British citizens but do need to show secure resident status, an address in the UK and prove they are "upstanding" members of society putting foreign national defendants at a disadvantage.

Defendants can also be required to regularly report to police stations but a greater level of surveillance can be provided by electronic monitoring (EM). Two forms of EM are available: curfew monitoring using radio-frequency technologies and location monitoring, using Global Positioning Systems (GPS), to monitor exclusion zones, curfews and attendance at appointment or provide trial monitoring which tracks individuals' movements 24/7 (Hucklesby and Holdsworth, 2016). No data are available on the number of foreign national defendants subject to EM bail. However, EM is already used for immigration bail with plans to increase its use to additional cohorts very soon (Home Office, 2022a; ICIBI, 2022). Consequently, it is likely that EM will be very widely used for foreign national defendants but whether this is as an alternative to pre-trial detention rather than as supplementary bail condition for those who would already be released is a more pertinent question.

Courts require all defendants to be released on EM bail to have suitable accommodation and will often also impose a residence condition. The householder or owner must consent to EM equipment being installed (Hucklesby and Holdsworth, 2016). The Community Accommodation Service (CAS) is available to defendants who do not have a suitable bail address (Hucklesby, 2011; MoJ, 2022b; Nacro, 2021). CAS provides accommodation but capacity issues limit availability. Foreign national defendants face a particular challenge because CAS requires payment for the accommodation and some of them will not have any financial resources available because of their immigration status (s. 115, Immigration and Asylum Act 1999).

Germany

As of 2021, about 13% of the resident population in Germany has a foreign nationality, 25% a migrant background (Statistisches Bundesamt, 2022). Unequal or discriminatory practices in the use of pre-trial detention may refer to various grounds, and defendants with a migrant background may be affected particularly. Whilst some racist practices by the police have been identified in Germany (Hunold and Wegner, 2020), only few studies (Ludwig-Mayerhofer, 1997; Oberwittler and Lukas, 2010; Schott, 2004) and no specific data are available to assess discriminatory practices in later stages of the criminal justice system. Some research exists on the nationality of those affected by pre-trial detention (Morgenstern, 2011, 2018) which shows that most of them are nationals of non-EU countries (often from Turkey and Arab States). Regularly published statistics, however, only refer to *sentenced* prisoners (Statistisches Bundesamt, 2021a and earlier),[2] this is the reason why Germany is missing in Table 13.1. Data for the nationality of pre-trial prisoners are available only for some years and only shows whether the person is of foreign nationality. Consequently, we know very little about foreign national pre-trial detainees and nothing about the treatment of individuals with German passports who have migrant backgrounds or who are labelled as migrants. Instead, our focus is on the more heterogenous group of foreign nationals, meaning those without a German passport. The latest data available (Aebi et al., 2017) show that Germany would be ranked high in Table 13.1 with 61% foreign nationals among the pre-trial prison population in 2016. This percentage has risen dramatically in the last 15 years (2008: 42%, 2013: 53%, Morgenstern, 2018) and, while in absolute numbers the German remand population has become smaller (2008: 7,081, 2016: 5,081), the number of foreign pre-trial detainees has increased (2008: 5,005, 2016: 8,308). This partly coincided with the "refugee crisis" in 2015/2016 when Germany registered almost 900,000 refugees in 2015 alone. After an initial societal and political climate of solidarity and understanding, critical and hostile voices became louder, accusing young male migrants of frequent criminal behaviour. Some incidents were extensively covered by the German and international media. During the 2015/2016 New Year's Eve celebrations, mass sexual assaults and numerous thefts were reported in several German cities. Suspects were mainly North-African man, often asylum seekers. Police coined the term "Nafris", which stands for "North African" but also for "North African Intensive Offender" (Morgenstern, 2017: 16).

While a longitudinal analysis is not possible due to scarce and scattered data, those available show that foreign nationals are overrepresented among all relevant sub-groups in the criminal justice system but to starkly different extents (Morgenstern, 2020): In 2020, foreign nationals formed 34% of all suspects in the Police Statistics (Bundeskriminalamt, 2021), 35% of all persons with a final court decision (convicted and sentenced, acquitted, other; Statistisches Bundesamt, 2021a), 35% of all prisoners serving a sentence persons (Statistisches Bundesamt, 2021b) as opposed to the more than 60% among pre-trial detainees (data for 2016) mentioned earlier. The gross overrepresentation of foreign nationals affected by pre-trial detention can therefore not be explained by developments in the other groups described. The difference between sentenced persons and those in pre-trial detention is particularly alarming. It indicates that many of those foreign nationals that have been in pre-trial detention either have not been convicted, sentenced to imprisonment or do not serve a prison sentence – at least not in Germany. How many of them are expelled from the country is unknown, but we can assume that many are convicted of offences that are not severe and are not punished with an unsuspended prison sentence.

A somewhat more recent study confirmed that foreign nationals run a much higher risk of being remanded in custody (Statistisches Bundesamt, 2021c). Of all those who received a final decision by a criminal court (convicted, acquitted, other) in 2017, 3.3% had spent time in pre-trial detention. This ratio was 1.9% for German defendants and 6.5% for foreigner nationals. In 2014, the values had been lower, 2.8% of the overall population; 1.7% in the case of German defendants and 6% in the case of foreign nationals.

Different possible explanations exist for the overrepresentation of foreign nationals in pre-trial detention. There are no indications that the type of offences committed differs significantly from those committed by Germans (Morgenstern, 2018). It is therefore the practice of ordering pre-trial detention and the reasons given that must be scrutinised. Generally (see also Chapter 5), the risk of flight was the most used ground for detention, supported by any evidence which may increase the expected sentence, thereby incentivising defendants to go into hiding or abscond. Other influential factors included accommodation, in the form a permanent postal address, and stable family bonds and employment or education, which were all viewed as stabilising if present and increasing the risk of absconding if missing. The significance of these factors increased for foreign nationals. According to our research, they do not *per se* run a greater risk of being detained, but the risk of absconding is linked to stable living conditions in Germany. Therefore, certain subgroups often cannot avoid detention: so-called travelling offenders, even for minor alleged offences, because of their insecure residency status or because they are in the country illegally. Judges reported not wanting to risk the trial not taking place. Even those who insisted that they took a proportionate approach to pre-trial decisions for foreign nationals said they would order an arrest warrant when defendants lacked social bonds (see Chapter 5). Certain groups of young men with Northern Africa and Arab backgrounds were at increased risk of detention because of the political/media pressure after the incidents mentioned earlier. As one defence lawyer exclaimed: "*Reason to detain? Nafri!*" (Morgenstern, 2017: 15).

"Foreign nationals" are not a homogenous group and different procedures exists for EU citizens which should result in less recourse to pre-trial detention. However, it is questionable, whether German courts accept and use detention-avoiding EU cooperation tools, namely to contact and summon foreign defendants in their home country. The DETOUR research found a mixed picture – judges were aware of the requirements and procedures but were hesitant about using them particularly for certain groups of defendants including travelling offenders, Eastern Europeans and those accused of financial crime. Some defence lawyers suggested that judges were too lazy to use the European mechanisms available.

Scepticism and sometimes ignorance, was clearly visible regarding the European Supervision Order (ESO), that aims to facilitate pre-trial supervision in the community "at home" within the European Union (see Chapter 14 for details). Most respondents were unaware of it. Only two had practical experience, which they did not want to repeat, because they found the procedure cumbersome. Others reported that they did not want to use it because it was bureaucratic and they would rather impose a financial surety. Whilst it can be assumed that the ESO has been used in a small number of cases (Morgenstern, 2017), no legal decisions have been published and no activities or publications by professional organisations are available. This means that the European mechanisms may alleviate the situation for some once they are properly implemented but are currently not very promising. They do not help for those who are not EU citizens, in Germany the majority of pre-trial detainees.

The Netherlands

Proportion of foreign nationals in pre-trial detention

According to Table 13.1, 24% of the pre-trial detainees in the Netherlands in 2020 were of foreign nationality. This rate does not differ significantly from 2015 and is and is higher than the proportion of foreign nationals in the general prison population (20%). The Netherlands are therefore in the middle range of European countries, with a proportion much lower than the neighbouring states of Belgium and Germany. However, foreign nationals are disproportionately detained pre-trial because only about 7.1% of Dutch residents hold foreign nationality (CBS, 2022). According to a recent quantitative study, 10% of all criminal cases referred to the Public Prosecutor's Office in 2012 (N = 18,274), foreign nationals were 1.7–2 times more likely to be in pre-trial detention than Dutch citizens when all measured, legally relevant variables were taken into account (Wermink et al., 2022).

Reasons for overrepresentation

Several related explanations can be given for this overrepresentation: 1) the legal grounds for pre-trial detention are clearly disadvantageous for foreign national defendants; 2) lack of a residence status increases the chances of pre-trial detention; and, 3) several obstacles stand in the way of using alternatives for this group.

Pre-trial detention can only be imposed when the alleged criminal offence carries a sentence of imprisonment of four years or more (see Chapter 8), but the criminal code mentions some exceptions to this "four years or more requirement". A pre-trial detention order can also be issued if it cannot be established that defendants have a permanent address or place of residence in the Netherlands and they are suspected of an offence which carries a sentence of imprisonment (Article 67, Subsection 2 CCP). Risk of flight legally is one of the main grounds for pre-trial detention in the Netherlands (Article 67a CCP), although in practice it is one of the least used (College voor de Rechten van de Mens, 2017). It entails a risk that suspects will abscond in order to evade criminal proceedings and subsequent punishment. According to the jurisprudence, the risk of flight must be substantiated with reference to the specific behaviour of defendants or specific personal circumstances. It may not be deduced solely from the severity of the punishment of the alleged offence or the fact that somebody is a foreign (European or non-European) national. If guarantees are offered by defendants, for example by putting up a financial guarantee, a custodial remand may not be based solely on the risk of flight (Corstens and Borgers, 2014; Janssen et al., 2013; ECtHR, *Letellier v. France*, 12369/86, 26 June 1991).

The Netherlands Institute for Human Rights (College voor de Rechten van de Mens, 2017) concluded that there were no sufficient grounds for applying "risk of flight" in the majority of cases. An example of the standard approach taken by Dutch courts is that:

> No fixed residence by the defendant can be established, he has no permit of residence (geldige verblijfstitel) in the Netherlands, and he has the opportunity to avoid criminal proceedings in the Netherlands [by absconding, eds.] and it is reasonably to be expected that he will make use of this possibility.
>
> (College voor de Rechten van de Mens, 2017: 25–26)

Many things remain unclear in the arguments used by the examining judge in this case, for instance, whether the suspect has no fixed residence or whether he is legally declared an "undesirable" foreign national, why there are indications that he will avoid criminal proceedings and why it assumed that he will make use of these possibilities. On similar grounds the European Court of

Human Rights (ECtHR) recently ruled on three Dutch cases of pre-trial detention (Hasselbaink v. The Netherlands, 73329/16; Maassen v. The Netherlands, 10982/15; Zohlandt v. The Netherlands, 69491/16; all decided by the ECtHR on 9 May 2021). The Court concluded that the decision to extend pre-trial detention in these cases was insufficiently substantiated because no additional information was provided by the court which simply referred back to its initial decision.

Compared to other jurisdictions, for example Germany, flight risk is in general used relatively scarcely as a ground for pre-trial detention in the Netherlands. Despite this, risk of flight was the first reason mentioned by respondents in the DETOUR study when they were asked to explain the higher proportion of foreign nationals in the Dutch pre-trial detention (Boone et al., 2017). This was particularly the case for foreign nationals who solely come to the Netherlands to commit crimes – so-called mobile bandits. Expedited proceedings (see Chapter 8) are used in these cases allowing for very swift trials. Defendants are kept in pre-trial detention whilst waiting for their trial to begin. A defence lawyer explained:

> In case somebody without documents steals a bicycle, you can be certain that he will be remanded in custody, the main idea being that it would be better if he serves his sentence immediately.
>
> (Boone et al., 2017: 41)

Most of these defendants were identified as coming from Eastern Europe, referred to as the "East-European route". In such cases, the actual ground for pre-trial detention used is risk of reoffending according to one of the prosecutors interviewed:

> What you do see, are Romanians, mobile bandits. They travel through all of Europe. They have lists in their pockets [of] what events are happening in Europe. These are typical cases for fast proceedings. You keep them two weeks in remand detention and, if possible, they are convicted after these two weeks for a longer period.
>
> (Boone et al., 2017: 42)

In 2013, the Amsterdam Court in Chambers held that, due to the principle of non-discrimination laid down in article 18 of the Treaty on the Functioning of the EU (TFEU) and the Directive on the right of free movement in the EU, EU citizens with a demonstrable address in another EU country cannot be remanded on the ground of flight risk (Rechtbank Amsterdam 10 December 2013, NBSTRAF 2014/25). At the time we conducted our DETOUR research, mixed feelings existed on the effect of this case law on the interpretation of flight risk as a ground of pre-trial detention. Some respondents were of the opinion that the flight risk for EU citizens should not be an argument for applying pre-trial detention, partly because of the principle of mutual recognition. According to them, the mere fact that defendants have no fixed place of residence in the Netherlands is not a sufficient reason to accept a risk of flight. They stated that judges should take account of whether it is possible to transfer defendants back to the Netherlands (for example, by using European Arrest Warrants), once they have left. Other respondents refuted the idea that this case-law really affected practice. One judge specifically indicated a lack of confidence in the procedures for transferring "mobile bandits" back to the Netherlands. He conceded that it might be contrary to the meaning of the EU-treaty but suggested that the flight risk should not be considered in in terms of "can I find them later on?", but in terms of "will they serve their sentence?" He was not convinced at all that "mobile bandits" would serve their sentences if they were not held in pre-trial detention, allowing them to flee the country and never return (Boone et al., 2017: 43).

The risk of flight and absence of a residence status are also obstacles to using non-custodial alternatives to pre-trial detention. Migrants without a residence status are largely excluded from all probation services (Boone and Kox, 2012). Financial bail is occasionally used but it is out of reach of defendants who do not have stable sources of income and housing. To qualify for electronic monitoring as an alternative for pre-trial detention, defendants need suitable accommodation and a place to charge equipment. These are requirements almost impossible for many foreign nationals to meet and are reasons for their overrepresentation in prison (Boone and Kox, 2012; Boone et al., 2017; Wermink et al., 2022). While the European Supervision Order (ESO; see Chapter 14) should make it easier to release foreign pre-trial detainees under the condition that alternative measures are supervised in their home countries, this mechanism is unfortunately still underused. A lack of knowledge, the bureaucracy involved and the length of the proceedings seem to stand in the way of a widespread use of the ESO (Lindeman et al., 2018).

Reducing effect of the interconnectedness of criminal policy and immigration policy

The relatively low proportion of foreign nationals in pre-trial detention in a comparative context can partly be explained by strong links between criminal and immigration policies. Judicial practitioners in the DETOUR study mentioned that suspects of relatively minor crimes who do not have residence status in the Netherlands are not subject to pre-trial detention but are instead immediately put in immigration detention. This may lead to individuals being detained in situations where "regular" suspects would have been released from pre-trial detention (Boone et al., 2017: 22).

Alternative measures for awaiting trial

Previous sections have underlined that the high numbers of foreign national defendants held in pre-trial detention are a European problem, which questions the human rights credentials of European states. Whilst the legal frameworks for pre-trial detention decisions are the same for everyone, the way they are applied differs for citizens and foreign nationals. The circumstances of foreign nationals, that is, that they are not citizens of the country in which they have allegedly committed an offence, means that the law is applied differently. A version of the legal criteria of risk of absconding/failing to appear is present in nearly every jurisdiction around the World as a reason for refusing release pending trial, yet it disadvantages foreign national defendants almost automatically. This is because defendants are assumed, simply because of their status, to have weak social/community ties in the country they allegedly committed their offence and strong social/community ties in their country of citizenship. The latter is assumed to pull them back to their country of origin whilst the former means they have no reason to stay. These factors added to assumptions and stereotypes about the trustworthiness of defendants, presumptions of guilt and defendants innate desire to avoid conviction and sentence, all compounded by racialised and gender stereotypes, act as powerful reasons for using pre-trial detention rather than exploring alternatives measures for this group. Problems and delays with accessing information from countries of origin and the work involved to confirm the identity of individuals, offending histories and their living circumstances add to the reasons not to release them. This applies equally to defence lawyers and criminal justice agencies, resulting in factually thin and unverified defence submissions to courts, which will inevitably make release less likely. It is also true that it will be easier to access this information in some circumstances than others, most notably for defendants who reside within the European Union. Information will be very difficult, if not impossible, to obtain from unstable states and war-torn countries where many non-EU defendants originate from.

The foreign national population in pre-trial detention is made up of many different groups. The most obvious and useful distinction may be between EU and non-EU citizens because the EU has already signalled its willingness to find alternatives for EU nationals and, theoretically, information exchange and mutual cooperation already exist. However, as the Dutch case study highlights, not all EU citizens are viewed equally by judges. For example, Eastern Europeans were identified as posing a particular flight risk. Stereotypes and discrimination against certain groups, for instance, Roma and other ethnic minorities, continue to impact upon pre-trial detention decisions.

Positively, the European Union has already identified the need for instruments of mutual cooperation to allow EU citizens to return home whilst awaiting trial via European Supervision Orders. However, these are little used and confidence in them appears to be low (Neira Pena, 2020, see Chapter

14). It is possible that judges and courts simply do not think it is appropriate that defendants are able to go home because it does not tackle the real or perceived problem of them failing to return to face trial. This is a challenge that the EAW is designed to tackle which sets out an extradition process. There is little doubt that the EAW is useful in some cases, but it probably provides additional reassurance in cases in which defendants would be released in any event, rather than facilitating the release of large numbers of those destined for pre-trial detention. Judges in the Netherlands demonstrated low confidence in the measures voicing very real concerns that it is too easy for defendants to disappear within EU borders. The more effective alternative to pre-trial detention may be in-country supervision and monitoring which is likely to be more palatable for decision-makers because the agencies and procedures will be familiar meaning that they will have more confidence in the effectiveness of the monitoring/supervision and enforcement.

Given that mitigating the risk of flight is a top priority for decision-makers in these cases, ensuring that defendants remain in the country is likely to be a very important factor in release decisions. Consequently, surrendering a passport and/or identity documents is an effective mechanism to facilitate this and is already used in such cases in England and Wales. However, the UK has sealed borders, unlike European countries within the Schengen zone. Whilst is it legally possible in Germany, judges tended to be sceptical of this approach (Morgenstern, 2017). Dutch judges seem all too aware of the consequences of the EU policy of free movement for tracing defendants from EU countries. This issue has even greater resonance when acknowledging that not all countries within the geographical zone are in the European Union and are, therefore, not party to the ESO or EAW.

Whilst it is technically possible for defendants to leave a country without a passport it is difficult to do so outside of the Schengen zone. No other bail condition provides such concrete assurances. "Money" bail whereby defendants or their sureties are required to promise or deposit a sum of money with the court prior to their release that is forfeited if they abscond, acts as a deterrent but does not prevent defendants' fleeing. It also has the disadvantage of relying on defendants having, or having access to, financial resources and personal bonds, resulting in considerable inequalities. In practice, any wider use of these conditions is only ever going to have a minimal impact of pre-trial detention populations because very few of those detained are likely to have the financial resources and/or social capital to take advantage of them.

Electronic monitoring may provide sufficient reassurance to decision-makers that defendants are being monitored continuously, in order to persuade them to release them. EM is now widely used across Europe to monitor pre-trial populations (Hucklesby et al., 2016), but we have no data about its use specifically with foreign national defendants. It is not available in every country (for example, in most parts of Germany and Ireland) and in others, it is questionable whether there is room for expansion given uptake varies considerably. EM should allay decision-makers fears about absconding but one challenge is that currently there are no procedures for EM to be used in a country that did not impose it and defendants cannot cross borders whilst being monitored. Consequently, defendants would need to stay in the country where their trial is going to take place requiring them to have stable accommodation (see the following text). Furthermore, EM is not full proof, the equipment can be removed at any time, although the authorities would be alerted.

Bail conditions are already used extensively across Europe to monitor behaviour to mitigate bail risks and provide alternatives to pre-trial detention. However, a significant disadvantage is that they are unlikely to be, or in the case of electronic monitoring cannot be, used unless defendants have an appropriate address where they can live and be monitored. Lack of accommodation is a very real barrier to reducing pre-trial detention for foreign nationals, but it does not apply to all defendants because some will be residents or have family or friends they can stay with. Even in countries which have accommodation provision, such as England and Wales, it is often not possible for foreign national defendants to access it. Finding a solution to this accommodation problem – both in terms of finding accommodation and getting decision-makers to accept it as fit for purpose – may reduce numbers in pre-trial detention. However, it may also lead to defendants being required to stay in court mandated accommodation rather than their own or the ESO being used. One potential option, which is being used in England and Wales with immigration cases were individuals do not have a stable address is to impose a condition of EM with GPS and allowing wearers to charge devices at specific building, such as probation offices. This deals with the practical issues of not having a place to live but not with ethical concerns.

We have only considered those non-custodial options which are currently in use in European countries. All of them have drawbacks which will limit their use and therefore the potential for them to significantly impact upon the number of foreign nationals in pre-trial detention. In order to consider more creative solutions to what will be an ongoing challenge, we need to know much more about the composition of the pre-trial population and the views of decision-makers about what measures would allay their concerns about the bail risks posed by foreign national defendants. Changing the culture of suspicion of these groups is a much harder challenge to meet.

Conclusion

It is clear from the aforementioned analysis that structural discrimination of foreign nationals exists with regard to remand decision-making in all three case-studies and beyond. When compared with general populations and populations of sentenced prisoners, foreign nationals are overrepresented in pre-trial detention. A range of factors will contribute to explaining the number of foreign national remand prisoners and these are likely to differ within and between countries. However, detailed research is hampered by a lack of available data. Of particular note is the dearth of data to uncover variations between different groups of foreign nationals, which is especially important given the intersections between nationality, race/ethnicity, gender, EU/Non-EU citizenship and residency. Foreign nationals are not a homogenous group. Any measures to reduce the use of pre-trial detention will need to account for these differences and provide alternatives which are tailored to defendants' circumstances but we currently do not have the knowledge to do so.

Working with the limited data which is available, this chapter suggests that the pre-trial process tends to treat all foreign nationals as a homogenous group, who are all assumed to be a flight risk, highly likely to abscond and not stand trial, therefore dodging justice and leaving victims in limbo, simply by virtue of being a foreign national, which itself is a complicated and contested term. These assumptions do not appear to be based on evidence, given the paucity of available data, but rather on stereotypes arising from the group's "otherness", inter alia, because of their country of origin and/or race and ethnicity. This is played out most notably in relation to Eastern Europeans who are widely identified as especially risky.

A particular trait ascribed to foreign nationals is that they all lack community ties in the jurisdiction where they are accused of committing an offence and that they have strong ties in their country of origin. Taken together these factors are considered to increase the likelihood of absconding, even when they have built a life in their adopted country. By contrast, many foreign nationals do have ties in the country of residence, even if they depend on informal labour markets and on relatives and friends for accommodation. Verifying community ties in all pre-trial decision-making is difficult because of a lack of time before the first court appearance, but it may be doubly difficult for foreign national defendants when they and others (family, employers, etc.) may not be easily contactable, speak the language and so on. A lack of trust in the authorities of other states, including criminal justice institutions and agencies, and concerns about immigration may also make accessing the necessary information more time consuming and difficult. The result is a pre-trial process where decisions are made on legally compliant and defensible criteria, that is, risk of flight, but which are based on assumptions and stereotypes which have no place in liberal democracies and which violate basic human rights principles of the presumption of innocence and the right to liberty.

Even the relatively small-scale comparative analysis of three European case studies in this chapter has demonstrated the interrelationship between criminal and immigration systems. At a macro-level, Germany's relatively liberal immigration policies and a higher resident immigrant population are linked to a greater level of overrepresentation of foreign nationals compared with the general population (61% against 13% in the general population) and the sparing use of prison for other groups. By contrast, the Netherlands uses pre-trial detention in the criminal justice system less as a result of stricter immigration enforcement and a lower resident immigrant population. Foreign nationals who are accused of offending are quickly transferred into the immigration system and expelled from the country instead of using pre-trial detention. On a micro-level, decision-makers are all too aware of their responsibility to ensure that the identities and immigration status of foreign national defendants are known before they consider whether to release them on bail for a criminal matter. Satisfying any concerns is particularly difficult when time is short to make enquiries of other government departments and overseas institutions. The "crimmigration" system is as omnipresent in the pre-trial process as it is in trial and post-trial procedures (Bowling and Westenra, 2020; Lousley, 2020; Stumpf, 2006).

A deep-seated culture where foreign nationals accused of committing offences are treated as a "suspect population", makes considering alternatives to pre-trial detention very difficult. A lack of trust means that decision-makers fail to consider the strong reasons many foreign national defendants will have for staying in the country, particularly if they have been residents for some time. Given the importance decision-makers attach to ensuring that defendants will stay in the country to stand trial, surrendering their identity papers may be an effective alternative for some of foreign nationals. This measure is already used in the England and Wales but German and Dutch decision-makers seem reluctant to impose it because of the ease of crossing borders in the Schengen zone. While electronic monitoring could theoretically also function as an alternative to pre-trial detention by monitoring the whereabouts of defendants, therefore allaying fears of absconding, it is underused for this group in Germany and the Netherlands because of the (assumed) lack of stable housing necessary to install the technical equipment. However, no bail conditions can prevent someone who wants to abscond doing so. Those who are detained never get the chance to prove their trustworthiness but some of those released inevitably disappear. As a result, countering decision-makers assumptions about the untrustworthiness of foreign nationals and the high likelihood that they will abscond is challenging.

European Union efforts for mutual agreements to enable foreign national defendants to be supervised in their own jurisdictions have not met with success, mainly because of a lack of trust in other jurisdictions' ability to monitor defendants' compliance and to ensure their return to face trial. In a climate of fear and suspicion fuelled by nationalistic tendencies, reducing high rates of pre-trial detention of foreign national defendants will be difficult. Shining a light on the issue is the beginning of the journey to ensure that the presumption of innocence and liberty is upheld for everyone.

Notes

1 www.politsei.ee/en/instructions/alien-s-passport-for-an-adult (accessed 10 January 2023).

2 In 2020, the largest national group of sentenced foreign national prisoners were Turkish nationals (14%), this roughly corresponds with their share of the foreign national resident population (www.destatis.de/DE/Themen/Gesellschaft-Umwelt/Bevoelkerung/Migration-Integration/Tabellen/nowcast-auslaendische-bevoelkerung-zeitreihe.html [accessed 29 November 2022]). EU citizens counted for 31% of all foreign national sentenced prisoners.

References

Aebi, M.F. and Tiago, M.M. (2021) *SPACE I – 2020 – Council of Europe Annual Penal Statistics: Prison Populations*, Strasbourg: Council of Europe.

Aebi, M.F., Tiago, M.M., Berger-Kolopp, L. and Burkhardt, C. (2017) *SPACE I – Council of Europe Annual Penal Statistics: Prison Populations. Survey 2016*, Strasbourg: Council of Europe.

Aliverti, A. (2018) 'Spotting foreigners inside the courtroom: Race, crime and the construction of foreignness', in A. Fili, S. Jahnsen and R. Powell (eds) *Criminal Justice Research in an Era of Mass Mobility*, London: Routledge: 85–99.

Aliverti, A. and Bosworth, M. (2017) 'Criminal justice adjudication in the age of migration', *New Criminal Law Review*, 20(1): 1–11.

Aliverti, A. and Seoighe, R. (2017) 'Lost in translation? Examining the role of interpreters in cases involving foreign national defendants in England and Wales', *New Criminal Law Review*, 20(1): 130–156.

Boone, M.M., Jacobs, P. and Lindeman, J.M.W. (2017) *DETOUR. Towards Pre-trial Detention as Ultima Ratio – 2nd Dutch National Report on Expert Interviews*, Vienna: Institute for the Sociology of Law and Criminology at www.uibk.ac.at/irks/publikationen/detour-publikationen/2nd-dutch-report_interview.pdf [accessed 10 January 2023].

Boone, M.M. and Kox, M. (2012) 'What works for irregular migrants in the Netherlands', *European Journal of Probation*, 4(3): 54–68.

Bowling, B., Parmar, A. and Phillips, C. (2012) 'Policing minority ethnic communities', in T. Newburn (ed) *The Handbook of Policing*, Cullompton: Willan Publishing.

Bowling, B. and Phillips, C. (2002) *Racism, Crime and Justice*, Harlow: Longman.

Bowling, B. and Westenra, S. (2020) '"A really hostile environment": Adiaphorization, global policing and the crimmigration control system', *Theoretical Criminology*, 24(2): 163–183.

Bundeskriminalamt (2021) *Polizeiliche Kriminalstatistik 2020* at www.bka.de/DE/AktuelleInformationen/StatistikenLagebilder/PolizeilicheKriminalstatistik/PKS2020/pks2020_node.html [accessed 29 November 2022].

CBS (Centraal Bureau voor de Statistiek) (2022) *Statistics Netherlands Database* at https://opendata.cbs.nl/statline/#/CBS/nl/dataset/03743/table?dl=72EFD [accessed 3 January 2023].

College voor de Rechten van de Mens (2017) *Tekst en Uitleg. Onderzoek naar de motivering van voorlopige hechtenis*, maart 2017 at file:///C:/Users/49176/Downloads/Onderzoek%20naar%20de%20motivering%20van%20voorlopige%20hechtenis.pdf [accessed 24 May 2023].

Corstens, G.J.M. and bewerkt door Borgers, M.J. (2014) *Het Nederlandse strafprocesrecht*, Deventer: Kluwer.

Griffiths, M. and Yeo, C. (2021) 'The UK's hostile environment: Deputising immigration control', *Critical Social Policy*, 41(4): 521–544.

Her Majesty's Inspectorate of Prisons (HMIP) (2006) *Foreign National Prisoners: A Thematic Review* at www.justiceinspectorates.gov.uk/hmiprisons/wp-content/uploads/sites/4/2014/06/Foreign-National-Prisoners-2005.pdf [accessed 17 December 2022].

Her Majesty's Inspectorate of Prisons (HMIP) (2012) *Remand Prisoners: A Thematic Inspection* at www.justiceinspectorates.gov.uk/hmiprisons/wp-content/uploads/sites/4/2012/08/remand-thematic.pdf [accessed 17 December 2022].

Home Office (2022a) *Immigration Bail* at https://assets.publishing.service.gov.uk/government/uploads/system/uploads/attachment_data/file/1102889/Immigration_bail_September_2022.pdf [accessed 15 September 2022].

Home Office (2022b) *Home Office Counting Rules 2022/23* at https://assets.publishing.service.gov.uk/government/uploads/system/uploads/attachment_data/file/1099880/hocr-complete-july-22.pdf [accessed 17 December 2022].

Hucklesby, A. (2011) *Bail Support Schemes for Adults*, Bristol: Policy Press.

Hucklesby, A., Beyens, K., Boone, M., Dünkel, F., McIvor, G. and Graham, H. (2016) *Creativity and Effectiveness in the Use of Electronic Monitoring: A Case Study of Five Jurisdictions*, Leeds: University of Leeds at http://emeu.leeds.ac.uk [accessed 9 September 2022].

Hucklesby, A. and Holdsworth, E. (2016) *Electronic Monitoring in England and Wales* at www.emeu.leeds.ac.uk [accessed 9 September 2022].

Hunold, D. and Wegner, M. (2020) 'Rassismus und Polizei. Zum Stand der Forschung', *Aus Politik und Zeitgeschichte*, 42–44: 27–32.

Hunter, G., Bhardwa, B., Dinisman, T., Moroz, A., Anastassiou, A. and Lynall, A. (2022) *Language Barriers in Criminal Justice System*, The Bell Foundation at www.bell-foundation.org.uk/app/uploads/2022/03/Language-barriers-in-the-criminal-justice-system.pdf [accessed 17 December 2022].

Independent Chief Inspector of Borders and Immigration (ICIBI) (2022) *An Inspection of the Global Positioning System (GPS) Electronic Monitoring of Foreign National Offenders March–April 2022* at www.gov.uk/government/publications/an-inspection-of-the-global-positioning-system-gps-electronic-monitoring-of-foreign-national-offenders-march-april-2022 [accessed 9 September 2022].

Janssen, J.H., van den Emster, F.W.H. and Trotman, T.B. (2013) 'Strafrechters over de praktijk van de voorlopige hechtenis. Een oordeel van de werkvloer!', *Strafblad*, 6: 430–444.

Lammy, D. (2017) *The Lammy Review: An Independent Review into the Treatment of, and Outcomes for, Black, Asian and Minority Individuals in the Criminal Justice System* at https://assets.publishing.service.gov.uk/government/uploads/system/uploads/attachment_data/file/643001/lammy-review-final-report.pdf [accessed 20 January 2023].

Light, M.T. and Wermink, H.T. (2021) 'The criminal case processing of foreign nationals in the Netherlands', *European Sociological Review*, 37(1): 104–120.

Lindeman, J.M.W., Jacobs, P. and Boone, M.M. (2018) 'De praktijk van de Europese toezichtmaatregel: begin van een meeromvattende invloed van de EU op de voorlopige hechtenis', *Strafblad*, 6: 30–34.

Lousley, G. (2020) 'Sentencing "unwanted" migrants: The border, racism and narrating punishability', *Critical Criminology*, 28: 209–224.

Ludwig-Mayerhofer, W. and Niemann, H. (1997) 'Gleiches (Straf-) Recht für alle? Neue Ergebnisse zur Ungleichheitsbehandlung ausländischer Jugendlicher im Strafrecht der Bundesrepublik', *Zeitschrift für Soziologie*, 26(1): 35–52.

Ministry of Justice (MoJ) (2020a) *Annual Prison Population 2020* at www.gov.uk/government/statistics/offender-management-statistics-quarterly-january-to-march-2020-2 [accessed 16 September 2022].

Ministry of Justice (MoJ) (2020b) *Freedom of Information Act Request 200914027* at https://assets.publishing.service.gov.uk/government/uploads/system/uploads/attachment_data/file/968080/FOI_200914027_prison_admissions_by_gender__nationality__offence_group_and_sentence_length.odt [accessed 15 September 2022].

Ministry of Justice (MoJ) (2021) *Ethnicity and the Criminal Justice System 2021* at www.gov.uk/government/statistics/ethnicity-and-the-criminal-justice-system-statistics-2020/ethnicity-and-the-criminal-justice-system-2020#defendants [accessed 16 September 2022].

Ministry of Justice (MoJ) (2022a) *Annual Prison Population 2022* at www.gov.uk/government/statistics/offender-management-statistics-quarterly-january-to-march-2022 [accessed 16 September 2022].

Ministry of Justice (MoJ) (2022b) *Community Accommodation Service – Tier 2 (Cas-2) – Policy Framework* at https://assets.publishing.service.gov.uk/government/uploads/system/uploads/attachment_data/file/1106711/cas2-policy-framework.pdf [accessed 13 December 2022].

Morgenstern, C. (2009) 'Estonia', in A. van Kalmthout, M. Knapen and C. Morgenstern (eds) *Pre-trial Detention in Europe*, Nijmegen: Wolf Legal Publishers: 287–324.

Morgenstern, C. (2011) 'Untersuchungshaft in Europa: Probleme im Rechts(tatsachen) vergleich', *Monatsschrift für Kriminologie und Strafrechtsreform*, 94: 452–473.

Morgenstern, C. (2017) *'2nd German National Report on Expert Interviews' Working Paper, DETOUR Project (Pre-trial Detention as Ultima Ratio)* at www.uibk.ac.at/irks/publikationen/detour-publikationen/2nd-german-report_interview.pdf [accessed 20 January 2023].

Morgenstern, C. (2018) *Die Untersuchungshaft. Eine Untersuchung unter rechtsdogmatischen, kriminologischen, rechtsvergleichenden und europarechtlichen Aspekten*, Baden-Baden: Nomos.

Morgenstern, C. (2020) 'Aktuelle Entwicklungen in Recht und Praxis der Untersuchungshaft in Deutschland', *Neue Zeitschrift für Kriminologie und Kriminalpolitik/Nouvelle Revue de Criminologie et de Politique Pénale*, 1: 19–28.

Nacro (2021) *Nacro Bail Accommodation and Support Service* at www.nacro.org.uk/services/bass/nacro-bass/ [accessed 10 December 2021].

Neira Pena, A. (2020) 'The reasons behind the failure of the European supervision order: The defeat of liberty versus security', *European Papers*, 5(3): 1493–1509.

Oberwittler, D. and Lukas, T. (2010) 'Schichtbezogene und ethnisierende Diskriminierung im Prozess der strafrechtlichen Sozialkontrolle', in U. Hormel and A. Scherr (eds) *Diskriminierung. Grundlagen und Forschungsergebnisse*, Wiesbaden: Springer: 221–254.

Parmar, A. (2019) 'Arresting (non)Citizenship: The policing migration nexus of nationality, race and criminalisation', *Theoretical Criminology*, 24(1): 28–49.

Prison Reform Trust and Hibiscus Initiatives (2018) *Still No Way Out – Foreign National Women and Trafficked Women in the Criminal Justice System – Full Report*, London: Prison Reform Trust at http://prisonreformtrust.org.uk/publication/still-no-way-out-foreign-national-women-and-trafficked-women-in-the-criminal-justice-system/ [accessed 15 September 2022].

Robson, M. (2020) *A Suspect Population? An Examination of Bail Decision-Making for Foreign National Women in Criminal Courts in England and Wales*, London: Griffins Society.

Schott, T. (2004) 'Ausländer vor Gericht', *Zeitschrift für Jugendkriminalrecht und Jugendhilfe*, 4: 385–395.

Statistisches Bundesamt (2021a) *Strafverfolgung*, Destatis: Wiesbaden.

Statistisches Bundesamt (2021b) *Strafvollzug – Demographische und kriminologische Merkmale der Strafgefangenen zum Stichtag 31.3*, Destatis: Wiesbaden.

Statistisches Bundesamt (2021c) *Personen mit Untersuchungshaft nach Staatsangehörigkeit (Sonderauswertung)*, Destatis: Wiesbaden at www.destatis.de/DE/Themen/Staat/Justiz-Rechtspflege/Tabellen/sonderauswertung-untersuchungshaft.html [accessed 3 Januar 2022].

Statistisches Bundesamt (2022) *Bevölkerung nach Nationalität und Geschlecht (Quartalszahlen)*, Destatis: Wiesbaden at https://www.destatis.de/DE/Themen/Gesellschaft-Umwelt/Bevoelkerung/Bevoelkerungsstand/Tabellen/liste-zensus-geschlecht-staatsangehoerigkeit.html [accessed 23 May 2023].

Stumpf, J.P. (2006) 'The crimmigration crisis: Immigrants, crime, and sovereign power', *American University Law Review*, 56: 367–419.

The Migration Observatory (2022) *Overview of UK's Foreign Born Population* at https://migrationobservatory.ox.ac.uk/resources/briefings/migrants-in-the-uk-an-overview/#:~:text=This%20briefing%20provides%20an%20overview,population%2C%20or%209.5%20million%20people [accessed 15 September 2022].

United Nations (UN) (2022) *International Migrant Stock: Table 3*, at www.un.org/development/desa/pd/content/international-migrant-stock [accessed 15 November 2022].

United Nations High Commissioner for Refugees (UNHCR) (2022) *Global Trends. Forced Displacement in 2021* at www.unhcr.org/62a9d1494/global-trends-report-2021 [accessed 22 November 2022].

Wermink, H., Light, M.T. and Krubnik, A.P. (2022) 'Pre-trial detention and incarceration-decisions for foreign nationals, a mixed-method approach', *European Journal on Criminal Policy and Research*, 28: 367–380.

Chapter 14

European aspects: human rights, cross-border policy and guidance for a responsible use of pre-trial detention

Christine Morgenstern and Ioan Durnescu

Introduction: "Two Europes" and their importance for pre-trial detention

This book not only seeks to identify common problems regarding pre-trial detention (PTD) and bail in the jurisdictions represented but also to contribute to an understanding of what Europe stands for in that area by highlighting distinctly European features. To this end, this chapter will explore the extent to which European legislation and policy have become important factors for the law and practice of PTD European states. Two European contexts – "two Europes" – have to be considered in this regard: the Council of Europe representing a group of currently 46 member states, and the smaller European Union with currently 27 member states. Traditionally, in the area of criminal justice, the Council of Europe is seen as the custodian of human rights for defendants and prisoners, with the European Convention on Human Rights (ECHR) as the assertive instrument and the European Court of Human Rights (ECtHR) and the European Committee for the Prevention of Torture and Inhuman or Degrading Treatment or Punishment (CPT) as influential actors (Snacken and van Zyl Smit, 2013).[1] The European Union often stands rather for a policy of making cross-border law enforcement more efficient, concentrating on a crime control approach and the relationship between different jurisdictions (Baker, 2013; Morgenstern, 2018). As this chapter will show, such a dichotomy may not prove correct regarding pre-trial detention, as several initiatives by the European Union in recent years have served the aim of restricting the overall use of pre-trial detention and, more specifically, its use against foreign nationals, namely EU citizens, in other EU member states (see also Chapter 13). With the European Union Fundamental Rights Agency (FRA), a body has been created in the Union to "*instil a fundamental rights culture across the EU*" (FRA-Homepage), which works on, inter alia, the presumption of innocence[2] and detention issues (European Fundamental Rights Agency, 2016).[3]

Remarkably, the European Commission also has funded several research and policy projects, including those of civil society initiatives, to further this

DOI: 10.4324/9781003159254-14

aim. Among them is the empirical study in the DETOUR project (see Chapter 1), two projects conducted by non-governmental organisations that focused on access to justice for pre-trial detainees (Fair Trials International, 2016, and the Prison Litigation project)[4] and the PRETRIAD project to explore and advance European judicial cooperation in pre-trial matters.[5]

Based on the findings of these projects, primarily the DETOUR project which both authors of this chapters were part of, and on decisions and reports by European actors, this chapter analyses the areas in which European influences are perceptible. In the next section, we will introduce norms and standards established by the ECtHR in the area of pre-trial detention, for example on defence rights or judicial reasoning in pre-trial matters, by examining country reports by the CPT on the treatment of pre-trial detainees as well as EU instruments on pre-trial decision-making and finding alternatives to detention. In the next section, we look at "European Law in action" and present practitioners' perspectives. As we will see, their assessment of European cooperation often is not very enthusiastic – our conclusion, however, is less sceptical and highlights the significance of European instruments for structural improvements for example in, but not limited to, middle and eastern European states.

European norms and standards

The Council of Europe

The European Convention and the jurisprudence of the European Court of Human Rights

The common normative background for this study is the European Convention of Human Rights with its basic values and guarantees. Often, comparable human rights standards can be found in domestic constitutional provisions and domestics statutes; those requirements may even reach beyond those of the ECHR. Nevertheless, in European comparative legal research the convention proves not only to be a valuable theoretical framework and valid yardstick for comparison, the jurisprudence of the ECtHR also provides rich material for comparative analysis. As the following overview shows, even in cases of (perceived) higher domestic standards, many convictions of member states in pre-trial matters show the importance of this European human rights monitoring.

The most relevant provision in practice is Article 5 ECHR, enshrining the right to liberty; a matter always relevant when someone is detained. Article 5 is violated when a person is detained unlawfully (without valid reasons) or without respect for the necessary procedural guarantees. Article 6 ECHR (the right to a fair trial) can be engaged or violated in various aspects regarding PTD; the most obvious being the presumption of innocence and the guarantee of effective legal defence, that is the right to defend oneself properly against a criminal charge and the right to effective legal counsel. Finally, Article 3 ECHR (the prohibition of torture, inhuman or degrading treatment or punishment) is relevant when prison conditions are so bad that they violate human dignity and are thus "degrading".

The influence of ECtHR case law is mentioned in the country chapters and can be traced for nearly all jurisdictions represented in this volume. Its decisions, over time, have affected the whole range of relevant human rights issues in PTD matters as the following (by no means exhaustive) overview shows: Austria, for example, has been convicted because of unjustified supervision of the communication between defence counsel and defendant (*Lanz v. Austria*, 24430/94, 1 January 2001). Belgium was the first country found to be in violation of Article 6 ECHR in a decision relating to insufficient access for the defence to case files while the defendant was in PTD (*Lamy v. Belgium*, 10444/83, 30 March 1989). Later, the so-called Salduz jurisprudence by the ECtHR (*Salduz v. Turkey*, 36391/02, 27 November 2008) was influential, and upheld in a case on access of defence lawyers to their clients during police interrogations (*Bouglame v. Belgium*, 16147/08, 2 March 2010).[6] Belgium was also convicted because of inhuman prison conditions that, among others, affected pre-trial detainees (*Vasilescu v. Belgium*, 64682/1225, November 2014).

Germany was convicted by the ECtHR, in both matters several times, because of insufficient access to files (*Lietzow v. Germany*, 24479/94; *Garcia Alva v. Germany*, 23541/94, both 13 February 2001; *Erdem v. Germany*, 38321/97, 5 July 2001) and the unacceptable length of detention (for example *El Khoury v. Germany*, 8824/09 and 42836/12, 9 July 2015). Lithuanian cases dealt, for example, with decision-making in cases with very long periods of PTD, in which no substantial reasons were given for the prolongation of detention (i.e. *Stašaitis v. Lithuania*, 47679/99, 21 March 2002), as well as in a case involving inhuman prison conditions (*Savenkovas v. Lithuania*, 871/02, 18 November 2008) or with insufficient access to files (*Albrechtas v. Lithuania*, 1886/06, 19 January 2016).

With regard to the Netherlands, no ECtHR involvement could be found for a long time in PTD matters. Since 2015, however, the court dealt with a few cases, and was critical of several practices. First, the "shocked legal order", a controversial ground for detention which can be the sole justification for detention in very serious cases, was critically assessed under Article 5. It was found to be acceptable under strict conditions, but the Court found that those were not fulfilled in the specific case because it was not substantiated well enough that indeed there was public outrage (*Geisterfer v. The Netherlands*, 15911/08, 9 December 2014; see Chapter 8). More recently, the Netherlands were convicted in three cases (*Hasselbaink v. Netherlands*, 73329/16; *Zohlandt v. Netherlands* 69491/16, and *Maassen v. Netherlands*, 10982/15;

all decided 9 February 2021) because of a violation of Article 5 ECHR due to what the Court held was a superficial substantiation of grounds for pre-trial detention, which could not sufficiently justify the infringement of personal liberty and freedom. Finally, Romania was convicted in a case in which (under old legislation) detention was not ordered by an independent judge (*Tase v. Romania*, 29761/02, 10 June 2008); because of the excessive use of PTD (*Pantea v. Romania*, 33343/96, 3 June 2003); and for inhuman prison conditions (*Cojan v. Romania*, 54539/12, 28 April 2015). In 2017, a pilot judgement in which the Court reacts to structural deficits, was delivered (*Rezmives and others v. Romania*, 61467/12 et al., 25 April 2017). In it, Romania was obliged to take measures to resolve the ongoing problems relating to conditions of detention in prisons and police cells, among them to reduce the use of detention, including pre-trial.

Only Ireland never was convicted by the Court in PTD matters.[7] Interestingly, however, the ECHR did play a role when the legal provisions for bail and PTD were amended and PTD for preventive purposes was introduced in 1996 (see Chapter 6): during the criminal policy debate preceding this change in 1996, the reform was justified partly with reference to Article 5 (1) lit. c ECHR, which explicitly allows for "the lawful arrest or detention . . . necessary to prevent his committing an offence".

The European Committee for the Prevention of Torture (CPT)

The activities of the Council of Europe's CPT, a body which visits all places of detention in member states of the Council of Europe and reports problems or possible risks regarding Article 3 ECHR has also had some impact in this field (Snacken and van Zyl Smit, 2013; Morgenstern, 2018). For many years, nearly all country reports by the CPT have been critical about the conditions for remand prisoners in the member states represented in this volume (including Ireland, CPT, 2015, 2020). In recent country reports, the detention conditions for remand detainees remain a prominent concern for the Committee because of overcrowding (e.g. in Belgium, CPT, 2022a and in Romania – in particular in police remand institutions – CPT, 2022b) and impoverished regimes for detainees having to stay up to 23 hours in their cell (e.g. Germany, CPT, 2022c). Hardly any state escapes critical comments concerning the way it deals with pre-trial detainees. Recent examples outside the scope of this book are France and Greece for particularly dire and overcrowded conditions (CPT, 2022e and CPT, 2021a), Switzerland for insufficient out-of-cell time (CPT, 2022d) or Sweden for the unduly strict separation rules for most remand detainees in (CPT, 2021b). Apart from the country visit reports, the CPT also publishes General Reports and the "CPT standards". In both, the PTD practice in Europe is described as problematic in many, in some respects in all countries.

The CPT is particularly critical about the restricted out-of-cell opportunities for remand detainees: in the 26th General Report of the CPT with a special section on remand detention, the Committee emphasises that

> prisoners cannot simply be left to languish for weeks, possibly months, locked up in their cells, and this regardless of how good material conditions might be within the cells [and] urges the 47 Council of Europe member states to use remand detention only as a measure of last resort and to provide remand prisoners with adequate detention conditions.
>
> (CPT, 2017: 31)

Three years later, the CPT reiterates that

> further steps [are] needed to reduce the use of remand detention.
>
> (CPT, 2021b: 65)

European human rights standards in PTD practice

As shown earlier, in all the countries represented in this study, human rights violations were found regarding PTD that had not been solved within the judicial system in the country concerned. Consequently, sometimes the practice had to be changed accordingly – for example following concerns raised by the CPT as mentioned earlier. Sometimes even legislation was altered, for example on access to files in Belgium or Germany or, following the Salduz jurisprudence mentioned earlier, in several states regarding the early access to a lawyer.

For everyday practice, however, European influences hardly play a role – usually, individual practitioners do not feel affected by these decisions and standards (see also Fair Trials International, 2016). Sometimes the notion transpired that domestic safeguards were enough, and that additional safeguards (for example on instructions and translations) were unnecessary and made things more complicated (see, for example, in Germany Morgenstern, 2017: 93). Nevertheless, both practitioners from Romania (Chapter 9) and Lithuania (Chapter 7) explicitly attributed progress towards a more restrictive use of PTD to jurisprudence of the ECtHR and its influence on younger practitioners, often during their training. Given the significantly decreased number of pre-trial detainees in these two countries, this impact must be emphasised and indicates the European contribution to the development of a different, human rights sensitive, legal culture.

The European Union

Mutual recognition, trust and knowledge

European cooperation in the criminal justice field is a gradual process and is influenced by various factors such as: globalisation of crime and crime structures, the fall of the internal borders between member states (especially after the 1980s), the development of the EU internal market law, etc. Negotiations between the member states on whether the EU competence should extend to criminal law have ended with a compromise formulated in the Maastricht Treaty (1993). It was for the first time that the Treaty established the Union competence in the justice and home affairs (the so-called third pillar), including in criminal matters. In 1999, the Amsterdam Treaty renamed and reformed this pillar into "police and judicial cooperation in criminal matters" and introduced a powerful tool for EU cooperation – the Framework Decisions. Even if the legislative framework has changed and the instrument of Framework Decisions no longer exists, the adopted instruments remain in force and the principle underlying the framework decisions, the principle of mutual recognition, remains to be of major importance for the understanding of cooperation and approximation within the Union.

The EU Framework Decisions oblige the member states in terms of results but they are free to determine their own ways of implementation, according to their traditions or institutional architectures. Therefore, the framework decisions need to be transposed into the national legislations before they can become active. Among the framework decisions that belong to the criminal justice family, two are of special interest for our research: The Framework Decision 2002/584/JHA on the European Arrest Warrant (EAW)[8]; and the Framework Decision 2009/829/JHA on the application, between member states of the European Union, of the principle of mutual recognition to decisions on supervision measures as an alternative to provisional detention (hereinafter European Supervision Order or ESO).[9] Under the principle of mutual recognition, a judicial decision produced in the course of criminal procedure in one Member State must be respected and given effect in the whole Union, that means in any of the other states. This requires mutual trust in each other's systems.

Trust here can be achieved not only in the form of trust in the functioning and efficacy of other state's law enforcement but also as trust in the respect for human rights during the criminal process. To achieve this, the European Union has set standards with regard to suspects' rights. It is beyond the scope of this chapter to go into details here, but it should be mentioned that following a "Roadmap on procedural rights", meanwhile six directives have been adopted and (mostly) transposed into national legislation[10]: on the right to interpretation and translation, the right to information, legal aid, on the right of access to a lawyer in criminal proceedings and on the right to communicate upon arrest, and on procedural safeguards on child defendants. Parts of them are important for PTD matters as they strengthen defence rights. In December 2022, the European Commission has adopted a soft law instrument to monitor the practice of member states, the Recommendation on procedural rights of suspects and accused persons subject to pre-trial detention and on material detention conditions. Its purpose is defined as setting out guidance for member states to take effective, appropriate and proportionate measures to strengthen defendant's rights when they are deprived of their liberty. The recommendation does not seek to create new thresholds or standards, but rather aims at consolidating the existing ones on international and Union level.[11] The instrument requires member states to "inform the Commission on their follow-up to this Recommendation within 18 months of its adoption" (Recommendation 87) so that the Commission can prepare a report, thus it can be viewed as only a weak monitoring tool.

The debates around the creation of the various instrument mentioned earlier, but also the research and policy projects funded by the European Commission have brought to light the urgent need for mutual knowledge about the relevant legal requirements, cultures and traditions in the different member states as it is the first step towards mutual trust and then a functioning system of mutual recognition. In the following section, we highlight how the two relevant framework decisions and other forms of Europeanisation are implemented in domestic law and practice.

The framework decisions

By far the most popular framework decision in the EU at least in criminal matters is the FD 2002/584/JHA on the European Arrest Warrant (EAW). In brief, the EAW is a simplified cross-border judicial surrender procedure by which one person can be surrendered for the purposes of prosecution or executing a custodial sentence or detention order to another EU Member State. Representing progress from the former complicated and lengthy extradition procedures, the EAW provided strict time limits for the procedure (60 days without the consent of the person, 10 days with the consent of the person), suspended the double criminality check for 32 categories of offences as long as they are punishable of at least three years of imprisonment in the issuing state, introduced some procedural guarantees and limited the number of grounds for refusal.

As mentioned in several of the country chapters in this volume as well as in the chapter on foreign nationals (Figure 13.1), one of the major problems of the criminal justice systems in Europe is the overrepresentation of foreign nationals in European prisons. One reason behind this reality is the lack of available alternatives to PTD for this group of offenders. The European Arrest Warrant is sometimes seen as a means of overcoming that problem at least for those offenders who are residing legally in another state of the EU than the state conducting the criminal investigation – in principle, it should be possible to summon them and if they do not appear for trial, to issue an arrest warrant, instead of detaining them in the respective country.[12]

In order to respond to this issue, the European Union Council adopted an additional framework decision, the European Supervision Order (ESO).[13]

One of the expectations of it is that the judiciary will treat non-residents (that have a fixed residence in another EU state) in the same manner as residents, by opening up alternatives to pre-trial detention for everybody. Unfortunately, only very limited statistics exist to assess the number of defendants who could potentially profit from such a possibility – often, only the number of foreign nationals in prisons is counted, only sometimes we find separate data for EU- and non-EU citizens in European prisons. But even this distinction is not always significant, as third country nationals could be included in the scope of the ESO as legal residents in another EU Member State. According to SPACE I statistics for 2021 (Aebi et al., 2022), the percentage of EU-citizens among the overall foreign prison population in our country sample lies between 27 and 32% in Austria, Belgium, Germany, Lithuania and Romania, it is higher in the Netherlands with 45% and Ireland with 60% (owing in part to the border to Northern Ireland as formally part of the United Kingdom as well as a high proportion of UK citizens in Ireland, with UK still counted as EU citizens in 2021). While the absolute numbers are low in Lithuania, Romania and Ireland, they are in their thousands in the other jurisdictions. Given the fact, that many prisoners in each system are pre-trial detainees and that foreign nationals are overrepresented here (Chapter 13), we can assume that the potential beneficiaries of such an instrument to avoid pre-trial detention in cross-border cases in the EU are numerous – and not only these defendants, also the prison systems could benefit from non-custodial solutions here.

Like the EAW, the ESO is based on the procedure of forwarding a uniform certificate together with the supporting documents from the issuing state to the executing state. The defendant may be transferred for supervision to the Member State in which he or she is lawfully and ordinary residing. The transfer is also possible to a third state but only if this Member State consents to this procedure.

In order to facilitate the communication between the member states, the Framework Decision provides that a central competent authority should be established in each Member State. The certificate will be thus forwarded from the competent authority in the issuing state to the competent authority in the executing state. Article 8 of the ESO provides that at least the following supervision measures shall be supervised by all member states:

(a) An obligation for the person to inform the competent authority in the executing State of any change of residence, in particular for the purpose of receiving a summons to attend a hearing or a trial in the course of criminal proceedings.
(b) An obligation not to enter certain localities, places or defined areas in the issuing or executing State.
(c) An obligation to remain at a specified place, where applicable during specified time.

(d) An obligation containing limitations on leaving the territory of the executing State.
(e) An obligation to report at specified times to a specific authority.
(f) An obligation to avoid contact with specific persons in relation with the offence(s) allegedly committed.

In the case where the nature of the supervision measure is incompatible with the law of the executing state for the same offence, the measure may be adapted, but the outcome should be as close as possible to the initial decision and never worse for the person. As opposed to the EAW, where consent is not always required for surrender, ESO provides that transfer may take place only upon the consent of the person.

Although the law governing the monitoring of the supervision measures falls under the authority of the executing state, all the subsequent decisions are taken by the issuing state: renewal, review or withdrawal, modification, issuing an arrest warrant or any other enforceable judicial decision having the same effect. As in the EAW procedure, the ESO provides for the same suspension of the double criminality check and almost the same grounds for refusal.

The framework decision's use

As mentioned earlier, the EAW is well-known and popular: Since 2005, the number of EAW issued in the EU increased from 6,894 to 16,144 in 2015.[14] In 2019, 20,226 EAWs were issued which signals quite a significant increase from the previous years. According to the EAW statistics for 2021, due to the COVID-19 pandemic, the number has decreased significantly to 15,938, but it is expected that this will change again.[15]

A factor that has hampered the use of the EAW in recent years are bad detention conditions, particularly in pre-trial detention, as mentioned earlier. Concerned about prison conditions that amounted to inhuman treatment (and thus were in violation of Article 3 ECHR), the European Court of Justice (ECJ), as the Union's highest court held, in the influential Aranyosi and Caldararu judgement (C-404/15 and C-659/15 PPU, ECLI:EU:C:2016:198), that member states can reject an EAW request when they are convinced that the prison conditions would amount to inhuman treatment for the suspect in question. While the ECJ for a long time seemed to prioritise European cooperation according to the principle of mutual recognition, and did not accept a rejection of the EAW because of human rights issues, it now explicitly referred to the ECtHR and CPT's assessments mentioned earlier and stated that, when deciding on EAW, the judicial authorities in the issuing state must assess the "real risk of inhuman or degrading treatment" in the executing state.

In the DETOUR study and according to the country reports in this volume, there seems to be consensus that the EAW generally works well in almost all jurisdictions and contributes significantly to the realisation of "Europe without borders" (particularly positive responses came from Lithuania, Bikelis and Pajaujis, 2017, and Romania, Oancea and Durnescu, 2017). It should be mentioned, however, that reservations about the possibility to avoid PTD by applying the EAW have also been expressed, namely in Germany (Morgenstern, 2017) and Belgium (Maes and Deblock, 2017, for the Flemish part). In the DETOUR study, participants in different jurisdictions mentioned difficulties localised in certain jurisdictions and procedures – for instance, England and Wales, France, Malta or Cyprus were mentioned several times as using lengthy procedures or demanding additional guarantees from the executing states prior to surrender. The lengthy procedure, however, in some jurisdictions may also be caused due to hearings and reviews demanded by suspects (Hammerschick et al., 2017).

Generally, difficulties relate to insufficient information available to judges prior to making a decision. For instance, when assessing the risk of absconding, some prosecutors in the Netherlands would like to have more information on the social background of the person or on whether the person has a job or other ties in the Netherlands (Boone et al., 2017). Another group generally seemed to be reluctant to use means of European cooperation, as, for example, some critical remarks by German defence lawyers indicate who complained about unwilling and Eurosceptic judges:

> [O]n every occasion you talk about a unified Europe, but when you look at detention judges' decisions, you would find often enough arrest warrants saying "He does not have a fixed abode in the Federal Republic of Germany" and then they are not fussed about this person having in the neighbouring country Poland the same address for 20 years, because they are too lazy and too comfortable or too delicate to respect this and to get that information.
>
> (Interview 26, lawyer; Morgenstern, 2017: 99)

If the EAW was mostly described as a successful instrument, the same does not apply to the ESO. Several member states were very reluctant to transpose it into domestic legislation – due in 2012, the last state, Ireland, only did so in 2021.[16] The use of the ESO in the EU is still at its infancy in general. For instance, 16 incoming cases and 18 outgoing cases were registered in the Netherlands from the moment of transposition until September 2017 (Beun, 2017); in Germany only two cases were mentioned during the DETOUR research until 2016 (Morgenstern, 2017, 2018) and no other cases have been recorded nor any judicial decision published ever since. Twenty-four cases were transferred to Romania between 2018 and 2021, most of them related to France (Stan, 2022). This reluctant use is not limited to the states represented in this study – Spain, for example, a keen user of the EAW, received two ESO requests and issued seven in 2019, the year in which this instrument was used the most to date; in Italy the statistics do not reveal the direction the ESO travels but mentions only three ESO procedures in total in 2019 (Neira Pena, 2020).

This means that in most jurisdictions, the ESO still is hardly known by the stakeholders and rarely used in practice. This reality might be explained by the novelty of the tool – at least in its transposed version. Although several projects from the beginning tried to promote the new instrument (see, for example, European Fundamental Rights Agency, 2016 and for a more recent overview PRETRIAD, 2021), most practitioners interviewed in the DETOUR project mentioned no training or other systematic awareness campaign they would have been aware of. In this respect, the Netherlands could be a good example to follow. As mentioned in Article 7 of the FD, the Netherlands designated one single central competent authority – Public Prosecution Service/the Centre for International Assistance in Criminal Matters (CILA). The CILA processes all incoming and outgoing requests of ESO and decides independently on the incoming requests. This kind of institutional arrangement facilitates the cooperation at the European level and creates expertise.

Critics argue that the initial lack of commitment on the part of the Member States in the transposition phase may have affected the judiciary or, in general, have impacted on the action of the competent issuing authorities of the member states and their discretion on deciding whether or not to issue a ESO (Min, 2015) or they have argued that a lack of common standards for pre-trial detention has impeded mutual trust in that matter (Neira Pena, 2020; Martufi and Peristeridou, 2020b). For a long time, neither Member States nor the European Union's institutions including the ECJ seemed to be eager to change this, and whether the aforementioned soft-law recommendation by the commission is a remedy is doubtful – in short: the ambitious project of the ESO lacks parenthood and a sponsor.

In the empirical research, more tangible reasons were given and administrative burden and time pressure were mentioned as obstacles in many jurisdictions (Austria, Lithuania, Ireland). Judges said that

> there are more important things than to saddle myself with additional work and with tremendous efforts and delays. . . . I'd rather follow the acceleration order and deal with the case next week and the thing is done.
> (interview 11, judge, Hammerschick and Reidinger, 2017: 83)

or simply

> I am deterred by all the bureaucracy.
> (interview 10, judge, Morgenstern, 2017: 99)

Most prosecutors and judges expressed real concerns regarding the time they have available in the investigation phase. Taking the ESO option seems to add even more pressure on the short time available and the other resources. For instance, ensuring translation is not always straightforward and costs time and money. Besides these structural difficulties, judges and prosecutors mentioned also various practical issues such as the certificate arriving very late, the absence of the person in the executing state or factual mistakes in the certificate (Hammerschick et al., 2017).

Therefore, instead of using the ESO, some judges stated that they would take an accelerated procedure and pass the sentence as soon as possible in rather easy cases. In more complicated cases, where evidence needs to be collected from many jurisdictions or when there are many offenders involved, this speedy procedure is not possible. Cases such as drug trafficking or human trafficking therefore seem to be the right candidates for the use of the ESO. Due to the time needed in these cases, the prosecution or the judge could use it to allow the suspects to return to their home countries under some control that would ensure their presence in court when needed.

The lack of control or the lack of information regarding the manner in which the supervision order is conducted in other jurisdictions were other important obstacles mentioned. Practitioners ask

> how can it be guaranteed that he comes back to trial, that's something he most likely won't do. That's totally unrealistic.
>
> (interview 7, public prosecutor, Hammerschick and Reidinger, 2017: 84)

Judges are therefore just "*happy that I have the person here on-site*" (interview 16, judge, Morgenstern, 2017: 99), and not willing to take any risk by using the new and cumbersome instrument.

Awareness-raising campaigns and better information about member states practices as well as clear competencies or clearing houses for potential ESO cases have been suggested to overcome the problems mentioned here – both in studies and policy projects (see, most recently, PRETRIAD, 2021) as well as by participants in the DETOUR study. Probably, a grassroot approach would help showing when and how concrete ESO cases can be successful. Here, efforts will be required by "*nagging defence lawyers*", as one Dutch lawyer described himself and his actions that lead to an ESO being processed, eventually sparing his client pre-trial detention.[17]

European law in action: what does Europe stand for in PTD matters?

Comparative research is beneficial for problems that can be found everywhere, despite distinct legal systems. While comparative criminal justice research was long seen as mainly academically interesting and often assigned to fundamental research without immediate benefit, this has changed in the field of criminal justice: cross-border cases must increasingly be solved in a globalised world. In Europe, two supranational actors must be included in such a comparison, the Council of Europe, and the European Union, who, with policy initiatives, standard- and norm-setting, jurisprudence and monitoring reports shape or at least influence the law in action in European jurisdictions.

Regarding the responsible use of pre-trial detention by the respective member states, the extent to which these initiatives have been beneficial to a European practice in conformity with the fundamental rights of the defendants is disputed (Morgenstern, 2014, 2018; Martufi and Peristeridou, 2020a, 2020b).

In our study, we can show – without neglecting shortcomings such as very long procedures and sometimes perhaps rather reluctant decisions – that the European Court of Human Rights generally is seen as serving as the European Human Rights conscience and support structure, including in pre-trial matters. Its jurisprudence has prompted practical changes in many countries, such as better possibilities to access files for the defence or stricter rules for review regarding the substantiation of decisions and the prolongation of detention. While Western European jurisdictions and their practitioners and scholars may sometimes be oblivious or even arrogant towards the necessity and impact of this court, in middle and Eastern European states, liberal developments and changing professional cultures were clearly attributed to its work. As it happens, in many cases the CPT reports mention the ECtHR jurisprudence when visiting a country. Moreover, the ECJ is making reference to the need to consult CPT reports or ECtHR cases when conducting the human rights check. This new reality demonstrates that human rights instruments available in "both Europes" began to cooperate closely and create a solid reference framework that hopefully will contribute to enhancing the human rights standards during the pre-trial stage.

As for the European Union, we explained earlier that several legislative instruments have been developed to facilitate the transfer of judicial decisions and ultimately to facilitate the transfer of defendants. In our research, we discovered how reluctant practitioners are to use those possibilities – mainly because they fear the amount of bureaucracy involved and some kind of path dependency or inertia. However, they often did not know about the relevant instrument, the ESO and its procedure, and could therefore not be sure of how much more work they would actually have. Sometimes they said that they did not think that authorities in the other European states would cooperate properly. Unfortunately, on several occasions this fear was confirmed in reality, namely with regard to detention conditions or to slow and cumbersome procedures. Here, some clearly had mixed experiences with the EAW. Others, however, had no experience at all.

We therefore agree that mutual understanding – required for mutual recognition as the indispensable tool for co-operation in the European Union – still is underdeveloped in pre-trial matters. Whether the latest initiative of the EU Commission, the Recommendation on procedural rights of suspects and accused persons subject to pre-trial detention and on material detention conditions (8 December 2022, C [2022] 8987 final) may change this, and how or whether a stronger EU regulatory framework could help (Martufi and Peristeridou, 2020b) remains to be seen.

Our conclusion therefore is that "the unknown" was feared and that, as banal as this may sound, practitioners still desperately need knowledge and support, particularly with regard to information and communication between the different national authorities. Even our small-scale workshops during the DETOUR project showed that once a Romanian judge and an Irish public prosecutor, a German defence lawyer and her Dutch colleague start to chat, mutual understanding begins to grow. The European Commission is therefore right to support this kind of work, as these seemingly minor steps are important to create informal networks feeding into more formal ones (via professional associations, for example). Ultimately, success (or failure) will depend on people – if nobody starts to use the instruments available, perhaps in an adapted form to suit their needs, they will be dead on arrival. Our favourite quote in this context, already mentioned earlier, stems from a Dutch lawyer during one of our workshops, who applied for the use of an ESO over and again until he succeeded: "*You just have to nag them until they finally start to use it*". He also said that he provided necessary information about the instruments, something that should not be necessary for the judiciary for professional reasons. In reality, however, judges' reluctance to follow advanced training is yet another uniform result in our country sample. This was often justified by the lack of time, lack of resources or simply the lack of opportunities. This is where member states should come in and make sure that these resources are made available to those who need them.

Summing up, it should be emphasised that exchange and communication both on the national level (between professional groups and between colleagues) and the European level is pivotal: problems and general attitudes are comparable to such a degree that inter-European cooperation should be possible, as we do not live in different worlds. PTD, on the other hand, is an example of a problem that must be solved not by blindly adopting foreign approaches, but by recollecting the basic rights and values in question: freedom, the rule of law and equal treatment.

Based on out study, it becomes obvious that there are solutions for a more responsible use of PTD and its alternatives in Europe. However, they are often not simple or unidimensional. Perhaps looking at PTD and its alternatives from a holistic perspective including legislation, practice, routines and mindsets could provide us with more tools to deal with them effectively both at the EU and national level. In particular, the problem of non-nationals and other minorities in pre-trial detention requires common European efforts.

Notes

1 For the sake of completeness, it should be mentioned that the Council of Europe through its Committee of Ministers has adopted several recommendations that should inform criminal policy in the member states and set standards for a responsible use of detention and for adequate prison conditions. A special instrument, the Recommendation Rec (2006) 13 on the use of remand in custody, tries to distill the main principles and interpretations by the court with regard to PTD and emphasises the need to use it as an ultima ratio. Equal stipulations can be found in the Council of Europe Recommendation (2006) 2-rev on the "European Prison Rules" (revised in 2020) and Council of Europe Recommendation (99) 22 on "Prison overcrowding and prison population inflation". While the European Prison Rules are influential for the overall prison practice in Europe (see, for example, Snacken and van Zyl Smit, 2013), this is hardly the case for the special recommendation on PTD (Morgenstern, 2018).

2 European Agency for Fundamental Rights at https://fra.europa.eu/en/publication/2021/presumption-of-innocence (accessed 3 January 2022).

3 European Agency for Fundamental Rights at https://fra.europa.eu/en/content/criminal-detention-database (accessed 3 January 2022).

4 European Prison Litigation Network at www.prisonlitigation.org/eupretrial-rights/ (accessed 14 December 2022).

5 PRE-TRIAD at www.pretrial-detention.org/ (accessed 14 December 2022).

6 In the Bouglame case, Belgium was not convicted because the appellant later had been acquitted, the court nevertheless repeated the indispensability of early access to a lawyer.

7 While the first ECtHR case ever dealing with PTD was an Irish case (*Lawless v. Ireland*, Nr. 3, 332/57, 1 July 1961), Ireland was not convicted because the Court accepted restrictions of the suspect's rights because of a declared public emergency threatening the life of the nation; the suspect was a member of the IRA.

8 Council Framework Decision of 13 June 2002 on the European arrest warrant and the surrender procedures between member states – Statements made by certain member states on the adoption of the Framework Decision [2002] OJ L 190/1.

9 Council Framework Decision 2009/829/JHA of 23 October 2009 on the application, between member states of the European Union, of the principle of mutual recognition to decisions on supervision measures as an alternative to provisional detention [2009] OJ L 294/20.

10 Directive (EU) 2016/1919 of the European Parliament and of the Council of 26 October 2016 on legal aid for suspects and accused persons in criminal proceedings and for requested persons in European arrest warrant proceedings; Directive (EU) 2016/343 of the European Parliament and of the Council of 9 March 2016 on the strengthening of certain aspects of the presumption of innocence and of the right to be present at the trial in criminal proceedings; Directive (EU) 2016/800 of the European Parliament and of the Council of 11 May 2016 on procedural safeguards for children who are suspects or accused persons in criminal proceedings; Directive 2010/64/EU of the European Parliament and of the Council of 20 October 2010 on the right to interpretation and translation in criminal proceedings; Directive 2012/13/EU of the European Parliament and of the Council of 22 May 2012 on the right to information in criminal proceedings; Directive 2013/48/EU of the European Parliament and of the Council of 22 October 2013 on the right of access to a lawyer in criminal proceedings and in European arrest warrant proceedings, and on the right to have a third party informed upon deprivation of liberty and to communicate with third persons and with consular authorities while deprived of liberty.

11 C (2022) *8987 final* at https://commission.europa.eu/system/files/2022-12/1_1_201158_rec_pro_det_en.pdf (accessed 3 January 2023).
12 For legal problems to issue an arrest warrant in these cases, for example, in Germany, see Morgenstern (2018: 508).
13 Council Framework Decision 2009/829/JHA of 23 October 2009 on the application, between member states of the European Union, of the principle of mutual recognition to decisions on supervision measures as an alternative to provisional detention [2009] OJ L 294/20.
14 European Union. E-Justice at https://e-justice.europa.eu/content_european_arrest_warrant-90-en.do (accessed 3 January 2023).
15 EAW Statistics 2019 and 2020 at https://commission.europa.eu/law/cross-border-cases/judicial-cooperation/types-judicial-cooperation/european-arrest-warrant_en#eaw-statistics-2020 (accessed 3 January 2023).
16 European Judicial Network at www.ejn-crimjust.europa.eu/ejn/EJN_Library_StatusOfImpByCat/EN/39 (accessed 3 January 2023).
17 During a discussion at a DETOUR workshop with practitioners (Brussels 2017), see Hammerschick et al., 2017.

References

Aebi, M.F., Cocco, E., Molnar, L. and Tiago, M.M. (2022) *SPACE I – 2021 – Council of Europe Annual Penal Statistics: Prison Populations*, Strasbourg: Council of Europe.

Baker, E. (2013) 'Governing through crime? The case of the European Union', in T. Daems, S. Snacken and D. van Zyl Smit (eds) *European Penology?*, Oxford: Hart Publishing.

Beun, M. (2017) *Expert Opinion on the ESO*, unpublished manuscript presented at the CEP Expert meeting, Brussels, 26 September 2017.

Bikelis, S. and Pajaujis, V. (2017) *DETOUR – Towards Pre-trial Detention as Ultima Ratio. Second National Report on Lithuania*, Vienna: IRKS at www.uibk.ac.at/irks/publikationen/detour-publikationen/2nd-lithuanian-report_interviews.pdf [accessed 3 January 2023].

Boone, M.M., Jacobs, P. and Lindeman, J.M.W. (2017) *DETOUR. Towards Pre-trial Detention as Ultima Ratio – 2nd Dutch National Report on Expert Interviews*, Vienna: IRKS at www.uibk.ac.at/irks/publikationen/detour-publikationen/2nd-dutch-report_interview.pdf [accessed 3 January 2023].

CPT (2015) *Report to the Irish Government on the Visit to Ireland Carried Out by the European Committee for the Prevention of Torture and Inhuman or Degrading Treatment or Punishment (CPT) from 25 January to 16 September 2014, CPT/Inf (2015) 38*, Strasbourg: Council of Europe.

CPT (2017) *Remand Detention. Extract from the 26th General Report of the CPT*, Strasbourg: Council of Europe.

CPT (2020) *Report to the Irish Government on the Visit to Ireland Carried Out by the European Committee for the Prevention of Torture and Inhuman or Degrading Treatment or Punishment (CPT) from 23 September to 4 October 2019, CPT/Inf (2020) 37*, Strasbourg: Council of Europe.

CPT (2021a) *30th General Report of the CPT, 1 January–31 December 2020*, Strasbourg: Council of Europe.

CPT (2021b) *Report to the Swedish Government on the Visit to Ireland Carried Out by the European Committee for the Prevention of Torture and Inhuman or*

Degrading Treatment or Punishment (CPT) from 18 to 29 January 2021, CPT/Inf (2021) 20, Strasbourg: Council of Europe.

CPT (2022a) *Rapport au Gouvernement de Belgique relatif à la visite effectuée en Belgique par le Comité européen pour la prevention de la torture et des peines ou traitements inhumains ou dégradants (CPT) du 2 au 9 novembre 2021, CPT/Inf (2022) 22*, Strasbourg: Council of Europe.

CPT (2022b) *Report to the Romanian Government on the Visit to Ireland Carried out by the European Committee for the Prevention of Torture and Inhuman or Degrading Treatment or Punishment (CPT) from 10 to 21 May 2021, CPT/Inf (2022) 6*, Strasbourg: Council of Europe.

CPT (2022c) *Report to the German Government on the Visit to Ireland Carried Out by the European Committee for the Prevention of Torture and Inhuman or Degrading Treatment or Punishment (CPT) from 1 to 14 December 2020, CPT/Inf (2022) 18*, Strasbourg: Council of Europe.

CPT (2022d) *Rapport au Conseil fédéral Suisse relatif à la visite effectuée en Suisse par le Comité européen pour la prevention de la torture et des peines ou traitements inhumains ou dégradants (CPT) du 22 mars au 1er avril 2021, CPT/Inf (2022) 9*, Strasbourg: Council of Europe.

CPT (2022e) *31st General Report of the CPT, 1 January–31 December 2021*, Strasbourg: Council of Europe.

European Union Agency for Fundamental Rights (2016) *Report on Criminal Detention and Alternatives: Fundamental Rights Aspects in EU Cross-Border Transfers* at https://fra.europa.eu/en/publication/2016/criminal-detention-and-alternatives-fundamental-rights-aspects-eu-cross-border [accessed 13 February 2023].

Fair Trials International (2016) *A Measure of Last Resort? The Practice of Pre-trial Detention Decision-Making in the EU* at www.fairtrials.org/articles/publications/a-measure-of-last-resort-the-practice-of-pre-trial-detention-decision-making-in-the-eu/ [accessed 3 January 2023].

Hammerschick, W., Morgenstern, C., Bikelis, S., Boone, M., Durnescu, I., Jonckheere, A., Lindeman, J., Maes, E. and Rogan, M. (2017) *DETOUR – Towards Pre-trial Detention as Ultima Ratio. Comparative Report* at www.uibk.ac.at/irks/publikationen/detour-publikationen/comparative-report_detour.pdf [accessed 3 January 2023].

Hammerschick, W. and Reidinger, V. (2017) *DETOUR – Towards Pre-trial Detention as Ultima Ratio. 2nd Austrian National Report on Expert Interviews Vienna: Institute for the Sociology of Law and Criminology* at www.uibk.ac.at/irks/publikationen/detour-publikationen/2nd-austrian-repor_interviews.pdf [accessed 4 January 2023].

Maes, E. and Deblock, M. (2017) *DETOUR – Towards Pre-trial Detention as Ultima Ratio*. Report on (Dutch-speaking) expert interviews (Flanders), in DETOUR-Towards Pre-trial Detention as Ultima Ratio. 2nd Belgian National Report on Expert Interviews. Brussels: INCC-NICC.

Martufi, A. and Peristeridou, C. (2020a) 'The purposes of pre-trial detention and the quest for alternatives', *European Journal of Crime, Criminal Law and Criminal Justice*, 28: 153–174.

Martufi, A. and Peristeridou, C. (2020b) 'Pre-trial detention and EU law: Collecting fragments of harmonisation within the existing legal framework', *European Papers*, 5: 1477–1492.

Min, B. (2015) *The European Supervision Order for Transfer of Defendants: Why Hasn't it Worked? Penal Reform International, 25 September 2015* at www.penalreform.org/blog/the-european-supervision-order-for-transfer-of-defendants/ [accessed 3 January 2023].

Morgenstern, C. (2014) 'Die Europäische Überwachungsanordnung – Überkomplexes Ungetüm oder sinnvolles Instrument zur Untersuchungshaftvermeidung von Ausländern?', *Zeitschrift für Internationale Strafrechtsdogmatik (ZIS)*, 9: 216–235.

Morgenstern, C. (2018) *Die Untersuchungshaft. Eine Untersuchung unter rechtsdogmatischen, kriminologischen, rechtsvergleichenden und europarechtlichen Aspekten*, Baden-Baden: Nomos.

Morgenstern, C., assisted by Eva Tanz (2017) *DETOUR – Towards Pre-trial Detention as Ultima Ratio. 2nd German National Report on Expert Interviews*, IRKS: Vienna at www.uibk.ac.at/irks/publikationen/detour-publikationen/2nd-german-report_interview.pdf [accessed 3 January 2023].

Neira Pena, A. (2020) 'The reasons behind the failure of the European supervision order: The defeat of liberty versus security', *European Papers*, 5(3): 1493–1509.

Oancea, G. and Durnescu, I. (2017) *DETOUR – Towards Pre-trial Detention as Ultima Ratio. 2nd Romanian National Report on Expert Interviews*, IRKS: Vienna at www.uibk.ac.at/irks/publikationen/detour-publikationen/2nd-romanian-report_interview.pdf [accessed 3 January 2023].

PRETRIAD (2021) *Recommendation Paper on the Application of the Council Framework Decision 2009/829/JHA at EU Level* at www.pretrial-detention.org/uploads/1/3/0/4/130474014/d3.2_%E2%80%93_recommendation_paper_on_the_application_of_the_council_framework_decision_2009829jha_at_eu_level_compressed.pdf [accessed 3 January 2023].

Snacken, S. and van Zyl Smit, D. (2013) 'Distinctive features of European penology and penal policy-making', in T. Daems, S. Snacken and D. van Zyl Smit (eds) *European Penology?*, Oxford: Hart Publishing.

Stan, S. (2022) *Conference Presentation During the Final Conference for the PRETRIAD Project*, unpublished manuscript presented at Final Conference of the PRETRIAD project, Berlin, 12 May 2022.

Chapter 15

Conclusion

Pre-trial detention as *ultima ratio* – European practice between aspiration and reality

Mary Rogan, Walter Hammerschick and Christine Morgenstern

Researching European approaches to pre-trial detention and bail

This book deals with pre-trial detention and bail practice in eight European jurisdictions. Central to the analysis is a human rights sensitive approach, which emphasises a restrained use of detention, whereby the deprivation of liberty in the pre-trial and trial phase of criminal proceedings must be a means of last resort – the ultima ratio of state action. This entails that pre-trial detention is an exception only allowed for when there are well-assessed grounds and risks which leave no other choice than to be addressed with this measure most intrusive for the lives of people in general, here aggravated by the fact that the ones affected are legally innocent. In this volume, we have pointed out that in the countries included, we share common legal values expressed in International and European conventions but also in the national legislations. The practice observed and partially expressed by the available statistical data, namely by pre-trial detainee rates, however, indicates considerable differences how these common legal values are reproduced in practice. While there are factors possibly explaining some of the differences between countries such as crime rates, different approaches to a welfare state regime etc., the dimension and the quality of the differences nevertheless suggest different understandings and differing approaches to the application of pre-trial detention, to the use of alternatives and in the end to the presumption of innocence, the presumption in favour of liberty, the ultima ratio principle and to the principle of proportionality. Our findings point towards the significance of legal traditions and professional cultures of those who are deciding and influence the decision-making in the pre-trial phase. In this concluding chapter, we will devote some more attention to the differing legal culture because it indicates that legal changes aiming at a reduced application of pre-trial detention will only produce humble outcomes in the best case, if the mindset of the practitioners is not in line with these changes.

Of course, there is no quantitative benchmark which can be adapted to diverse national settings providing an orientation towards the "adequate"

DOI: 10.4324/9781003159254-15

pre-trial detention rate. The best we can do is to identify important factors which we argue are influences behind more or less extensive reliance on detention before trial. This is what we aim at in this chapter. To fulfil this aim, we explore these influences, drawing common themes arising out of the respective national practices. Drawing on these reflections, we advocate for knowledge exchange amongst practitioners within and across jurisdictions and awareness-raising essential in order to trigger and foster developments with the objective of mitigating excessive pre-trial detention. The value of this kind of comparative approach is seen first and most directly when we consider the application of the European human rights frameworks and criminal justice policy in the domestic setting. A second comparative layer highlights the merits of a European perspective: while the European Convention on Human Rights (ECHR) and its substantiation by the jurisprudence of the European Court of Human Rights (ECtHR) help to delineate the normative European Human Rights framework for pre-trial detention and the rights of suspects in all member states and may help to create a shared European understanding, cooperation tools within the European Union aim at solving practical cross-border problems. To achieve this aim, the European Union equally strives for the strengthening of common values and common standards. Only when we understand domestic practices in European jurisdictions can we fully appreciate these pan-European approaches. We therefore need to learn about each other, with each other and from each other. This has to be considered a main mechanism for improving cross border cooperation.

The material provided here supports this approach. While the research conducted relies in large part on interviews with practitioners rather than quantitative assessments of the variables influencing pre-trial detention, these insights from those working directly within the field along with comparative analysis of legal instruments and policy as well as statistical data provides a useful basis upon which to draw conclusions about what leads to higher or lower rates of pre-trial detention. The perspective of those working directly in every-day decision-making has real value and importance. Other studies may well wish to build on the qualitative approach to explore influential factors in a more quantitative way. Here, we have shared the experiences of those who work in this field, providing our analysis of the ways they speak about the various approaches to decision-making. Though of course, the way people talk about their decision-making is not always the same as their decision-making in practice, we argue that our approach provides useful insights into how choices at the pre-trial stage are made. The experiences and perspectives shared through the empirical research in this book, along with the examination of literature and legal analysis, have provided a firm basis for understanding the difference we see across countries. These factors warrant further research, but they also provide a basis for policy reform and changes in legal practice. While efforts to address high pre-trial detention rates are clearly most urgent, our work suggests that there also remains much room for improvement in countries where rates are low, given the evidence of upwards pressure on pre-trial detention rates, something noted in Ireland, for example, or the overrepresentation of marginalised groups in Austria and Germany, and the central importance of a restrained approach to the use of detention generally.

Four factors shaping pre-trial detention and bail practice in Europe

The comparative analysis presented in this book suggests that there are important recurring themes in our analysis of the factors influencing the use of pre-trial detention; we want to highlight four of them in this concluding chapter. Although criminal proceedings must be thought of as reactions to a crime committed – or at least alleged – and as retroactive in nature, pre-trial detention can be based on a preventive ground. The first of these practice-shaping factors therefore is the role of the risk of offending ground. The way in which this ground is used and its comparative importance amongst the grounds on which pre-trial detention can be ordered is one of the most critical factors behind the use of detention. Additionally, the use of the risk of absconding ground is highly relevant in the case of foreign defendants, most notably those from outside the European Union. Secondly, professional roles and cultures are relevant. Here, we have identified the ways in which prosecution and defence lawyers work as being important. We argue, in particular, that what we identify as "procedural economics" – the pressures on prosecution and defence practitioners of an organisational, administrative or logistical nature – can influence how pre-trial proceedings operate and, by extension, the use of detention. Thirdly, we also suggest that the presence of alternatives to detention which are viewed as legitimate and are embedded in domestic legal culture plays an important role in avoiding detention. It is notable in this regard that we see comparatively restrained use of pre-trial detention in England and Wales where rates of incarceration are otherwise high. There, as with Ireland, the long-established and deeply-rooted culture of using "bail", a catch-all term used to describe a flexible alternative to which a variety of conditions on liberty can be attached, is influential in avoiding the use of detention. Conversely, in places where there are few alternatives, or few alternatives viewed as credible, pre-trial detention is reported to be more likely to be used. While the presence of alternatives is evident as an influential factor across countries, the type and use of alternatives needs further assessment and interrogation. Conceptually, the purpose of alternatives is opaque in some instances, and confused in others, operating on the borderlands of both punitive sanctions and mechanisms for securing the proceedings. Concerns have also been raised by many practitioners in the countries examined here about whether the use of alternatives impinges upon the presumption of innocence. This situation suggests a difficult scenario: alternatives may assist in minimising the use of detention but may also have the effect of infringing the presumption of innocence. A key issue to emerge from this work is therefore that of what we expect alternatives to do. This question needs a conceptually clear answer from policymakers acting in this field. The fourth aspect we want to emphasise is related to the question of alternatives. How can we, within Europe and in particular within the European Union, enhance a system that avoids pre-trial detention for non-nationals? Our analysis demonstrates the nature of the problem (as noted earlier concerning the ground of risk of flight) but also that the cooperation tool developed, the European Supervision Order (ESO), has hardly been used and that its potential as a means of avoiding detention remains unrealised.

In this chapter, we explore these factors in greater depth, providing analysis from across the jurisdictions explored here. We also examine the implications of this analysis for policy, practice and research. We argue that there is greater scope at European Union and domestic level to ensure that detention is a last resort pre-trial, particularly with respect to the use of the risk of offending ground and the position of foreign defendants. We also advocate for efforts outside of the legislative sphere. In the first instance, a lack of comparable data was an issue across the work presented here, and, in many countries a lack of even basic data on the use of pre-trial detention was very striking. In order to ensure a robust evidence base for any policy efforts, these shortcoming needs to be addressed at national and international levels.

The research presented in this work also indicates a key role for legal culture and the training of practitioners. Evidence from Ireland in particular, and also England and Wales, suggests that once a sense of the "right" approach – that is, a restrictive one – to pre-trial detention is shared across prosecution and defence it plays a role in creating a more restrained approach to the use of detention, with both sides making efforts to use alternatives where possible. The transplantation of legal culture is exceedingly difficult, but European-wide initiatives to support knowledge and experience sharing both amongst practitioners at domestic level and across countries could reap benefits. The creation of a Europe-wide legal culture which seeks to ensure pre-trial detention is truly ultima ratio may be difficult, but could be beneficial for the reduction of the use of detention.

Risk of offending as a driver for extensive recourse to pre-trial detention

The research presented in this work suggests that certain factors are the most important when it comes to the choice of detention or liberty at the pre-trial stage. Foremost amongst these factors is the risk of offending ground. Countries where this ground is predominant – that is, the most frequently used ground for the imposition of pre-trial detention, or is to the forefront of judicial concerns, have higher rates of detention than those where this ground is not so influential. While further research is necessary to test this hypothesis in a quantitative way, this work suggests that the risk of offending ground's prominence in some contexts shapes actors' views, approaches and practices in fundamental ways. When the risk of offending ground is prominent, it acts as a frame of reference or a lens by which the pre-trial decision-making process is viewed, and one which has detention in clear view. A key point of contrast in this respect can be found between the common law jurisdictions represented here (England and Wales, and Ireland) and civil law systems. However, it should also be noted that Germany, which has lower rates of pre-trial detention than many of its continental neighbours, also demonstrates less reliance on the risk of offending ground than these other countries. This suggests further that the risk of offending ground acts as a pull towards higher rates of pre-trial detention. In both England and Wales and Ireland the risk of offending ground is a relatively recent introduction, coming in the case of Ireland only in the mid-1990s, being codified in England and Wales in the 1970s. While this ground exists in both these jurisdictions, a striking feature of both of them is how comparatively little hold they have on the imaginations of the actors in the process. In other places reviewed in this book, the risk of offending ground is far more prominent in the thinking of the legal actors. It is more important for actors in these places to consider the risk of offending before trial than the likelihood of the defendant to turn up for trial. The effect of the weight which is given to the reoffending ground is considerable. From the analyses presented here, the risk of offending ground acts as something like an anchor – dragging the calibration of the balance of the assessment in favour of a preventive, risk-averse approach which, we argue, is more likely to make prosecutors push for detention and judges to apply it. The prominence of this ground is not only important in practical terms, but also from a cultural perspective. The salience of the risk of offending ground seems to influence how actors see both defendants and the purpose of the proceedings. Considering risk of offending in a pre-eminent fashion seems to influence prosecutors and judges' thinking in a more general way. By focusing on risk of offending, and potential further harm, actors may become more risk-averse, and therefore have a lower threshold for seeking or imposing PTD, and greater fears about what might happen if the proceedings do not result in detention. This legal culture is also influenced by a lack of shared understanding or interconnection between prosecution and defence actors, something returned to in more detail later.

The question of what grounds are used in pre-trial detention proceedings is a critical one. Historically, detention has been used at the pre-trial stage to secure the proceedings and to provide as close to a guarantee as possible that a defendant will not abscond or will not interfere with witnesses or evidence. By introducing a risk of offending ground, a new calculation must be made, one which seeks to assess, with limited tools, how likely it is that the person will commit offences. While such an assessment is indeed a difficult task, a critique of the decisions about pre-trial detention often heard from defence lawyers refers to a lack of thorough risk assessment. Introducing this ground, and, more particularly, giving it pre-eminence, we may lose sight of those original objectives for pre-trial detention. A zealous application of this ground, on the basis of the experiences reported in this work, may be an important driver towards higher rates of pre-trial detention and non-adherence to the principle that pre-trial detention should be *ultima ratio*.

While the risk of offending ground merits particular assessment in analyses of why pre-trial detention rates are higher or lower, the risk of absconding ground appears to be a driver of higher rates in certain settings. When defendants are foreign nationals, particularly, though not exclusively, if they are from outside the European Union, the risk of absconding ground takes on a particular significance given the potential to flee across borders and out of the reach of the criminal justice system. We see in this volume many examples of pre-trial detention rates which are influenced by the use of detention in the case of foreign defendants. Across countries, participants reported that their concerns of flight were heightened in the case of foreign defendants and their experience was that pre-trial detention was more likely in such circumstances. Participants mentioned that it was a critical aspect of the weighing process by which pre-trial detention was decided, and few links to the country in which the proceedings would be held was an important factor in favour of detention. This is quite pronounced in Austria, where the proportion of foreigners in the pre-trial detention population is very high. Austria's particular location with multiple borders plays a role, but participants reported clear concern with the concept of people crossing borders specifically to commit crimes and then leave again. The case of Austria and, to a lesser extent, Germany also indicates that pre-trial detention practice concerning foreign nationals may partly be influenced by general preventive motives, demonstrating the functionality and "grip" of the criminal justice system, often to the detriment of human rights. The extent to which European instruments such as the ESO or the European Arrest Warrant (EAW) impacted on how practitioners view a defendant's nationality will be explored further later.

Roles, tasks and practical constraints in pre-trial decision-making

Another important influence on pre-trial detention rates emerging from this analysis is the methods of working and attitudes of the relevant players, as well as the interplay between those actors. Defence lawyers play a critical role in promoting the importance of the presumption of innocence and in suggesting alternative ways of addressing concerns other than through the use of detention. An active defence is an important protective factor against the use of pre-trial detention. Across all countries, we see, however, pressure on defence lawyers. They are pressurised in terms of limited time to prepare for proceedings, sometimes limited access to their clients when they are in custody, and limited resources. They also face obstacles when seeking to suggest alternatives to custody when limited alternatives exist. This is particularly the case for vulnerable and as such "difficult" (in the sense of requiring extra time or consideration) clients, namely foreign nationals, persons with addictions or other mental health issues or homeless persons. Judges expect defence lawyers to put forward potential alternatives which are realistic, credible and tailored to the individual circumstances of the person and the alleged offence. The fact that the judges themselves have a responsibility to look for and assess the applicability of alternatives hardly becomes visible in most jurisdictions. Sometimes judges appear to be somewhat detached from practical questions and investigations into the feasibility of particular alternatives, or conditions which might be tailored in such a way that they address prosecution concerns. Some judges would appear to view their role as one of adjudicating on the efforts of prosecution and defence to refute or put forward alternatives, rather than being obliged to conduct their own examination of the appropriateness of alternatives which enable release. Our research reveals, that, in several countries, there is also often more room for activity of the defence lawyers. A factor possibly limiting the potential of the impact of defence lawyer is the organisation of legal aid. Models of funding which do not sufficiently ensure their adequate remuneration bear a higher risk of lower quality defence activities. Supporting defence lawyers in their role is another mechanism by which the use of pre-trial detention can be addressed.

This work also highlights the pressures faced by prosecutors and indeed judges. Prosecutors across all countries report heavy workloads, with many cases in any given day. What we term "procedural economics" seems to play a role in increasing the use of detention. With many cases to prosecute, especially in settings where risk of offending is a preeminent consideration, seeking detention may become routine or the norm. For judges, detention can also be the most straightforward and "cleanest" solution – the case is essentially finalised at the pre-trial stage at least and can be moved off the judicial desk. There is work required in fashioning alternatives. Often, reports must be obtained to assess a person's suitability for an alternative, which may create delays. There may be a risk that the person comes back before the court and the judge will then be obliged to deal with breaches, taking up more precious court time. In systems under pressures of time and resources, the full effects of procedural economics are unknown, but our analysis suggests they do play a role as reported by participants active in these processes across Europe.

There is also little time for the decisions on pre-trial detention. This means that there is limited opportunity to collect sufficient and high-quality information on suspects, which information will support the assessment of whether alternatives are suitable. It is widely agreed by practitioners and experts that this kind of information serves a better quality of decisions. There is however some tension between the need for a speedy decision and good quality information. Prosecutors and judges themselves generally neither have the time nor the competency to collect this information on their own. The involvement of expert organisations collecting this kind of information with staff specifically qualified to carry out such (social) inquiries and assessments is an approach only practiced in a few countries. In the Netherlands, the probation service is involved in pre-trial proceedings this way, in Austria and Germany juvenile justice procedures take advantage of a court aid providing this kind of services. Practitioners sometimes refer to the problem that the reports may not be completed in time before the decision on pre-trial detention. This indeed will happen sometimes, but then the reports are nonetheless still valuable for subsequent hearings and decisions and should not be discounted as a result of this early time pressure.

In continental European countries, we also see in some cases that it is expected from prosecutors that they will seek detention rather than agree or at least accept the implementation of alternative measures. Though this pressure is also felt in England and Wales and Ireland, it is less intense, with participants in Ireland in particular reporting that prosecutors did not see their role as being one to pursue detention at all costs. In these jurisdictions, we see prosecutors being open to agreeing alternatives and working with defence lawyers to come up with solutions which avoid the use of detention. A notable finding of this work is the differences we have identified in legal cultures between continental European systems and common law ones. Even in the otherwise punitive and risk-averse context of England and Wales, the use of pre-trial detention still is seen by practitioners as something which should be exceptional, and its overuse is viewed as a problem, as evidenced by the investigation of the House of Commons Select Committee on Justice investigating what it sees as a worryingly high levels of pre-trial detention (House of Commons Justice Committee, 2023). While numbers are increasing in both England and Wales and Ireland, practitioners nonetheless continue to see alternatives to detention as viable, and, for many cases, to be preferred. In short, there is a legal culture in these places which sees detention as something that the defendant must be argued *into*, whereas in continental jurisdictions, detention is more something that the defendant must be argued *out of*. While this is a simplification, the prism or lens by which detention is viewed in these jurisdictions is an important feature of the findings presented here. The liberty lens or the detention lens can shape how the proceedings operate and, ultimately, whether detention is prioritised or alternatives are prioritised. This work suggests that an important factor which differentiates both approaches is the backgrounds of prosecutors and defence lawyers and the shared experiences and training between them. In both England and Wales and especially Ireland it is common for legal practitioners, particularly barristers who advocate in court to have a shared background in terms of their training and, even more pertinently, shared daily experiences. There are no specialised "tracks" to become prosecutors or judges in these jurisdictions at the training stage, with practitioners selecting to go into prosecutorial offices as a career path rather than a training method. More than this, legal practitioners may act on behalf both of the prosecution and defence in different cases. Within the course of a single day, legal practitioners may be acting on behalf of the prosecution in a case, and then seeking alternatives to custody for a defendant in another. The effects of this situation are difficult to quantify and are somewhat intangible, but we see from the Irish research presented here in particular, participants report a kind of shared understanding of the "rules of the game": that detention, at least in some cases, should usually be avoided and be a measure of last resort.

Bail and (the lack of) alternatives to pre-trial detention

Our analysis deals with "alternatives" to pre-trial detention, using this term as generic one to cover both Continental European models of "milder measures" (as opposed to pre-trial detention) and "bail models" as for example in Ireland or England and Wales. We found that in principle, most European jurisdictions provide for several types of alternative measures in the law: most often these are different forms of judicial supervision with conditions and financial bail to guarantee compliance with the procedure (in particular, appearing in court), in some states house arrest and electronic monitoring are options as well. They are, however, often hardly used. Dealing with the issue of alternatives, we found the largest discrepancies between the systems represented in this study; not only between the two different systematic approaches, but also with regard to the acceptance or rejection of non-custodial measures to achieve the aims of securing the proceedings. This refers to practitioners and academics alike, as we find stark warnings against potential net-widening effects, for example from the Belgian experience, but also suggestions to explore further the possibilities of electronic monitoring (for example, in the chapter on the Netherlands) or Bail Support Systems (as in the chapter on England and Wales). Risks that the maxim of innocent until proven guilty is threatened because of the use of conditions designed to address "off ending behaviour" or because unduly harsh or unnecessary conditions are attached to bail have to be considered carefully. Leaving these reservations aside, there seems to be consensus that a careful use of the alternative options may help to avoid pre-trial detention for a significant proportion of suspects and defendants and therefore must be encouraged.

European cooperation: promises and limits

The importance of European aspects has become visible in our study as most European jurisdictions have been influenced by the jurisprudence of the ECtHR, strengthening a suspect's rights and – at least usually – aiming at restricting the use of pre-trial detention. In particular, the chapters on Romania and Lithuania highlight the European impact not only on law-making and criminal policy but also on education, training and ultimately the culture of legal professionals.

Our research also suggests that the promise of reduced use of detention through the European Supervision Order (ESO) has not yet been realised. There was agreement across the countries represented here that this tool has some potential as a mechanism for reducing the use of detention on the grounds of a risk of flight. There was, however, evidence of low awareness of the ESO in most jurisdictions. One barrier to the use of this tool is time. In proceedings which are to be decided quickly, there is limited opportunity to deploy a tool which needs input from other countries' supervision authorities, requiring reports, contacts, communication and so on, all of which takes time. The need to act quickly may also mean that it becomes hardly possible or viable to use the ESO.

The European Arrest Warrant, a well-established and better-known instrument, does however, provide some comfort for prosecutors and judges in the case of European Union nationals. Those from outside the European Union face much higher barriers to being permitted to be at liberty than those from within. As we describe later, particular attention must be given to this category of defendants in any serious effort to reduce pre-trial detention rates. The potential for the use of the ESO may be limited, but most practitioners agree that it has a largely unrealised potential so far. Practitioners are broadly well-disposed to it, but lack of awareness, lack of familiarity and, in some cases, lack of time lessen the likelihood of its use. The problems restricting transborder cooperation within the EU in general, not least little trust in the capacities and standards in other member states, definitely also affects the ESO.

What is to be done? Perspectives for curbing the recourse to pre-trial detention

Overall, the contributions in this work indicate a number of important factors which we suggest play a role in contributing to higher or lower usage of detention at the pre-trial stage. First, the grounds on which pre-trial detention may be ordered are of obvious importance, but, more subtly, the effect of the priority which is given to those grounds in law and in practice deserves attention. In countries where the risk of offending ground is highly prominent in the approach and mindset of prosecutors and judges, we see pre-trial detention being used more frequently. While quantitative assessment of this hypothesis would be deeply valuable, the qualitative work presented here indicates that the risk of offending ground has an important effect on the thinking of prosecutors on judges. The high stakes of trying to prevent crimes seems to encourage an approach which favours detention as the most effective way to reduce this risk. In places where the risk of absconding has the greater hold on the legal imaginations of the practitioners, a bigger space or greater opportunity exists for the implementation of alternatives. Where the focus is on ensuring that the person turns up for trial, alternatives such as financial guarantees, and regular signing on with the police become more viable and credible. The aim of pre-trial detention in law and practice is therefore very important: if it is primarily or almost totally to prevent crime, detention becomes a more prominent option; if it is to secure the proceedings, alternatives become more acceptable, with the important exception of the case of foreign defendants. Our findings therefore suggest that the purpose of intervention, in both law and practice, at the pre-trial stage is important. This must be addressed not only by lawmakers but also and perhaps foremost in the education systems for the eventual decision-makers, in law school curricula, training programmes or professional events.

We also suggest that an active defence is an important protector against the unnecessary use of detention, but that pressures on defence lawyers can militate against the most effective execution of their role. We also suggest that the role of the prosecution is highly significant. The attitude of the prosecution may be almost determinative of the proceedings in some instances, and the pressures on them to act quickly and with a heavy workload may also create a certain momentum towards the use of detention. Besides the importance of the prosecution's attitude and approach, we see the critical role of the interplay between prosecution, defence and judges. The relative importance of each of these bodies in the legal culture and the context of the courtroom also plays an important role from the evidence presented here. A nexus between prosecution and judges can create a more detention-focused mindset, with the defence becoming less influential. Where there is a shared understanding of the approach to pre-trial detention amongst the actors, we see a greater space for the use of alternatives.

The work presented further suggests that there is some conceptual opacity regarding the purpose of alternatives. Alternatives to custody are sometimes expected to do a huge amount of work: prevent crime, secure the proceedings, and, where social interventions are used, address the causes of offending behaviour, while at the same time respecting the presumption of innocence. Alternatives seem to be used more readily in places where they are seen as genuinely credible. Bail has such a well-entrenched status in England and Wales and Ireland that it is seen as a genuine alternative or default option. In this regard, it is notable that there, the term "pre-trial detention" is not a natural or commonly used phrase, whereas bail is very much common parlance. This perhaps small point does suggest a difference in mindset – the common law jurisdictions analysed here start from the premise of liberty and reasons for it to be denied, while the continental European countries are more inclined to focus on detention and reasons why it should be avoided. This is an important difference. The legal culture in a jurisdiction is therefore an important focus both for research and action in the area of pre-trial detention.

Policy recommendations: ensuring pre-trial detention is truly ultima ratio

There are several important research, policy and practice recommendations arising out of the work presented here. These recommendations are made both to the national and the European-wide levels. Turning first to the question of data. A lack of up-to-date, comprehensive or comparable information on the use of pre-trial detention and, most especially, alternatives thereto, was a notable and recurring feature of the analysis on the jurisdictions explored here. We noted that often despite publishing data for example on the composition of the whole prison population by ethnic origin or nationality, these data are unavailable for the remand population. This lack of a robust evidence base for how pre-trial detention proceedings operate is a problem for research, but also for the development of policy and evaluation of practice. The very useful SPACE data compiled on behalf of the Council of Europe (see Chapter 1) tells us some important basic and interesting things about detention, but there is very limited comparable data on alternatives and on the proceedings.

We advocate for the development of more timely and more comprehensive information on pre-trial detention and its alternatives to be made publicly available. Specifically, we suggest that domestic authorities and European-wide bodies make the following information readily available:

- The length of pre-trial detention categorised by offence type and the background characteristics of the defendant.
- The overall frequency by which alternatives are used when compared to detention, and then broken down by alternative type.
- The frequency with which alternatives to custody are breached and the outcomes of those breaches.
- The frequency with which pre-trial detention is ended before a trial started.

We encourage Europe-wide bodies to seek and support the development of the publication of these statistics. At a basic level, this information would support reflection and the evaluation of policy, but it would also allow firmer conclusions to be drawn on why there are differences in pre-trial detention rates across countries, to support learning across borders. With common "minimum standards" being a keyword in the context of cross border co-operation (e.g. European Commission, 2022: 9) more and comparable data become a requirement.

Our second recommendation concerns the legislative bases for pre-trial detention. First, we advocate for strict adherence to the grounds for imposing pre-trial detention. Pre-trial detention must be carefully restricted to being used only where it is absolutely necessary to ensure that the trial can take place, and evidence can be secured. A very careful weighing process must be carried out to be absolutely certain that no alternative, or combination of alternatives can fulfil this aim. Secondly, where the risk of offending ground is to be used, it must be done so very sparingly and with great care. This ground is in clear conflict with the presumption of innocence, and a very high bar must be in place before detention can be ordered on this basis. The offences anticipated must be serious and the evidence of their likelihood very strong. There must be a very high threshold before detention can be ordered in such circumstances if pre-trial detention is truly to be ultima ratio. Authorities must also ensure that the grounds for imposing pre-trial detention are used in true compliance with the relevant legislation, and ensure that it is not used for extra-legal purposes such as to address concerns that a person does not have a permanent address, or to address a person's social needs. The position of foreign defendants needs particular attention and review. The work presented here suggests that practitioners find that judges and prosecutors have particular concerns about flight in the case of non-national defendants, and especially those from outside the EU. While there is a legitimate base for such concerns about a person's ties to the jurisdiction and ability to evade justice in these cases, all too often detention becomes a kind of default way to meet these concerns. Authorities must work to find ways to ensure that detention is not used unnecessarily in these situations. Even if often there may be well-grounded reasons why non-nationals have a higher risk of pre-trial detention, the boundaries to a situation of discrimination are fluid and must be carefully reviewed.

We also advocate for adequate resourcing for defence lawyers. These professionals play an essential role in keeping the presumption of innocence alive in pre-trial proceedings, and in advocating for and proposing specific and workable alternatives to detention. When under pressure for time, with limited opportunities to engage with their client, and minimal resources for obtaining reports from bodies or organisations which might be able to support a person in complying with any pre-trial obligations, defence lawyers are hamstrung and constrained in their ability to perform this important role. Particular attention must be given to adequate pay, good working conditions and effective access to both clients and bodies which can support the implementation of alternatives to custody. Considering the precarious living conditions of many of the people endangered by pre-trial detention it is of utmost importance that legal aid systems ensure the functioning of legal protection.

We also see a role for greater connections to be made between prosecutors and defence lawyers. Having opportunities to share experiences, practices, and common challenges seems to play a role in reducing the focus on detention and open up a space to explore alternatives in suitable cases. The practice of "bail on consent" in England and Wales and Ireland is striking in this regard, as it shows a well-accepted willingness to work together to avoid detention when possible.

These practices which seem to reduce the use of pre-trial detention in England and Wales and Ireland are the product of a particular legal culture, where risk of offending has been a relative late-comer to the options for imposing detention and, in Ireland, was unconstitutional for many decades. This thinking has had a lingering effect, where the risk of not turning up for trial remains the most important factor in decision-making at the pre-trial stage. This emphasis or slant on proceedings is accompanied by a shared understanding of the process and its aims, and an openness to compromise, between prosecution and defence. Together, this creates a legal culture with a greater willingness to deploy alternatives. Legal cultures are built in very specific settings, over long periods of time and because of particular experiences. They are not transplanted easily. Any efforts to implement policies from other countries must always take account of these particular factors, which may not provide fertile ground for the introduction of new approaches (Jones and Newburn, 2007). However, we suggest that there are things which cross-European institutions such as the Council of Europe and the European Commission could do to promote a European-wide legal culture which ensures pre-trial detention is a measure of last resort. Based on the experiences described in this work, important features of this culture include: an emphasis at the pre-trial stage on the likelihood of turning up for trial; very strong restrictions on the use of a risk of offending ground; real protections in constitutional or other rights-protecting laws for the presumption of innocence and the right to liberty; and opportunities for prosecution and defence lawyers to interact more informally, to share experiences, training and perspectives. We advocate for training for all players in the process: judges, prosecutors and defence lawyers should have the benefit of education and support regarding human rights standards and the importance of ensuring that detention is a measure of last resort. These efforts will be incremental and progress may be slow, but, given the importance of legal culture as uncovered in this research, targeting the viewpoints, perspectives and attitudes of the participants in the legal decision-making process could yield important benefits.

We also posit that there is a need for much deeper reflection and consideration on the role of probation or other social services at the pre-trial stage. There are unresolved questions about the use of social work-oriented alternatives. Involving probation or related services is attractive in the sense that support can be offered to the defendant which may be very valuable for example, drug treatment, training and so on. However, requiring people to participate in programmes, meet with a supervisor regularly or organise their lives in a particular way is an infringement on the right to liberty and on the presumption of innocence. It is important to tread carefully when requiring defendants to do offence-focused type of work in the absence of a criminal conviction. We have not found robust evaluation of these types of interventions and we call for further research into and assessment of the involvement of social services at the pre-trial stage. There is, however, a clear need for supports for people to meet the terms of their conditional liberty, for example, through the provision of accessible information about the terms of conditions and the requirements concerning attendance in court. The provision of special support for foreign national suspects is a particularly challenging but pertinent task.

Pre-trial detention in Europe: not yet the ultima ratio

Late in 2022, following decades of European initiatives to curb the use of pre-trial detention and to help member states to achieve this aim, the European Commission adopted a recommendation to member states, called "Minimum Standards for procedural rights of suspects and accused persons subject to pre-trial detention". The principles and recommendations sound very familiar and have been repeated over and again, not least in this volume – to name just the first "general principle" that reads:

> Member States should use pre-trial detention only as a measure of last resort. Alternative measures to detention should be preferred, in particular where the offence is punishable only by a short sentence of imprisonment or where the offender is a child.
>
> (European Commission, 2022: 10)

Has nothing been achieved so far? We would argue that progress indeed has been made in some regards but that in all jurisdictions represented in this volume, there is still much room for improvement. In this work, we have brought together assessments and experiences of the decision-making process for detention at the pre-trial stage in eight jurisdictions. Though there are considerable differences in forms of political governance, legal contexts, national histories and penal policies, we see important common themes. Across the countries studied, there are common grounds for the use of detention. Differences in practice emerge in how those grounds are used, with the risk of offending ground being an important driver. Differences also exist regarding the relative positions or dominance of the players in the proceedings. Where prosecutors and defence lawyers share a similar understanding of the correct approach to pre-trial decision-making, rates seem to be lower. Given the high rates of pre-trial detention in many countries and the particular use of detention in the case of foreign defendants in all countries, we cannot say detention is the ultima ratio at the pre-trial stage in the countries studied here. This is concerning in light of the need to use detention sparingly and the significant human rights concerns associated with its use, especially at the pre-trial stage, along with the social and economic costs involved. There is a clear and pressing need for national and cross-European efforts to address the overuse of the risk of offending ground and the overuse of detention for foreign defendants. These efforts should also support the creation of greater faith and trust in alternatives to detention. Underlying all these efforts is a deep need for better data to support evaluation and assessment of policy and practice.

The development of a European legal culture which favours the use of pre-trial detention as a measure of last resort requires a commitment to addressing these issues, but also, as this work as shown, dedication to sharing experiences and learning across borders, to fulfil European ideals of commitment to human rights and social inclusion.

References

European Commission (2022) *Commission Recommendation of 8.12.2022 on Procedural Rights of Suspects and Accused Persons Subject to Pre-trial Detention and on Material Detention Conditions, C(2022) 8987 Final*, Brussels at https://commission.europa.eu/document/b59ddb88-b9c3-420c-98d5-622807f8729b_en [accessed 3 February 2023]

House of Commons Justice Committee (2023) *The Role of Adult Custodial Remand in the Criminal Justice System, Seventh Report of Session 2022–23*, House of Commons at https://committees.parliament.uk/publications/33530/documents/182421/default/ [accessed 14 February 2023].

Jones, T. and Newburn, T. (2007) *Policy Transfer and Criminal Justice: Exploring US Influence Over British Crime Control Policy*, Maidenhead: Open University Press.

Index

Note: Page numbers in *italics* indicate a figure and page numbers in **bold** indicate a table on the corresponding page.

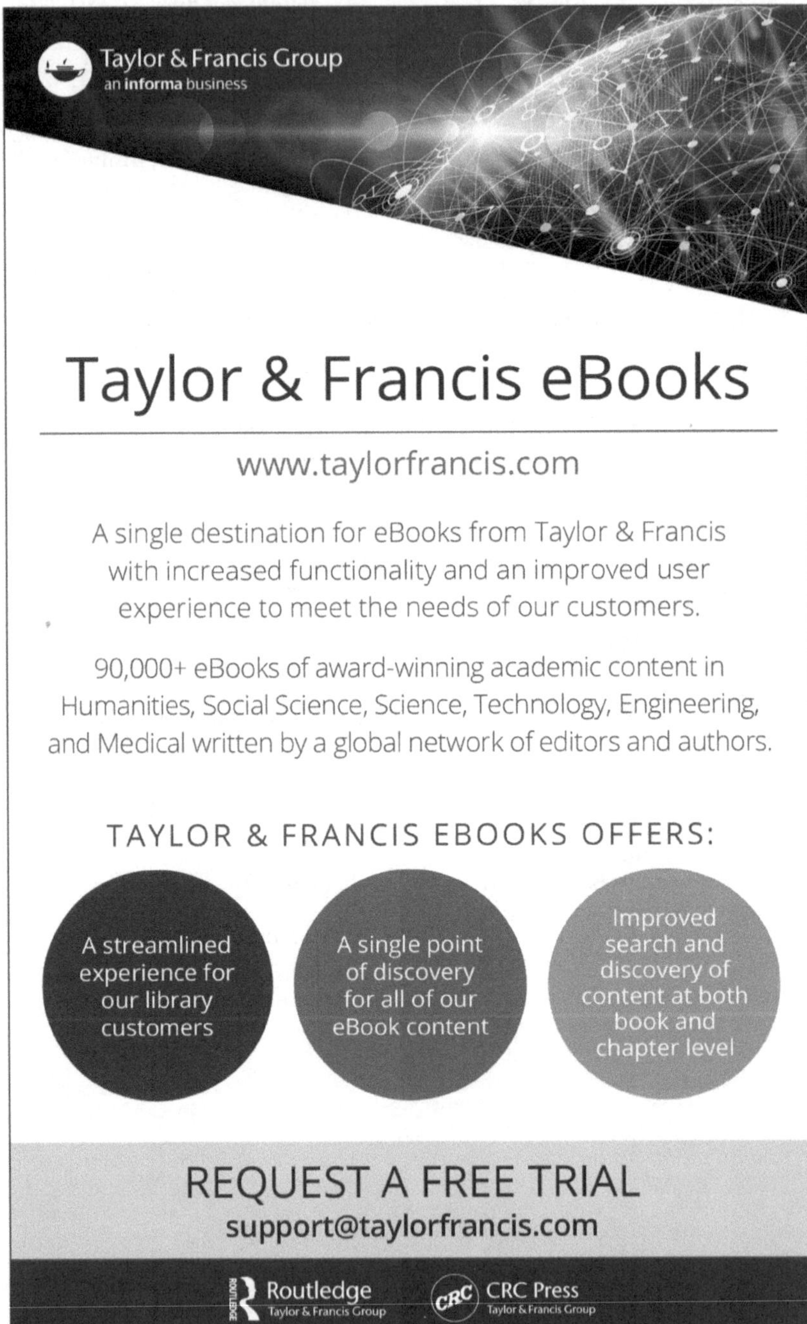
Taylor & Francis Group
an informa business
Taylor & Francis eBooks
www.taylorfrancis.com
A single destination for eBooks from Taylor & Francis with increased functionality and an improved user experience to meet the needs of our customers.
90,000+ eBooks of award-winning academic content in Humanities, Social Science, Science, Technology, Engineering, and Medical written by a global network of editors and authors.
TAYLOR & FRANCIS EBOOKS OFFERS:
A streamlined experience for our library customers
A single point of discovery for all of our eBook content
Improved search and discovery of content at both book and chapter level
REQUEST A FREE TRIAL
support@taylorfrancis.com
Routledge
Taylor & Francis Group
CRC Press
Taylor & Francis Group

FSC
www.fsc.org
MIX
Papier | Fördert gute Waldnutzung
FSC® C083411

Kolibri 360 GmbH
Ferdinand-Jühlke-Straße 7
99095 Erfurt, Deutschland
produktsicherheit@kolibri360.de